MW01068977

The Power of the Gospel

The
POWER
of the
GOSPEL

A Year in Romans

R.C. SPROUL

 LIGONIER MINISTRIES

The Power of the Gospel: A Year in Romans
© 2024 by the R.C. Sproul Trust

Portions of this devotional were previously published under the
following title:
Romans: An Expositional Commentary
© 2009 by R.C. Sproul

Published by Ligonier Ministries
421 Ligonier Court, Sanford, FL 32771
Ligonier.org

Printed in China
RR Donnelley
0001024
First printing

ISBN 978-1-64289-592-6 (Hardcover)
ISBN 978-1-64289-593-3 (ePub)

Cover design: Ligonier Creative
Interior design and typeset: Katherine Lloyd, The DESK

Ligonier Ministries edited and adapted Dr. R.C. Sproul's original material to
create this volume. We are thankful to Mrs. Vesta Sproul for her invaluable
help on this project.

Library of Congress Control Number: 2023938698

CONTENTS

Romans 1

PAUL, A BONDSERVANT OF JESUS CHRIST, *called to be an apostle, separated to the gospel of God which He promised before through His prophets in the Holy Scriptures, concerning His Son Jesus Christ our Lord, who was born of the seed of David according to the flesh, and declared to be the Son of God with power according to the Spirit of holiness, by the resurrection from the dead. Through Him we have received grace and apostleship for obedience to the faith among all nations for His name, among whom you also are the called of Jesus Christ;*

To all who are in Rome, beloved of God, called to be saints:

Grace to you and peace from God our Father and the Lord Jesus Christ.

First, I thank my God through Jesus Christ for you all, that your faith is spoken of throughout the whole world. For God is my witness, whom I serve with my spirit in the gospel of His Son, that without ceasing I make mention of you always in my prayers, making request if, by some means, now at last I may find a way in the will of God to come to you. For I long to see you, that I may impart to you some spiritual gift, so that you may be established—that is, that I may be encouraged together with you by the mutual faith both of you and me.

Now I do not want you to be unaware, brethren, that I often planned to come to you (but was hindered until now), that I might have some fruit among you also, just as among the other Gentiles. I am a debtor both to Greeks and to barbarians, both to wise and to unwise. So, as much as is in me, I am ready to preach the gospel to you who are in Rome also.

For I am not ashamed of the gospel of Christ, for it is the power of God to salvation for everyone who believes, for the Jew first and also for the Greek. For in it the righteousness of God is revealed from faith to faith; as it is written, "The just shall live by faith."

For the wrath of God is revealed from heaven against all ungodliness and unrighteousness of men, who suppress the truth in unrighteousness, because what may be known of God is manifest in them, for God has shown it to them. For since the creation of the world His invisible attributes are clearly seen, being understood by the things that are made, even His eternal power and Godhead, so that they are without excuse, because, although they knew God, they did not glorify Him as God, nor were thankful, but became futile in their thoughts, and their foolish hearts were darkened. Professing to be wise, they became fools, and changed the glory of the incorruptible God into an image made like corruptible man—and birds and four-footed animals and creeping things.

Therefore God also gave them up to uncleanness, in the lusts of their hearts, to dishonor their bodies among themselves, who exchanged the truth of God for the lie, and worshiped and served the creature rather than the Creator, who is blessed forever. Amen.

For this reason God gave them up to vile passions. For even their women exchanged the natural use for what is against nature. Likewise also the men, leaving the natural use of the woman, burned in their lust for one another, men with men committing what is shameful, and receiving in themselves the penalty of their error which was due.

And even as they did not like to retain God in their knowledge, God gave them over to a debased mind, to do those things which are not fitting; being filled with all unrighteousness, sexual immorality, wickedness, covetousness, maliciousness; full of envy, murder, strife, deceit, evil-mindedness; they are whisperers, backbiters, haters of God, violent, proud, boasters, inventors of evil things, disobedient to parents, undiscerning, untrustworthy, unloving, unforgiving, unmerciful; who, knowing the righteous judgment of God, that those who practice such things are deserving of death, not only do the same but also approve of those who practice them.

WEEK 1

1

Paul: Bondservant

PAUL STARTS BY GIVING HIS NAME, but he then seeks to define who he understands himself to be. This self-identification is not just Paul's introspection or self-evaluation; the Holy Spirit superintends the Apostle's writing, which is how we know that this is a true and accurate description of the author of the epistle.

Paul identifies himself as **a bondservant of Jesus Christ** (v. 1a). I have never been satisfied with that English translation of this second phrase. Some translations have, "Paul, a servant of Jesus Christ." *Bondservant* is an improvement, but I think the proper translation should read, "Paul, a slave of Jesus Christ." The Greek word that Paul uses here is *doulos*. A *doulos* was not a hired servant who could come and go as he pleased. A *doulos* was a person who had been purchased, and once purchased he became his master's possession.

This idea of the *doulos* in Scripture is always connected to another descriptive word, *kurios*.

In the New Testament, the title "lord" or *kurios* is used in three ways. There is a simple, common usage, where calling someone *kurios* is like addressing him as "sir," a polite form of address. The supreme use of *kurios* refers to the sovereign God, who rules all things. *Kurios*, "the name which is above every name" (Phil. 2:9), is the name given to Jesus, whom the Father calls the King of kings and the Lord of lords. There is yet a middle usage of the term *kurios* in the New Testament. It is used to describe a slave owner, which is an apt description of Jesus, and it is from this that Paul describes himself. He is not just a servant but a slave.

Paul, in addressing believers, said, "You are not your own. For you were bought at a price" (1 Cor. 6:19–20). We have been purchased by the blood of Jesus Christ (Acts 20:28). There is a paradox here: when the New Testament describes our condition by nature, as fallen people, it describes us as slaves to sin. There is also irony here: when Christ sets us free from slavery to the flesh, He calls us to the royal liberty of slavery to Him. That is why we call Him Master. We acknowledge that it is from Him that we get our marching orders. He is the Lord of our lives. We are not our own. We are not autonomous or independent. Unless people understand their relationship to Christ in these terms, they remain unconverted.

Application
Everyone born of the Spirit is set free from slavery to sin and belongs to a new master. We are now slaves of Jesus Christ, a service in which we find true freedom—the freedom to do what is good and holy. This liberating work of the Holy Spirit was not only for our first being set free from sin by the Lord. The Holy Spirit is at work in our daily obedience to Christ, our new master. Let us walk in humble reliance on the Spirit every day as faithful servants in our freedom from sin.

2

Sent and Separated

PAUL MAKES A SIGNIFICANT AFFIRMATION ABOUT himself and his mission: **called to be an apostle** (v. 1b). In the early chapters of Acts, the church gathered to elect a new Apostle, and it set forth the criteria for apostleship. The first criterion was having been a disciple of Jesus during His earthly ministry; the second was having been an eyewitness of the resurrection; and the third and most important criterion was having been directly and immediately called by Jesus (Acts 1:20–26).

In the ancient world, an apostle was like an ambassador who spoke on behalf of the king. The ambassador's message carried with it the authority of the one who sent him. The word *apostolos* in Greek means simply "one who is sent." "He who hears you hears Me, he who rejects you rejects Me, and he who rejects Me rejects Him who sent Me" (Luke 10:16).

People often say, "I like to know what Jesus says; it is Paul I do not want to listen to." Almost all we know about Jesus is that which comes through Apostolic authority, so such remarks set Paul against Matthew, or Paul against John. That may not be done with impunity because all the Apostolic writings carry the delegated authority of Jesus Himself. That is what it means to be an Apostle. That is why the New Testament church is built on the foundation of the Apostles.

In the three criteria for apostleship, Paul fails the first two tests: he had not been a disciple of Jesus during Jesus' tenure on earth, nor had he been an eyewitness of the resurrection of Christ. That is why there were some in the early church who seriously challenged the Apostolic authority of Paul. The supreme qualification for Apostolic authority was a direct and immediate call by Jesus. I believe that is why, in the book of Acts, the account of Paul's conversion on the road to Damascus, where Christ called him to be His Apostle, is repeated three times. It is to remind the people that Paul is an authentic agent of revelation. He speaks with the authority of Jesus.

The next thing we learn about Paul is that he had been **separated to the gospel of God** (v. 1c). In Latin, *separated* means "segregated," set apart from the multitude to a specific, sacred, consecrated task. The phrase Paul uses involves a part of speech in the Greek language called the genitive, which indicates possession. He is not saying, "I have been commissioned to announce a message or good news about God." Rather, he is saying that the gospel that he has been separated and called to proclaim is God's gospel. God is the Author and owner of it. Paul is simply the messenger whom God has called and set apart to proclaim to people a message that comes from God Himself.

Application

God used the Apostle Paul mightily, and he is a lesson of God's grace. Paul himself reminds us, "I was formerly a blasphemer, a persecutor, and an insolent man; but I obtained mercy" (1 Tim. 1:13). This was the Paul whom God had set apart. Just like Paul, we have been delivered from our former sins in Christ, and God calls us into His service for the advancement of the gospel.

3

The Promised Gospel

PAUL HAS BEEN SEPARATED FOR THE GOSPEL **which He promised before through His prophets in the Holy Scriptures** (v. 2). Sometimes we make an artificial separation or distinction between the Old and New Testaments. We talk about the Old Testament as law and the New Testament as gospel, as if there were no law in the New Testament and no gospel in the Old Testament. Paul says at the very beginning that the gospel is not a novelty; it is the same gospel that was promised numerous times before.

The first time the gospel was promised in the Old Testament was in the context of a curse. As a result of the fall, God cursed Adam and Eve as well as the serpent. God said that the Seed of the woman would crush the serpent's head, and in the process the seed of the serpent would bruise the man's heel. Centuries before Christ was delivered to the cross, where He crushed the head of Satan while being bruised for our iniquities, the gospel of Christ was given in the promise of the curse of the enemy. That is the *protoeuangelion*, the first proclamation of the gospel (Gen. 3:14–19).

Paul, an expert student of the Old Testament, was aware of that, which is why he said that this gospel is what God "promised before through His prophets in the Holy Scriptures." The "sacred writings" is the actual phrase he uses here. Many people today have lost confidence in the trustworthiness of sacred Scripture. However, God has not lost confidence in the power of the sacred Scriptures. He has invested the Scriptures with the power of the Holy Spirit. He declared to Isaiah, "My word . . . shall not return to Me void" (Isa. 55:11). When God utters words, the earth melts. Paul is not reticent about where his authority lies with respect to the gospel that God "promised before through His prophets in the Holy Scriptures."

Our Lord Himself, after His resurrection, as He walked with people on the road to Emmaus, opened up the Old Testament text to them "beginning at Moses and all the Prophets" (Luke 24:27), showing that they should not have been surprised by His resurrection. Jesus' identity was still hidden from these people. When they sat down to break bread together, Jesus left them, and they then realized who He was. Their response was, "Did not our heart burn within us while He talked with us on the road, and while He opened the Scriptures to us?" (v. 32). It is good for our hearts to burn when we see the power of sacred Scripture authenticating God's truth.

Application

As Christians, we ought to be as the Bereans were. When Paul and Silas brought the gospel to the Jews in Berea, "they received the word with all readiness, and searched the Scriptures daily to find out whether these things were so" (Acts 17:11). The Bereans examined the Scriptures daily to know whether Jesus was indeed the Christ. When we come to know Jesus as the Christ through God's Word, we ought to endeavor all the more to encounter Him there.

4

Jesus Christ Our Lord: Seed of David

THIS GOSPEL FROM GOD, PAUL CONTINUES, is that **concerning His Son Jesus Christ our Lord** (v. 3a). In this brief passage, Paul calls Jesus the Son of God, and he calls Him the Messiah of Israel, which is what the term *Christ* means. *Jesus Christ* is not His name. *Jesus* is His name. His full name would be Jesus bar Joseph or Jesus of Nazareth. The word *Christ* is His title, and the title *Jesus Christ* means "Jesus Christos," or "Jesus Messiah." God's Son is the Christ, **who was born of the seed of David according to the flesh** (v. 3b). This is important to the Jew, because the Old Testament prophecies of the coming Messiah said that He would be from the lineage of David. Luke spends much time on the nativity of Jesus, bringing us to Bethlehem, the city of David, because the Old Testament prophesied that the Messiah would be born from the loins of David. He was to be David's son yet at the same time David's Lord.

Paul reminds the recipients of this epistle that Jesus Christ was descended from David *kata sarka,* "according to the flesh." This is another important phrase in the New Testament. The Greek language uses two different words to refer to the physical nature of our humanity, words that are sometimes, but not always, used interchangeably. The more common word for *body,* or the physical makeup of people, is the word *sōma*. When psychiatrists and psychologists talk about psychosomatic illnesses, they are referring to illnesses that have their genesis in some aspect of one's psychology. It is not that the illnesses are not real—they are real, and they affect the *sōma,* the body.

In addition to the term *sōma,* there is the word *sarx,* which also refers to the physical dimension of human life. Paul says elsewhere that he did not meet Jesus in the flesh. He met Him in the power of His resurrection on the road to Damascus, but he never met Him personally during His incarnation in this world. That is what Paul is getting at here. Elsewhere the term *sarx* is loaded with theological content. It is used to describe our fallen, corrupt nature. When Jesus said, "That which is born of the flesh is flesh, and that which is born of the Spirit is spirit" (John 3:6), or, "The flesh profits nothing" (6:63), He was talking about our fallen condition, not about our skin and bones. He was talking about our corrupt nature, which Scripture frequently sets in contrast to the spirit.

Application

When we study the Bible, we must carefully determine the meanings of words. Words can have multiple meanings. The same word in one context can mean something different in another context. Therefore, one principle that ought to guide our interpretation of Scripture is to study words in their context. Paying close attention to context helps us interpret Scripture using Scripture.

5

Jesus Christ Our Lord: Son of God

CHRIST DID NOT RECEIVE HIS DEITY from Mary or from Joseph. He brought His deity with Him from heaven. With respect to His divine nature, of course, He is the Logos of heaven. He was born of the seed of David according to the flesh and declared to be the Son of God. Paul summarizes the whole life and work of Jesus here: He is "born of the seed of David" (v. 3) and **declared to be the Son of God with power** (v. 4a).

Paul makes clear in his next breath the way in which the declaration was made: **by the resurrection from the dead** (v. 4b). When God the Holy Spirit raised the corpse of Jesus from the tomb, God was announcing to the world the sonship of Jesus. By what evidence do we believe that Jesus is the Son of God? By the testimony of God, who has declared Him to be His Son through the power of the resurrection. Paul debated with the philosophers on Mars Hill at the Areopagus, where a monument was erected to an unknown god: "These times of ignorance God overlooked, but now commands all men everywhere to repent, because He has appointed a day on which He will judge the world in righteousness by the Man whom He has ordained. He has given assurance of this to all by raising Him from the dead" (Acts 17:30–31).

As we will see later in Romans 1, Paul labors the point that God has manifested Himself so clearly to every human being that nobody has an excuse for denying Him. When Jesus is declared to be God's Son through the power of the resurrection, that declaration may be all that we ever get. We might be like Thomas and say, "Unless I see in His hands the print of the nails, and put my finger into the print of the nails, and put my hand into His side, I will not believe" (John 20:25). We do not want to say that to God on judgment day, because He has manifested the reality of Jesus through the power of the resurrection. This is the appeal that Paul is making here. He is saying, "I'm not the one declaring to you that Jesus is the Son of God. God has declared that to you by the Holy Spirit in the power of the resurrection."

Application

The resurrection of Jesus Christ is the bedrock of the Christian faith. In it, Jesus was powerfully declared to be the Son of God, and in it, we also place our confidence for our own bodily resurrections. Hebrews 1:2 tells us that "in these last days [God has] spoken to us by His Son." As those who have been spiritually raised to newness of life, let us always look for God's definitive Word to us in Him.

6

Called of Christ

PAUL SAYS THAT JESUS IS THE SOURCE of his apostleship: **Through Him we have received grace and apostleship** (v. 5a). But he does not stop there: the Apostles had received grace and apostleship **for obedience to the faith among all nations for His name, among whom you also are the called of Jesus Christ** (vv. 5b–6). Paul moves quickly from his own call as an Apostle to the call shared by every Christian in the church at Rome and by every Christian in every church in every age. The Bible calls them elect, "the called-out ones." The church is the *ekklēsia*, a Greek word that comes from the verb *kaleō*, meaning "to call," and the prefix *ek-*, meaning "out of." Every Christian is called out of the world, out of bondage, out of death, and out of sin, and into Christ and into His body. Paul is not the only one who has been called. All who are truly part of the church have been called out, separated by the power of the Holy Spirit.

What are you called to be? **To all who are in Rome, beloved of God, called to be saints** (v. 7a). That is your vocation.

"What are you studying?"

"I'm studying to be a saint. Do you think it will ever happen?"

"It has already happened if you are in Christ Jesus."

You are already numbered among the saints. The word for *saint* in the New Testament is the word that means "sanctified one," one who has been set apart by the Holy Spirit and called inwardly by Christ to Himself. If you put your trust in Christ, you are right now a saint. You are set apart. You are part of the invisible church, which is beloved of God.

Application

The church in Corinth was rife with sin. Yet it was to this church that Paul wrote, "To the church of God which is at Corinth, to those who are sanctified in Christ Jesus, called to be saints" (1 Cor. 1:2). Often, we might feel more like sinners than saints, but the reality is that while we do sin, we are saints *right now* in Jesus Christ, and this is our calling throughout the Christian life.

WEEK 2

1

Grace and Peace

PAUL EXPRESSES HIS TRADITIONAL GREETING: Grace to you and peace (v. 7b). In Old Testament times, the Jews greeted one another the same way they do today: *Shalom aleichem*, "Peace be unto you." The response to the greeting was *Aleichem shalom*, "Peace also to you." Our Jewish friends say prayers for the peace of Jerusalem, and the Jewish benediction for centuries has been this: "The LORD bless you and keep you; the LORD make His face shine upon you, and be gracious to you; the LORD lift up His countenance upon you, and give you peace" (Num. 6:24–26). This peace is "not as the world gives," said Jesus in His final will and testament before leaving the world (John 14:27). He left us His peace, a peace that transcends earthly peace, a peace that is permanent and eternal, one in which the warfare between the sinner and God is over.

Isaiah was directed by God to say:

"Comfort, yes, comfort My people!"
Says your God.
"Speak comfort to Jerusalem, and cry out to her,
That her warfare is ended,

That her iniquity is pardoned;
For she has received from the Lord's hand
Double for all her sins." (Isa. 40:1–2)

That cry is pronounced for every Christian, which is why Jesus is the consolation of Israel. He is our Paraclete—our Comforter—because He is the One who comforts us; He gives us the peace of God that cannot be revoked. It is not an uneasy truce. God does not rattle the sword every time He is distressed with our behavior.

Having been reconciled, justified, we possess that peace right now—and forevermore—which is integral to the Apostolic greeting, "Grace and peace." They go together because the peace of God is not something we can ever earn or merit or deserve. The peace that comes from God is by His grace. Paul wishes that his friends in the church at Rome would receive the grace of God.

Application

Consider the significance of what it means to have peace with God through our Lord Jesus Christ. Is this peace something that you experience even when confessing your sin to our loving heavenly Father? Just as Paul extended his greeting of "grace and peace" to the Romans, may our experience of this grace and peace create in us a longing for it to be extended to others as they come to saving faith in Christ even through us.

2

Paul's Thanksgiving and Vow

PAUL CONTINUES HIS GREETINGS and opening comments to the church at Rome with a thankful heart: **I thank my God through Jesus Christ**

for you all, that your faith is spoken of throughout the whole world
(v. 8). The word that Paul uses for "thank" is *eucharistō*, from which
the church gets the term *Eucharist*. The word was used to describe
the celebration of the Lord's Supper. A profound spirit of thanksgiving lay at the heart of the Supper in the primitive Christian church,
thanksgiving for what God had wrought in the work of Jesus Christ.

Paul conjoins the words *universe* and *cosmos* to say that the Roman
Christians' reputation for faith has been broadcast throughout the cosmos, or universe. In a sense, Paul is using hyperbole, but it is important
to pause and pay attention to his use of the term *world*, one of many
times in the Bible, particularly in the New Testament, where it occurs.
When we think of the world, we typically have in mind the entire
planet. We think of the continents and all the people who live in far-off
places. But when first-century people spoke of the world, they were
speaking of the known world, which, in their case, was the Mediterranean world. Therefore, Paul is expressing joy that people throughout
the Mediterranean world are talking about the faith of the Roman
Christians; their faith had made an impact.

Paul follows this note of thanksgiving by swearing a vow—**for
God is my witness** (v. 9a). From time to time, the Apostles swore an
oath to guarantee the trustworthiness of what they were saying, just
as we do in a courtroom when we say, "I swear to tell the truth, the
whole truth, and nothing but the truth, so help me God." Paul does
that here. He is eager that the recipients of his epistle understand the
depth of passion he feels in his grateful heart for the remembrance
that is being published throughout the known world concerning their
faith, and he demonstrates his eagerness by swearing a vow. The
basic purpose of Paul's vow is to assure the Roman Christians that
his desire to come visit them is not casual. He has made mention of
them constantly in his prayers, and he has been hoping and planning
that somehow, through the will of God, he will make it to Rome. He
had no idea when he wrote those words that the manner in which he

would finally make it to Rome would be in chains as a prisoner of the Roman government.

Application

Is your faith, like that of the Romans, known "throughout the whole world," at least in your little corner of it? Your faith can make an impact. God can use your faith and good reputation to draw others to Himself. Pray that God would do this in your life, giving you boldness and helping you live out your faith in a way that is seen by others and that leads to His praise.

3

The Euangelion *in the Old Testament*

"FOR GOD IS MY WITNESS," whom I serve with my spirit in the gospel of His Son, that without ceasing I make mention of you always in my prayers, making request if, by some means, now at last I may find a way in the will of God to come to you (vv. 9–10). We noted before that Paul identifies himself as one separated as an Apostle and called by God to preach the gospel. I said that the phrase "the gospel of God" (v. 1c) did not mean the gospel *about* God, but rather the gospel that is *the possession* of God. God owns that gospel. He is the One who invented the gospel and commissioned Paul to teach it. The gospel did not originate with Paul; it originated with God. Here, Paul uses the same structure to refer not to the gospel of God but to the gospel of God's Son, Jesus Christ. The gospel is the possession of Jesus, but even more, Jesus is the heart of the content of the gospel.

The word for "gospel" is the word *euangelion*. It has that prefix *eu-*, which comes into English in a variety of words. We talk about *euphonics* or *euphonious* music, which refers to something that sounds good. We talk about a *eulogy*, which is a good word pronounced about someone at his or her funeral service. The prefix *eu-* refers to something good or pleasant. The word *angelos* or *angelion* is the word for "message." Angels are messengers, and an *angelos* is one who delivers a message.

This word *euangelion*, which means "good message" or "good news," has a rich background in the Old Testament. There, the basic meaning of the term *gospel* was simply an announcement of a good message. If a doctor came to examine a sick person and afterward declared that the problem was nothing serious, that was gospel or good news. In ancient days when soldiers went out to battle, people waited breathlessly for a report from the battlefield about the outcome. Once the outcome of the battle was sure, marathon runners dashed back to the people to give the report of the conflict. That is why Isaiah wrote, "How beautiful upon the mountains are the feet of him who brings good news" (Isa. 52:7). The watchman in the watchtower would look as far as the eye could see into the distance. Finally, he would see the dust moving as the runner sped back to the city to give the report of the battle. The watchmen were trained to tell by the way the runner's legs were churning whether the news was good or bad. If the runner was doing the survival shuffle, it indicated a grim report, but if his legs were flying and the dust was kicking up, that meant good news. That is the concept of *gospel* in its most rudimentary sense.

Application

Have you ever had to deliver bad news? It's difficult. But imagine yourself like one of those marathon runners whom Isaiah pictured. In Christ, you've been given a message of good news, an announcement of victory, that Jesus has defeated sin, Satan, and death in His triumph on the cross. Imagine the rush of Isaiah's messenger. May this be true of us when we reflect on and share the gospel.

4

The Euangelion *in the New Testament*

WHEN WE COME TO THE NEW Testament, we find three distinct ways in which the term *gospel* is used. First, we have four books in the New Testament that we call Gospels: Matthew, Mark, Luke, and John. These books are biographical portraits of Jesus. *Gospel* in this sense describes a particular form of literature. Second, during the earthly ministry of Jesus, the term *gospel* was linked not particularly with the person of Jesus but with the kingdom of God. John the Baptist is introduced as one who comes preaching the gospel, and his message is "Repent, for the kingdom of heaven is at hand!" (Matt. 3:2). Jesus did the same in His parables, proclaiming, "The kingdom of God is like . . ." On the lips of Jesus, the gospel was about the dramatic moment in history when, through the long-awaited Messiah, the kingdom of God had broken through in time and space. The good news was the good news of the kingdom. Third, by the time the Epistles were written, particularly the Pauline epistles, the term *gospel* had taken on a new shade of understanding. It had become the gospel of Jesus Christ. *Gospel* had a clear content to it. At the heart of this gospel was the announcement of who Jesus was and what He had accomplished in His lifetime.

In addition to the person and work of Jesus, there is also in the New Testament use of the term *gospel* the question of how the benefits accomplished by the objective work of Jesus are subjectively appropriated to the believer. First, there is the question of who Jesus was and what He did. Second is the question of how that benefits you and me. That is why Paul conjoins the objective account of the person and work of Jesus (particularly to the Galatians) with the doctrine of justification by faith alone, which is essential to the gospel. In preaching the gospel we preach about Jesus, and we preach about how we are brought into a saving relationship with Him.

The gospel is under attack in the church today. I cannot stress enough how important it is to get the gospel right and to understand both the objective aspect of the person and work of Jesus and the subjective dimension of how we benefit from that by faith alone.

Application

In what ways have you seen the gospel attacked in the church or in society? Is the objective or subjective dimension of the gospel attacked more frequently? Now consider your role in the kingdom to defend the gospel and take some time to reflect on these two dimensions. Rehearse a succinct gospel presentation that incorporates both aspects and anticipates the common attacks that you have heard.

5

Encouraged Together

PAUL HAS A DEEP YEARNING, a passion in his soul, to meet the Roman Christians face-to-face: **that I may impart to you some spiritual gift, so that you may be established** (v. 11). Paul is not referring to starting out in the Christian faith but to becoming confirmed, built up, and edified in it. Nor is he writing about charismatic gifts here but about establishing believers in confidence and maturity in their faith. This is why Paul wrote the letter to the Romans, and it is why, in the providence of God, his letter is given to us—that the faith that has taken root in our souls may be established so that we may grow to maturity and full conformity to the image of Christ.

Paul adds this reason to his desire to visit them: **that I may be encouraged together with you by the mutual faith both of you and me** (v. 12). He makes that comment in passing, so I do not want to labor it, but I do want to mention that Paul was such a tremendous pastor, as well as a theologian, a missionary, and an evangelist, because his heart was involved. When he wrote to the church at Corinth recalling the experiences he had shared with the Corinthian Christians, he mentioned specifically that he had been with them in their trials and afflictions (1 Cor. 2:3). Paul did not just preach at or to people. He longed to be with the Roman Christians, not just so that he could encourage them but so that they could encourage him.

Every pastor needs to be encouraged. So often, the work of the pastorate is an exercise in discouragement. The pastor is fair game for all criticism, and every Sunday afternoon people have roast pastor for dinner. When a pastor stands at the door at the end of the service and speaks to fifty people, forty-nine will say, "Thank you, Pastor, for bringing the Word of God to us today. It ministered to me, and I appreciate that message I heard this morning." But there is one who says, "I cannot believe that awful sermon you preached this morning." When the pastor goes home, is he going to remember the forty-nine words of encouragement or the one word of discouragement? If other pastors are like me, that one remark will eat away at them for the rest of the day. That is why pastors have to be encouraged. Paul needed that kind of encouragement.

Application

God gives pastors a remarkable responsibility: to keep watch over our souls. And for this, they must give an account (Heb. 13:17). One of the ways that you can encourage your pastor is by listening to him, not only when he encourages you from God's Word but also when he does the hard work of calling you to repentance from God's Word.

6

Paul's Longing

NOW I DO NOT WANT YOU TO BE unaware, brethren, that I often planned to come to you (but was hindered until now), that I might have some fruit among you also, just as among the other Gentiles (v. 13). Paul refers to the Roman Christians as "Gentiles." I am sure that there were Jewish converts mixed in among the Gentiles there, but the Christian Jews had been expelled from Rome by the emperor Claudius a short time before this epistle was written, and Gentiles were primarily the ones left.

I am a debtor both to Greeks and to barbarians, both to wise and to unwise (v. 14). He does not say that he is a debtor to the Jew and the Greek but to the Greek and the barbarian. The Greeks were the highly cultured, civilized, intellectual elite of the ancient culture as distinguished from the rest of the Gentiles, who were pagan barbarians. Paul is in debt both to the high-minded Greek and to the barbarian, but he is not talking about a pecuniary obligation or debt; he does not owe them money. Paul is writing about a moral debt. He is burdened by an obligation that accompanied his office as an Apostle.

He had been set apart as the Apostle to the Gentiles, and he spends his life discharging that obligation. Ultimately, the debt Paul owes is owed to God and to Christ, but he transfers that indebtedness, that obligation, to the people who need to hear the gospel. To Paul's way of thinking, so long as he is alive he cannot pay that debt because he owes his life to every person he meets. Someone said to me, "R.C., I want you to know that I have decided to dedicate the rest of my life to serving Jesus." I have heard that many times from people, but it never gets stale. Such fervency of soul should be the heartbeat of every believer. Once again Paul reaches down into his soul to speak of the depth of his passion: as much as is in me, I am ready to preach the gospel to you who are in Rome also (v. 15). Paul is saying, "Every fiber of my being is ready to preach the gospel to you. I cannot wait to get there."

Application

God has given you specific gifts for the work of ministry in the church. Paul was compelled to serve Christ with all his life. We are called to do the same. Feeling this eager compulsion to serve our Lord is one of the signs that the Spirit is at work in us. Pray that God would only strengthen this desire in you, even if it is already strong but especially if it is weak.

WEEK 3

1

Not Ashamed

IT SHOULD BE FOR THE PASTOR as it was for Paul: **For I am not ashamed of the gospel of Christ** (v. 16a). If we think our culture is hostile to the gospel, the first-century culture Paul lived in was much more so. Yet Paul was not ashamed of the gospel; he gloried in it. "Let the one who boasts boast in the Lord" (2 Cor. 10:17, NIV). Paul enjoyed nothing more than being known as a Christian.

Jesus warned us that if we are ashamed of Him before men, He will be ashamed of us before His Father (Mark 8:38; Luke 9:26). That is the real crunch for many Christians. They want to be Secret Service Christians. They do not want to be known as "holier than thou." They know that if they say one word to their friends about Christ, they will be accused of trying to shove the gospel down their throats. If we get rebuffed enough times, pretty soon we find ourselves tempted to be embarrassed about our faith, but not the Apostle. He could not wait to get to Rome because he was not ashamed of the gospel. The gospel is **the power of God to salvation for everyone who believes, for the Jew first and also for the Greek** (v. 16b).

God's power is invested in the gospel. God has promised that His Word will not return to Him void (Isa. 55:11). The foolishness of preaching is the method that God has chosen to save the world. That is why Paul said that he was not ashamed. He wanted to preach the gospel because it is the power of God to salvation. It is not the power of the preacher's eloquence or the power of the preacher's education; it is the power of God.

Application

There's no shame in the gospel. There's no shame in being a Christian. The world may think that the gospel is folly, but here Paul reminds us that it is the power of God. Have this very same conviction when you share it and especially when others try to shame you for believing it. The gospel of God—the gospel of Jesus Christ—is our only hope and our greatest joy.

2

Alien Righteousness

WE NEED THE POWER OF GOD for salvation, **for in it the righteousness of God is revealed from faith to faith** (v. 17a). In the gospel, the righteousness of God is revealed from faith to faith. This was the verse that the Holy Spirit used to awaken Martin Luther as he was preparing his lectures on the book of Romans. He glanced at a manuscript from Augustine and found where Augustine said that the righteousness here is not God's righteousness but rather it is the righteousness that He provides for people who do not have any righteousness. It is the righteousness He makes available by free grace to all who believe. Luther called it "alien righteousness." This righteousness is not our own; it is Jesus' righteousness.

Luther sought every means he knew within the confines of the monastery to satisfy the demands of God's law, yet he had no peace. Luther was an expert in the law of God, and every day he was in terror as he looked in the mirror of the law and examined his life against God's righteousness. We are not in terror, because we have blocked out the view of God's righteousness. We judge ourselves on a curve, measuring ourselves against others. We never judge ourselves according to the standard of God's perfection. If we did, we would be tormented as Luther was in the monastery. Luther, on realizing the truth that it is God's righteousness and not our own which saves us, said that it seemed as if the doors of paradise swung open, and he walked through. That is the reason he stood against kings and officials of the church. He refused to compromise. Once he had tasted the gospel of Jesus Christ and had been delivered from the pangs and torment of the law, nobody could take it from him.

Application

Salvation is by faith alone. But even our faith isn't ground for boasting. Our faith is in someone else's righteousness: Christ's righteousness. His righteousness is given to us as a gift, and our entire salvation rests on it from first to last. If you are trusting in Christ and in Christ alone, you stand, right now and forever, justified before God.

3

The Life of Faith

AS IT IS WRITTEN, **"The just shall live by faith"** (v. 17b), which comes from the Old Testament book of the prophet Habakkuk and is quoted three times in the New Testament: here in Romans 1:17, in Galatians 3:11, and in Hebrews 10:38. In its original context, Habakkuk was deeply distressed. The people of God were being invaded by pagans, the pagans were triumphing, and Habakkuk was confused. He asked God:

> You are of purer eyes than to behold evil,
> And cannot look on wickedness.
> Why do You look on those who deal treacherously,
> And hold Your tongue when the wicked devours
> A person more righteous than he? (Hab. 1:13)

Then Habakkuk stood in his watchtower and set himself on the rampart, waiting to see what God would say to him. The Lord answered:

> Write the vision
> And make it plain on tablets,
> That he may run who reads it.
> For the vision is yet for an appointed time;
> But at the end it will speak, and it will not lie.
> Though it tarries, wait for it. (2:2–3)

Do you ever feel tension because the promises of God do not show up when you want them to? You cry and say, "God, where are You in this?" That was the complaint of Habakkuk, and yet the God we worship is a promise-keeping God. He tells Habakkuk to be patient:

> Because it will surely come,
> It will not tarry.

> Behold the proud,
> His soul is not upright in him;
> But the just shall live by his faith. (2:3–4)

One who lives by faith is a righteous person in the sight of God. The righteous live by trust. When Jesus was in the Judean wilderness under the unbridled assault of Satan, lonely and hungry, Satan told Him to take stones and make them bread. Jesus said that He would not do that: "It is written, 'Man shall not live by bread alone, but by every word that proceeds from the mouth of God'" (Matt. 4:4). Anybody can believe *in* God. What it means to be a Christian is to trust Him when He speaks, which does not require a leap of faith or a crucifixion of the intellect. It requires a crucifixion of pride, because no one is more trustworthy than God.

When we do not trust God, it is because we transfer to Him our own corrupt qualities, but God does not have any of those corrupt qualities. You can trust Him with your life, and that is the theme of this epistle— the just shall live by faith—and from that vantage point, Paul opens up the depths and the riches of the whole gospel for the people of God.

Application

Are you distressed by our culture's dismissal of God? Like Habakkuk, perhaps you see things that make you begin to question God. But also like Habakkuk, we must trust the Lord and recognize that the tension we are feeling arises because we know that God is perfectly just and sovereign over the world that is unjust. His justice means, however, that He will one day certainly set all things right even as it sometimes seem to us that He is slow to act. As you wait for Him, grow more and more in your trust in Him.

4

Wrath Revealed, Truth Suppressed

BEFORE PAUL DEVELOPS THE THEME of the gospel, he says that **the wrath of God is revealed from heaven against all ungodliness and**

unrighteousness of men (v. 18a). It is perfectly appropriate for a holy and righteous God to be moved to anger against evil. A judge with no distaste for evil would not be a good judge. God is angry with two distinct things: ungodliness, or irreverence or impiety (from the Latin word *impiatos*), and unrighteousness. *Ungodliness* and *unrighteousness* are vast generic terms that cover a multitude of sins, but Paul is not talking about a multitude of sins here. He has in view one particular sin. It is a universal sin, one committed by every human being. It is the sin that most clearly expresses our Adamic nature, our corruption and fallenness in the flesh. Paul does not leave us to guess at the nature of this sin; God is provoked to an orgy of anger against the sin of those **who suppress the truth in unrighteousness** (v. 18b). The single sin that provokes God's wrath against the whole human race is the sin of suppressing truth.

The root of the Greek word translated *suppress* is *katacain*, which can also be translated as *to hinder, to stifle, to incarcerate, to put in detention, to obscure,* or *to repress.* We might think of a gigantic spring or coil that would require all the strength in our body to push down or compress. While we are pushing it down, it is resisting our strength and seeking to spring back up and recoil into its original position. By nature we take the truth of God and press it down. We force it into our subconscious, as it were, to get it out of our mind; yet despite all the strength we use to suppress it, we simply cannot eradicate it. We cannot get rid of it because it is always and everywhere pushing back up. The specific sin here is the suppression of truth.

What truth is being suppressed? Paul tells us: **because what may be known of God is manifest in them, for God has shown it to them** (v. 19). The truth that every human being suppresses is the truth of God, what God reveals of Himself in nature to the whole human race. This is not the truth of God that we learn through the Bible. We suppress that, too, but here Paul is writing of a truth that is known about God apart from the Bible, a knowledge of God that God makes manifest.

The Greek word is *phoneros*, which means "to show plainly." We use the term *phenomenon*, which is derived from that Greek word. The Latin text translates it as *manifestum*. The knowledge that God gives of Himself is not obscure. It is not buried with hidden clues that only an intellectual, elite group of people are able to discover after a painful and tedious search of sifting through the evidence. The truth that God gives of Himself is manifest. It is clear—so plain that it is clear to everybody.

Application

As you pray today, praise God for His holy and righteous wrath against evil and for His goodness in delivering you from His wrath. Believing on Christ, you can know that He died on the cross as an acceptable sacrifice for your sins. In our justification, He has given us His righteousness—even we who once suppressed the truth in unrighteousness. Let us all the more in light of God's love proclaim it.

5

The Visibility of the Invisible God

GOD HAS PLAINLY AND CLEARLY SHOWN Himself to everyone. **For since the creation of the world His invisible attributes are clearly seen** (v. 20a). The Latin word used for "clearly seen" is the root for our English word *conspicuous*; God has made His self-revelation conspicuous to everyone since the creation of the world. God does not pop a clue into history about His existence every three thousand years or so. Every moment since the dawn of creation, God has been manifesting Himself through **the things that are made** (v. 20b). God did not give us a world and just say, "Sit down and begin to think about where that world came from and reason from the cosmos back to God." We are to do that, but it is more than that. Every second, God is manifesting Himself through the things that are made so that His testimony to His nature is plainly evident.

Immanuel Kant, the great philosopher of the eighteenth century and perhaps the greatest agnostic of all time, revolutionized the world of philosophy by giving a systematic and comprehensive critique of the traditional classic arguments for the existence of God. Kant argued that you cannot reason from the visible things of the world back to the invisible God. According to Kant, God is in a realm not known through theoretical reason or empirical investigation. If Kant was right, then the Apostle Paul was wrong. If Paul was right, then Kant was wrong. It is time that the Christian church stopped rolling over and playing dead at the feet of Immanuel Kant and started showing the error of Kant's reasoning. In Romans Paul sets forth plainly that the invisible God, even though He cannot be seen because He is invisible, is clearly seen. God is not seen directly, but He is seen through the things that are made.

God reveals **His eternal power and Godhead** (v. 20c) to the whole world. This revelation does not give us all the specific details about the character and nature of God, but it certainly gives us knowledge of God in general. This revelation includes God's eternal power. God's self-existent, eternal being has been revealed in every leaf, every page, every raindrop, and every inch of the cosmos since the beginning of time. The temporal world is the vehicle of divine revelation, and by it all people are able to know that God exists. God's eternal power and His inherent attributes—immutability, omniscience, omnipresence, and all that fits deity—are made clear through nature. God is also revealed by His moral perfection, holiness, righteousness, and sovereign right to impose obligations upon His creatures without their permission or assent. God inherently has the right to command from His creatures what is pleasing to Him. Paul says that all these things are made clear to us.

Application

Believing that God exists isn't irrational. Romans 1:18–20 teaches us that we can reason to the existence of God from the things that He has made. As staggering as the beauty, power, and majesty of God's creation is, even more staggering is to think that in every way God is so much more. The things that He has made "are the mere edges of His ways" (Job 26:14). Scripture gives us an even fuller picture of who God is. May we study it regularly.

6

Without Excuse

PAUL EXPLAINS THE RATIONALE for the revelation of God's wrath: **they are without excuse** (v. 20d). Man has no basis for an *apologia* ("defense") to God's indictment. What answer will corrupt and fallen human beings try to give to God on the day of judgment? "God, I did not know You were there. If You had made Your revelation clear to me, I would have been Your obedient servant." People will be tempted to make a plea or excuse, but everyone stands without an excuse. There is no excuse of ignorance before God, not when He Himself has given us the information. A plea of ignorance is an empty plea and will have no effect.

Although they knew God, they did not glorify Him as God, nor were thankful (v. 21a). A well-known Dutch philosopher and theologian said about this text that although God has objectively revealed Himself to the human race, this general revelation yields no natural theology; that is, the revelation does not penetrate man's consciousness. Those who hold to this view cite John Calvin, who saw nature as a glorious theater that man cannot see because of his fallen condition. I think it is unfortunate that Calvin, the great Reformer, used that metaphor, because it is not consistent with everything else he taught about our response to general revelation.

Man's problem is not that the knowledge fails to get through in the sense of a cognitive awareness of the reality of God. God is angry because that knowledge does get through. It is what we do with the knowledge that provokes the wrath of God. Knowing God, we refuse to honor Him as God; neither are we grateful.

The most fundamental sin in our fallen, corrupt nature is the sin of idolatry, the sin of refusing to honor God as He is. We want to strip Him of His attributes, turn Him into a God made in our image, a God whom we can live with, a God whom we can be comfortable with. People say that God is a God of love, not a God of wrath, but that is not the God of Scripture. The God of love revealed in Scripture is also angry with sin. He is the God of justice, righteousness, and holiness. We cannot embrace the attributes of God that make us comfortable and reject the rest. When we do that, we join the throng of humanity that suppresses the truth of God and refuses to honor Him as God or be thankful.

Application

When you reflect on what God has done for you in Jesus Christ, gratitude is natural. But we cannot truly fathom how much God has done for us in Christ if we acknowledge only some of His attributes. The cross was a glorious display of God's love, but it was also a display of His wrath. That we are saved from His wrath, knowing that we deserve that wrath, is why we are so thankful.

WEEK 4

1

Fools

BECAUSE MEN REFUSED TO GLORIFY GOD AS GOD, THEY **became futile in their thoughts, and their foolish hearts were darkened** (v. 21b). Some of the most brilliant people come to very different conclusions about the nature of reality. Who was more brilliant than Thomas Aquinas or Aurelius Augustine? They were fiercely convinced of the reality of God, and their lives were driven by that conviction, which lay at the foundation of everything else they believed. Others of gifted intellect, such as Jean-Paul Sartre, John Stuart Mill, and Albert Camus, wound up on the other end of the spectrum, embracing nihilism à la Friedrich Nietzsche, saying that there is no meaning or significance in human experience. How can such brilliant people end up so far away? If, at the very beginning of the pursuit of knowledge, people categorically deny what they know to be true—the reality of God—then, frankly, the further away they will go from God. They have built their house on a lie so that their thinking becomes an exercise in futility, and their foolish hearts are darkened.

When Paul speaks of hearts that are dark, he uses the word *foolish*. To the Jew, the judgment of "foolish" is not an intellectual judgment; it is a moral judgment. That is why Jesus warned against calling people fools (Matt. 5:22). Don't say, "The fool has said in his heart, 'There is no God'" (Ps. 14:1). The fool is not only being stupid; he is also being wicked because he is denying what he knows to be true. The indictment on all people is this: they refuse to honor God as God. It is not that they fail to know God and therefore do not honor or thank Him. They do know God but will not honor Him or be grateful. That is the massive perdition in which we find ourselves as fallen human beings.

Their foolish hearts were darkened, and **professing to be wise, they became fools** (v. 22). There is an ongoing debate on television and in the newspapers between intelligent design and science. Intelligent design, many people claim, is not science. Yet the word *science* means "knowledge." If you know that God is the Author of all things, then you know that the affirmation of the existence of God is the purest scientific thought there is. To deny or exclude it is not to be scientific but to be foolish. It is ironic that those who refuse to acknowledge what they know to be true claim such activity in the name of wisdom. They call it *science* when actually it is foolishness—foolishness that betrays a heart of darkness. They do not become atheists, generally. They become idolaters. They become religious.

Application

The one who says in his heart that there is no God isn't merely being foolish. We must remember that he is also being sinful. Keep this in mind when you interact with nonbelievers. Belief in God is not morally neutral. Your friends and family who deny Him have darkened hearts, and they need the light of the gospel. Pray that the light of Jesus Christ shines in this darkness.

2

A Dreadful Exchange

THEY CHANGED THE GLORY OF **the incorruptible God into an image made like corruptible man—and birds and four-footed animals and creeping things** (v. 23). They exchange the truth of God—the majestic, self-existent, eternal God of heaven and earth—and begin to worship birds, bears, and totem poles. Can anything be more ridiculous than a religion that builds on a fundamental refusal to acknowledge what is known to be true? Can anything be more ridiculous than trading in the glory of God for the creature?

Therefore God also gave them up to uncleanness, in the lusts of their hearts, to dishonor their bodies among themselves, who exchanged the truth of God for the lie, and worshiped and served the creature rather than the Creator, who is blessed forever. Amen (vv. 24–25). (Even when Paul is talking about the wrath of God and the universal sin of fallen humanity, he cannot help but break into doxology, speaking about the Creator.) The word *exchanged* is a critical term here. It is the Greek word *metallassō*. I cannot help but read this text through the eyes of modern psychiatry, which works in terms of repression and suppression. What kinds of ideas do we tend to suppress or repress? We do not push down pleasant thoughts; we push down frightening thoughts and bad memories. But there is nothing more terrifying to a sinner than God.

In trying to explain the universality of religion, Sigmund Freud asked why it is that people are so incurably religious. He claimed that we have invented God to deal with things in nature that we find frightening. This is where Freud missed the point. If people are going to invent religion to protect them from the fear of nature, why would they invent a god who is more terrifying than nature itself? Why would they invent a holy god? Fallen creatures, when they make idols, do not make holy idols. We prefer the unholy, the profane, the secular—a god we can control.

Here in Romans, the Apostle brings us to the place where we have no excuse, where ignorance cannot be claimed, because God has so manifested Himself to every creature that every last one of us knows that God exists and that He deserves our honor and thanks and that He is not to be traded in or swapped for the creature.

Paul outlines the dreadful consequences that fall on a race of people who live by refusing to acknowledge what they know to be true about the character of God. The result is a futile mind, a blackened heart, and a life of radical corruption. People are exposed to God's displeasure so that their only hope is the gospel of His dear Son. This portion of Paul's letter is preparatory; it is the groundwork. If he had stopped here, we would be without hope, lost forever in our guilt and sin.

Application

Obviously, Freud was not on the Sea of Galilee when Jesus rebuked the wind and the waves (see Mark 4:35–41). Instead of experiencing the same calm that overcame the sea, the disciples experienced an escalation of fear because the holiness of Christ was made manifest. But it's precisely the holiness of Christ that we need to stand before a holy God without fear. Rejoice that God's love in Christ casts out fear, and seek to love others with the very same love (1 John 4:17–18).

3

Sin for Sin

MANY TIMES, IF NOT MOST TIMES, the sin we commit is a punishment for sin. When we sin, we are actually working out God's punishment for our sin. God gives us over to our sinful impulses. We become slaves to the things that we want to do. *(Fallen will outside of Christ)*

Paul gives a detailed description of how those sinful passions are manifested in concrete human behavior: **For this reason God gave them up to vile passions. For even their women exchanged the natural use for what is against nature** (v. 26). This is a text that we will not hear often on television in this day and age. There are two things I need to say about it. First, when the Apostle Paul describes the radical corruption of the human race, he sees the sin of homosexual behavior as the sin most representative of the radical nature of our fall. It is seen here not simply as a sin, nor even as a serious sin or a gross sin, but as the clearest expression of the depths of our perversity.

Second, when Paul introduces the sin of homosexual behavior, he first mentions females. Throughout human history, man has been the gender that seems most brutish, most without conscience and godliness. The woman has been understood as the fairer sex, but when Paul wants to describe the depth of the fall of the human race, he says that even the women exchanged the natural use for what is *contra naturam*, against nature, not simply against culture, or societal convention. In other words, when we become involved in homosexual practices, we are sinning not only against God but against the nature of things. All the debates today about whether homosexual behavior is acquired or inherently genetic can be answered here in this text. The Word of God says that such behavior is not natural. It is against nature as God has created it.

Likewise also the men, leaving the natural use of the woman, burned in their lust for one another, men with men committing what is shameful, and receiving in themselves the penalty of their error which was due (v. 27). When men and women engage in this kind of behavior, there are necessary, divinely appointed consequences. A price must be paid when people go that far to defy the law of God. The word *due* has all but disappeared from our culture and vocabulary, but it is one that has a very rich history in ethics. It goes back to the *Nicomachean Ethics* of Aristotle and on down through Western civilization, throughout which justice has been defined not only in the church but also outside the church as giving people what is due them. When people so act against God's law and the law of nature, He gives them what they earned.

Application

God has a clear design for the sexual relationship between one man and one woman in the context of a lawful marriage. This is a fundamental part of God's creation, which is why homosexual sin is against nature.

The staggering reality is that this is an expression of God's judgment. But sexual sin is not unforgivable. Pray to the Lord that those you know who are ensnared in sexual sin would repent and come to faith in Jesus Christ.

4

Filled with Unrighteousness

AND EVEN AS THEY DID NOT LIKE TO retain God in their knowledge, God gave them over to a debased mind (v. 28a), a mind that does not focus attention on whatsoever things are true, pure, lovely, and just (see Phil. 4:8). A debased mind is one in which the thoughts are filled with impurities, the desires of the flesh, lust, jealousy, and hatred against people. Such a mind is in love with the lie and flees from the truth. Our basic nature as fallen humans does not want to receive the knowledge of God, and when it does penetrate the mind, we do not want to keep it there. We see again God's use of judicial abandonment. It is as if He is saying, "If you want a mind fixed on debauchery, you can have it."

It is rare that human beings have a taste for and a love of hearing the Word of God. If we have any affection in our hearts to hear the things of God, it is possible only because the Holy Spirit has already rescued us from the condition that Paul is describing, which is basic to all humanity. If we have a desire to learn the things of God, then something has happened to plant that desire in our hearts. At one time, we had the mind of a reprobate and did not want knowledge of God.

Because they did not want to retain God in their knowledge, God gave them over to debased minds **to do those things which are not fitting; being filled with all unrighteousness** (vv. 28b–29a). If we ask people whether they believe man is basically good, the majority answer yes. Due to the impact of humanism on our culture, people believe that man is basically good and simply makes mistakes on occasion. Such thinking leads people to believe that they do not need Jesus. Yet there is nothing we need more than Jesus. We tickle our imaginations if we say that we are basically good. The people who need to hear the gospel are not merely tainted by unrighteousness; they are filled with unrighteousness. That is how Paul describes us in our natural condition. No one is merely mildly affected by error or bad habits or mistakes; man is saturated with unrighteousness.

Application

The idea that people are basically good strikes at the heart of the gospel. Every sin, even the most "minor" sin, is rebellion against God and a violation of His law. It's essential for people to recognize this to understand their need for the gospel. When you have opportunities to share the good news of Jesus Christ with people, make sure to bring this reality to bear so that they might see the horror of their sin and the beauty of the cross. *THE GOOD NEWS!*

5

List of Unrighteousness

UNRIGHTEOUSNESS IS A GENERAL TERM, but Paul wants to get more specific, so he begins to elaborate on the kinds of unrighteousness that fill us as fallen creatures. First is **sexual immorality** (v. 29b). Elsewhere the Apostle writes, "Fornication and all uncleanness or covetousness, let it not even be named among you, as is fitting for saints" (Eph. 5:3). A recent Gallup poll reported that the incidence of fornication and adultery among those who profess to be born-again Christians is not measurably different from that of unconverted pagans. Truly regenerate Christians do fall into these sins, but it should be a radical exception to Christian behavior, not a generally accepted practice. Today people get their behavioral cues not from what God says is acceptable but from the culture.

Some argue that condemning immoral behavior is old-fashioned, but that sort of thinking is why we have Christian parents giving their daughters birth-control pills, something that sends a message that sexual immorality is okay. Paul, however, puts sexual immorality at the top of the list of what constitutes our corruption. Sex is a beautiful thing. God designed it and gave it to His people, but He gave a context for it—marriage—and He is jealous that it be reserved for that context.

To sexual immorality Paul adds **wickedness** and **covetousness** (v. 29c). Covetousness is the sign of someone who does not want God in his thinking. When we covet someone else's property or prestige or job, we are saying, "God is not just in giving it to that person and not giving it to me." The minute we are envious and jealous of another, we have banished God from our minds. _Fact_

John Calvin had the highest view of human beings of any theologian in history, as far as I know. Some think otherwise in light of all that Calvin said about man's total depravity, but the reason why Calvin takes sin so seriously is that he takes people so seriously. The reason God takes sin so seriously is not that He is a bully or a killjoy who does not want His creatures to have any fun. God takes sin seriously because He knows how destructive sin is to this world and to our friends, to family, and to marriage. God has a better idea for what humans are to experience, and in His ultimate plan of redemption He will banish sin from His world altogether.

Application

It's easy to take our cues from culture instead of God. Is there any ground that you've given up in your thinking about what constitutes sexual immorality? Are you guarding yourself personally in this area? Christians are called to wage war against the flesh, and this is a lifelong battle, but commit yourself to continuing the fight, even if it's just at the heart level, with the Spirit's help.

6

The List Goes On

PAUL'S LIST GROWS: **maliciousness; full of envy, murder, strife, deceit, evil-mindedness; they are whisperers** (v. 29d). People whisper their plans because they cannot speak them aloud. Even in a fallen world, our plans are so evil that others will reject them, so we whisper. Paul also includes **backbiters** (v. 30a) on the list. Have people bitten us in the back? Have people slandered us? We must consider how many we have slandered and bitten in the back. This is not a problem only for pagans. As humans, we are given to this sort of behavior.

Next on Paul's list are **haters of God** (v. 30b). Who will admit to that—to actually hating God? He also adds **violent, proud, boasters,** and **inventors of evil things** (v. 30c). As if there were not enough temptations and sins to arouse our vile passions, we like to think up new ways to sin. Paul adds to his list **disobedient to parents** (v. 30d). When young people are disobedient to their parents, they are revealing their natural condition. Paul also includes those who are **undiscerning, untrustworthy, unloving, unforgiving, unmerciful** (v. 31). Despite the scope of his list, it is only partial. It is merely representative of our corruption. If Paul had enumerated all the sins that the Bible spells out, he could have filled the entire epistle and then some. He gives us a representative list that should be enough to stop every mouth and convict every conscience.

The worst indictment is not found in this list of heinous crimes against God. It is found in the conclusion of the chapter: **those who practice such things are deserving of death** (v. 32a). Paul says that fallen human beings not only do these things, but know better. God has planted in the mind of every creature made in His image a conscience that can discern the difference between good and evil. A normal person—a fallen person whose normal behavior is the abnormality of sin—knows that people who do these things are worthy of death.

It gets worse. Those who do those things **also approve of those who practice them** (v. 32b). There is honor among thieves. Misery loves company. If we can entice others to join us in our sin, we can get rid of the taboos rather than repent of our guilt. We seek to establish a new ethic.

Thanks be to God that Romans does not end here. The gospel, the good news, is coming. People who do not care about the good news might care if they digest the bad news first and realize what our Savior has done, what He has saved us from, what He has saved us for, and what He has saved us to. We are saved in order to be conformed to His image, to love the things He loves, and to hate the things He hates.

Application

Consider the list of sins that Paul gives us in today's reading. Despite the scope of his list, it is only partial. He gives us a representative list that should be enough to stop every mouth and convict every conscience. Look over this list again and pray to God to manifest the opposite of each sin in your life as one who is sanctified and being sanctified by the Lord.

Romans 2

THEREFORE YOU ARE INEXCUSABLE, O MAN, *whoever you are who judge, for in whatever you judge another you condemn yourself; for you who judge practice the same things. But we know that the judgment of God is according to truth against those who practice such things. And do you think this, O man, you who judge those practicing such things, and doing the same, that you will escape the judgment of God? Or do you despise the riches of His goodness, forbearance, and longsuffering, not knowing that the goodness of God leads you to repentance? But in accordance with your hardness and your impenitent heart you are treasuring up for yourself wrath in the day of wrath and revelation of the righteous judgment of God, who "will render to each one according to his deeds": eternal life to those who by patient continuance in doing good seek for glory, honor, and immortality; but to those who are self-seeking and do not obey the truth, but obey unrighteousness—indignation and wrath, tribulation and anguish, on every soul of man who does evil, of the Jew first and also of the Greek; but glory, honor, and peace to everyone who works what is good, to the Jew first and also to the Greek. For there is no partiality with God.*

For as many as have sinned without law will also perish without law, and as many as have sinned in the law will be judged by the law (for not the hearers of the law are just in the sight of God, but the doers of the law will be justified; for when Gentiles, who do not have the law, by nature do the things in the law, these, although not having the law, are a law to themselves, who show the work of the law written in their hearts, their conscience also bearing witness, and between themselves their thoughts accusing or else excusing them) in the day when God will judge the secrets of men by Jesus Christ, according to my gospel.

Indeed you are called a Jew, and rest on the law, and make your boast in God, and know His will, and approve the things that are excellent, being instructed out of the law, and are confident that you yourself are a guide to the blind, a light to those who are in darkness, an instructor of the foolish, a teacher of babes, having the form of knowledge and truth in the law. You, therefore, who teach another, do you not teach yourself? You who preach that a man should not steal, do you steal? You who say, "Do not commit adultery," do you commit adultery? You who abhor idols, do you rob temples? You who make your boast in the law, do you dishonor God through breaking the law? For "the name of God is blasphemed among the Gentiles because of you," as it is written. which is impossible

For circumcision is indeed profitable if you keep the law; but if you are a breaker of the law, your circumcision has become uncircumcision. Therefore, if an uncircumcised man keeps the righteous requirements of the law, will not his uncircumcision be counted as circumcision? And will not the physically uncircumcised, if he fulfills the law, judge you who, even with your written code and circumcision, are a transgressor of the law? For he is not a Jew who is one outwardly, nor is circumcision that which is outward in the flesh; but he is a Jew who is one inwardly; and circumcision is that of the heart, in the Spirit, not in the letter; whose praise is not from men but from God. By Regeneration

WEEK 5

1

Hypocrisy

PAUL HAS JUST FINISHED GIVING an indictment on all people. How long can he torment us with the oppressive character of the law and of our sin before he gives us some relief? After Jonathan Edwards preached one of his stirring sermons on the judgment of God and the threat of eternal damnation in hell, one of the parishioners cried out, "But, Mr. Edwards, is there no mercy with God?" Edwards reminded the people that they had to wait till the following Sabbath before they got that part of the message. The same is true here as we come to Romans 2. If we hope to get that good news now, our hopes are in vain, because the Apostle is not finished with the bad news yet. Before we get to the gospel, the good news of justification by faith alone, we must be brought kicking and screaming, if necessary, before the holy standard of God's law so that we might be duly persuaded of our need for the gospel.

Paul continues his somewhat relentless indictment of our sinfulness: **Therefore you are inexcusable, O man** (v. 1a). In light of all that he has just spread out before us of the universal rejection and suppression of God's manifest self-revelation, which everybody knows with clarity, and in light of God's eternal power, deity, and holiness, the sins that people practice are worthy of death. People not only continue to practice these sins, but also encourage others to do so. Therefore, man is without excuse. We might think that the "O man" is a generic address to any human being, but it was a common form of address in antiquity used between Jews. When Paul uses "O man," he is clearly addressing Jewish people.

Whoever you are who judge, for in whatever you judge another you condemn yourself; for you who judge practice the same things (v. 1b). The sin of hypocrisy is in view here. Paul is chastising his kinsmen according to the flesh, Israel, for their judgmental attitude toward the Gentiles. He is basically saying, "Who do you think you are? You condemn the Gentiles, yet practice the very same things they do." That is the essence of hypocrisy. It is the particular threat of doom to any preacher who dares to stand in a pulpit and correct sinners in the congregation, because he is himself a sinner and runs that very risk of condemning others for doing the very things that he does.

Even though these words are specifically addressed to Jews, there is a more universal application of the text. What was true for Israel is true for us—if we condemn other people for doing the very things that we do, then, by our condemning them, we are showing our awareness of the wrongness of certain activities, and we are in effect condemning ourselves.

Application

Take a moment to reflect on a sin you've pointed out in someone else's life that you've also committed. Although Paul's statements are directed to his kinsmen, they can just as easily apply to Christians today. Remember Jesus' words: "Why do you look at the speck in your brother's eye, but do not consider the plank in your own eye?" (Matt. 7:3).

2

No Escaping the Truth

THE ONE THING WE CAN BE CONFIDENT OF is that the just judgment of God is always according to truth: **But we know that the judgment of God is according to truth against those who practice such things** (v. 2). Nobody can stand before the judgment seat of God and complain, "That's not fair." Our consciences tell us that every last person, at some point, will be held accountable before his Creator—believer and nonbeliever alike. Even though the believer passes from condemnation, he will still have to stand before God and be judged, and that judgment will harbor no secrets. It will be perfect and accurate, for it will be according to truth.

Every time we read in the Scriptures descriptions of the judgment before the presence of God, we see that the human response is always silence. Every mouth will be stopped. We will see the futility of debate. The discussion is over when God renders His verdict, for we know that His judgment will be according to truth. **And do you think this, O man, you who judge those practicing such things, and doing the same, that you will escape the judgment of God?** (v. 3).

The deepest hope harbored in the hearts of corrupt humanity is that somehow we will escape. As W.C. Fields lay in his hospital room on his deathbed, a friend came to see him and was shocked to find Fields reading the Bible. Fields was not known for his religious devotion. When Fields' friend asked him why he was reading the Bible, Fields replied, "I'm looking for loopholes." Everyone thinks there is going to be a loophole, a way of escape from an omniscient, holy, righteous God, but there is no way to escape the judgment save through the way that that holy God has given to the world, which is the way of the cross. We do not want that way; we want to find a way to escape, yet there is none.

Or do you despise the riches of His goodness, forbearance, and longsuffering . . . ? (v. 4a). Paul's rhetorical question is essentially asking, "Do you take the goodness of God lightly? Do you take it for granted? Do you assume that because God is good He will not judge?" That is the most pervasive religious myth in our culture today. God is viewed as a cosmic bellhop at our beck and call. He is a celestial Santa Claus. All we have to do is come and ask Him for what we want, and He will provide it for us.

A judge who refuses to punish evil is not a good judge; he is an unjust judge. A corrupt judge is not good, but God in His goodness, the One who judges all and does what is right, promises judgment against evil. Do we so despise His goodness that we assume that there is no room in His goodness for justice? That is folly. If God is good, then He will judge, and He will judge according to truth. We ought not to despise the riches of His goodness and forbearance. In His patience, God is forbearing. He puts up with our rebellion and sin. He knows every sin we have ever committed, but He has not exposed them all. He has not visited His wrath on us for all those sins, but we wipe our foreheads and say, "God is good that He will never deal with my sins." "Do you despise the riches of His goodness," Paul asks, **not knowing that the goodness of God leads you to repentance?** (v. 4b). What comes next is one of the scariest verses in the Bible.

Application

We make judgments about others all the time, but we must apply the same standard of judgment to ourselves that we apply to others. This way we guard ourselves from thinking that we are more righteous than we actually are. God's judgment is surely coming, and we must not misinterpret His patience as apathy over sin. Look to the cross, where we have a sure answer about what God thinks of sin—and where we have a sure hope of being delivered from ours.

3

Judged by Works

IN ACCORDANCE WITH YOUR HARDNESS **and your impenitent heart you are treasuring up for yourself wrath in the day of wrath and revelation of the righteous judgment of God** (v. 5). God considers every sin we commit in thought, word, and deed. Each one is exposed to God's perfect judgment according to the truth. In explaining our sin in relation to God's wrath, Paul uses a banking metaphor: If we begin to save our money, taking a small portion of each paycheck and putting it in the bank, we are building up, slowly but surely, a treasure; we are saving up for a rainy day. Just so, every time we sin, we add an indictment against ourselves, treasuring up wrath against the day of wrath. Do we really believe that? I do not think the world believes it. Every day that we sin without repenting, we are depositing future wrath into the account of God's judgment.

God "will render to each one according to his deeds" (v. 6). Our justification is by faith alone, but our rewards in heaven will be distributed according to our works. That is why our Lord told His followers, those who are justified by faith alone, to treasure up things in heaven (Matt. 6:20; Luke 12:33). Augustine said that in distributing rewards according to our levels of obedience, God is crowning His own works in us. On the day of judgment, we will be judged according to our works. God will subject our lives to the closest scrutiny.

Paul makes a distinction: God will give **eternal life to those who by patient continuance in doing good seek for glory, honor, and immortality** (v. 7). Those who gain eternal life are those who set their hearts on heaven, **but to those who are self-seeking and do not obey the truth, but obey unrighteousness—indignation and wrath** (v. 8). The Bible says that God is not just angry at our sin; He is indignant about it. It is an affront to God when we live our lives in constant defiance of and rebellion against His law. When we rebel against God, we attack His dignity, which makes Him indignant. Who do we think we are, as His creatures, to do what we want to do rather than what God commands us? Those who are self-seeking and do not obey the truth but practice unrighteousness will know God's indignation and wrath, and there will be **tribulation and anguish, on every soul of man who does evil, of the Jew first and also of the Greek; but glory, honor, and peace to everyone who works what is good, to the Jew first and also to the Greek. For there is no partiality with God** (vv. 9–11). We cannot come before God and say, "I was a member of a church," or, "I am a descendant of Abraham." That counts for nothing. God will render to every person according to his deeds; there is no partiality with God.

Application

We must be careful not to lose hope. Our works are not the basis of our justification, but the Lord will weigh them and reward us for our good works for Christ. This should motivate us to good works and not discourage us. Far from teaching that what we do doesn't matter, Paul affirms that our lives do have consequences though we rest everything on Christ's righteousness to be saved.

4

Our Need for Christ

THIS IS A VASTLY MISUNDERSTOOD TEXT: **For as many as have sinned without law will also perish without law, and as many as have sinned in the law will be judged by the law (for not the hearers of the law are just in the sight of God, but the doers of the law will be justified; for when Gentiles, who do not have the law, by nature do the things in the law, these, although not having the law, are a law to themselves, who show the work of the law written in their hearts, their conscience also bearing witness, and between themselves their thoughts accusing or else excusing them) in the day when God will judge the secrets of men by Jesus Christ, according to my gospel** (vv. 12–16). FAITH/Belief

The point is not that the Jews, who had the law, were sinning against God while the Gentile pagans, who did not have the law, were obeying the law. Paul is saying that those who have the law perish with the law, and that those who do not have the law perish without the law. People demonstrate by their actions, by what the philosophers call the *ius gentium* (the law of nations), that even if they have never read the Ten Commandments, God has written His law on their hearts. Their behavior reveals that they know in their hearts the difference between right and wrong. Both Jew and Greek have consistently defied God, and they will be judged according to the light they have been given. The Jews will have a greater judgment because they have greater light, but the Gentiles are not without light.

We know God both mediately, through nature, and immediately, through the sense of His deity that we have in our souls. God has revealed Himself to the human heart such that everyone knows what is right and what is not right. We show the work of the law written in our hearts because our consciences bear witness against us.

Our thoughts will accuse or excuse us in the day when God will judge the secrets of men by Jesus Christ, according to the gospel, because essential to the gospel is the announcement that Christ has been appointed the perfect Judge of the earth. We will be judged by Christ on the day of judgment. The Father has delegated that role to His Son, and He will reveal the secrets of our hearts. Jesus Himself warned His own generation that what they did in secret would be made manifest. All skeletons in all closets will be revealed. That is why we need to be covered. That is what redemption is all about—a divine cover-up. The last thing we would want to do is appear before God like Adam and Eve after they sinned, naked and uncovered.

It is absolutely essential that we gain the cloak of the righteousness of Christ so that when every secret is made manifest in the judgment we will be covered by the perfection of Christ's righteousness. Our righteousness will not do it.

Application

God has given everyone a conscience. No one can claim ignorance on the day of judgment for doing what is known to be wrong and not doing what is known to be right. Think about your own life apart from Christ or even when you sin as a Christian. In a strange way, it is a beautiful thing to stand self-condemned. Only by acknowledging our sin and our deserved condemnation can we ever hope to have a yearning for Christ's cloak of righteousness as our covering.

5

Masters of Masquerading

PAUL CONTINUES ADDRESSING THE ISSUE of hypocrisy and the law: **Indeed you are called a Jew, and rest on the law, and make your boast in God, and know His will, and approve the things that are excellent, being instructed out of the law, and are confident that you yourself are a guide to the blind, a light to those who are in darkness, an instructor of the foolish, a teacher of babes, having the form of knowledge and truth in the law** (vv. 17–20).

Can we not extrapolate the critique that Paul gives to his kinsmen, Israel, and apply it to today's church? We rely on the Word of God and on our doctrine. We are confident in our calling as guides to the blind, as lights to those who are perishing in darkness. We instruct the foolish; we are the teachers of infants. We have the form of knowledge and truth. Elsewhere Paul rebukes people for having a form of godliness but lacking the substance of it (2 Tim. 3:5). The outward form is there, but that form is an empty shell, and once God bores through that shell and examines the heart beneath the external form, there is no internal reality. That is the judgment that Paul is giving to Israel, but it also has application to us.

You, therefore, who teach another, do you not teach yourself? You who preach that a man should not steal, do you steal? You who

say, "Do not commit adultery," do you commit adultery? You who abhor idols, do you rob temples? You who make your boast in the law, do you dishonor God through breaking the law? (vv. 21–23). We have the law of God—what are we doing with it? We boast of it while we break it. Here is the clincher: For "the name of God is blasphemed among the Gentiles because of you," as it is written (v. 24). The Gentiles were blaspheming God for the way that the Jews were treating them. Non-churchgoers frequently complain that the church is full of hypocrites. We have heard that, and maybe we have even said it. I once heard a minister respond to that complaint, saying, "Yes, it is, and there is always room for one more." He went on to say, "If you ever find a perfect church, do not join it; you will ruin it."

Hypocrisy is a damnable thing, which is why our Lord was constantly rebuking the Pharisees, the masters of masquerading, who pretended to have a form of righteousness that they really did not possess. Christians do not pretend to be perfect. The church is filled with sinners, and being a sinner is the first qualification for joining a church. We have to be sinners to get in because it is not a place for perfect people. One reason why people call us hypocrites is that they notice that we are not perfect, but actually it is the hypocrite who claims to be more righteous than he is. That is a serious matter, and it is what Paul is talking about.

Application

It is vital to have a high standard for behavior within the church, but this can lead to a practical problem if we are not careful also to place a high value on grace and mercy. If we fail to appropriately value grace and mercy, we can inadvertently lead people to feign righteousness out of a belief they will be utterly rejected if they are honest about their sins. May we not let the holy standards that we rightly set create an ungracious environment in the church.

6

Signs of the Covenant

FOR CIRCUMCISION IS INDEED PROFITABLE **if you keep the law; but if you are a breaker of the law, your circumcision has become uncircumcision. Therefore, if an uncircumcised man keeps the righteous requirements of the law, will not his uncircumcision be counted as circumcision?** (vv. 25–26). Paul explains the difference between outward circumcision and inward circumcision: **he is not a Jew who is one outwardly, nor is circumcision that which is outward in the flesh; but he is a Jew who is one inwardly; and circumcision is that of the heart, in the Spirit, not in the letter; whose praise is not from men but from God** (vv. 28–29). In other words, Paul is saying, those on the outside might be more sensitive to the spirit of the law than the Jews were, even though the outsiders did not know the letter of the law.

Paul uses circumcision as his illustration. Circumcision is very important to Paul's understanding of redemption and of the law and the gospel. In the Old Testament, circumcision was the sign that God gave to His people of His covenant promise. God commanded Abraham to have the foreskin of his flesh cut off, a very crass thing. Breaking the covenant would cut off God's people from blessings and bring the curse of judgment. God was communicating His promise in a sign so base, so primitive, that the least of the people in the nation could grasp it in its graphicness.

When we look to the New Testament, we see that Christ received the curse of God when He hung on the tree, when He took upon Himself the corporate sins of His people. Paul reminds the Christians at Rome that the fact that they are circumcised does not guarantee the blessing. The same could be said for us and our sign of the new covenant, baptism. Baptism in itself does not save anybody (nor does joining the church). Baptism is an outward sign of what God promises to do inwardly. The ultimate question is not whether we are baptized outwardly but whether we are baptized inwardly. Do we possess the spiritual reality that the sign points to?

Application

Christians might be tempted to think that they are in good standing with God because they've been baptized or go to church and participate in the Lord's Supper. But genuine faith ought to be the reality underneath all these things. We must have a personal trust in Christ and in Christ alone, never looking to these things as though merely participating in external rites were enough. It is Christ who is everything.

Romans 3

WHAT ADVANTAGE THEN HAS THE JEW, *or what is the profit of circumcision? Much in every way! Chiefly because to them were committed the oracles of God. For what if some did not believe? Will their unbelief make the faithfulness of God without effect? Certainly not! Indeed, let God be true but every man a liar. As it is written:*

> *"That You may be justified in Your words,*
> *And may overcome when You are judged."*

But if our unrighteousness demonstrates the righteousness of God, what shall we say? Is God unjust who inflicts wrath? (I speak as a man.) Certainly not! For then how will God judge the world?

For if the truth of God has increased through my lie to His glory, why am I also still judged as a sinner? And why not say, "Let us do evil that good may come"?—as we are slanderously reported and as some affirm that we say. Their condemnation is just.

What then? Are we better than they? Not at all. For we have previously charged both Jews and Greeks that they are all under sin.

As it is written:

> *"There is none righteous, no, not one;*
> *There is none who understands;*
> *There is none who seeks after God.*
> *They have all turned aside;*
> *They have together become unprofitable;*
> *There is none who does good, no, not one."*

"Their throat is an open tomb;
With their tongues they have practiced deceit";
"The poison of asps is under their lips";
"Whose mouth is full of cursing and bitterness."
"Their feet are swift to shed blood;
Destruction and misery are in their ways;
And the way of peace they have not known."
"There is no fear of God before their eyes."

Now we know that whatever the law says, it says to those who are under the law, that every mouth may be stopped, and all the world may become guilty before God. Therefore by the deeds of the law no flesh will be justified in His sight, for by the law is the knowledge of sin.

But now the righteousness of God apart from the law is revealed, being witnessed by the Law and the Prophets, even the righteousness of God, through faith in Jesus Christ, to all and on all who believe. For there is no difference; for all have sinned and fall short of the glory of God, being justified freely by His grace through the redemption that is in Christ Jesus, whom God set forth as a propitiation by His blood, through faith, to demonstrate His righteousness, because in His forbearance God had passed over the sins that were previously committed, to demonstrate at the present time His righteousness, that He might be just and the justifier of the one who has faith in Jesus.

Where is boasting then? It is excluded. By what law? Of works? No, but by the law of faith. Therefore we conclude that a man is justified by faith apart from the deeds of the law. Or is He the God of the Jews only? Is He not also the God of the Gentiles? Yes, of the Gentiles also, since there is one God who will justify the circumcised by faith and the uncircumcised through faith. Do we then make void the law through faith? Certainly not! On the contrary, we establish the law.

WEEK 6

1

The Oracles of God

WHAT ADVANTAGE THEN HAS THE JEW, or what is the profit of circumcision? (v. 1). If Paul were writing today, he might mention church membership or baptism as that which does not guarantee salvation. Many place their confidence in the fact that they have been baptized or have joined a church, but our Lord gave weighty, ominous warnings about that. The church is a community where there are always tares growing along with the wheat (Matt. 13:24–30). Jesus warned that people honor Him with their lips, but that their hearts are far from Him (15:8). Making a verbal confession of faith is no guarantee of salvation. What is in the heart determines our redemption.

So what advantage has the Jew? Paul has downplayed circumcision, so we would expect him to answer his question by saying that there is no advantage. Instead he answers, **Much in every way!** (v. 2a). Just so, there is advantage to us in receiving baptism and being a member of a Christian church. There are a multitude of advantages to that in every conceivable manner.

Chiefly because to them were committed the oracles of God (v. 2b). There is a technical point here. The actual word that Paul uses is *first*, not *chiefly*—"First, to them were committed the oracles of God." Some who stand against the authority of Scripture have said that the fact that Paul uses *first* shows that he could not possibly have been inspired by the Holy Spirit, since it suggests that there will be a long list of advantages, but he gives only one. The word translated *chiefly* is a form of the word *protos*, which in Greek means "first"—not necessarily in sequence but in the order of importance. It is the word Jesus used when He said,

"Seek first the kingdom of God and His righteousness, and all these things shall be added to you" (Matt. 6:33). The translator has it right when he renders the word *chiefly*. There are many advantages to being a Jew, but the main advantage is that Jews were given the oracles of God. The Apostle is pointing out the tremendous advantage that Jews had over the Philistines, the Syrians, and the Babylonians—the Word of God.

God has chosen the foolishness of preaching as His method of saving His people, and He has invested His power in the Word. The power is not in the preacher. The power is not in the program. The power is not in the liturgy. The power is in the Word because it is attended by the Holy Spirit. The Word can cut through our minds and hardened hearts; it can pierce our souls and bring us to Christ. There is much advantage where the Word of God is preached, just as there was advantage to the Israelites in possessing the oracles of God.

Application

While church attendance does not save us, we must not neglect it. In worship, we hear God's Word, and where God's Word is preached, there is power. God ordinarily uses the preaching of His Word to save individuals and to sustain them in the faith. Be sure that you are regularly attending to the preaching of God's Word in worship so that you can avail yourself of the means through which the Holy Spirit works with power in your sanctification.

2

The Integrity of God

FOR WHAT IF SOME DID NOT BELIEVE? **Will their unbelief make the faithfulness of God without effect?** (v. 3). If a majority of those baptized never come to faith, does it mean that we should do away with baptism? Do we say that since baptism does not guarantee salvation, there is no advantage to it? Baptism is simply a visible expression of God's promise to all who believe. Those who do not believe in no way diminish the value of the promise that God makes to those who do believe. If everyone is a covenant breaker, that does not destroy the integrity of God in His part of the covenant.

Paul exposes the Jews' thinking. If people do not believe in the significance of circumcision or in the oracles of God, does that unbelief destroy the faithfulness of God? Will such unbelief make the faithfulness of God without effect? **Certainly not! Indeed, let God be true but every man a liar** (v. 4a). The Bible makes that condemnation—all men are liars. We are all promise breakers. God is the only perfect promise keeper. That is how we live as Christians: we trust that God is not like us. We break our promises and lie to each other, but God cannot lie. Because His eternal being and character are truth, it is impossible for God to lie. Just because we lie does not mean that God does. Because we ignore His Word does not mean that His Word becomes worthless. Paul warns against ever allowing such thinking into our heads.

Paul cites a passage from Psalm 51, the great penitential psalm of David that he composed after being confronted by Nathan for his adulterous relationship with Bathsheba: **As it is written: "That You may be justified in Your words, and may overcome when You are judged"** (v. 4b). David was driven to his knees, and he wrote the greatest psalm of repentance ever penned:

Have mercy upon me, O God,
According to Your lovingkindness;
According to the multitude of Your tender mercies,
Blot out my transgressions. . . .

For I acknowledge my transgressions,
And my sin is always before me.
Against You, You only, have I sinned,
And done this evil in Your sight—
That You may be found just when You speak,
And blameless when You judge. (Ps. 51:1, 3–4)

That is true confession. In true repentance, there is no rationalization. There is no attempt to minimize guilt. There is no attempt at self-justification, which is the human tendency. Even when we confess our sins, we always hold back something, some of the gravity of it, but not so with David.

David understood that if God responded to his actions according to the law and to His own character of righteousness, God had every right to do so and to punish David in whatever way He chose, so David threw himself on the mercy of the court. That is why David asked God to deal with him not according to His justice but according to His tender mercy. That was David's only hope, and that is our only hope in the presence of a holy God.

Application

Paul makes use of Psalm 51 in our passage today. It is a psalm that models repentance for us. In repentance, we go before God in the understanding that He is righteous and will judge sin. That's why we ask Him for His mercy. God can be merciful to us because He has justly condemned us in Christ. It is only in Christ that we are rescued from judgment. Praise God that He is faithful to judge and also that the judgment that we deserved landed on Christ.

3

A Just Judge

BUT IF OUR UNRIGHTEOUSNESS DEMONSTRATES the righteousness of God, what shall we say? Is God unjust who inflicts wrath? (I speak as a man.) Certainly not! For then how will God judge the world? (vv. 5–6). Even when we sin, our unrighteousness indirectly bears witness to the righteousness of God. How would we ever recognize sin for what it is if we did not have a standard by which to judge it?

Nobody is really a relativist. The culture claims to be morally relative, yet the person who says that there is no morality is the first one to scream foul when somebody steals his wallet. We know better than that, but we excuse our sinfulness and say, "After all, boys will be boys; to err is human, and to forgive is divine. Everybody is entitled to one mistake." We have this moral entitlement program in our culture, but God does not entitle us to any mistakes, not to one sin.

We begin to think that God is glorified in our sinfulness, so we might as well continue in sin that grace may abound. This is how distorted we are. We say, "Let God be God. I will be who I am. I am just being myself. At least I am honest about it; at least I am an honest sinner." There is no such thing, and Paul warns against that sort of thinking. It is silly, too, for then how would God judge the world? If God were unjust for inflicting wrath, He would never be able to judge the world. Nothing could be more obvious than that, yet nothing is more repugnant to the culture and, in many cases, to the church than the idea that God is capable of judging people by pouring out His wrath.

The Bible says that salvation is being saved from the wrath to come. No preacher in the history of the world spoke more ominously about the certainty of the wrath of God than Jesus. God will not hold back His wrath forever. Every person is going to have to face the judgment of God. We will either face it on our own or face it with God's appointed defense attorney, Jesus. It is because God is righteous that He is wrathful. His wrath is not a manifestation of a lack of righteousness; rather, it is a manifestation of the fullness of the righteousness in Him.

Application

We all too often find ways to excuse our sins. Even though God is faithful to forgive us, we ought never to run into sin presumptuously. Reflect on whether you have sinned in such a manner recently. If you have, confess your presumption to the Lord and rely on His grace for a more profound sense of the sinfulness of sin. If you have not recently sinned presumptuously, thank Him for His preserving Spirit, for it's only by grace that you stand.

4

A Just Condemnation

FOR IF THE TRUTH OF GOD HAS INCREASED **through my lie to His glory, why am I also still judged as a sinner? And why not say, "Let us do evil that good may come"?—as we are slanderously reported and as some affirm that we say** (vv. 7–8a). Paul was accused of antinomianism, of so despising the law of the Old Testament and being so intoxicated by the primacy of grace and the sweetness of the gospel that he had completely dispensed with the law of God. Such slander went around the community, where people said that this Jewish teacher was denying the law of God. Paul never denied God's law. He always understood the proper relationship between the law of God and the gospel of God. Paul is not saying:

> Free from the law,
> O blessed condition;

We can sin all we want

And still have remission.

There is no room in Paul's theology for the carnal Christian, one who takes Christ as Savior but does not take Him as Lord. That would be nonsense to the Apostle. We cannot put that slander at his feet. He never said, "Let us do evil that good may come." Paul never entertained the idea that the end justifies the means. Rather, he said that **their condemnation is just** (v. 8b). Those who twist his teaching, the Apostolic word, and accuse him of teaching antinomianism will be condemned, and justly so.

Paul is about to develop the universal guilt of the human race. Jew and Gentile—every last one of us—are under the weight and condemnation of sin. He will turn to the Old Testament to spell that out in detail before he reaches the crescendo, where he brings every human being before the divine tribunal, showing that all need the gospel.

Application

The grace of God should be so pronounced in your telling of the gospel that people understand that His grace is not something that they could ever earn. Those who want to hold on to their self-righteousness will be offended. Others may question whether you're saying that how we live doesn't matter. This is how people who opposed Paul wrongly interpreted his words. God's grace cannot be earned, but when we receive it, we want to live a life of obedient gratitude in response.

5

All under Sin

WE ARE NOT READY TO HEAR the gospel until we first understand the indictment against humanity that comes down to us from God Himself.

The view of humanity that we see in Romans 3:10–20 is on a collision course with everything that our culture tells us about our natural condition. People today profoundly disagree with the Apostle Paul's assessment of our condition, but we must not be caught up in what we as fallen people think of ourselves. What matters is God's assessment of our condition.

What then? Are we better than they? Not at all. For we have previously charged both Jews and Greeks that they are all under sin (v. 9). When the Apostle Paul says that we are all under sin, he means that sin is not something that just scratches us on the surface. Sin is not tangential to our lives. The weight of sin is so heavy that it presses down upon us. We are under a weighty burden of guilt as a result of our sin. The force of what Paul is saying in verse 9 is that because of our sin, each one of us, under the verdict of the law, is exposed to the judgment of God.

When we are succeeding, we say that we are "on top" of things. With respect to our performance of obedience before God, we are not on top; we are underneath it, and the law hangs like the sword of Damocles over our necks. We are under an awesome weight of sin and a burden of guilt before God. I desire that we come to a greater capacity to feel the weight of that burden, because we have become experts at denying it. We dodge it so that we do not feel the burden. Not one person in a thousand has a complete comprehension of the weightiness of this matter.

Paul, in order to buttress his claim and defend this grim assessment of our condition, does not rest on his own insights or experience but goes back into the pages of the Old Testament. The quotations that follow are not found in one particular place. Paul is going to give us an amalgamation of several texts, most of which are from the Psalms and some from the prophet Isaiah. Everything that Paul is about to quote is taken from the sacred Scriptures of the Old Testament. Paul sets it before us in a kind of chronological order. The Old Testament references are not just loosely laid together; rather, the second judgment follows from the first, and the third from the second, and so on throughout the indictment.

Application

Our sins are heavy; that's why when we as Christians sin, we don't take it lightly. We know the cost of sin. Go to the Lord in prayer. If you trust in Christ alone for your salvation, thank Him that, in Christ, you are no longer under sin's condemnation, but also pray that it would be put to death in your life.

6

There Is None

IF WE WERE IN GOD'S COURT RIGHT NOW, the charges would sound like this: **As it is written: "There is none righteous, no, not one"** (v. 10). Not one person, when judged against the standard of God's perfect righteousness, can be seen to be righteous, yet our self-description of righteousness leads us to suppose that we can pass the judgment of God on judgment day based on our own performance.

When we evangelize, we sometimes ask, "If you were to die tonight and stand before God, and God were to say to you, 'Why should I let you into my heaven?,' what would you say?" Ninety percent of those asked give a works-righteousness answer: "I would say to God, 'I tried to live a good life. I belonged to a church. I gave to charity. I never did anything really bad.'" That is a pretense of righteousness that has no substance to it. There is none righteous, and in case we do not get it, the emphasis follows: "no, not one." There is no exception to this universal judgment.

Since there is none righteous, it follows irresistibly that **"there is none who understands"** (v. 11a). In view here is a failure to understand the things of God. If we as fallen creatures do not want to have God in our thinking, and if we dismiss Him and develop a worldview that fits our performance, how can we not end up with complete inability to grasp the truths of God? Who among us understands the sweetness of God? Who among us, even in a converted state (if indeed we are converted), hungers and thirsts to understand the deep things of God? How many professing Christians have you heard say, "I do not need to study the Scriptures; I do not want to get involved with theology"?

Application

Most people would probably admit that they are not perfect, but many might still believe that they can point to something in themselves that will acquit them before God in judgment. This isn't an uncommon way of thinking, so take a moment and imagine that you are evangelizing someone who thinks like this. What would you say?

WEEK 7

1

No Seekers

"**THERE IS NONE WHO SEEKS AFTER GOD**" (v. 11b). No one in his natural condition seeks after God. Seeking after God is the business of the believer. The moment we become a Christian is the moment when our quest for God begins. Before our conversion, we were fugitives from God; we fled from Him. Churches today structure worship, teaching, and preaching toward the pagan to help him find what he is desperately searching for and just cannot seem to uncover, but it is foolish to structure worship for unbelievers who are seeking after God when the Bible tells us that there aren't any seekers. It manifests a failure to understand the things of God. If we understood the things of God, we would know that there is no such thing as unconverted seekers.

Thomas Aquinas was asked on one occasion why there seem to be non-Christians who are searching for God, when the Bible says that no one seeks after God in an unconverted state. Aquinas replied that we see people all around us who are feverishly seeking for purpose in their lives, pursuing happiness, and looking for relief from guilt to silence the pangs of conscience. We see people searching for the things that we know can be found only in Christ, but we make the gratuitous assumption that because they are seeking the benefits of God, they must therefore be seeking God. That is the very dilemma of fallen creatures: we want the things that only God can give us, but we do not want Him. We want peace but not the Prince of Peace. We want purpose but not the sovereign purposes decreed by God. We want meaning found in ourselves but not in His rule over us. We see desperate people, and we assume that they are seeking for God, but they are not seeking for God. I know that because God says so. No one seeks after God.

How desperately was Paul searching for God while on his way to Damascus to destroy the followers of Jesus? He was no more searching for God than I was when God stopped me in my path one night and brought me sovereignly to Himself. I knew then that I did not come to Christ because I was seeking Him. I came to Christ because He sought me. No one seeks after Christ until he has first been found by Christ—that begins the seeking of the kingdom. That is why Jesus says to those who come to Him, "Seek first the kingdom of God and His righteousness, and all these things shall be added to you" (Matt. 6:33). That is meaningful only to the believer.

Application

While we are living in unbelief, we do not seek God. If we do seek God, it is a clear indication that the kingdom is ours. Yet it is important to remember the distinction between seeking after God and seeking after His benefits. Jesus promises Christians that all things are added to us when we seek the kingdom first (Matt. 6:33), but let us be careful that we are seeking for the right reasons.

2

Unprofitable Good

"THEY HAVE ALL TURNED ASIDE" (v. 12a). Those in the Christian community were called *people of the Way* before they were called *Christians* (a term of derision used for them at Antioch) because Jesus identified Himself as the way: "I am the way, the truth, and the life. No one comes to the Father except through Me" (John 14:6). Do we believe that? Do we believe that there is only one way? The culture tells us that there are many ways. God says that there is only one. If there are none righteous and no one understands and no one seeks after God, where would we expect people to go except out of the way? If they have turned aside, if they have no understanding of the things of God, if they are not searching after God, and if there is no righteousness, the net result is this: **"They have together become unprofitable"** (v. 12b).

Paul concludes this section of the indictment: **"There is none who does good, no, not one"** (v. 12c). Some argue, "It is one thing to say that people are not righteous, but surely you are not going to say that no pagan ever does anything good! We have seen pagan soldiers lay down their lives for their brothers on the battlefield and pagan mothers sacrifice themselves to save their children." John Calvin called this "civic righteousness."

From our perspective, there are good deeds, but if we define goodness the way God does, the verdict comes out a little differently. From a biblical standpoint, there are two aspects to a good deed. When God weighs our actions, He weighs whether they correspond outwardly to His law. God requires honesty, and we are honest if we do not cheat on our income taxes or steal. It is good that we do not steal; it is good that we do not cheat—so far, so good. We have that external conformity to the law of God. But when God evaluates our behavior, not only does He judge the outward action, but He also considers the work, the inward motivation. Therefore, for people to do good in God's sight, they not only have to do something that externally conforms to His law, but also must be motivated in that action by a heart that is trying to please God, a heart that loves Him completely, with the whole mind.

Application

We cannot possibly turn our affections to God and God-glorifying good works without His help. Even as Christians, we can find it difficult to discern our true motives, but we can find encouragement when we genuinely ask ourselves whether we desire to please God at all. This desire manifests a heart that loves Him, and we cannot have this heart unless He has given it to us.

3

The Things We Say

PAUL GIVES A LIST OF METAPHORS to describe the extent to which we are not righteous but have gone astray and the extent to which we do not understand the things of God. In this relentless indictment, he begins to use parts of the body, principally the throat, the mouth, and the tongue, to show our corruption. **"Their throat is an open tomb"** (v. 13a). Jesus had said to the Pharisees, "You are like whitewashed tombs which indeed appear beautiful outwardly, but inside are full of dead men's bones and all uncleanness" (Matt. 23:27); in other words, "If I open your mouth and look down your throat, I see corruption and death."

Paul moves from the throat to the tongue: **"With their tongues they have practiced deceit"** (v. 13b). The Bible says that all men are liars. We are deceitful. By nature we do not love truth. We use truth only when it advances our self-interest. Apart from that, our lips are full of deceit: **"The poison of asps is under their lips"; "whose mouth is full of cursing and bitterness"** (vv. 13c–14). The adder, or asp, is one of the deadliest reptiles in the world. Not only is its bite fatal, as was the case with Cleopatra, but it is exceedingly painful. The Bible describes our tongues as sacs of venom; we are like pit vipers. The words we use destroy, maim, and poison; they are vituperative.

I rarely heard my father curse. If he hit his thumb with a hammer, he might have said a bad word. Today I live in a world where lots of people I know cannot speak a sentence without vulgarity or blasphemy. Gratuitous language is so much a part of the warp and woof of our society. We take for granted that we are people whose mouths are full of cursing and blasphemy and filthy talk. That is who we are; it is our nature. It is not just that we let a bad word slip every now and then; our mouths are filled with such talk. Mouths filled with cursing and bitterness demonstrate sheer paganism.

Application

It isn't hard to find vulgarities that are tolerated and celebrated in our society, especially in our entertainment. Scripture calls us to be careful with our speech, and part of that is being careful with what we watch and hear. Be mindful of what you are watching and what you are listening to; it might just have its influence on you and cause you to lose control of your tongue, which is "a fire, a world of iniquity" (James 3:6).

4

The Things We Do

PAUL MOVES FROM THE THROAT, the mouth, the lips, and the tongue to the feet: **"Their feet are swift to shed blood"** (v. 15). In our bitterness and propensity for violence, we run toward it; we cannot wait to spill blood. What kind of being would be worthy of a description like this: **"Destruction and misery are in their ways"** (v. 16)? Many think that Paul is quoting nothing more than antiquated texts from the Old Testament that seem to depict God as vengeful. Such thinking predominates in our sophisticated world, where we consider ourselves more civilized than those who lived in the past.

Somebody did a calculation of the violence in warfare during the last two thousand years of Western civilization, measuring the number of wars and the magnitude of violence in each. The most peaceful century in the history of Western civilization was the first century, which was the century that witnessed the coming of the Prince of Peace. The second most peaceful century in history was the nineteenth century, which is why people became so optimistic at the end of it. They thought that through science and education, warfare was over. They did not anticipate that there would be more violence and warfare in the first quarter of the twentieth century than in any full century before it. This was before World War II, before the slaughter of millions in the Soviet Union or Red China, before Vietnam, before Korea, and before the world wars that have broken out across every aspect of the globe in the last twenty-five years. Far and away the most violent century in recorded human history was the twentieth century because the way of peace we have not known.

The conclusion of this biblical rehearsal of God's assessment comes down to the bottom line: **"There is no fear of God before their** eyes" (v. 18). The most frightening thing of all is that the pagan is not afraid of God. Of course, inherent in the fear that Paul mentions is a sense of reverence. We are by nature irreverent people. We have no sense of awe, no desire to honor God or to glorify Him as God. We are not naturally afraid of God, but He scares me sometimes. I know that I am redeemed; I know that now there is no condemnation for those who are in Christ Jesus, but I know that God is holy, so even though I am covered by the Savior, I am still frightened at times by the character of God, and with good reason. Yet Old Testament wisdom literature says, "The fear of the LORD is the beginning of wisdom" (Prov. 9:10).

Application

The first great sin that we read about in Scripture after the fall was violent. God does not take violence lightly. It is one of the main reasons that He flooded the earth (see Gen. 6:11–13). We ought to fear the Lord as holy. Whenever you witness violence, real or choreographed, remember God's hatred of it, but also look forward to the absence of it in the new heavens and new earth.

5

All the World Guilty

NOW WE KNOW THAT WHATEVER THE LAW SAYS, it says to those who are under the law, that every mouth may be stopped, and all the world may become guilty before God (v. 19). Every time the New Testament describes with vivid imagery the scene of the final judgment where God's verdict comes down in His courtroom, the response of those on trial is silence.

I had a friend who did his PhD at Harvard in neurological studies—advanced studies on the function of the brain—and he once said that the brain is more incredible than the most vast computer system in the world. Every experience we have and every word we speak is recorded in our brains. Concerning the judgment day, he said, "I think that in the last day God is going to take our brain out of our head, put it on a table there in His courtroom, plug in a recorder, and punch 'rewind.' We are going to have to sit there and listen to our brain replay everything we have ever done, said, and thought. The prosecuting attorney doesn't have to say a word."

After such a recitation, what would there be to say? What use is there in arguing with God, when God says that He has weighed us in the balance and found us wanting? God will say, "I cannot find any goodness. I search your soul, and I do not see righteousness. I see the poison of snakes in your mouth. I give you My law, and you break it at every point."

Here is the conclusion of this segment of the epistle, a conclusion that no sane person dare miss: **Therefore by the deeds of the law no flesh will be justified in His sight, for by the law is the knowledge of sin** (v. 20). If we are paying attention to the law, we know that it will not justify us. We know that we will never be able to get into heaven on the basis of our works, because the law reveals to us our filthiness. The law teaches us that by the works of the law, no flesh, no human being, will ever be justified in God's sight. Why, then, do people continue to hope that their good deeds are going to be good enough to satisfy the demands of God? We must despair of that. We must not rest on our works as grounds for our justification because by the works of the law no flesh will be justified in His sight. We are not without hope forever, for God has provided for us to receive our justification by faith and not by works, which we will begin to examine next.

Application

That description of the final judgment day is horrifying. It's especially horrifying if we do not have an advocate before God. We cannot be justified by our works. This is something that we must believe if we are to believe the gospel. Whose works will you call to your defense before God? According to our passage today, our works won't provide a defense—our mouths will be stopped. We need the righteousness of another.

6

Justification Defined and Defended

THE CONTROVERSY OVER JUSTIFICATION resulted in the sixteenth-century Protestant Reformation, which focused on the material cause of the doctrine of justification. The controversy involved this simple question: how can an unjust person ever hope to stand before the just judgment of God? In other words, how are we saved? This is a matter of eternal consideration. The Reformation was not a tempest in a teapot or a question of theological shadowboxing. At stake in the controversy, in which many paid with their lives, was this doctrine that is central to the New Testament gospel. In this day and age, however, there are few professing Christians who can even define the meaning of the term *justification*.

Martin Luther insisted that justification by faith alone is the article upon which the church stands or falls, and if the church does not get this right, the church ceases to be an authentic church. If the church denies or obscures the doctrine of justification by faith alone, it is no longer a Christian body. We need to be clear as to what the word *justification* means and what the doctrine is all about.

In justification God makes a legal declaration, what we call a *forensic* declaration. Forensics has to do with judicial judgment or declaration. The New Testament shows us that in the act of justification, God makes a judicial declaration about a person's status before He makes His judgment. What happens in justification is not merely a pardon; it is an act whereby God declares a person to be just. Justification is that act by which God judicially declares a person to be righteous in His sight.

In the sixteenth century, both Roman Catholics and Protestants agreed that in the final analysis, the act of justification is something God does, and it is a judicial declaration. Both sides, Roman Catholic and Protestant, agreed that justification does not happen until God declares a person righteous. The issue then and now is this: on what grounds does God make that declaration? Why would God look at us, when He sees one who is dead in sin and trespasses, and say, "You are a just person," when manifestly we are not just people? The good news of the gospel is that God pronounces people just, astonishingly enough, while they are still sinners because of the righteousness of Christ.

Application

The book of Romans sets before us the bad news before it gets to the good news. In a sense, the bad news is part of the good news, but what comes first in Paul's presentation of the good news is a clear articulation of the doctrine of justification by faith alone. If you trust in Christ alone, praise God that He has declared you righteous in Him.

WEEK 8

1

Justification Declared

IN THE ROMAN CATHOLIC VIEW, God will never pronounce a person just or righteous until, by the help of God's grace and Christ, that person actually becomes righteous. If God were to judge us tonight, what would He find? Would He find sin in our lives? Could He possibly declare us just if He considers only the righteousness that He finds in us today? Remember what the Apostle Paul said: "By the deeds of the law no flesh will be justified in His sight" (3:20). That is precisely why the ground for our justification cannot be found in us or in any righteousness inherent in our souls. That is why we need so desperately what Martin Luther called a *justitia alienum*, an alien righteousness, a righteousness that comes from outside ourselves. Luther called this righteousness *extra nos*, outside or apart from us.

In simple terms, this means that the only righteousness sufficient for us to stand before the judgment of God is the righteousness of Christ. The doctrine of justification by faith alone is only theological shorthand for the affirmation that justification is by Christ alone, by His righteousness, which is received by faith. When Paul speaks here about justification, he is not talking merely about pardon, and he is not talking about God's declaration of what He finds in us and in our behavior. He is talking about something else altogether.

One of the slogans formulated by Luther and widely repeated in the sixteenth century was a little Latin phrase: *simul iustus et peccator*. *Simul* is the root from which we get the word *simultaneously*, which means "at the same time." *Iustus* means "just" or "righteous." When we put the words together, we get "at the same time righteous." *Et* means "and," and *peccator* is the word for "sinner." If somebody is without sin, we say that he is *impeccable*. We use the term *peccadillo* to describe a little sin. The point of Luther's slogan was this: the Christian is someone who is at the very same time righteous and sinner. How can that be? While we are sinners, we are also righteous in God's sight by virtue of the legal transfer God made by assigning to us the righteousness of Jesus, if we put our trust in Christ. By virtue of this transfer, or the imputation of the righteousness of Christ to us, we are declared to be righteous while still sinners.

That is the good news—we can be declared just by God while we are still sinners. That is the heart of the gospel.

Application

Being a Christian doesn't make sinning easier; it makes it harder. Before becoming a Christian, a person may have to deal with the worldly sorrow that comes from committing a sin without any real hatred for the sin itself. After becoming a Christian, the person experiences a Spirit-wrought wrestling with temptation, and if we succumb to temptation, we experience a profound hatred for sin. It's critical that in all this we never forget that we are righteous in Christ but sinners in practice and thus that we continue to turn from our sins.

2

Justification by Faith

WE DO NOT HAVE TO WAIT TO BECOME perfectly righteous before we are acceptable to God. This is the point that the Apostle is laboring to make in this section of the epistle. **But now the righteousness of God apart from the law is revealed, being witnessed by the Law and the Prophets** (v. 21).

When we get to Romans 4, Paul is going to show that the doctrine of justification by faith alone is not a novelty. It is not a new doctrine announced by Jesus during His incarnation, nor is it one that the Apostle Paul created during his ministry. This doctrine of the gospel is rooted in the testimony of the Old Testament. The whole point of the law is to drive us to this One who possesses the righteousness that we do not have. We find it in the teaching of the prophets. Paul will show us in Romans 4 that we are justified today on this side of the cross the same way that people in the Old Testament were justified. To give us a heads-up of what is to come, Paul mentions here in Romans 3 that this is **even the righteousness of God, through faith in Jesus Christ, to all and on all who believe** (v. 22a).

When we claim that justification is "by faith" or "through faith," we have to be careful that we do not misunderstand that. To be justified by faith is not to be justified because we have faith, in the sense that our faith now is the supreme work that makes us righteous. The language here of being justified by faith or through faith simply means that faith is the means by which we lay hold of Christ. It is the means by which the righteousness of Christ is bestowed upon us.

Application

Perhaps the most beautiful phrase in Romans 1–3 is found in the words "But now." These two words have a reality in the history of God's work of salvation in the coming of the Lord Jesus Christ, but we each come to know Him personally when God takes hold of our lives through the Spirit. What is that "but now" moment in your life? In what ways is God's redemptive grace at work in you? Reflect on this and praise Him for it.

3

Faith as Instrumental Cause

THE ROMAN CATHOLIC CHURCH DEFINES FAITH as important and indeed essential to justification. Faith is the foundation for justification, but the instrumental cause of justification, according to Rome, is the sacrament of baptism. To understand the idea of an instrumental cause, we have to go back before Jesus to the philosopher Aristotle, who examined different ways that change is brought about. He said that the word *cause*, in and of itself, is too vague. We need to be more specific if we are going to be scientific in discerning various types of causes.

Aristotle used a piece of sculpture as an illustration. A piece of sculpture starts out as a block of stone; it has no beautiful shape. How does the block of stone change into a gorgeous statue, such as one created by Michelangelo? Aristotle said that there is a *material cause*, the stuff out of which something is brought to pass; the material cause in the case of the sculpture is the block of stone. Then there is the *formal cause*, which is the idea that the sculptor or artist has before he creates his piece of art. An artist has a sketch, or even just an idea in his head, and he follows that blueprint in order to produce the sculpture. That is the formal cause. The *efficient cause* is the one whose work brings about the change. In the case of the sculpture, the efficient cause is the sculptor. The *final cause* is the purpose for which something is made. In the case of the sculpture, the final cause might be to beautify an emperor's garden. Aristotle also spoke of the *instrumental cause*, which is the means by which the sculptor shapes that stone into a beautiful statue. The instruments that the sculptor uses are the chisel and the hammer. The instrumental cause of Rembrandt's paintings was his brushes. The instruments are the means by which the change takes place.

Rome says that the instrumental cause of justification is baptism, in the first instance, and the sacrament of penance, in the second instance. If someone loses his justification through mortal sin, he can have it restored through the sacrament of penance, which includes doing works of satisfaction. In the sixteenth century, Rome declared that the sacraments are the means by which a person is made righteous, but the Reformers said that the instrumental cause of our justification is not the sacraments. Faith is the only instrument by which one is linked to Christ and receives His righteousness.

Application

Our faith is not the meritorious basis for our justification. Rather, Christ and His righteousness alone merit our justification. Faith, however, is the means by which we take hold of His righteousness. God requires it of us, but He also gives it to us as a gift (see Eph. 2:8–10). Thus, the gospel is all of grace. This is the message that saves and the one that God is pleased to use to grant sinners the ability to believe in Christ through the work of the Spirit. Proclaim it boldly.

4

The Double Transfer

IT IS VITALLY IMPORTANT FOR US to understand what faith is—why we call people to faith and why the New Testament calls us to faith. Faith means that we place our trust in Christ and His righteousness. We do not trust our own righteousness because we do not have any. When we trust Christ's righteousness on our behalf and embrace Him, then God legally transfers His righteousness to us. A double transfer is involved in salvation. Christ dies for our salvation, but He also lives for our salvation. Our sins are transferred to Jesus, and He died for us on the cross to bear those sins.

This is a legal transfer. God did not reach down into our souls and grab a hunk of sin and place it on the back of Jesus. God assigned our guilt to His Son. He transferred it from us to Christ, but that is only half the transaction. The other half is that He took Christ's righteousness and assigned it to us when we believed so that now when God looks at us, knowing that all our righteousness is as filthy rags, we will not perish. He has given us the cloak of the righteousness of Jesus. That is the righteousness of God that Paul introduced in Romans 1, the righteousness not by which God Himself is righteous but that which He makes available to all who put their trust in Christ. **For there is no difference; for all have sinned and fall short of the glory of God, being justified freely by His grace through the redemption that is in Christ Jesus** (vv. 22b–24).

Paul is talking about the grace by which God freely gives the righteousness of Christ to a sinner, one who is at the same time just and sinner, through the redemption that is in Christ Jesus, **whom God set forth as a propitiation by His blood, through faith, to demonstrate His righteousness, because in His forbearance God had passed over the sins that were previously committed, to demonstrate at the present time His righteousness** (vv. 25–26a).

Application

"Justified freely by His grace" (v. 24). Meditate on those words for a moment. Feel the weight of what they mean. Allow them to strip you of any self-righteous pride, but also let them fill you with the exuberant joy that comes from knowing that God loves you in His only begotten Son. Jesus has taken your sin and given you His righteousness.

5

Propitiation and Expiation

A STORM OF CONTROVERSY AROSE WHEN the Revised Standard Version appeared in English. The words *expiation* and *propitiation* were removed from the English text based on the reasoning that people in this day and age do not use words like that, and that if people are going to understand the New Testament, such strange terms must be eliminated. We must never get rid of the words *propitiation* and *expiation*. Those are two of the most glorious words that we find anywhere in the New Testament.

Propitiation means to satisfy the demands of justice. In biblical terms, it means to satisfy the demands of God's wrath. God places sin and evil under His judgment and decrees that He is going to pour out His wrath upon it. In New Testament terms, what we are saved from is God. We are saved by God from God, from the wrath that is to come. Propitiation satisfies completely the demands of God's wrath and justice, which is what the cross was all about. Christ as our substitute took upon Himself the wrath that we deserve, to pay the penalty that was due for our guilt to satisfy the demands of God's justice. In His work of propitiation, Jesus did something on a vertical level, something with respect to the Father, satisfying the justice of God for us.

Expiation has to do directly with us. The prefix *ex-* means "away from" or "out of." One of the benefits of justification is the remission of sin, our sin being removed from us. Our sin goes away. After a close friend's wife had fought cancer for several years, he told me, "She is in her fourth remission." For the time being, at least, the cancer had gone away. It had been removed. If we buy something on our credit card, a bill will come, requesting us to remit payment. When we send in the payment, the money is transferred from our account to the merchant. When the New Testament speaks about expiation, it is referring to the sense in which Christ removes our sin from us and takes it away. The psalmist tells us, "As far as the east is from the west, so far has He removed our transgressions from us" (Ps. 103:12).

In the work of Christ, there is propitiation and expiation. We must not lose these words, *propitiation* and *expiation*. They so richly capture the essence of the gospel that stands upon what Christ did on the cross in paying for our guilt and in His life of perfect obedience in earning the righteousness that He freely gives to us.

Application

One way to think about propitiation and expiation is through the shape of a cross. The vertical beam of the cross can be thought to represent our justification with God. It is through the cross that Christ makes propitiation for our sin. The horizontal beam of the cross can be thought to represent how far our sin is separated from us, just as Psalm 103 teaches us: "As far as the east is from the west" (v. 12).

6

The Just and the Justifier

GOD SET FORTH CHRIST AS A propitiation by His blood through faith, **that He might be just and the justifier of the one who has faith in Jesus** (v. 26b). There is no such thing as cheap grace. The gospel is not simply an announcement of pardon. In justification, God does not merely decide unilaterally to forgive us our sins. That is the prevailing idea, that what happens in the gospel is that God freely forgives us of sin because He is such a loving, dear, wonderful God, and it does not disturb Him that we violate everything that is holy. God never negotiates His righteousness. God will never lay aside His holiness to save us. God demands and requires that sin be punished. That is why the cross is the universal symbol of Christianity. Christ had to die because, according to God, the propitiation had to be made; sin had to be punished. Our sin has to be punished.

In the drama of justification, God remains just. He does not set aside His justice. He does not waive His righteousness; He insists upon it. We cannot be justified without righteousness, but the glory of His grace is that His justice is vicariously served by a substitute that He appointed. God's mercy is shown in that what saves us is not our righteousness. It is someone else's. We get in on someone else's coattails—that is grace. That somebody, our Redeemer, is perfectly righteous and has fulfilled the justice of God for us perfectly. That is the glory of justification. God demonstrates that He is both just and justifier. If all He did was maintain His righteousness without extending the imputation of that righteousness to us, He would not be the justifier. He is both just and justifier, which is the marvel of the gospel.

Application

Grace is not cheap. Grace is costly. Its cost is seen at the cross. The notion of cheap grace comes with the danger of misunderstanding the

Christian life. If we disconnect God's forgiveness of our sin from the cross through which Christ accomplished it, we fail to see the cost of forgiveness. This might lead us into an antinomian mentality, wherein we think that we can sin freely because we've been freely forgiven. Take time to pray to God that you might always keep the cross in sight and strive for greater holiness in gratitude for what Christ has done.

Romans 4

WHAT THEN SHALL WE SAY THAT ABRAHAM OUR FATHER *has found according to the flesh? For if Abraham was justified by works, he has something to boast about, but not before God. For what does the Scripture say? "Abraham believed God, and it was accounted to him for righteousness." Now to him who works, the wages are not counted as grace but as debt.*

But to him who does not work but believes on Him who justifies the ungodly, his faith is accounted for righteousness, just as David also describes the blessedness of the man to whom God imputes righteousness apart from works:

> *"Blessed are those whose lawless deeds are forgiven,*
> *And whose sins are covered;*
> *Blessed is the man to whom the LORD shall not impute sin."*

Does this blessedness then come upon the circumcised only, or upon the uncircumcised also? For we say that faith was accounted to Abraham for righteousness. How then was it accounted? While he was circumcised, or uncircumcised? Not while circumcised, but while uncircumcised. And he received the sign of circumcision, a seal of the righteousness of the faith which he had while still uncircumcised, that he might be the father of all those who believe, though they are uncircumcised, that righteousness might be imputed to them also, and the father of circumcision to those who not only are of the circumcision, but who also walk in the steps of the faith which our father Abraham had while still uncircumcised.

For the promise that he would be the heir of the world was not to Abraham or to his seed through the law, but through the righteousness of faith. For if those who are of the law are heirs, faith is made void and the promise made of no effect, because the law brings about wrath; for where there is no law there is no transgression.

Therefore it is of faith that it might be according to grace, so that the promise might be sure to all the seed, not only to those who are of the law, but also to those who are of the faith of Abraham, who is the father of us all (as it is written, "I have made you a father of many nations") in the presence of Him whom he believed—God, who gives life to the dead and calls those things which do not exist as though they did; who, contrary to hope, in hope believed, so that he became the father of many nations, according to what was spoken, "So shall your descendants be." And not being weak in faith, he did not consider his own body, already dead (since he was about a hundred years old), and the deadness of Sarah's womb. He did not waver at the promise of God through unbelief, but was strengthened in faith, giving glory to God, and being fully convinced that what He had promised He was also able to perform. And therefore "it was accounted to him for righteousness."

Now it was not written for his sake alone that it was imputed to him, but also for us. It shall be imputed to us who believe in Him who raised up Jesus our Lord from the dead, who was delivered up because of our offenses, and was raised because of our justification.

WEEK 9

1

Salvation Old and New

SINCE RIGHTEOUSNESS COMES ONLY THROUGH FAITH in Christ Jesus, Paul asks, "Where is boasting then?" (3:27a). Paul answers his question emphatically—boasting is excluded. Since our justification is by faith alone, by no merit in us or endeavors of our works, there is no room whatsoever for boasting, save in Christ. In this section of the epistle, Paul is going to bring forth exhibit A to prove his case. He does not do it by an abstract exposition of doctrine but by a historical reconnaissance. He reaches back to the Old Testament to the person of Abraham, who was known to the Jews as the father of the faithful. Paul looks to Abraham as the supreme example of how a person is justified by faith and not by works.

Before we get into the exposition of Romans 4:1–8, it is important to understand that salvation occurred in the Old Testament in the same manner that it occurs in the New Testament. When Paul speaks of Abraham's justification as being by faith, that is shorthand for saying that Abraham was justified by the righteousness of Christ. The only difference between our justification and Abraham's is that Abraham looked forward to the Promised One. He trusted in the promise of the Redeemer, whereas we look backward to the work of Jesus. The only difference is the time frame of where the object of faith is. Abraham's faith looked forward and our faith looks backward, but the ground of Abraham's justification was exactly the same as ours, namely, the person and work of Jesus.

That is very important to understand, because the dominant

theology in our country today tends to see a strong disjunction between salvation in the Old Testament and salvation in the New Testament. The Old Testament is viewed as the age of law, and the New Testament is viewed as the age of grace; therefore, God's way of salvation differed in the two covenants. Paul refutes that idea right here when he brings forward as his example of the doctrine of justification by faith not someone from the New Testament but someone from the Old Testament, Father Abraham.

What then shall we say that Abraham our father has found according to the flesh? For if Abraham was justified by works, he has something to boast about, but not before God (vv. 1–2). Abraham was excluded from boasting because he was not justified by works, any more than we are.

Application

The hymn "Rock of Ages" includes this brilliant line: "Nothing in my hand I bring, simply to Thy cross I cling." We can't cling to and take hold of the cross if we are holding on to our own sense of righteousness. Pray that even as you strive for greater measures of holiness in this life, you will never let go of the cross. AMEN

2

Abraham Believed

FOR WHAT DOES THE SCRIPTURE SAY? "**Abraham believed God, and it was accounted to him for righteousness.**" **Now to him who works, the wages are not counted as grace but as debt** (vv. 3–4). Here Paul cites a statement found in Genesis 15, where God appeared to Abraham and told him that He would be his shield and his very great reward

(v. 1). Abraham was staggered by that announcement because he was one of the wealthiest men on earth. What do you give a man who has everything? To the Jew you give progeny. You give him sons. Abraham had plenty of cattle, livestock, and property, but he had no son, so he said, "Lord GOD, what will You give me, seeing I go childless, and the heir of my house is Eliezer of Damascus?" (v. 2). God told him, "This one shall not be your heir, but one who will come from your own body shall be your heir" (v. 4).

This staggering promise that God gave to Abraham in his old age resulted in Abraham's believing God (v. 6). He trusted the promise of God. Abraham's faith was not without some admixture of wavering or doubt—"Lord GOD, how shall I know that I will inherit it?" (v. 8)— but God put him to sleep and gave him a magnificent theophany, a visible manifestation of the invisible God. God, because He could swear by nothing greater, swore by Himself in the drama of that vision (vv. 12–21).

What we are mainly concerned about in Genesis 15 is that Abraham believed God, and it was counted to him as righteousness. That is, Abraham was reckoned or considered by God to be righteous, not because of any righteous deeds that Abraham had performed but simply because he believed the promise.

Application

There is an important distinction to be made between doing and believing. Often, we might be tempted to think of faith as the basis for our justification, that one thing that we had to do to be justified. While it is true that faith is the instrument of our justification—how we take hold of our justification—it is not a meritorious work that we exercise for our justification. Saving faith acknowledges that we are empty before God and believes that He freely justifies in Christ.

3

Faith as Trust

PAUL'S ARGUMENT IN ROMANS 4 IS SOMEWHAT problematic because of the way in which the Apostle James deals with the issue in his epistle:

> Was not Abraham our father justified by works when he offered Isaac his son on the altar? Do you see that faith was working together with his works, and by works faith was made perfect? And the Scripture was fulfilled which says, "Abraham believed God, and it was accounted to him for righteousness." And he was called the friend of God. You see then that a man is justified by works, and not by faith only. (2:21–24)

On the surface, it would seem that there could be no clearer repudiation of the doctrine of justification by faith alone.

In order to reach a resolution, we must first examine the context in which the statements were made and ask, "What question is the author trying to answer?" James tells us what question he is trying to answer: "What does it profit, my brethren, if someone says he has faith but does not have works? Can faith save him?" (v. 14). That was one of the most critical questions of the sixteenth-century Reformation. When Martin Luther insisted that justification is by faith alone, people took that to mean that all one has to do is give intellectual assent that Jesus is the Savior of the world. That is not what Luther meant, however.

If, before I was a Christian, you had asked me if I believed in God and that Jesus was His Son, I would have said yes, but I had no personal relationship with Christ; I had no saving faith whatsoever. It was merely an intellectual assent to an abstract proposition. James writes here in this text, "You believe that there is one God. You do well. Even the demons believe—and tremble!" (v. 19). All that does is qualify us to be demons. Anybody can believe in the existence of God. Satan believes. The demons know that God exists and they tremble before Him, but they do not put their trust in God for salvation. Luther had to spell out the ingredients of saving faith, which include not only the data, the content to believe, but also the intellectual assent to the propositions. If we have the content and the assent but if that is all we have, we are not going to be justified. That is the point that James is making in his epistle.

The third and most critical element of saving faith that Luther delineated was what he called *fiducia*, personal trust in Christ. *Fiducia* is necessary for salvation. We can believe that Jesus can save us without having saving faith. We have to trust that He does save us, and we put our trust in Him alone. When we do that, we are justified by God and begin to do good works—not to gain righteousness before God but to thank Him for His free grace, His forgiveness, and His declaration that we are righteous in Christ. When James says that we are justified by works (James 2:24), He means that works "justify"—demonstrate the authenticity of—our profession of faith.

Application

Do you *trust* in the Lord Jesus Christ alone for your salvation? People can be easily confused by the language of belief. When you share the gospel with your friends and loved ones, make sure to communicate that you are not simply trying to get them to believe in God's existence or acknowledge who Christ is—although these things are important—but also that you want them to have a right response to the gospel of grace: absolute dependence on Christ alone for salvation.

4

Counted Righteous

THE REFORMERS ADDED A FOOTNOTE TO the formula of justification by faith alone. The full phrase is this: "Justification is by faith alone but not by a faith that is alone." The point is that if we have true faith, it will immediately and necessarily be manifested in a changed life. If no change follows from our profession of faith, all we have is a profession of faith. We do not possess the real thing, because real faith always issues in some degree of obedience. Works flow necessarily from faith, but the point of the gospel is that the works that flow from faith are in no way the grounds of justification. God declares us just in His sight the moment true faith is present, before a single work flows from our faith.

God does not have to wait to see our behavior before He knows if the faith we profess is authentic. We may need to see the works, but God does not. When James references Abraham, he quotes from Genesis 22 where Abraham offers up Isaac on the altar. When Paul references Abraham, he quotes from Genesis 15. Paul's point is that God did not have to wait until Mount Moriah (Gen. 22) to know whether Abraham's faith was authentic. The moment Abraham believed, God counted him righteous. We are the ones who do not know that his faith was authentic until we see how he responds to the test that God gives him in Genesis 22. There is nothing in James about merit attending the obedience of Abraham; James is describing Abraham's obedience as proof that his profession of faith is real and valid. This is difficult, but it resolves the apparent problem between these two writers of sacred Scripture.

If the ground of Abraham's justification were his works, then Abraham's justification would not be by grace. If his works had been good enough to make him just in the sight of God, if Abraham had brought the merit of his own works to the table—even if he had that merit with God's help—then his justification would not have been reckoned as grace but as debt. In other words, God would owe him justification, which is what Paul is demolishing here in verses 3 and 4.

But to him who does not work but believes on Him who justifies the ungodly, his faith is accounted for righteousness (v. 5). This does not mean that our faith itself is the righteousness that is the grounds for our salvation. Faith only lays hold of Christ. Faith is the instrument by which we are linked to Jesus. Only Christ's righteousness is the grounds of our justification. When God declares His legal judgment of our status in His sight, when He sees faith, He counts us righteous— even when we are still in ourselves sinners.

Application

It has been observed that Paul defends himself in Romans against the charge that his teaching promotes licentiousness. In chapters 6–8, he therefore makes it clear that while salvation is not based on our works, true faith will result in a changed life that pursues holiness. Christians often face the charge of preaching licentiousness, as though we were teaching that it doesn't matter how someone lives. To receive this accusation is a good sign that you are rightly communicating the nature of God's free grace, and it is an opportunity to clarify that saved people do good works as a consequence of salvation, not to earn salvation.

5

The Blessedness of Imputation

PAUL THEN ARGUES HIS POINT FROM DAVID: **just as David also describes the blessedness of the man to whom God imputes righteousness apart from works** (v. 6). In our day, the doctrine of justification has been battled afresh within certain so-called evangelical circles, which shows that they are not truly evangelical. Anyone who challenges *sola fide* cannot do that and legitimately be counted as an evangelical, because justification by faith alone is at the very heart of historic evangelicalism. Be that as it may, there are many who call themselves evangelicals but whose profession of evangelicalism is a false profession because they deny the *evangel* that defines evangelicalism.

The gospel is that we are righteous on the basis of the righteousness of Jesus, which is transferred to our account—what Martin Luther called a *justitia alienum*, an alien righteousness, one that is *extra nos*, outside of us. It is Christ's righteousness that justifies us. All we bring to the table is our trust in Him and His righteousness. If we add one ounce of our own righteousness as our confidence, we repudiate the gospel. That is why Paul cites David: **"Blessed are those whose lawless deeds are forgiven, and whose sins are covered; blessed is the man to whom the LORD shall not impute sin"** (vv. 7–8). There is no greater blessedness under heaven than to have God in His mercy and grace transfer the righteousness of Jesus to our account.

It disturbs me not a little bit that many modern commentators, seeking to be relevant to the culture, prefer to translate the word *blessed* as the word *happy*. If any word would cheapen the concept that is before us, I can think of no word that would cheapen it more than *happy*. The terms *happy* and *happiness* have been used to such a superficial degree that they have lost the force of their import. We say that "happiness is a warm puppy," but the kind of happiness in view in such adages is miles away from the happiness contained in the biblical word *blessed*.

We tend to cheapen the word *blessed* by saying, "Bless you, my friend" or "God bless you." Yet the highest experience and joy of the human soul is to experience that blessedness that only God can give. So when Paul is talking here about the gospel, about justification by faith alone, he calls attention to this great beatitude, to the supreme state of blessedness, by calling attention to David. If we transformed that into the oracular form, David could be saying, "How blessed is the one who receives the imputation of the righteousness of Christ."

Application

David's gratitude for forgiveness is evident in these lines from the Psalms. Take a moment and dwell on what he has said, that if you have trusted in Christ, your sins are covered, and you are *blessed*. Pray to the Lord with a heart of thankfulness in response to this reality.

6

Sign and Seal

DOES THIS BLESSEDNESS THEN COME UPON **the circumcised only, or upon the uncircumcised also?** (v. 9a). This blessedness of which David spoke is not for Jews only. It is not tied to the Old Testament sign of the covenant, which is circumcision. Paul comes back again to Abraham: **For we say that faith was accounted to Abraham for righteousness. How then was it accounted? While he was circumcised, or uncircumcised? Not while circumcised, but while uncircumcised** (vv. 9b–10).

Abraham had faith before he was circumcised. His son Isaac had faith after he was circumcised. The faith to which circumcision pointed was not tied to the time in which circumcision was rendered. The point is that the sign of the covenant is the sign of all the benefits that God promises to His people who believe.

Circumcision is the sign of the old covenant, baptism the sign of the new covenant—but both are also seals. **And he received the sign of circumcision, a seal of the righteousness of the faith which he had while still uncircumcised, that he might be the father of all those who believe** (v. 11a).

That term *sealing* in the Scriptures is very important. The New Testament Greek word for "seal" goes back to the idea of the signet ring of the king. When the king issued a decree at the end of a document, he put wax on the paper and then took his ring and pressed it down into the wax, and it became the seal that identified the promise of the king. The Scriptures tell us that those who are in Christ are sealed by the Holy Spirit. We are not just saved; we are sealed. God has put His indelible mark upon us. In the sacraments, God guarantees the consequences of justification to all who believe, not to all who receive the sign.

Abraham received the sign of circumcision, a seal of the righteousness of faith, that he might be **the father of circumcision to those who not only are of the circumcision, but who also walk in the steps of the faith which our father Abraham had while still uncircumcised** (v. 12). The circumcised Jew is justified by faith alone. Those who are uncircumcised are justified the same way—through the imputation of the righteousness of Christ.

Understanding justification by faith alone is not hard. Anyone can grasp it intellectually, but to get it in the bloodstream is extremely difficult because the voices all around us are saying, "No, that is too easy. You have to earn it. You have to deserve it." Our righteousness accomplishes nothing. The only thing we can ever merit is eternal damnation. If God were to give us what we earn, what we deserve, we would perish from His wrath, but thanks be to God that He gives to us what was earned by His Son. Jesus got what He did not deserve; we got what He did deserve—the righteousness that is by faith.

Application

The signs and seals of the new covenant reinforce the importance of being a member of a local church. While we receive baptism only once, we partake of the Lord's Supper regularly, but only if we are connected to a church. The sacraments of the church are an important part of a vibrant faith because they are means of grace, reminders to us of our justification that provide us with greater measures of assurance.

WEEK 10

1

Faith or Wrath

PAUL IS SO CAUGHT UP IN THE DOCTRINE OF justification by faith alone that he just cannot seem to let go of it. He labors it all through Romans 3 and 4. Sadly, in light of church history, perhaps the Apostle did not labor it enough, because in every generation there are those who stand up and oppose this essential truth of the gospel.

Paul continues to press home his example of Abraham: **For the promise that he would be the heir of the world was not to Abraham or to his seed through the law** (v. 13a). Abraham and his seed are the heirs of God, joint heirs with Christ.

Actually, the only proper heir of God the Father is God the Son. God the Son alone is worthy to inherit the kingdom that His Father promised, but through the gift of faith and through that righteousness that is by faith, those who are adopted into the family of God become His heirs also. Later in the epistle, Paul will give more details about what it means to be an heir of God, but here he introduces the concept to us and reminds us that the heirs of Abraham and his seed do not receive the promised inheritance through the law but through faith: **For if those who are of the law are heirs, faith is made void and the promise made of no effect** (v. 14). If we could receive the kingdom of God through the law, it would vitiate the primary importance of faith. If we could receive the gifts of God apart from faith—through our works and striving and attempts at merit—then we would, in effect, empty the significance of faith, which is indeed the solitary instrumental cause of our justification. The promise of God to Abraham and his seed has no effect apart from faith.

Why does Paul come to such a grim conclusion about those who think that justification comes through the works of the law rather than through faith alone? He answers that question for us: **because the law brings about wrath** (v. 15a). What the law effects for sinners is not salvation, justification, or forgiveness; it is the wrath of God. If we put our confidence in the law, the only thing we can hope to gain by it is the wrath of God. If we seek to base our salvation on our merit, the only thing we will ever merit is God's wrath.

Application

Take a moment to reflect on the Ten Commandments. It doesn't take long to realize the many ways that we have violated them, both in what we've done and in what we haven't done. Even our good works fall short of God's glory. This is why the law can never justify us, and to seek to be justified by it is anti-gospel. Rejoice that it is through faith in Christ and His righteousness that God has made a way for your justification—without it, we're lost.

2

Transgressing the Law

For where there is no law there is no transgression (v. 15b). If God had not set any standards or imposed obligations on us, then we would be autonomous. We would be free to do whatever we want to do. As Russian novelist Fyodor Dostoyevsky said, "If there is no God, all things are permissible." We live in a society that seeks to banish the very concept of sin from human consciousness, but in order to do that, we must first banish God from the equation.

In setting forth the Shorter Catechism, the Westminster divines provided a simple definition of sin. The question in the catechism asks,

"What is sin?" The answer given is, "Sin is any want of conformity unto, or transgression of, the law of God." That gets at it succinctly. The somewhat archaic language in this phrase simply means "a lack of conformity to the law of God." If God imposes a law or a rule for our behavior, saying, "You shall do this" or "You shall not do that," we fail to conform to His standard of righteousness if we don't conform to that law or if we disobey that commandment. In one sense, this failure to conform calls attention (not always but sometimes) to what we call *sins of omission*. We commit sins of omission when we fail to do those things that we ought to have done, things that God commands us to do. Not only are there negative failures or omissions, but there are also sins of commission, actual transgressions of the law of God.

The law of God is what demonstrates our falling short of His glory. When we break the law of God—something we do, have done, and continue to do—the problem is not simply that we have violated some moral, abstract standard that we call law. The law of God is a personal matter. When we sin, we do not just sin against some abstract norm or piece of legislation. We sin against the One whose law it is. We do violence to Him, to the Author of our very life. That is why sin is such an egregious matter in His sight. If we seek to find our salvation through the law, we are on a fool's errand, because the only consequence of that law for us is exposure to His wrath. We must banish from our minds forever any thought of justifying ourselves by our behavior, good deeds, merits, or work. Just as Dante posted above the entrance to hell the words "Abandon hope, all ye who enter here," so we should abandon all hope of entering the kingdom of God by virtue of our obedience to the law.

Application

By the Spirit's work, our sins against God and His law are accompanied by conviction. When you sin against the Lord, recognize your sin. Then, in grief for and hatred of your sin, turn from it to the mercies of God that are in Christ, pressing on for greater measures of faithfulness.

This is true repentance and, as called in the Westminster Shorter Catechism, a "saving grace" (WSC 87).

3

According to Grace

Therefore it is of faith that it might be according to grace, so that the promise might be sure to all the seed (v. 16a). This is a complicated sentence. Paul emphasizes our justification when he says, "Therefore it is of faith." Next we have a purpose clause, something that gives us a reason. Why is it by faith? "It is of faith that it might be according to grace." When we really grasp this doctrine of justification by faith alone, we grasp with it the sole graciousness of our redemption.

The New Testament gives us the exhortation to make our election sure. We are called not to vacillate, not to waver in our confidence, but to be sure of our status before God and of our receiving the promises of God. Suppose that our salvation depended on our obedience to the law of God. How sure would we be of our salvation? How sure *could* we be of our salvation? If we had to look at the law of God and then look honestly at our own life, any assurance that we had scraped hold of would be demolished in an instant.

The Apostle says that justification is by faith so that it might be of grace so that all the seed of Abraham—all those who come after him and follow in his way—may be sure. The surety belongs to **those who are of the faith of Abraham, who is the father of us all (as it is written, "I have made you a father of many nations") in the presence of Him whom he believed—God, who gives life to the dead and calls those things which do not exist as though they did; who, contrary to hope, in hope believed, so that he became the father of many nations, according to what was spoken, "So shall your descendants**

be" (vv. 16b–18). Abraham is not simply the father of Isaac and his progeny or the father of the Jews, but also the father of the Gentiles who trust in the same promise that he embraced by which he was counted righteous before God.

Application

If you have faith in Jesus Christ, you are a child of Abraham. Even more, you are a child of God (John 1:12). You are a coheir with Jesus Christ and have been given the Holy Spirit as a guarantee of your inheritance (Rom. 8:17; Eph. 1:13–14). Rest in this reality, and know that by God's gift of faith it is sure.

4

Faith That Justifies

SOMETIMES PEOPLE GET THIS MIXED UP and think that saving faith is a leap into the dark. People are told, "Just close your eyes, take a deep breath, make a leap of faith, jump into the darkness, and pray that Jesus will be there to catch you." Jesus never calls people to jump into the darkness. He calls them to jump out of the darkness. He never asks us to crucify our intellect to become Christians. Faith is not believing the absurd or the foolish. Faith is ultimately trusting what is preeminently trustworthy. There is tension when it comes to staking our life on God, which is why Paul writes that Abraham believed "God, who gives life to the dead and calls those things which do not exist as though they did; who, contrary to hope [or against all hope], in hope believed" (vv. 17b–18a). That would seem to give some credence to the idea that true faith is faith that believes against the evidence and against all reason. Here is Abraham who, against all hope, hoped. Is that a leap of faith, or did he have a reason for it, against all earthly indicators?

Abraham's body was for all intents and purposes dead: **not being weak in faith, he did not consider his own body, already dead (since he was about a hundred years old), and the deadness of Sarah's womb. He did not waver at the promise of God through unbelief, but was strengthened in faith, giving glory to God** (vv. 19–20). Abraham was one hundred years old, and his wife was barren, but God said that Sarah would have a child. Eliezer of Damascus would not be Abraham's heir; one from Abraham's loins would be his heir (see Gen. 15:2–4). Abraham looked at himself and his wife and saw a hopeless situation. "How can I possibly believe that promise?" Then he looked at the One who had made the promise and realized that there was nothing hopeless about it. The only thing hopeless was the idea that the promise would *not* come to pass, because it is impossible for God to lie. It is impossible for God to break a promise.

Application

Don't rest your assurance of salvation in the strength of your faith. Paul uses Abraham as a model of faith, and his faith was not always strong. A strong faith or a weak faith in the unbreakable promises of God is still faith in the One who is all-powerful, and it's His power that saves us, not the power of our faith. If you find yourself struggling with doubts about your faith, pray to the Lord that He will strengthen your faith, that your assurance would rest in Christ alone.

5

Fully Convinced

IN OUR SIN, WE PROJECT ONTO the character of God our own character. We break promises, and we live in the midst of people who break promises routinely. Therefore, we question how, since we are so accustomed to broken promises, we can trust this One who promises us things against all earthly evidence.

Abraham was dealing with God, and the God he was dealing with can say, "Let there be . . ." Abraham put his trust in the promise of God. That is what it means to be a Christian. Our only hope in life and death is trusting in the Word of God. There is nothing else to trust in. Everything this world offers passes away. Abraham did not waver at the promise of God through unbelief, but was strengthened in faith, giving glory to God, **and being fully convinced that what He had promised He was also able to perform** (v. 21).

When Vesta and I were offered our second teaching appointment at a Christian college in Boston, we sought a realtor to help us secure a home. A woman who was connected to the college was also a real estate agent, and she took us around Hamilton, Massachusetts, so that we could look for a place to live. At the end of that day we went back to her house, and I met her husband, who was sitting on the couch, watching a Boston Celtics game. There were all kinds of medicine bottles in front of him, and he explained that he had not been feeling well. I talked to him that evening and watched the game with him. After we returned to Pennsylvania to prepare for the move to Boston, I got word that the man I had met that night had been diagnosed with cancer of the pancreas, and that his condition was terminal. God gave me an enormous burden for him, and not a night went by, even before we moved to Boston, that I did not wrestle with God for that man's life.

After we moved to Boston, I went every day to Massachusetts General Hospital to visit him. The only thing I could do was read the Bible to him and put ice on his lips. When he could no longer talk, he would just point at the Bible, and I would read to him from Hebrews: "Because [God] could swear by no one greater, He swore by Himself" (6:13). Through his last breath, that man trusted the promises of God. When he died, I saw the valiant death of a Christian who believed God, and it was counted to him for righteousness. He was like Abraham, who did not waver. His faith was strengthened, he gave glory to God, and he became fully convinced that what God promised He was able to perform.

Application

Do you have a burden for your loved ones who do not know the Lord? Prioritize being in constant prayer for them, even that God may be pleased to work through you in bringing them to faith. As the Apostle Paul writes, "Behold, now is the accepted time; behold, now is the day of salvation" (2 Cor. 6:2). Strive to see this day in the lives of your loved ones.

6

Raised for Our Justification

WITHOUT THE IMPUTATION OF CHRIST'S MERIT to us, we lose everything. It is only by His righteousness that we have any standing in the presence of God. I mentioned earlier that there is a double imputation in our salvation. God reckoned or imputed our sin to Christ in His work for us and in His atoning death upon the cross. When we say that Jesus died for us, we mean that His death was vicarious, He did something for us in our place as our substitute, and that God accepted the transfer of our guilt to His Son. The imputation is dual in the sense that while our sin is reckoned to Christ, His righteousness is imputed to us. He gets our guilt; we get His merit. This double imputation is the great benefit of redemption that Christ won for us.

It would seem that once we have that double imputation by virtue of the life and death of Jesus, our justification would be secure, but there is one more element that we have not yet addressed, and that is the resurrection of Christ, which Paul introduces at the end of chapter 4: **It shall be imputed to us who believe in Him who raised up Jesus our Lord from the dead, who was delivered up because of our offenses, and was raised because of our justification** (vv. 24–25). We could understand how the Apostle would say that Jesus was raised for His own vindication, to declare to the world that His conviction by an earthly court of accusers was fraudulent and that death could not hold Him. That Jesus was raised for His own vindication is an essential element of the resurrection of Jesus, but here Paul is saying that Christ was raised for *our* justification. To understand that, we want to revisit what happened on the cross for our redemption.

With respect to our condition of guilt before God, the language of indebtedness. What is the nature of the debt that we owe God because of our sin? We have a moral debt with God, and when a moral transgression has taken place, the offended person is under no obligation to accept the payment of a substitute on behalf of the guilty. But Christ laid down His life for His sheep on the cross. He offered Himself in His perfect righteousness and took upon Himself the sin of His people. If Jesus had stayed dead, we would have no justification, but when the Father raised the Son from the dead, He said to the world, "I accept this payment for the debtors who cannot pay." The resurrection of Jesus is not simply for His vindication; it is for our justification, because it is God's demonstration to His unjust people that He accepts the payment in full for the moral debt they have incurred.

Application

When you think about the gospel, what comes to mind most prominently? Often, our minds go to the cross, that our sins are dealt with in the death of Christ. This is good news, but there is more to the gospel. Today's passage underscores this fact. Just as our sins are imputed to Christ, so His righteousness—the merit of His sinless life—is imputed to us, and His resurrection is rich in significance for us; it was for our justification. When you share the gospel or preach it to yourself, remember that it is even better news than merely being forgiven. In your justification, you have Christ's righteousness.

Romans 5

THEREFORE, HAVING BEEN JUSTIFIED BY FAITH, *we have peace with God through our Lord Jesus Christ, through whom also we have access by faith into this grace in which we stand, and rejoice in hope of the glory of God. And not only that, but we also glory in tribulations, knowing that tribulation produces perseverance; and perseverance, character; and character, hope. Now hope does not disappoint, because the love of God has been poured out in our hearts by the Holy Spirit who was given to us.*

For when we were still without strength, in due time Christ died for the ungodly. For scarcely for a righteous man will one die; yet perhaps for a good man someone would even dare to die. But God demonstrates His own love toward us, in that while we were still sinners, Christ died for us. Much more then, having now been justified by His blood, we shall be saved from wrath through Him. For if when we were enemies we were reconciled to God through the death of His Son, much more, having been reconciled, we shall be saved by His life. And not only that, but we also rejoice in God through our Lord Jesus Christ, through whom we have now received the reconciliation.

Therefore, just as through one man sin entered the world, and death through sin, and thus death spread to all men, because all sinned—(For until the law sin was in the world, but sin is not imputed when there is no law. Nevertheless death reigned from Adam to Moses, even over those who had not sinned according to the likeness of the transgression of Adam, who is a type of Him who was to come. But the free gift is not like the offense. For if by the one man's offense many died, much more the grace of God and the gift by the grace of the one Man, Jesus Christ, abounded to many. And the gift is not like that which came through the one who

sinned. For the judgment which came from one offense resulted in condemnation, but the free gift which came from many offenses resulted in
justification. For if by the one man's offense death reigned through the
one, much more those who receive abundance of grace and of the gift of
righteousness will reign in life through the One, Jesus Christ.

Therefore, as through one man's offense judgment came to all men,
resulting in condemnation, even so through one Man's righteous act the
free gift came to all men, resulting in justification of life. For as by one
man's disobedience many were made sinners, so also by one Man's obedience many will be made righteous.

Moreover the law entered that the offense might abound. But where
sin abounded, grace abounded much more, so that as sin reigned in death,
even so grace might reign through righteousness to eternal life through
Jesus Christ our Lord.

CHRIST

WEEK 11

1

Consequences of Justification: Peace

PAUL IS LOOKING AT THE DOCTRINE OF JUSTIFICATION as something that has already taken place: **Therefore, having been justified by faith** (v. 1a). The great truth of the *therefore* is that we can be justified now, contrary to what the Roman Catholic Church claims. Those who put their faith in Jesus Christ do not have a prolonged wait for their justification. The moment they believe in Jesus and put their trust in Him, God declares them just, once and for all. "Having been justified" refers to an action in the past, to something that has been accomplished. The work of Christ is finished. Justification is a past action. We received it the moment we believed.

The first consequence is that, having been justified by faith, **we have peace with God through our Lord Jesus Christ** (v. 1b). Peace comes through our peace agent, the peacemaker, the Prince of Peace. He is the medium, the means, through which this peace is given to us.

When I was about six years old, my family was temporarily living in an apartment in Chicago. One summer afternoon, I was playing stickball in front of our apartment. Home plate was a manhole cover in the middle of the street. I was delighted to be up at bat until my turn was rudely interrupted by a spontaneous outcry of great noise and carrying on. I was completely amazed to see people running out of buildings and aproned ladies pounding on pots and pans with wooden spoons. They were screaming and yelling in unrestrained jubilation. I had no idea what was going on except for the fact that my stickball game had just been ruined. I was not happy about it until my mother came out of the apartment building and rushed over to me with tears streaming down her face, crying, "It's over! It's over!" She grabbed me and hugged me. This was the joy of VJ Day, the end of World War II.

There is a strong contrast between the peace we experience during conflicts in this world and the peace about which Paul is writing in Romans 5. Paul is writing about the end of the worst of all possible wars. The vast majority in our country today are engaged in a war of cosmic proportion. The New Testament repeatedly describes the natural condition of fallen people as one of enmity with God. By nature we regard God as our enemy, but few people will own up to that. They feign a kind of indifference about all things religious, yet the heart of man is recalcitrant. It has become hardened to the point that it no longer pulsates with any spiritual life whatsoever. The Scriptures tell us that in our natural condition we do not want to have God in our thinking.

Being justified, we have peace with God, and God has taken the initiative to bring about that peace. We did not surrender and sue for peace; God conquered us, and in His gracious mercy He enabled us to be reconciled to Him through the work of His Son. When God enters into a peace treaty with His people, it is a permanent peace. He may be displeased with us, and we may grieve Him, but once we have peace with God through the work of Jesus Christ, that peace is ours forever.

Application

We might not often think about our time before becoming Christians as characterized by warfare with God. Scripture declares, however, that this was our natural condition. If in our natural condition we were enemies of God and friends to sin, how much more should we flee from sin as Christians now that we are reconciled to Him and have peace with Him?

2

Consequences of Justification: Access, Part 1

THE SECOND CONSEQUENCE OR BENEFIT OF justification is another that we should never take lightly: **we have access by faith into this grace in which we stand** (v. 2a). We have access to the Father. Jews looked back on the whole scope of redemptive history, back to the dawn of creation where God made human beings in His image to be a little lower than the angels, and saw that the best thing Adam and Eve experienced was unlimited access to God. They rushed to commune with Him until that communion was ruined by the first transgression. After that, instead of rushing to their Creator when He entered the garden, they fled from His presence and hid themselves because they had become aware of their nakedness and were overcome with a sense of shame. If our sin is not covered, if our shame has not been removed, there is no way that we can be anything but fugitives.

Despite that unbelievable work of condescension, of mercy and grace, still there were penalties that had to be paid: "In the day that you eat of it you shall surely die" (Gen. 2:17). Adam and Eve suffered spiritual death immediately, but the judgment of physical death was postponed. God let His creatures live, covered, in His presence, but with no further access to the garden of Eden. They were expelled, driven out of Paradise into the darkness. After that, earthly governments were established. The very essence of government is legal force, which we will examine in more detail when we get to Romans 13. The first appearance in sacred Scripture of the power of the sword is found with the sentinel that God placed at the entrance to the garden of Eden. God put an angel by the garden with a flaming sword, which was meant to be an instrument of coercion to prevent creatures tainted by sin from entering back in. The significance of that loss is reiterated through the Old Testament Scriptures.

A critical moment in the history of Israel occurred when God summoned Moses to Mount Sinai. Moses was to go up on the mountain to receive the law by which God was to constitute the Israelites as a nation of His people. Only Moses was allowed to go up the mountain. If others so much as put one finger or foot on that holy mountain, they were to be executed. Even those who would simply witness the mountain shaking with thunder, lightning, earthquake, volcanic eruption, and cloud when God appeared would be required to go through days of cleansing and purification.

Application

When we sin, we sometimes see the cost of our sin right away. Maybe it was some harsh words spoken to a spouse that can't be unsaid. Something is lost, and our relationship with the person we sinned against is threatened. Remember the cosmic scale of this loss when experienced by humanity in Adam, and in light of God's mercy and grace demonstrated in His seeking reconciliation with us, seek to be reconciled quickly with those against whom you've sinned.

3

Consequences of Justification: Access, Part 2

WHEN THE NOMADIC TRIBES OF ISRAEL encamped, they set up the camp in a circle, according to the tribes, and at the very center of that circle was the tabernacle. The point of the circle was to ensure that no one tribe had greater access to the presence of God than any other tribe. The glory of the people of Israel was in the tabernacle because it manifested the presence of God. The people were comforted because God was in their midst. In this gracious condescension God dwelt with His people, but even in that grace there was a limit. At the core of the tabernacle in the center of the camp was the *sanctus sanctorum*, the Holy of Holies. Contained in the Holy of Holies was the ark of the covenant, a chest, on which was the mercy seat, and in the chest were copies of the Decalogue, some manna from the wilderness, and Aaron's rod that had blossomed. It was on top of the mercy seat, the *kapporeth*, where the blood of the offering was sprinkled on the Day of Atonement. From among the whole nation of Israel only one person, the high priest, was allowed inside the Holy of Holies. Others could stand in the holy place or in the outer court; they could come that close to God but no farther. Even the high priest could go in only after going through elaborate ablutions and rites of purification, and even then he entered the Holy of Holies in a spirit of fear and trembling. One tradition says (we don't know whether it's accurate) that the great high priest would have a rope tied around one of his legs and bells strung on his cassock so that if he had a heart attack and fell over while inside, the bells would ring, and he could be dragged out by the rope. No one else was allowed to go in, even to save the great high priest's life.

We see the same picture over and over again, the picture of no access. One of the most intricately designed parts of the tabernacle was the curtain, or the veil, which later became the veil of the temple that separated the holy place from the Holy of Holies. The veil was composed of very thick drapes that could not be broken. Nothing could break through that barrier that separated the people from the immediate presence of God until Golgotha, until that day in Jerusalem when the sun was blotted out of the sky in the middle of the day and it became pitch black as night. On that day, when Christ was the curse on the cross, there was an earthquake. During that earthquake the wall of separation came crashing down through the work of the Mediator, the Savior. When He rose from the dead, He entered into the heavenly sanctuary, into the heavenly Holy of Holies, where He gives us access.

Application

The Puritan Thomas Watson wrote, "Jesus Christ went more willingly to the cross than we do to the throne of grace." As Christians, we have been given access to God, and it has come at a great price. Let our lives be characterized by a constant communion with God in prayer because it is what Christ has secured for us and will be our joy for all eternity.

4

Consequences of Justification: Access, Part 3

WHEN WE COME TOGETHER FOR WORSHIP on Sundays, we no longer come to that mountain that was shaking with thunder and lightning and hidden in clouds:

> But you have come to Mount Zion and to the city of the living God, the heavenly Jerusalem, to an innumerable company of angels, to the general assembly and church of the firstborn who are registered in heaven, to God the Judge of all, to the spirits of just men made perfect, to Jesus the Mediator of the new covenant. (Heb. 12:22–24)

We come to the presence of God. We have access to His presence. There is no more veil. The angel's sword of flame has been doused with the blood of Christ, and God welcomes us into His presence.

There is no greater human experience than to have an overwhelming sense of being in the presence of God. The greatest of Christians testify that the times they recall of having an acute sense of being in the presence of God can be numbered on one hand. If we have tasted it, we have had a taste of heaven, a taste of the presence of divine glory that Christ opened up for us.

Our justification is not just about forgiveness or the imputation of the righteousness of Christ. It is not just about escaping the judgment of divine wrath, though it includes all that. In our justification we have peace that passes all human understanding. While once we were barred from admittance into the immediate presence of God, now we are called to enter into His presence boldly. Yet there is a difference between boldness and arrogance; we are never to enter into the presence of God arrogantly. Many speak flippantly about their relationship to Christ or God as that of pal or peer, but if Jesus Christ walked into our presence, everyone would be on his face in a posture of submission and adoration, overwhelmed by Christ's glory.

"We have access by faith into this grace" (v. 2a). Faith and grace are inseparably related. The most unmerited favor that any creature, any sinner, can experience is the grace of being allowed into the presence of God. How would we feel if we received a written invitation for a personal audience with God? What would we wear? What would we say? That engraved invitation comes to all who are justified. It is a fruit of our justification. That is the grace in which we stand in Christ Jesus and in which we rejoice in the hope of the glory of God.

Application

Do you think of worship as coming into God's presence? Understanding worship in this way helps us worship rightly in reverence and awe. While the overwhelming sense of being in the presence of God might be rare, worship is indeed coming into His presence. Meditate on this as you prepare for the Lord's Day and as you go to worship, and perhaps the sense of God's presence will be more and more real to you.

5

Consequences of Justification: Hope, Part 1

THE THIRD CONSEQUENCE OR BENEFIT OF JUSTIFICATION that Paul mentions in the beginning of chapter 5 is the **hope of the glory of God** (v. 2b). Elsewhere Paul tells us that the triad of Christian virtues consists of faith, hope, and love, and the greatest of these is love (1 Cor. 13:13). The word *hope, elpis* in the Greek, is one of the richest terms we find anywhere in the New Testament. It is the gift that God gives to every person justified by faith. It is a hope that radically differs from our normal understanding of hope.

If we are asked, "Do you think the Steelers are going to win?" we might reply, "I don't know, but I hope so." Such a use of the word *hope* expresses the desire that certain things will come to pass, but we have no assurance that they will. Not so with the biblical concept of hope. The Bible describes hope with a metaphor: hope is the anchor of our souls. Our souls are not tossed to and fro by every wind of doctrine. We have stability in our lives because, in the midst of the tempest, there is an anchor, and that anchor is the hope that God the Holy Spirit has shed abroad in our hearts. It is a hope that cannot possibly be ashamed, as we will consider more fully in the next study. It is a hope that carries with it God's assurance; it is a hope that cannot fail. In one sense, our faith looks backward so that we put our trust in what Christ has done for us. In another sense, our hope looks forward with the same assurance to what He will do when He completes His work of redemption in us, a work that cannot fail.

Those are the three things that Paul tells us are the fruit of our justification—peace with God, access to His presence, and the hope of His glory, which is shed abroad in our hearts. It is important to note that these benefits come to us "through our Lord Jesus Christ" (v. 1b). Just as our justification is by faith and grace because of Christ, the benefits of peace we enjoy come through His ministry to us. He is the Prince of Peace. He has effected our reconciliation with the Father, and we receive the legacy of His peace. The access we have and the benefits we gain through Christ are things "in which we stand" (v. 2a). Our standing before God is as those covered with the righteousness of Christ and declared just in His sight; we have had our sins remitted and our guilt satisfied by Christ's atoning death.

Application

Many times, we can become discouraged in our present struggles. When you begin to feel such discouragement come over you, remember that even in your present struggle, God has given you a faith that can look backward and forward—backward to the reality of what Christ has done for you and forward to the glory that will be yours, giving you certain hope in the present.

6

Consequences of Justification: Hope, Part 2

HERE WE WILL LOOK MORE FULLY AT that third benefit: "we . . . rejoice in hope of the glory of God" (v. 2). There are three words in this little phrase that are vitally important to understand properly. The first is the word "rejoice." That translation, "rejoice," does not quite get it; the meaning is more than simply "rejoicing." The actual word that Paul used is not the normal word for "joy" or "rejoicing"; it is the word more often translated *boasting*. In both the Greek and Latin texts, we see a play on words: we "glory now in glory." We have a sense of celebration and ecstasy beyond normal levels of joy, and the target of our joy is the hope directed toward the manifestation of the glory of God.

The second word, *glory*, comes from the Greek noun *doka* or *doxa*. From it we get the word *doxology*. When we sing the Doxology, we sing praises to the majesty of God; we glorify God. We are in the activity of glorifying the One who possesses glory, which is the play on words in both the Latin and the Greek. Paul is saying that once we are justified, one of the things that delights us and causes joy to fill our souls is to contemplate who God is. Our greatest delight is in His character and glory.

The Old Testament frequently speaks about the nature of God. He manifests His glory. The word for "glory" in the Old Testament is *kabod*, sometimes rendered *kavod*. In the original Semitic language, the word meant "weightiness" or "heaviness." When we speak about the glory of God, we speak about One whose very being is not light or insignificant; it is substantive and heavy. We use similar language in everyday situations. When someone says something that we think is profound, we might shake our heads and say, "That was heavy." We also use the term to indicate something that should be taken seriously. There is a link in the original languages between the weightiness or dignity of God and His august nature. God's glory is tied to His dignity or gravity.

The purpose of worship is to ascribe glory to God, to honor and revere Him, to adore Him in the excellence of His being. Augustine was not narrow in his selection of the sort of music that is fitting for worship. He pointed out that there are different music strains and styles, but no matter what type of music we use in the celebration of God's glory, there ought to be some connection between the glory of God and what Augustine called the *gravitas*, gravity or weightiness, in the means by which we worship Him. Sometimes we get too familiar in the way we worship God, forgetting who He is, the weightiness of His very being. Part of this particular benefit of justification is the delight we take in glorifying God, for once faith has taken hold of our hearts, we perceive the things of God in a way totally different from how we did in our natural state. Something is created in our souls the moment we come to faith that involves the dimension of *hope*, the third word that we'll look at next.

Application

Take some time to hide God's Word in your heart in order to shape the way that you meditate on the wonder of worship. Memorize Hebrews 12:28–29: "Therefore, since we are receiving a kingdom which cannot be shaken, let us have grace, by which we may serve God acceptably with reverence and godly fear. For our God is a consuming fire."

WEEK 12

1

Hope Misunderstood

THE TRIAD OF CHRISTIAN VIRTUES—faith, hope, and love—are all important. As important as love is (1 Cor. 13:13), we know that faith is not unimportant. We have been working closely on the significance of faith, and we understand the importance of love, but so often that third element in this triad of virtues, hope, gets overlooked in Christian experience.

If there is any word in Romans 5 that we might radically misunderstand, it is *hope*. There is always an element of doubt that clouds our understanding of Paul's use of the word. When we use the word *hope*, typically we use it to describe a wish or a desire that something will take place, something that we are not sure will actually happen. That is not the way that the word functions in the New Testament. When we are regenerated by the Holy Spirit, we are born anew to a hope that forms the basis for our confidence in living out the Christian life. The only difference between hope and faith is that faith looks to what has already taken place, and we put our trust in it. Hope is merely faith looking forward.

I mentioned earlier that the metaphor used in the New Testament to describe the nature of hope is that of an anchor. Hope, we are told, is the anchor of the soul. We frequently find this nautical image in the New Testament. The unstable are compared to boats that have no anchor, tossed to and fro with every wind of doctrine. Such people are characterized by vacillation and uncertainty, but the hope planted in the soul by the Holy Spirit is not like that. This hope gives a foundation and stability and assurance. Hope is the anchor that keeps us from being blown about. It is the hope that God is surely going to do in the future every single thing that He has said He will do.

The fruit of justification is that kind of hope. Justification, in a sense, is the down payment for all that God promises us in His work of redemption. Hope is created by the Holy Spirit within us. Elsewhere Paul will speak about God's giving to us the "earnest" or down payment of the Holy Spirit, which gives us total assurance for the future. Hope is not taking a deep breath and hoping that things are going to turn out all right. It is assurance that God is going to do what He says He will do.

Application

Where do you turn when life seems to be tossing you to and fro? It is important to notice that the Christians in Ephesus were tossed to and fro and carried about by "every wind of doctrine" (Eph. 4:14). Be sure that when doubts assail you, you rehearse truth to yourself. The great remedy to false doctrine is true doctrine, for which you must go to God's Word.

2

Glory in Tribulations

NOT ONLY THAT, BUT WE ALSO GLORY IN TRIBULATIONS (v. 3a). There is nothing more unnatural than to enjoy afflictions or tribulation. Tribulation is something that we desperately seek to avoid. Once we have been justified, however, we have a whole new perspective on tribulations. We no longer see suffering as an exercise in futility, something that takes away our hope. Once we have the anchor on our soul, it holds when tribulation comes. It is not that we have the capacity of a Stoic to grin and bear it; it goes beyond endurance to rejoicing in tribulations.

Paul was not a masochist. He is not saying that tribulation is a joyful, pleasant, pleasurable experience. Rather, he is saying that because we have been justified, even the tribulations and afflictions we experience can be an occasion for joy. Above all, the fruit of justification is the presence of joy in the Christian's life. We have found the pearl of great price, and no matter how much pain we have to go through, as bad as things may be, these things are not worthy to be compared with the joy that God has set before us in Christ. If we lose everything the world can give us, we still possess that priceless pearl of our justification. Because God has redeemed us, we are able to rejoice no matter what life brings. Once we are reconciled and justified, we can rejoice even when people slander us and wound us deeply. We can glory in it because of Christ and our justification. We glory in tribulation because we know what tribulation does. Paul understood because he believed in the sovereignty and providence of God. There are no accidents in this world. No matter how many injustices are heaped upon us this side of heaven, they do not mean anything compared to the crown of glory that God has prepared for His people. Paul is saying that when we go through afflictions and tribulations, we can glory in them, not because we enjoy pain but because we know what tribulation yields. For most people, tribulation breaks the spirit, leads them to despair, and causes them to abandon all hope. Not so for the Christian.

Application

We can look back on many times in our Christian lives when we did not endure tribulations with hope or joy. We must constantly remind ourselves of the good that God works through our tribulations. Be diligent to take your suffering to Him in prayer so that you will have faith and hope that your tribulations are working out His good intentions for you, knowing full well that He loves you.

AMEN

3

The Fruit of Tribulation

TRIBULATION PRODUCES PERSEVERANCE (v. 3b). Tribulation puts muscle on our souls. Tribulation makes it possible for the people of God to persevere rather than to give up. Tribulation produces perseverance; **and perseverance, character** (v. 4a). An easy life does nothing to produce character. Character is forged in the crucible of pain. Character is built when we have no alternative but to persevere in tribulation. Those who come out on the other side are those in whose souls God has built character. The result of character is **hope** (v. 4b)—there it is again. Authentically joyful people are those who know where their hope is. They have been through the crucible. They have been through afflictions, persecution, and rejection from their friends. They have been through pain. They have identified with the humiliation of Christ. They have been crucified with Christ and raised in His resurrection and now participate in His exaltation. That is the hope that Christian character produces.

What about the result of that hope? Here is the best part: **Now hope**

does not disappoint (v. 5a). Other translations say that hope "does not make us ashamed." It is embarrassing that the world's idea of hope is to invest it in some particular enterprise only to see that enterprise fail. When it fails, we are dashed to pieces, but the hope that we have from God will never disappoint. It will never embarrass us. We will never have to be ashamed for putting our confidence and trust in Christ. If you put your trust in anything else but Christ, you are destined for disappointment and embarrassment. Hope in Christ is the only hope that never shames us. The New Testament tells us that if we are not in the faith, if we do not believe, we are without hope and destined ultimately to disappointment.

All of us struggle with the weaknesses of the flesh and sin. One of the many things I am ashamed of is that I still have a hard time dealing with disappointments and unrealized expectations. When I travel across the country and arrive at my destination, tired and just wanting to get to the hotel room to take a nap, and I find that the hotel has mislaid my reservation, I find myself in a fit of "hotel rage." Infants are quick to cry and scream, and almost every time it is because they are disappointed. They did not get what they wanted. They were looking forward to something that did not happen, and they cannot handle it. That tendency does not leave us as we grow older. One of the hardest things to deal with in life is disappointment when our hopes have been dashed into pieces. Yet the hope we have of the glory of God and for the ultimate victory of His kingdom will never let us down. Nobody is going to cancel that reservation or let it fall between the cracks. We can rely absolutely on God. That is what we learn when we understand the gospel and our justification. This is just one more fruit.

Application

Perseverance is a great and precious promise of the gospel. Knowing that we will persevere in the Christian life is a source of great confidence, assured that nothing can come between our salvation and our

Savior. We can know for certain that we will endure to the end in faith. Reflect often on God's promise that you will persevere. It will enable you to bear tribulation, pressing onward for greater character and hope.

4

Love Poured Out

PAUL GIVES ANOTHER REASON FOR HOPE: **the love of God has been poured out in our hearts by the Holy Spirit who was given to us** (v. 5b). Paul is not saying that affection for God will prevent us from experiencing disappointment or shame, even though such affection is one of the most important fruits of salvation that the Holy Spirit kindles within our hearts. Here Paul is not talking about our love for God; he is talking about God's love for us. The love of God is a love that the Holy Spirit sheds abroad. God's love for the justified is no mere feeling; neither are the gifts that God gives us or the benefits that He pours upon us. It is God's affection that God puts inside us, His love for us. That is what fuels our hope and gives us confidence that we will not be ashamed. It is what enables us to persevere and endure tribulations and afflictions. The love that God pours out is no small portion; it is an outpouring of divine love, lavished upon us. He pours His love for us into our souls to such a degree that even if the rest of the world hates us, we can know that He loves us and has given us hope that we will never be ashamed. It is one of the works of the Holy Spirit.

Salvation is not like receiving just one gift under the Christmas tree but gift after gift all wrapped up together. The first package we find is our justification, and when we open that package, we find inside it another—peace with God. Inside that package is access into His presence, and inside that gift is the ability to rejoice in glorifying the glory of God. Inside that package we find that there is joy in the midst of tribulation, and that very tribulation gives us another gift—perseverance. Tear off the ribbon from that gift, and there is another one, which is the character that perseverance gives us, and within that gift is hope that will never embarrass or disappoint us. Finally, we open one more present, and it is the love of God poured profusely into our hearts by the grace of God. All these are the gift of our justification. Do we wonder, then, at that doxological writing of the Apostle Paul, who rejoices in these things over and over again? For Paul, Christmas never ends.

Application

The reason that our hope isn't just an empty wish is found in the love of God, and God's love has very concrete expressions. In history, we see it most expressly in the person and work of Jesus Christ, but Paul mentions here the Holy Spirit's work in our experience of God's love. We don't merely conjure up our own feelings of being loved by God, but God Himself assures us of His love by the Spirit. Ask for this assuring love and be encouraged more and more to live for Him.

5

The When of the Atonement, Part 1

AFTER SHOWING US THE BENEFITS THAT accompany justification—peace with God, access to God's presence, and hope—Paul turns his attention to the atonement of Christ: **For when we were still without strength, in due time Christ died for the ungodly** (v. 6). At this point, Paul discusses the *when* of our atonement, the point in history at which the redemption of the people of God was accomplished. Paul speaks of the *when* of this accomplishment in two ways. The first is with respect to us. At what point in our personal history did Christ offer Himself on the cross? Paul tells us first that Christ offered Himself "when we were still without strength." Let's look at that before we look at the second way, the temporal aspect of the atonement.

One of the cardinal doctrines of biblical Christianity has to do with original sin and its impact on our spiritual strength. This issue has provoked a battle in every generation throughout church history. Virtually every church confesses some doctrine of original sin, but as we have seen, this original sin does not refer to the first sin committed by Adam and Eve but to the consequences of that sin by which God visited corruption upon the entire human race. All the progeny of Adam and Eve are born in a state of spiritual death and moral corruption. The debate comes in with regard to the degree of that corruption. To what extent have we fallen from our original righteousness?

Augustine waged this battle in antiquity against the heretic Pelagius, who denied the fall altogether. The cardinal point that Augustine taught was that the ravages of sin are so great and penetrate so deeply within our souls that we are left in a state of spiritual death. Spiritual death means that even though we are still alive biologically, even though we have faculties that remain intact—a brain, a mind, affections, a will—our humanity has been so damaged by the fall that our state, by nature, is one of moral inability.

The idea of moral inability is this: we have been plunged so deeply into sin that we do not have the moral capacity to incline ourselves in any way to the things of God. If God in His mercy and grace were to offer us complete forgiveness and salvation in Jesus Christ but do nothing to work in our hearts, we would never exercise that option. We simply do not have the moral capacity. We have the volitional power to choose what we want in any circumstance, but sin is so deep that we no longer have any desire for God or any want for the gospel or for Christ.

Application

Think about the last person who was rude or dismissive toward you. How do you feel toward that person? As sinners, we have a hard time loving those who have sinned against us. God, however, loved us in such a way that He sent His Son to die for us. Remember this the next time you are offended. It just might change the way you react, allowing you to love even your enemy as Christ commands us.

6

The When of the Atonement, Part 2

UNLESS THE HOLY SPIRIT EMPOWERS THE WORD of preaching and the outreach of evangelism, no one will come to Christ. That is the point that Jesus made when He said, "No one can come to Me unless the Father who sent Me draws him" (John 6:44). Paul is teaching this same principle. He is saying that Christ died for the ungodly while we were still without strength. The strength that Paul has in view is clearly spiritual strength. We have no strength in and of ourselves to effect our salvation.

God did not wait for us to exercise our wills, incline ourselves to Him, repent of our sins, or get ourselves in such a state that it would be appropriate to provide an atonement for us. No, while we were still in this state, which Paul later, in his letter to the Ephesians, describes as spiritual death, while we were dead in trespasses and sin (Eph. 2:1), Christ died. That is the *when* with respect to our human condition.

Concerning the historical *when*: "A decree went out from Caesar Augustus that all the world should be registered. This census first took place while Quirinius was governing Syria" (Luke 2:1–2). It is an integral part of the Christmas narrative in Luke, but the point here is that Christ came into the world in real time in real history. It did not happen outside space and time. Christ came in the fullness of time. He was born on the exact date and in the exact place that the Father had decreed. Throughout the whole Old Testament—in the activity of God's ministering to His people, in creating a nation for Himself out of Israel, in giving them the Law and the Prophets, in ministering to them through their entire sojourn—God was ripening history for the moment that Christ would come. He came "in due time."

When we read in the Gospel narratives about the death of Christ, we find political machinations going on behind the scenes. Caiaphas, Pilate, and Herod all give their advice. The soldiers conspire. The Sanhedrin gets involved; they pay money to Judas to make sure that all would take place. God knew from the foundation of the world that this was the day because He had ordained it. All these things came together in the concurrence of divine providence so that on a specific date Christ would die.

Application

The reason for God's love for us is not found in us. Scripture emphasizes that we were dead in trespasses and sin with nothing that would move God to love us, and yet He did. Take a moment to meditate on this great love of God in Christ and appreciate the riches of Reformed theology in exalting this love in faithfulness to the Scriptures.

WEEK 13

1

The Scope of the Atonement

WHEN YOUNG MEN ARE EXAMINED FOR ORDINATION, they are asked, "Do you believe in limited atonement?" In other words, do they believe that Christ did not die for everybody? The standard answer they give is that Christ's death is sufficient for all but efficient only for some. It is valuable enough to cover the sins of all, and in that sense it is universally sufficient, but it is efficient, that is, it effects salvation, only for those who believe. I have no quarrel with that, but it is not limited atonement. Every Arminian believes that Christ's atonement is sufficient for all and efficient only for believers.

The question about the scope of the atonement is this: what was God's eternal purpose in designing the death of His Son? From all eternity, God had a plan of salvation. Did He plan to save everybody? If God is God and if God is sovereign and if saving everybody was His eternal plan, then nothing could defeat that plan, and every human being would be saved, but manifestly the Scriptures teach that not everybody is saved. Do we doubt that God has the power and the right to save everybody? If God had determined to save everybody in the world, everybody would be saved.

There is in Scripture, from Genesis to Revelation, a doctrine of election. We may not like the doctrine, and if we do not, it is because we do not understand it. I do not know how people could have affection for Christ in their hearts and not rejoice at the unspeakable grace of God to include them in salvation and make certain that they would be saved. And if God has chosen only some to be saved, it makes sense that Christ would die only for those whom He chose (Rom. 9:1–24). Indeed, Jesus said that He laid down His life for only His sheep (John 10:15).

The idea of limited atonement deals with the question of God's design. Did God intend to save a remnant of the world and send His Son to die for those people to ensure their salvation? That is what *limited atonement* means. It means "definite atonement." The atonement of Christ was not just to make salvation possible. If that were the case, Christ could have died and never have seen the travail of His soul and been satisfied. If the efficacy of Christ's death depends on us, Christ would have no fruit from His death; but while we were powerless in our souls to incline ourselves to the things of God, in due time Christ died for the ungodly.

Application

Have you ever struggled with the doctrine of election? Often, we fail to see the goodness of God and acknowledge the sinfulness of man when considering such questions. If we keep these two things in place, the wonder of salvation can captivate us. Christ died for sinners. This is the good news that we get to share with others.

2

Our Helplessness

FOR SCARCELY FOR A RIGHTEOUS MAN WILL ONE DIE; **yet perhaps for a good man someone would even dare to die** (v. 7). The words that Paul uses are translated *righteous* and *good*, but John Calvin believed that since there is no distinction between a righteous person and a good person, Paul was using a *hendiadys*. *Hendiadys* is the name given to two different words used to refer to the same thing. Martin Luther, on the other hand, was convinced that Paul was making a distinction. Although a good man would necessarily have to be a righteous man, the idea here is that *righteous* is somewhat formal. A righteous person might be somebody who obeys the law and does what is right so that his behavior provokes a certain measure of respect. Although we can respect people that we think are morally upright, it is rare that we would lay down our lives just because we respect their character.

When we talk about "good" people, we are speaking about more than their moral activity, more than their conformity to principles of righteousness. A good person is the sort who produces in us a certain love and concern. When we say, "He is a good fellow," we mean that he is a nice guy. He is a kind person. He is the sort of person for whom we would be willing to go the extra mile to reciprocate his affection and kindness toward us. Paul is saying that rarely will anybody die for a righteous man, although maybe someone will die for a loved one or for someone who has shown personal kindnesses. Even pagans, on occasion, might be willing to jump on a hand grenade for such a person, but in the case of the atonement, Jesus did not die for righteous people or for good people; He died for godless people.

In the heart of every corrupt human being, even in one who is partially sanctified, there remains a little buzz that seeks to persuade, "I was not that bad." Rarely do we come to a full conviction of our helplessness and wickedness. All the power of our psychology is at work every minute to suppress full admission of our guilt and hopelessness. When people repeatedly give me reasons other than the sovereign grace of God as to why they are Christian while their friends are not, I begin to wonder if they are in the kingdom at all, because they certainly have not yet been convinced of their helplessness and sin.

Application

Acknowledging our helplessness and sin is good. First, it does justice to the truth. Second, it convinces us of our need for Christ. Third, it can lead to greater measures of humility in our faithful obedience to Him. Strive to remember the joyous reality that if you trust in Christ, you are a child of God, but that like any child, you are dependent. This may guard us from presumption and keep us relying on God's grace for our sanctification.

3

God's Love for Sinners

BUT GOD DEMONSTRATES HIS OWN LOVE TOWARD US, **in that while we were still sinners, Christ died for us** (v. 8). There is a shift in language here from the generic *ungodly* to the specific *for us*. While we were in a state of sin, God set forth *for us*. Again and again in his epistles, Paul speaks of the specific work of grace that Christ does for the believer. When he talks about *us*, he is talking about those who are in Christ Jesus. He is talking about Christians.

What about the love of God? "God demonstrates His own love toward us." There are two aspects to consider concerning this clause. The first is how theology distinguishes among three distinct types of God's love. The first type of divine love is the *love of benevolence*. The word *bene* means "good" or "well." The word *volens* has to do with the will. The Bible tells us that God's basic attitude toward the world, toward fallen humanity, is one of goodwill. God is not unkind or mean-spirited; the basic posture of the Creator toward the world is one of goodwill, and every person in the world experiences it in one way or another. The fact that people are alive is an indication of God's goodwill. Every moment that a sinner continues to exist in this world, he does so only by virtue of the goodwill of God, by God's forbearance and patience. God loves everybody in the sense that His goodwill flows toward all.

The second sense of divine love is God's *beneficence*. His benevolence refers to His goodwill, whereas His beneficence refers to His good acts. The Bible tells us that God's rain falls on the just and the unjust (Matt. 5:45). All people, repentant or not, believers or not, receive certain kind acts from the hand of God. In that sense, they all experience God's beneficent love.

When we talk about the unconditional love of God, the love that never fails, we are talking about His *complacent* love, the third type of divine love. God's complacent love is the delight He takes, supremely, in His Son. God's love for His Son is without measure or qualification; He loves His Son fully and perfectly. The love that the Father has for His Son extends beyond His Son to those who belong to His Son. Therefore, only believers receive God's complacent love. They do not receive it because of anything in them but only because God gives gifts to His Son. From all eternity He has loved His Son and planned to give Him a portion of humanity so that His Son might be the firstborn among many brothers. God loves His Son with the love of complacency, and He demonstrates that complacent love for us in that "while we were still sinners, Christ died for us."

Application

Understanding that God's basic attitude toward fallen humanity is one of goodwill gives us insight into the posture that we as Christians ought to adopt toward the world. God is not unkind and mean-spirited, so let us also not be unkind and mean-spirited. Through the church, may God awaken more people to the reality that all creatures enjoy His goodness, but especially to the truth that His saving love can be found only through faith in Jesus Christ.

4

Wrath Satisfied

THE SECOND ASPECT OF GOD'S DEMONSTRATING "His own love toward us" (v. 8) is quite technical, so I will mention it briefly. Old creeds present God's anger, *ira Dei*, as something that needs to be assuaged so that sin is repaid through the satisfaction offered by His Son's atoning sacrifice, but a debate emerged in twentieth-century German theology about the atonement. Some theologians were opposed to the classic doctrine of the atonement as the Son's satisfying the wrath of the Father. The effects of the debate are that today, some theologians scoff at any idea of an atonement that provides satisfaction for our sins. They say that God does not need satisfying and that His love is so great that it cancels His wrath.

Several years ago at a Christian booksellers convention, I was asked to give the keynote address to six thousand people, and I decided to speak on the urgency of the gospel. Titling my talk "Saved from What?" I went back to the rudimentary concept of salvation, and I told them that if we look at the concept of salvation in the Bible, we see that the most rudimentary meaning of salvation is to be rescued from some calamity. If we are restored from sickness, we are saved from the effects of that illness. If we experience victory in battle, we are saved from the ignominy of defeat. That is the way in which the Greek word for "salvation" is used in the New Testament; for example, anytime someone is rescued from catastrophe, he experiences salvation, but then there is the grand doctrine of salvation that speaks of salvation in the ultimate sense, in which we are rescued from the worst of all possible catastrophes—God's wrath.

Many churches do not believe that anymore. Many believe in a god who has no wrath, but if God has no wrath, there is no need for Christ. Unbelievers say, "That's fine for you, but I do not need Jesus," yet there is nothing in heaven or on earth they need more than Jesus. As long as people are unconcerned about the wrath of God, they feel no need to come to Jesus. If God is real, so is His wrath, and the biblical view of salvation is rescue from wrath.

In my address at the booksellers convention, I said, "Do you want to know what you are saved from? In a word, you are saved from God." They just gasped, and to this day when I attend that convention, people come up to me and say, "I had never thought of that until I heard your message." It is God who saves people from God because His wrath is stored up against the day of wrath, and He most certainly will demonstrate it to the impenitent. But He has demonstrated His love toward believers "in that while we were still sinners, Christ died for us."

Application

The wrath of God is an essential part of the good news. Let us ponder this truth often, remembering that one day we will stand before the judgment seat of Christ, the One who is also our Mediator and the One who bore the punishment of God's wrath in the place of His people. Christ has delivered you from the fear of condemnation on that day.

5

Enemies

PAUL BEGINS THIS SECTION WITH A COMPARISON: **For if when we were enemies we were reconciled to God through the death of His Son, much more, having been reconciled, we shall be saved by His life** (v. 10). The theme of this verse has to do with reconciliation. One absolute, essential precondition for reconciliation is estrangement, because without estrangement there is no need for reconciliation. The fact that through Christ we have been reconciled to God is one of the central motifs of the New Testament.

Sinclair Ferguson has said that there is almost a universal repudiation of the idea that human beings have a natural enmity toward God. I can think of nothing that provokes more anger from unbelievers than when we tell them that they hate God. They deny it emphatically. "I might be indifferent to God, but I do not hate God," they say. But if people are indifferent to the Lord God Almighty, the One who created them and has given them every blessing they receive, what is that except hatred? We do not sense the weight of our natural hostility toward God. The New Testament speaks about reconciliation because reconciliation to God is so greatly and earnestly needed. We are estranged from Him. Not only are we at enmity with God, but God is at enmity with us. God is the natural enemy of corrupt sinners.

There is a love that God displays to creatures indiscriminately, but at the same time the Scripture is replete with descriptive terms that tell us how God's face is steadfastly set against the wicked. He is too holy to even look at us, so great is that gulf of estrangement. There is a big difference in the driving force of the estranged parties. Driving our opposition toward God is evil. His estrangement from us is founded on a holy opposition to sin. We must understand that difference and not project onto God's character the same unjust grounds for enmity that we are guilty of ourselves. It is not right for the creature to be estranged from the Creator, but if the creature is sinful, it is right and proper for the Creator to be estranged. He is holy and we are not. Paul is declaring here the glorious work of redemption in which God takes the initiative for our reconciliation.

Application

We can be assured of our future experience of God's saving love because of our present standing in it in Christ. This is not something that God revokes. If we are saved by grace alone, we are kept by grace alone. Remember this as you live out the life of reconciliation, striving to be holy and never doubting in your mind this blessed reality.

6

Enemies Reconciled

ON THE CROSS BY HIS WORK of propitiation, Jesus reconciled the Father to the Father's people. On Good Friday when Christ paid for our sin and made atonement for His people with the perfect sacrifice and satisfied God's wrath completely, that was the end of the estrangement on God's part. We were reconciled in the sense that God, the injured party, was satisfied. God was reconciled toward us while we were still estranged from Him. In this drama of reconciliation, Christ satisfied the righteousness and holiness of His Father. On the day that God became satisfied and was no longer in opposition to His people, we did not automatically change. We do not experience that reconciliation until our opposition and hostility toward Him end—when we are regenerated by the Holy Spirit, our hardened hearts are broken, and we are brought joyfully into a loving relationship with the Father through the Son.

It is one thing to experience the reconciliation that comes through the death of Christ, but how much greater is the reconciliation that occurs through the life of Christ. We can look at that in two ways. Christ's life of perfect obedience to the law, by which His righteousness was merited and earned, is now given to us who have no righteousness of our own. We can say that it is the life of Christ even more than the death of Christ that is the ground of our justification. That is true, but I am not sure that it is what Paul is talking about here when he says, "How much more, having been reconciled, we shall be saved by [Christ's] life." Paul has already introduced the idea not only that we are justified by the death of Christ but also that Christ was raised for our justification. We are reconciled because we have a Mediator who not only died for us but also was raised from the dead and continues to make intercession. He is our peacemaker. He lives forever, continuing in that role, representing us before the Father. As wonderful as was that once-for-all death on the cross, how much greater is that reconciliation that we realize and experience because He lives and ever intercedes for us.

Application

Take a moment to pray after this week's study through the nature of the atonement. Praise the Father, Son, and Holy Spirit for your deliverance, that the Father set His love on you in Christ before the foundation of the world, that Christ secured your salvation by living for you in perfect obedience and dying as your substitute, and that the Spirit has sealed you as the surety of all that is yours in Christ (Eph. 1:3–14)

WEEK 14

1

Rejoicing in Reconciliation

I WANT TO EXPLORE A LITTLE more the meaning of this term *reconciliation*. Paul said in Romans 1 that the substance of our universal guilt and corruption before God is this: our proclivity for idolatry, the sin of exchanging the truth of God for the lie, serving and worshiping the creature rather than the Creator. When we first looked at that, I made mention of a word that Paul used, *metallassō*, which indicates an exchange or a swap. We trade the glory of the eternal, immortal, everlasting God for the glory of corruptible things, creeping things, bugs and snakes and idols of all sorts. The word *metallassō* has the prefix *meta-*, which means "with." One thing is traded for something else. The same root is found in the word *reconciliation*. There, it is not *metallassō* but *katallassō*, a verb (the noun form is *katallagē*). That is the word that Paul is using here when he says, "We were reconciled to God through the death of His Son, much more, having been reconciled [again, the form of *katallassō*], we shall be saved by His life" (v. 10). **And not only that, but we also rejoice in God through our Lord Jesus Christ, through whom we have now received the reconciliation** (v. 11). Reconciliation is a substantive reality. It is a gift that God has given to His people through the death and resurrection of Christ.

The result of reconciliation is unspeakable joy. The Christian life from beginning to end is meant to be a life of joy. We have much to be happy about. There is no room for the sourpuss in the kingdom of God. There is nothing dour about our redemption. If we were to suffer to a degree that nobody else has ever been called to suffer—a modern-day

Job sitting on the dung heap—we would have no right to say anything different from what Job declared: "Though He slay me, yet will I trust Him" (Job 13:15). No affliction so dire, no sorrow so deep, no pain so intense, is worthy to be compared to the glory of that *katallagē*, that reconciliation, that we have received in the Beloved.

Application

It is often hard to maintain this perspective in our everyday lives. To help us interpret our present suffering rightly so that it might not steal our joy, we must look to the great source of our joy constantly. Never stop reminding yourself of what God has done for you in Jesus Christ. Pray that the Spirit would give you unshakable joy as you look at your life from an eternal vantage point.

2

Death through Adam: Realism

BEGINNING IN VERSE 12, PAUL INTRODUCES a most difficult concept: **Therefore, just as through one man sin entered the world, and death through sin, and thus death spread to all men, because all sinned— (For until the law sin was in the world, but sin is not imputed when there is no law. Nevertheless death reigned from Adam to Moses, even over those who had not sinned according to the likeness of the transgression of Adam, who is a type of Him who was to come** (vv. 12–14). There is so much in that text that it keeps the theologians busy studying and arguing. It is one of the most important texts in the Bible because it talks about the fall of the entire human race through Adam.

One man, Adam, brought sin. With that sin came death, which came on the whole human race because all have sinned, but not up to the similitude of Adam's sin. Even babies sometimes live only a few hours. Death is the penalty for sin. Without sin there can be no death, and without the law there can be no sin. Death was in the world before God gave His law through Moses. Since Adam's fall, all creatures have died because all have sinned, and they sinned before the Law of Moses was given.

There can be no sin unless there is law, because sin is defined as the transgression of God's law. If there is no law, there can be no foul, but if there is a law, then a penalty is incurred when we break the law. Since the penalty for sin is death, and since death reigned from Adam to Moses, there is a sense in which everybody in the world somehow broke the law in Adam. That is the point here in Romans 5. Through one man sin and death came into the whole world. Somehow we are related to Adam.

People ask, "How can God blame me for sinning when all I am doing is what comes naturally? I was born in sin, and when I sin, I am just acting according to the nature I was born with. How can God hold me responsible for acting out a nature He gave me before I was even born?" The answer is that they sinned in Adam. They reply, "How can God hold people responsible for what Adam did when they were not even there in the garden?" Several answers have been given through the ages.

A common explanation is the doctrine called *realism*. Realism operates on the premise that the only way that God could justly and morally condemn us for what Adam did was if we were really there participating in the act. We were really there, so that when he sinned, we sinned, because we were really there.

Application

Realism isn't the only explanation for our fallen natures and guilt in Adam. But imagine that you had been there in the garden. What would you have done differently? Many of us think that we'd do better than Adam did. We need to remember that Adam did not have a fallen inclination toward sin, yet he was disobedient to God. It is a mighty presumption to think that we, who do have sinful inclinations, could have succeeded where he failed. Let us rejoice that Christ did.

3

Death through Adam: Federalism

CLASSIC REFORMED THEOLOGY REFERS TO *FEDERALISM* as distinguished from realism. Adam was the federal head of the whole human race. The name Adam, which comes directly into English from the Hebrew term *adam*, means "mankind." What Adam did in the garden was not simply for himself but for all those whom he represented. God appointed him during his probation in Eden to act for himself and for all his progeny. People do not like that. They say, "No damnation without representation," but indeed, there was representation, which is the whole point here. People squirm under this and say, "I did not choose my representative."

When Parliament changed the rules of the game and imposed taxes on the colonists without giving them representation in Parliament, the colonists protested because it was a violation of British law. The colonists were not just rebelling against the crown; they were calling the crown to obey the law. We can have no confidence that our interests will be represented by someone chosen for us by someone else. That is why we want to be able to elect our governing representatives. In the American electorate, we listen to the candidates and their positions on the issues. We hear their campaign promises. We become persuaded that candidate X is the one who can most accurately represent us, and we cast our vote. Later we are annoyed that the elected candidate does not do what he said he was going to do, but he is our representative because we put him there.

How could it be just for God to appoint one man to represent all kinds of people when the people do not even have a voice in the election? There is a big difference between King George, our congressmen or senators, and God. When God selects our representative, He makes that selection infallibly and impeccably. Nowhere in time and space have we been more perfectly represented than we were in the garden of Eden by the representative that God selected to act in our place. Since that is true, we can never curse God and say that it is not fair. When we complain about being misrepresented by Adam, all we do is prove the perfection of that representation. Those who do not like that say, "It is not appropriate for God to accept the representation of one person for another," but if they want to hold to that principle consistently, then they must also reject their representation by Christ. The principle of representation is at the very heart and soul of our salvation. We must be careful not to reject that principle because if we do, we have rejected our only hope of salvation.

Application

Remember this concept of federal headship when you are sharing the gospel with others. The "unfairness" of God's arrangement with Adam is not an uncommon objection, and the best way to answer that objection is with the good news of Jesus Christ. Just as Adam was our representative, so Christ is a representative. We might not have had any choice in the matter when it comes to Adam, but we are called to put our faith in Jesus Christ. Pray that the Spirit might enable this in the hearts of others.

4

Death through Adam: The View of Jonathan Edwards

THERE IS PERHAPS A DEEPER COMBINATION of realism and federalism expressed in the profound thinking of the Puritan divine Jonathan

Edwards. He put forth the identity theory. We would need to have some idea of Platonic philosophy to really understand this. The idea is that in the garden we were present, not because our souls were there but because we were there in the mind of God, and what is present in the mind of God is present in reality. In Edwards' great treatise on original sin, he said that if the Bible never taught a universal plunge of the human race into ruin at the beginning, in Adam, and if there were no such account of the fall in the Scripture, reason would require that we posit such an event. How else could we explain the universality of sin in the human race? Our culture is schizophrenic on this point. People do not want to acknowledge the reality of sin but of mistakes. They want to say that the origin of sin is environment and that people become corrupt because they are reared in a flawed culture.

Jean-Jacques Rousseau thought that man was born free and now is everywhere in chains. The idea behind his thinking is that we are born neutral and innocent, and we sin because we are overwhelmed by the corrupting influences all around. Edwards said that if this were the case, we would expect at least 50 percent of the population to stay in that state of innocence. We have to look beyond the external influence of fallen society and cultural inducements to sin to explain the universality of it. The question, therefore, is this: if we were all born innocent, how did society become so corrupt? Society comprises people. It is not as if 5 percent are evil and they seduce the other 95 percent. One hundred percent are evil because we are born in that fallen state. In Adam, sin and death and destruction came into the whole world.

That is Paul's premise here when he turns our attention away from Adam to the new Adam, the new representative. The new Adam did not succumb to the enticements of the serpent but lived a life of perfect obedience, not just for His own sake but for the sake of the people whom He came to represent, to reconcile, and to save.

Application

Look around. The universality of sin is one of the easiest realities to verify. That people attempt to explain it away is more evidence of it. When we acknowledge our sins, we acknowledge that God's Word is true in its testimony about us, that we are fallen in Adam and desperately need a new Adam. Do not try to explain away or rationalize your sin, but take it often before God, trusting that He has dealt with your sin in Christ.

5

Imputation and Justification

SOME YEARS AGO, I WAS TEACHING A COLLEGE COURSE in theology at a Christian school in Massachusetts, and we came to the section of theology called *soteriology*, which focuses attention on salvation and how it is acquired. Part of that course involved covering the so-called famous five points of Calvinism, summarized by the popular acrostic TULIP. The acrostic stands for the fairest flower in God's garden.

I began teaching at the beginning of TULIP, with T, which stands for *total depravity*. There were about thirty students in my class, and I explained the doctrine of total depravity, showing them that sin is not simply tangential to our existence. Sin is not the blemish on our exterior; sin penetrates to the very core of our humanity, despoiling us in body, mind, and will and rendering us in a state of moral inability. So much are we captivated by this bondage to sin that we no longer have within us the moral capacity to incline ourselves to the things of God. I labored through all of that for the college students, and at the end of the discussion about total depravity, I asked for a show of hands as to how many were persuaded of this doctrine.

There was no hesitation; every hand went up. On the top left corner of the blackboard I wrote the number 30, and then I wrote a message to the janitor: "Please do not erase."

Class resumed the following Monday, at which time I started on the U of TULIP, *unconditional election*. When I got through and asked how many agreed with it, there was quite a bit of attrition. Once we got to L, *limited atonement*, there was wholesale abandonment of their convictions. I said to them, "It's QED (*quod erat demonstrandum*); it is automatic. If you understood the doctrine of total depravity, you would have to believe in unconditional election or limited atonement even if the Bible didn't teach it. If you do not believe in irresistible grace, you would have to assume it once you understood the nature of our fallen condition."

Application

The universality of sin and the doctrine of total depravity go hand in hand, one affirming that truth that all humanity is sinful and the other that every aspect of our humanity is sinful. If you or someone you know struggles with the doctrines of grace, also known as the five points of Calvinism, studying the doctrine of total depravity may be a good starting place to embracing all the doctrines of grace because total depravity is evident to us if we are honest about the way the world is and about our own hearts.

6

Imputation and the Gospel

THE EVANGELICAL WORLD WAS SHOCKED BY an initiative some years ago called Evangelicals and Catholics Together (ECT). Very well-known members of the Christian evangelical community joined forces with representatives of the Roman Catholic community to declare their joint effort in combating what we call common-grace issues: the issue of relativism in the culture, the issue of the destruction of marriage and the family, the issue of abortion, and so on. Historically, Protestants have argued for the legitimacy of joining hands with people of any theological persuasion in arenas of what we call common grace—ministering to the very basic human needs of people. But the ECT document went beyond this joint activity and declared to the world that its signers shared a common faith in the gospel.

I along with several other evangelical leaders publicly protested the document because we saw in it the compromise of the gospel of justification by faith alone. This was a very painful time for me because it involved breaking ranks with some very close friends and comrades. The protest provoked a second ECT article in which people agreed that faith is necessary for justification but said that there are other matters that still need to be discussed, such as imputation. I responded to the architects of that particular document and said, "If you do not have justification by faith alone, you do not have the gospel, and if you do not have imputation, you do not have justification by faith alone."

I have labored this point for a reason: there is no place in the Bible where the doctrine of imputation is set forth more clearly and centrally than here in Romans 5. I can find no other way to make sense of the way in which Paul says that we sinned in Adam than to understand this assertion putatively, that is, we sinned in Adam by imputation. Paul labors the point that Adam's sin is reckoned and transferred, that is, imputed, to the entire human race. We know that he is talking about imputation here because he spends time drawing the remarkable contrast that just as one man's offense and sin were reckoned to the entire human race, so another man's righteousness, in a similar manner, was imputed to all who believe.

Application
When we deny imputation in Adam, then we deny imputation in Christ. Understood this way, God's covenant with Adam is not an occasion for

voicing a complaint but an occasion for praise. God is pleased to receive the righteousness of another on our behalf. Take a moment to reflect on this reality, and then go to the Lord in a prayer of praise and adoration.

WEEK 15

1

Universal Death

EVEN THOUGH THERE IS AN ONGOING CONTROVERSY between Arminians and Calvinists about the extent of original sin, one thing that these groups agree on is that Adam's sin produced a ruinous effect for the entire human race. There is no way that we can avoid the thrust of what Paul is teaching in Romans 5 about the consequences of the fall of Adam and Eve. Paul ties the universal extent of the sin of Adam to the universality of death: "Therefore, just as through one man sin entered the world, and death through sin, and thus death spread to all men, because all sinned" (v. 12). This is where it is important to make another distinction, that between original sin and actual sin.

Actual sin occurs when we do something that transgresses the law of God. A baby in the crib, though it bears the weight of original sin, does not bear the weight of the guilt of actual sin because actual sin requires a conscious awareness of right and wrong and an actual violation of law. An infant in the crib does not know anything about the law of God. Has not God planted in the human heart the law of nature (*lex naturalis*) so that we learn from nature itself without ever hearing about the Ten Commandments? Yes, that is true. God does reveal His law in ways and places other than the Ten Commandments. Nevertheless, for sin to be involved, one must have some kind of discernment, a conscious understanding, of the prohibition, which we are saying that an infant does not have. Until people reach an age of accountability, they have not yet committed actual sin even though by nature they are sinners.

If that is the case, if there is a period of time between birth and accountability before a person commits actual sin, why is it that people die? How do we account for babies' dying in infancy? Since death is the punishment for sin, and if an infant is incapable of actual sin, how is it possible for the infant to die in his crib? Again, it makes sense only in the way that Paul argues here—that death reigned from Adam to Moses. Before there was any law in the world, there was still sin as a result of the imputation of Adam's sin.

Application

Death is not part of God's natural order of everything at the beginning. It entered history because of Adam's sin. This reality helps us understand that death is unnatural, the penalty for sin, and even an enemy, as it is called in the New Testament (1 Cor. 15:26). Knowing this, we grieve death, especially the death of infants, but we also have hope that Christ will ultimately destroy death.

2

Imputation: A Hill to Die On

IN AUGUSTINE'S DEBATE WITH PELAGIUS, he argued that at creation, before the fall, Adam had two abilities. He had what Augustine called the *posse peccare*, the possibility of sinning and the ability to sin. The word *peccare* means "to sin." We use the word *impeccable* for someone who is without any stain or blemish. We talk about little sins or *peccadilloes*, a word that comes from the Latin root *peccare*. Augustine said that in creation Adam and Eve were made with the ability to sin, the *posse peccare*, but they also had the ability not to sin. They were not yet fallen or corrupt. Adam and Eve had the power to resist temptation and not fall into sin; they had the *posse non peccare*, the power or the ability not to sin. They also had the ability to live forever, the *posse non mori*.

After the fall, Adam's progeny lost the *posse non peccare*, the ability not to sin. Since the fall, no mere human being has had inherent power to live a perfect life. Nobody can live without sinning, just as nobody can live without dying. Augustine said that the curse of the fall is this: we are now in a state of *non posse non peccare*; it is not possible not to sin. Likewise, we have the *non posse non mori*, which is the inability not to die.

Paul is arguing that because of Adam's sin, both sin and death are universal because the guilt of Adam is reckoned to the whole race. We are dealing unassailably with the doctrine of imputation in its worst possible manifestation. The imputation of guilt from one person to all whom he represents leads us to ruination, our present estate as fallen and corrupt sinners.

In contrast is imputation in its best possible manifestation, the imputation of someone else's righteousness to us. The very essence of the gospel is that someone else's righteousness counts for us. If we get rid of imputation, we have no basis for any hope in standing before the judgment seat of God. We stand before God's judgment either with our righteousness or with someone else's. If we have to stand before God with our own righteousness, which the Bible says is nothing but filthy rags (Isa. 64:6), we have no hope. Take away the imputation of the Savior's righteousness, and there is no good news left to the gospel. We are on our own. Nothing we can bring to the table is enough to escape the wrath of a holy God. Give me the imputation of Christ or give me death. I'd be happy, proud, and honored to die on that hill.

Application

J. Gresham Machen was instrumental in the founding of Westminster Theological Seminary and the Orthodox Presbyterian Church.

Not long before he died on January 1, 1937, he telegrammed a message to his friend and fellow professor John Murray: "I'm so thankful for the active obedience of Christ. No hope without it." May we rest in this hope, knowing that Christ's righteousness is our righteousness through imputation.

3

The Covenant of Works

THERE IS ANOTHER ISSUE IN THE ONGOING CONTROVERSY of our time that is tightly related to the issue of imputation. It has to do with the covenant of works. Historic Reformed theology often goes by the name of *covenant theology*, which stands in contradistinction from the modern theology called *dispensationalism*. Dispensationalism divides redemptive history into seven time frames, seven ways in which God judges people. Dispensationalists want to "rightly divide" the Word of truth, so they divide up the Bible into these seven time frames instead of looking at the structure in which the Bible itself is written, which is covenant.

In the Old Testament, God made a covenant with Noah (Gen. 6:18). After God destroyed the world by flood, He promised never to do it again; He put His rainbow in the sky. Then God called Abraham out of the land of paganism, and He said, "I am the LORD, who brought you out of Ur of the Chaldeans, to give you this land to inherit it" (15:7). In the framework of that promise is a covenant that God made with Abraham. God called a people for Himself after Abraham's covenant was passed on to Isaac and Jacob. Then Jacob's descendants were called into bondage, and God brought the descendants of Abraham together and added to the covenant He had made with Abraham by giving them the Decalogue and the blessings and the curses that follow the law. God also made a covenant with David and his house, the promise to restore his kingship forever.

Over and over again we see God establishing covenants in the Old Testament, but the first covenant we encounter is the covenant of works. God made that covenant with Adam and Eve on behalf of the whole world. In it He set before them the promise of blessedness: they could eat of the tree of life and live forever if they were obedient. They were told that they must not eat from the tree of the knowledge of good and evil lest they die. What happened to Adam and Eve in the garden is surrounded with the structure of an agreement, a promise of either destruction or blessing, depending on how they performed. That is why it is called a covenant of works. Those who worked righteousness would live, but those who worked disobedience would perish along with all their progeny.

Application

It should astound us that God covenants with us. After Adam sinned, God still extended His grace, and this is especially seen in His continued commitment to His people in the various covenants that He made as He brought to fulfillment the promises to crush the serpent in Christ (see Gen. 3:15). See yourself as part of this grand story if you trust in Him. Meditate on the fact that from the beginning, even from all eternity, God set His love on you in Christ, and rejoice in this reality today.

4

The Covenant of Works and Imputation

IN RECENT YEARS, PEOPLE HAVE RAISED a protest against the covenant of works: "God does not owe His creatures any promise of redemption whatsoever, so the fact that He enters into a covenant with Adam and Eve is a matter of grace." That is true, but it is not the point of the distinction between the covenant of works and the covenant of grace. The point of the distinction is this: Adam and Eve failed the covenant of works, and when that failure took place, God did not destroy the human race but added a promise of redemption, which would come through the Seed of the woman. The promise pertained to One who would crush the head of the serpent even while His heel would be injured in the process. God's promises to Abraham, Isaac, and Jacob, to Moses, to David, and to all the rest were promises to pour out His blessing upon people on the basis of His preserving, redeeming, saving grace.

The Bible teaches that justification is by faith alone, yet ultimately there is only one way that anybody is ever saved in the presence of God, and that is through works. The question is not *whether* we are going to be saved through works; the question is *whose* works. We are saved through the works of the One who alone fulfilled the terms of the covenant of works. That is why it is not just the death of Christ that redeems us, but also the life of Christ.

By one man's disobedience we were plunged into ruin, but by the obedience of one man, the new Adam, we are justified. Saying that we are justified by faith alone is simply shorthand for saying that we are justified by Christ alone. Justification by faith alone means that we cannot make it on the basis of our works, but only by trusting in someone else's works. Our works will never save us, but Christ's works are perfect, and they meet all the requirements of the covenant of works.

There is a connection between the covenant of works and imputation. If we take away the covenant of works and imputation, we take away the significance of the perfect act of obedience of Jesus. Without the imputation of the righteousness of Christ, there is no justification, and without justification, there is no gospel. Paul shows the centrality of Christ's perfectly obedient life as the only possible ground for our salvation, which comes by imputation.

Application

At the heart of God's covenant promises to His people is the promise that He will be their God, that they will be His people, and that He will even walk and dwell among them (see Lev. 26:11–12; Ezek. 37:26–28). This promise was richly fulfilled in the Son of God's becoming man and dwelling among us and in the Spirit's indwelling us (John 1:14; Rom. 8:9). Know that through the Spirit, God is with you, just as Jesus promised that He would also be (Matt. 28:20).

5

Why the Law?

MOREOVER THE LAW ENTERED **that the offense might abound** (v. 20a). This is a purpose clause, which is one that gives a reason why a certain action takes place. The purpose of this clause is to show why the law became part of the equation of justification. Death reigned from Adam to Moses, but then God added to the covenant He had made with Adam and Noah. To Abraham, Isaac, and Jacob He added the whole of the Old Testament law. God added the law so that sin might abound.

Why would God want sin to abound? We would think He would want it to abate, to see it ebb and disappear from His creation. The law comes and reveals to us our helpless condition; the law reveals the reality of sin. We must remember the principle that the Scriptures set forth: where there is no law, there is no sin. By definition, sin is a transgression of the law of God, yet we have this inherited corruption from our father Adam, and God gives law that we may see the extent of our sin. There is also a true sense in which the added laws incite us to sin. So desperately wicked are we in our hearts that every time God adds a new law, we take it as an occasion to further our rebellion and disobedience. We see that happen with our children at times. The more rules we give them, the more determined they are to break them.

Paul makes a contrast: **But where sin abounded, grace abounded much more** (v. 20b). This is not just a comparison. It is not like an equation with sin and grace on either side of it. Paul might have said, "Where sin abounded, grace abounded, so five pounds of sin, five pounds of grace." It is not a comparative; it is a superlative. There really is no comparison. Where sin abounds, Paul says, grace does much more abound. The scales are not equal. Sin is far outweighed by the grace that God gives. That is true in our lives. We live in the presence of a superabundance of grace that is far greater than the depths of our disobedience.

Application

May the abundance of God's grace stagger us. One of the ways to see the extent of God's grace is by looking at its cost. There is no way to measure the infinite value of Christ's death as a penalty for sin or God's imputing to us Christ's righteousness. This should give us profound assurance in the Christian life, not to live however we want, but knowing that when we sin, God's grace to us in Christ can never be exhausted.

6

The Reign of Sin and the Reign of Grace

PAUL ADDS PARENTHETICALLY: **so that as sin reigned in death, even so grace might reign through righteousness to eternal life through Jesus Christ our Lord** (v. 21). Paul is not saying that sin reigned unto death so that wherever sin is in power, it results in death. He has already told us that death is one of the consequences of sin. Where there is no sin, there is no death. He is not talking about the mere presence of sin; he is talking about its reign, about sin's exerting its power and authority. The reign of sin may be found in the face of death because in death we see the exaltation of sin, the empowering of it, into this world.

One of Paul's favorite contrasts in his writing is the suffering and pain we experience as not being worthy of comparison to the glory that awaits us when we pass from this world. Our destiny is not to become citizens in the realm of sin under the power of death. The power of that enemy has been vanquished, and by grace God has much more poured upon us the gift of righteousness, which gives us the ultimate benefit of justification—eternal life through Jesus Christ our Lord.

We can see now why the gospel is so important, why the doctrine of justification by faith alone can never be negotiated. In it the glory of the grace of God is made manifest. While we were still sinners, Christ took upon Himself the curse of that reigning death and defeated the grave by His righteousness, which is imputed to us by faith if indeed we put our trust in Him. Sin reigns in death, but Christ triumphs over death. Death is but a moment; the triumph lasts forever.

Application

God's mercy and grace overcome the reign of sin and death. This is precisely why Christians can walk in newness of life. Though we might experience the presence of sin, we have been freed from its power. In preparation for your study of Romans 6, which explores this theme in depth, pray that God will transform you more and more in righteousness through the power of the Spirit's working through His Word.

Romans 6

WHAT SHALL WE SAY THEN? SHALL WE CONTINUE *in sin that grace may abound? Certainly not! How shall we who died to sin live any longer in it? Or do you not know that as many of us as were baptized into Christ Jesus were baptized into His death? Therefore we were buried with Him through baptism into death, that just as Christ was raised from the dead by the glory of the Father, even so we also should walk in newness of life.*

For if we have been united together in the likeness of His death, certainly we also shall be in the likeness of His resurrection, knowing this, that our old man was crucified with Him, that the body of sin might be done away with, that we should no longer be slaves of sin. For he who has died has been freed from sin. Now if we died with Christ, we believe that we shall also live with Him, knowing that Christ, having been raised from the dead, dies no more. Death no longer has dominion over Him. For the death that He died, He died to sin once for all; but the life that He lives, He lives to God. Likewise you also, reckon yourselves to be dead indeed to sin, but alive to God in Christ Jesus our Lord.

Therefore do not let sin reign in your mortal body, that you should obey it in its lusts. And do not present your members as instruments of unrighteousness to sin, but present yourselves to God as being alive from the dead, and your members as instruments of righteousness to God. For sin shall not have dominion over you, for you are not under law but under grace.

What then? Shall we sin because we are not under law but under grace? Certainly not! Do you not know that to whom you present yourselves slaves to obey, you are that one's slaves whom you obey, whether of sin leading to death, or of obedience leading to righteousness? But God be thanked that though you were slaves of sin, yet you obeyed from the heart that form of doctrine to which you were delivered. And having been set free from sin, you became slaves of righteousness. I speak in human terms because of the weakness of your flesh. For just as you presented your members as slaves of uncleanness, and of lawlessness leading to more lawlessness, so now present your members as slaves of righteousness for holiness.

For when you were slaves of sin, you were free in regard to righteousness. What fruit did you have then in the things of which you are now ashamed? For the end of those things is death. But now having been set free from sin, and having become slaves of God, you have your fruit to holiness, and the end, everlasting life. For the wages of sin is death, but the gift of God is eternal life in Christ Jesus our Lord.

WEEK 16

1

Life and Sanctification

AS WE COME TO ROMANS 6, Paul is still in the midst of this contrast between life and death, but the basic theme now sounds a new note. Here we find a theological distinction between justification and sanctification. We can see the transition. That is likely why those who divided the epistle into chapters made a division at the beginning of Romans 6—the attention turns toward another consequence of justification, which is sanctification, our growth in personal holiness.

What shall we say then? (v. 1a). Paul interrupts his discourse; there is a pregnant pause here. He has just developed all these fantastic benefits that flow from our justification, the rich fruits that accrue to us as a result of the gospel, and after explaining all of that, he comes to the *so what?* How are we to respond to it? What shall we say to this supremacy and triumph of grace over sin and death?

Paul knows how sinful people think. He has just given the argument that where sin abounds, grace much more abounds, so the logic seems simple: if we want more grace, then we should commit more sin. Therefore, he says, **Shall we continue in sin that grace may abound?** (v. 1b). He asks the question rhetorically and then supplies the answer, and we cannot miss the impact it makes: **Certainly not!** (v. 2a). My translation (NKJV) is weak here. Some translations are even weaker, supplying simply, "No." My favorite is this one: "Shall we continue in sin, that grace may abound? God forbid" (ASV). In other words, we must not even think about it. Paul is not simply expressing a denial of that premise; the force of his language signals Apostolic abhorrence.

Paul would be appalled if he heard any true Christian say, "If I keep getting grace when I sin, I am just going to keep on sinning that grace may abound." God forbid.

Application

Notice that sanctification is a *consequence* of justification. It naturally flows from our declaration of righteousness in Christ. When we rest our salvation on Christ alone, we experience a radical reorientation toward sin and desire holiness. Search your heart for a love for Christ and desire to please Him in obedience. This desire is a great assurance and one that we should often return to in our fight against sin. Though we will not be perfect, let us pursue this desire with the Spirit's help.

2

The Charge of Antinomianism

AT THE TIME OF THE REFORMATION in the sixteenth century, Martin Luther was charged with antinomianism. *Anti* means "against" or "opposed to," and *nomos* is the Greek word for "law." *Antinomian*, therefore, means "being opposed to the law of God" or "against the law of God." The Roman Catholic Church feared that people would take the doctrine of *sola fide*, justification by faith alone, as a license for sin. If justification is by faith alone without any works, the layperson is going to understand it simply to mean that he is saved by grace, by faith alone, so he can live however he wants to live. It was critical to the sixteenth-century Reformers to answer that charge because they had the same concern. They reminded their friends in the Roman Catholic Church that Paul addresses this question in Romans 6.

Luther responded to the charge by explaining that we are justified by faith alone but not by a faith that is alone. Justification by faith alone, as we have seen, is shorthand for justification by Christ alone and by His righteousness, but justification by faith alone was never intended by God as a license for sin.

Every time the gospel is preached, the demon of antinomianism knocks at the door and says that if we are justified by faith, then works do not count, and that if works do not count, then works do not matter. Certainly, no work we do will ever contribute to our justification; in that sense, our works do not count. Yet that is not the same thing as saying that they do not matter, because we are justified *unto* good works. We are not justified by our sanctification, but we are justified *unto* sanctification. The fruit of true faith, the fruit of true justification, will always be conformity to the image of Christ. That is what Paul is beginning to spell out for us.

Rome believes that faith is necessary and indispensable to justification. An orthodox Roman Catholic can say, "Yes, I believe that justification is by faith," but he must choke on the word *alone*, because his communion teaches that justification is by faith plus works. The Roman Catholic view is that faith + works = justification. You have to have the works or there is no justification, because the works are part of the ground for that justification. The Reformation view, the biblical view, is that faith = justification + works. The works are there, but they are on the other side of the equation. The antinomian view is that faith = justification – works, which is the heresy that Paul abhors here at the beginning of Romans 6.

Application

When you are tempted to sin, fight any presumptive urge to find comfort in running to it in your justification. Such a blessedness, purchased by Christ to remedy our problem of sin before a holy God, is no grounds for sin. Instead, go to the Lord in prayer, praising Him for your justification and its great price, and ask Him for deliverance from your temptation, trusting that the Spirit will help (1 Cor. 10:13).

3

Carnal Christianity?

A CONTROVERSY BROKE OUT IN THE UNITED STATES several years ago within dispensational circles that became known as the *lordship-salvation controversy*. The division arose between Zane Hodges and Charles Ryrie. Hodges said and taught emphatically that people could be converted to Christ, put their trust in Him as their Savior, and never produce a single work of obedience, yet still be saved. He insisted that if we argue for producing the fruit of righteousness, we are mixing work with faith and thereby destroying the gospel. Ryrie was less militant. He said that if we have true faith, eventually we will begin to show some change in our pattern of living. Distinct from Hodges, Ryrie said that if we have true faith, good works are inevitable at some point. That is a less militant form of antinomianism.

The gospel teaches us that if we have true faith in Jesus Christ, works of obedience are not only inevitable but immediate, because a justified person is a changed person. Justification is the fruit of faith, and faith is the fruit of regeneration. We cannot have saving faith unless the Holy Spirit has changed the disposition of our souls. Therefore, only the regenerate have faith. All the regenerate are changed. We cannot have the Holy Spirit changing the disposition of our hearts and bringing us to faith but then leaving us hanging there with no change in our lives.

The doctrine of carnal Christianity—that one can have true faith without ever having any good works—went like wildfire through the Christian community. Used to represent this view is an analogy of a chair and a circle. Concerning an unconverted person, self is on the chair or throne and Christ is outside the circle. Concerning the converted person, Christ is now inside the circle but self is still on the throne. For the Spirit-filled person, Christ is on the throne and the self has been removed. The metaphor teaches that we can have Christ in our lives—we can be converted—without having Christ on the throne of our lives.

We cannot receive Christ as Savior without at the same time bending our knees to His lordship. This does not mean that we believe we are perfect, but it does mean that at the moment we believe, we are changed. Our lives are turned around, and the beginning of the process of sanctification has taken place. Justification does not produce the fullness of sanctification, but it initiates it immediately. If we have made a profession of faith but there is absolutely no evidence of change in our hearts and lives, then we need to ask whether that profession of faith was genuine. True faith always and immediately produces change.

Application

Sometimes our fight against sin meets frustration, and growth in our sanctification can seem painfully slow. Instead of letting discouragement get the best of us, let us praise God that He is at work and continue to fight against sin. This posture toward God in our sanctification is from faith, knowing that He is truly working in us, even if the timing doesn't seem right to us. Never stop pressing toward the goal of greater Christlikeness, knowing that God's will is for your sanctification (1 Thess. 4:3).

4

Baptized into Christ

HOW SHALL WE WHO DIED TO SIN LIVE ANY LONGER IN IT? (v. 2b). When we come to Christ, when we are born anew, the old man is put to death. Nevertheless, the old man keeps kicking and screaming. In a very real sense, we are crucified with Christ, so the new life in Christ is just that—new. "If anyone is in Christ, he is a new creation; old things have passed away; behold, all things have become new" (2 Cor. 5:17).

Paul continues in a metaphorical way: **Do you not know that as many of us as were baptized into Christ Jesus were baptized into His death?** (v. 3). We have lost touch with the riches of the sacraments that God has given to His people. Martin Luther used to say, when the devil would tempt him, "Get away from me! I'm baptized!" Baptism is not what saves us, but in our baptism God gives us a tangible sign of His promise of redemption. All the processes that are wrought through the redeeming work of Christ are contained in that sign. Baptism is a sign of our being regenerated by the Holy Spirit. It does not effect regeneration, but it is a sign of it. It is the sign of God's promise that all who believe will, in fact, be justified. It is a sign of our sanctification. It is the sign of our being indwelt by the Holy Spirit. It is a sign of our glorification. It is a sign of our identification with Christ. We are in Christ, and He is our champion.

Paul says that if we are believers, if we have received the grace of justification, baptism is a reminder of our union in the death and burial of Christ. We are not only baptized into His death and burial, but also baptized into His resurrection. All these things are part of what is being communicated graphically with the sign of baptism.

One of the people I want to meet when I get to heaven is the minister who baptized me in the Methodist church. He was a beloved pastor to my family when I was a small boy, and I long to have the opportunity to sit down and tell him that during the first seventeen years of my life I looked like a child of hell, but then God quickened my soul. All the promises that were communicated to me in baptism were realized the moment I believed and understood my burial and resurrection in Christ.

Application

Westminster Larger Catechism 167 calls us to consider how to properly reflect on and even "improve" our baptism. We are to look back to our baptism in times of temptation or when witnessing the beautiful moment when someone else is being baptized with heartfelt thankfulness for it and what it means. We have been united with Christ by grace in our baptism. This should humble us and cause us to greatly pursue after new life, especially with our brothers and sisters in Christ.

5

Newness of Life

IN A VERY REAL SENSE, we have already died and been buried, and we are already participating in the resurrection of Christ. "Do you not know that as many of us as were baptized into Christ Jesus were baptized into His death?" (v. 3). **Therefore we were buried with Him through baptism into death, that just as Christ was raised from the dead by the glory of the Father, even so we also should walk in newness of life** (v. 4). We are resurrected people. We already have the down payment of eternal life in our souls by having been given the sealing of the Holy Spirit. How can someone in Christ Jesus, someone who participates in the power of His resurrection, continue in sin that grace may abound? It is not possible.

Chapter 6 begins, as we have seen, with a rhetorical question: "Shall we continue in sin that grace may abound?" Paul answered not only with denial but with abhorrence, saying, "God forbid." Paul's great concern is that those who have been justified have been justified *unto* holiness. We have not been justified *by* our holiness or *through* our holiness but *unto* it so that we might grow in conformity to the image of Christ.

To make sense of what Paul is teaching here, it is important to look again at how strongly he articulates the idea of our mystical union with Christ. By the Holy Spirit, every person who believes in Christ is joined to Christ spiritually. If we are believers, we are in Christ and Christ is in us. The invisible church is made up of all who are in Christ Jesus, all who participate in this mystical union with Him. In this text Paul takes the idea of our mystical union further. He tells us that not only are our sins imputed to Christ in His death on the cross, the benefits of His resurrection transferred to us, and the benefits of His righteousness imputed to us by legal transaction, but also there is a real spiritual union with our Savior. In a spiritual sense, we died with Him on Calvary. When He went to the cross, He went not for Himself but for His sheep. He did a work that we could not possibly do for ourselves. It was our sin that He was carrying in His death, so when He died, He did not simply die for us; we, by virtue of this spiritual union, died with Him.

"Therefore we were buried with Him through baptism into death, that just as Christ was raised from the dead by the glory of the Father, even so we also should walk in newness of life" (v. 4). In a very real sense, we who are in Christ share in the power of His resurrection not merely after we die and go to heaven but right now, because everyone who believes savingly in Jesus Christ has already been raised from spiritual death.

Application

At this moment, united to Christ by faith, you have died with Him, and you have been raised with Him. The power of His resurrection is yours in the Christian life. While we still have to fight indwelling sin, the dominion and power of sin has been broken in our lives, so let us strive in the resurrection power of Christ through the Spirit to see more and more of our sin die, that we might walk in greater newness of life.

6

Dead on Arrival

WHEN WE CONSIDERED IN AN EARLIER STUDY our condition of original sin, we used the biblical metaphors of death and slavery. By nature we are born into this world DOA, dead on arrival, spiritually although alive biologically. We have no inclination whatsoever in our souls toward the things of God—no interest, no passion, no love. We are dead. Because we are spiritually dead, we are slaves to the sinful impulses and lusts that drive our behavior. We are not just participants in sin; such a description is far too weak. The Bible teaches us again and again that we are slaves to sin. Sin is not only in our nature, but also our master.

The great Augustine on occasion used the metaphor of Satan's riding a horse. Before conversion we, the horse, have one rider—Satan. He has the bit in our teeth. He is in control of the reins. When he turns our head in a certain direction, that is the direction we go. When he says, "Whoa," we stop, and when he says, "Giddyup," we go, because he is our master, and we are his slave. Augustine went on to say that once we are converted by the power of the Holy Spirit, it is not as if Satan is sent back to the stables so that the only one riding us now is Jesus. Satan gives up the reins reluctantly. He will do everything he can to get that bit back in our mouth and to recover us as a slave. He hates to lose a slave. We have to fight against the enticements of Satan throughout our whole Christian life because he is furious that we have left his design, but something radically new has happened—we have gone through a spiritual resurrection. What does the Bible say? "If anyone is in Christ, he is a new creation; old things have passed away; behold, all things have become new" (2 Cor. 5:17). The Spirit of God has raised our souls from the dead.

Paul elaborates on this idea in his letter to the Ephesians, particularly in chapter 2: "You He made alive, who were dead in trespasses and sins, in which you once walked according to the course of this world, according to the prince of the power of the air, the spirit who now works in the sons of disobedience, among whom also we all once conducted ourselves in the lusts of our flesh" (vv. 2:1–3). That is Paul's description of spiritual death and slavery. He is referring to regeneration, and the idea of regeneration lies beneath everything Paul is teaching here in Romans 6. The justified are people who have been changed, and they have been changed supernaturally.

Application

The nature and necessity of regeneration is at the heart of Reformed theology. If you or someone you know struggles with Reformed theology, one of the best places to start is the biblical witness that we are spiritually dead apart from Christ. Only God can cause us to have spiritual life. This realization creates a humble heart of dependence on God and eyes to see the lavish extent of His saving grace in the whole Christian life.

WEEK 17

1

Regeneration

MARTIN LUTHER, IN EXTOLLING THE WONDERS of spiritual rebirth or regeneration, said that regeneration is the greatest miracle of all. I quibble with the Reformer there. I do not think regeneration is a miracle, because regeneration is invisible. A tight definition of *miracle* in the biblical sense is "something that happens in the external, perceivable world that only God can bring to pass, such as bringing life out of death or something out of nothing." Regeneration is hidden. It takes place in the soul of a human being so that we cannot see it. Regeneration is every bit as supernatural as any outward miracle, however, and that is what Luther was getting at. Regeneration is not something that we can do for ourselves.

We had no influence in our physical birth or conception. When it comes to spiritual rebirth, we have even less influence. Only God has the power to raise a human soul from spiritual death to spiritual life, so we define *regeneration* as "that supernatural work of God the Holy Spirit that happens supernaturally and immediately in the soul of a human being." By *immediately* we mean without the use of any means, without intermediary devices. The Spirit works directly, and He works monergistically, which is to say that He is the only One operating in this endeavor. Regeneration is not a joint venture between us and God. The flesh, which is all we are before conversion, can do nothing.

Only God can raise somebody from the dead, both physically and spiritually, so here in Romans 6 Paul is saying that we have been raised from the dead. We have a new genesis. *Gennaō* means "to be," "to become," or "to happen," and *regeneration* refers to a new or a second occurrence of the original genesis. We had a genesis when we were born; then we have a new genesis, a rebirth, only this time it is a spiritual birth wrought by the supernatural work of God the Holy Spirit.

Application

God's monergistic work of regeneration ought to lead us to great humility and gratitude. God worked in us through His Spirit not for something in us but solely by His grace. Meditate on this truth regularly, that it may work in you a deep humility and gratitude. Pray boldly that God will use this spiritual demeanor so that others may come to know the great privilege of what it is to be born again.

2

Consider What Has Happened to You

THINK OF THE BLESSINGS THAT WE HAVE RECEIVED in our lifetimes. Think of how many times we have grumbled about what we did not get. Think of how many times we have lacked contentment and been dissatisfied with the hand that God has dealt us, and then look around the world and see the vast multitudes who have no idea what it means to be born of the Spirit. If we are living in a hovel or are living through constant chronic pain and illness but have received the supernatural work of regeneration in our souls, we have no reason to do anything but praise God for the rest of eternity because we have received the pearl of great price. We have been raised from the dead already. We are already going to live into eternity because the sting of death has been removed. Death cannot destroy what God has regenerated.

We have newness of life. Our lives have been changed. That is why I spend time explaining the pernicious doctrine of the lordship-salvation controversy, that people can have Jesus as Savior and not as Lord. How can somebody dead be made alive, yet not be different? How can somebody in slavery be released from bondage, yet not be changed? The biggest change that we will ever go through in life takes place when we are reborn. We have changed from spiritual death to spiritual life, from bondage to freedom. "Where the Spirit of the Lord is, there is liberty" (2 Cor. 3:17).

Paul is asking us to consider what has happened. We died with Christ; we were raised in the power of His resurrection. In a sense, there is a strange combination of the imperative and the indicative. Since this is the way we are, then we must behave that way. We must live as people who have a new life, because if we are regenerate, we do have new lives, and if we are justified, we are new creations. Now that God has rescued us from death, He expects us to live for Him the rest of our days.

Application
James calls God's law "perfect" and "the law of liberty" (1:25). In Christ, we are set free from our bondage to sin to begin to see obedience to God's law as freedom. God created us for obedience to Him,

and it is not until we have been liberated from our spiritual bondage that we can experience the freedom for which we were originally created and newly created.

3

The Old Man

FOR IF WE HAVE BEEN UNITED TOGETHER **in the likeness of His death, certainly we also shall be in the likeness of His resurrection, knowing this, that our old man was crucified with Him** (vv. 5–6a). By "old man," Paul is talking about the former human nature, the nature that we brought into this world where our humanity was dead in sin. That person, the old person with a singular disposition toward sin whose heart was a heart of stone, is the one who was crucified with Christ. Christ did not just die for our sins; He died for our sinfulness. He did not just die for our sin legally, bearing our guilt; He died to kill our original sin, our moral inability. Our dead, corrupt, fallen nature was crucified with Christ on the cross. My old man received the curse of God on Calvary.

I put question marks in my Bible, and I have one after these words: "knowing this, that our old man was crucified with Him," **that the body of sin might be done away with** (v. 6a). By saying "body of sin," Paul is describing our physical body. He uses the Greek word *sōma*, which is not the usual term used to describe our corrupt nature, our flesh, which, as I have already indicated, is *sarx*. Here he is talking about our physical body, the body of sin.

Let me tell you what Paul does not mean. Paul does not equate sin with physicality. We tend to think of sins simply in terms of physical appetites and acts of disobedience that immediately involve our body—gluttony, sex, drunkenness. Yet we have a mind of flesh. Sin is something in our thoughts. Sin is something deeply rooted in our souls. Some try to bifurcate the human person and say that the physical part is sinful and the spiritual part is good, the way Plato did, but that is not the way. Paul may be using the expression "body of sin" similarly to the way we talk about a body of literature comprising several volumes. I am still not sure what Paul means by the "body of sin." It is likely that he is just talking about the mass of sin that we have to deal with. The mass of sin that describes our fallen condition, what Augustine called a mass of perdition, is crucified with Christ and done away with.

Application

Before coming to know Christ, we served the master of sin. When we are tempted to go back into servitude to sin, we must look not at sin's present enticement or temptation but to its track record. This is what Paul calls us to recognize later in Romans 6. When tempted to return to former sins, ask, "What fruit did you have then in the things of which you are now ashamed?" (v. 21a).

4

Slaves No Longer

I HAVE BEEN TOLD THAT ONE OF the penalties for murder in some sectors of the ancient world was to tie the murdered, decaying corpse onto the murderer, who had to drag it everywhere on his person while it was rotting. Can you imagine anything more ghastly than having a dead body tied to you? Some think this is what Paul is speaking of here when he refers to the body of sin. The sin nature that we brought into this world is like a putrid, decaying, corrupted corpse, a body of death that we still have to carry around with us until we go to heaven. Even though we have been reborn, even though we have been let out of prison and set free from slavery, we still sin and fall. Yet that does not mean that we are unchanged. We are changed, and the old man is dying daily. He dies the death by inches, but each day that we live in the grace of God, the new man, which has been raised with Christ, is being strengthened and is growing, and the old man is dying more and more. In a very spiritual way, it died already on the cross, but at the same time it is still kicking and screaming, and we have to deal with it to our life's end.

Paul's intent is clear: **that we should no longer be slaves of sin** (v. 6b). It is one thing to be a sinner; it is another to be a slave of sin. We all sin, but if we have been born of the Spirit, we are no longer slaves to that sin. We can no longer say to God, "I cannot help it. I am dominated by the power of sin." If we are still in a condition of slavery to sin, then we are not regenerate. Of course, we have besetting sins, those that cause us to fail over and over again, but we are called to resist those sins. The greatest Christians fight against such sins all their spiritual lives, yet in the final analysis we have been set free, and we now have the power of God at our disposal so that we can have victory over every sin.

I believe it is possible for a Christian after conversion to live a perfect life, but let me qualify that. I think it is hypothetically possible that we can live the rest of our days without sin, but it is certain that we will continue to struggle with sin. There is so much weakness left in us, and we are bombarded with so many opportunities for sin. But the God who raised us from spiritual death has given us the grace to resist. No longer do we sin under compulsion as slaves. We have been set free, but our liberty is extremely weak. We are not accustomed to the power of the resurrection. Our comfort zone is still back in the graveyard of spiritual death even though we have been set free by the power of the Holy Spirit.

Application

Indwelling sin is a reality with which every Christian struggles. Yet we must resist it and not grow discouraged, remembering the promise that is ours as Christians. In 2 Corinthians 3:18, Paul describes our promised transformation this way: "We all, with unveiled face, beholding as in a mirror the glory of the Lord, are being transformed into the same image from glory to glory, just as by the Spirit of the Lord."

5

Reckoned Dead

CORPSES IN THE CEMETERY ARE NOT struggling with temptation. The battle is over. Saints in heaven are not exposed to sin. Once we die, the battle is over. That's why Paul says, **For he who has died has been freed from sin. Now if we died with Christ, we believe that we shall also live with Him, knowing that Christ, having been raised from the dead, dies no more** (vv. 7–9a). Jesus died once, and He would not have died even that once had He not been willing to receive in His own person the imputation of our sin. Death had no claim over Him because He was sinless, but He died one time, "once for all" (v. 10). The work of Christ was finished on the cross.

Death no longer has dominion over Him (v. 9b). Death did not have dominion over Christ for very long. He was vulnerable to death only because of the imputation of sin, but after He paid the price for our sin, death became powerless. The dominion of death was gone. People say that the resurrection of Christ is impossible because they determine possibilities on the basis of probabilities based on what they observe. We have never seen anybody come out of the grave. People die and stay dead, so people come to the conclusion that the resurrection could not have happened, but that is not the way that the Bible looks at it. The Bible says that death could not maintain dominion over Christ. For God, raising His Son from the dead was easy.

For the death that He died, He died to sin once for all; but the life that He lives, He lives to God (v. 10). The life He lived and the life He gives are not like vapor that passes away. The Christ who is alive lives forever. Death is no longer a threat to Him. **Likewise you also, reckon yourselves to be dead indeed to sin, but alive to God in Christ Jesus our Lord** (v. 11). Here Paul is making application of our union with Christ and His death and resurrection. Just as our Savior defeated death and sin, not just for Himself but for us, we are to reckon ourselves dead to sin but alive to God.

Application

We must hold fast to our identity in Christ. So often, we define ourselves by the wrong things. Whether we define ourselves by the things of the world or even by the sins with which we struggle, we lose sight of our deeper identity in Christ. It is only by holding fast to this identity that we might see ourselves as we truly are to have victory over sin. In Christ, we are alive to God but dead to sin.

6

Slavery and Bondage

WE HAVE LOOKED AT THE FACT that we ought to consider ourselves dead to sin because we have been crucified with Christ, and in the passage before us now, Paul brings that to a conclusion: **Therefore do not let sin reign in your mortal body, that you should obey it in its lusts** (v. 12). We reckon ourselves dead with Christ in His crucifixion and do not allow ourselves to be under the dominion of sin. The conclusion is that we are called to guard against allowing sin to rule over us.

Paul has set forth more than once in the epistle our natural condition of original sin. By way of review, original sin is described by two basic metaphors in the New Testament. One is the metaphor of death. By nature we are spiritually dead in our sins. In our natural condition, we have no life with respect to the things of God, no vitality whatsoever. The second metaphor is the one that Paul is developing here in Romans 6, the metaphor of slavery and bondage. We are by nature in bondage to sin.

We have to be very careful when we read the New Testament to try to read it with virgin ears. We do not want to bring to the text all the baggage from the secular culture around us. One of the most destructive ideas we tend to bring is the pagan notion of free will, which holds that every time we have a moral option before us, we have the power to say yes or no; the will is basically in a state of indifference. That idea is as American as apple pie and Chevrolet and baseball, and it is as heretical as can be. It is not just unbiblical; it is antibiblical. The notion of that kind of freedom cannot be found anywhere in sacred Scripture.

We are free in the sense that we have a will and the power of volition; by nature we have the capacity to make choices according to our desires. The problem is that the desires of our hearts by nature are only wicked continually. By nature we have no inclination toward the things of God. Therefore, as Augustine argued against Pelagius, we are in a state of moral inability. We have no ability to do the things of God.

We must not think that we have the moral power to incline ourselves to the things of God. Jesus made it clear to Nicodemus that unless a man is born again, he cannot even see the kingdom of God, let alone take steps to enter it (John 3). Before our rebirth by the work of the Holy Spirit, we are in prison through our sinful impulses. The Bible is not the only place we learn that. We can know it just by looking at the world around us as well as our own hearts.

Application

There are many ways to define freedom. It is misleading when we define it as moral indifference. We are not indifferent to the gospel. In our fallen condition, we cannot respond to it. Only by the Spirit's working in our hearts can we hear it with faith. If the Spirit has worked in this way in your life, give praise to the Lord in prayer. If not, go to Him anyway and ask for the gift of faith.

WEEK 18

1

Made Alive

AND DO NOT PRESENT YOUR MEMBERS AS **instruments of unrighteousness to sin, but present yourselves to God as being alive from the dead, and your members as instruments of righteousness to God** (v. 13). We have been made alive. Paul is addressing believers, those no longer in their original state of sin but raised from the dead and set free from bondage and slavery. That is our condition now. When we sin now, even though the freedom we have from sin and bondage is real and the power of the Holy Spirit is there, we still struggle. We will experience this conflict until the day we die. In fact, Paul speaks in other places about the intense warfare that continues between the old man, who was completely flesh, and the new man, who now has the power of the Holy Spirit indwelling him and enabling him to move toward the things of God. As Christians, we still sin, but we do not have to. Every time we are presented with a temptation, God gives us a way out. He promises us the present power of the Holy Spirit if we will simply cooperate.

The Christian life after conversion is synergistic, not monergistic. Our regeneration, our rebirth, was the work of one person, God. It was not a joint venture; but from the moment we take our first breath of regenerated spiritual life, our effort is also involved. That is why the Apostle elsewhere says, "Work out your own salvation with fear and trembling; for it is God who works in you both to will and to do for His good pleasure" (Phil. 2:12b–13). God is working, and we have to work. Our work, indeed, is the fruit of God's work in us.

Paul is speaking here to free people, to those whom God has regenerated, but still we are tempted and have weaknesses. We bring a lot of baggage into the Christian life, sinful patterns of behavior, and they do not disappear overnight. What disappears is the bondage. Now we have the responsibility to cooperate with the grace that God makes available to us. We are to make diligent use of the means of grace and make sure that our souls are being regularly fed by the Word of God. We have responsibility to be on our faces before God earnestly on a regular basis and never to miss the corporate worship of the people of God unless we are absolutely indisposed.

All these means of grace God has given us to help us in our pilgrimage.

Application

Quietism is a belief that can be summarized in the popular slogan "Let go and let God," as though we were to cease our efforts so that the Spirit might fully work in our lives. This view of sanctification is not biblical. Though God is ultimately the One who works in us, we are plainly called to strive after holiness. Make every effort to put sin to death and to live unto righteousness in your sanctification.

2

Set Free for Righteousness

WE ARE NOT TO OBEY SIN ANYMORE. Paul personifies sin as if it had an individual existence, as if it were a tyrant that would try to enslave us again. We are not to let that happen. We are not to let our minds be instruments of sin. We are not to let our legs be instruments of sin; we must not be swift to shed blood. We are not to let our lips be instruments of sin; we must guard our tongues. We must not allow ourselves to be enslaved once again to sinful patterns. Instead, Paul says, we are to offer ourselves to God. We are to present ourselves to God as resurrected people. Our minds, mouths, ears, eyes, and feet are to be used as tools in our toolkit for offering our whole person to God.

Later in the epistle Paul will say, "I beseech you therefore, brethren, by the mercies of God, that you present your bodies a living sacrifice, . . . which is your reasonable service" (12:1). Instruments, or tools, are means by which certain works are accomplished. The sculptor has a chisel by which he creates a statue. The painter has his brushes and the paint, and the brushes are the instruments he uses to create the painting. The pool player has the cue stick. The baseball player has a bat. All these tools or instruments are used to bring about a desired effect. We can use such tools for good or for evil. We can use our minds for sin or for righteousness. We can use our speech to blaspheme or to praise. We can use our legs to walk in sin or to walk in righteousness.

Paul says that the whole person has been raised from spiritual death and is called to a new kind of slavery. He continues this metaphor of slavery when he calls us to be slaves of righteousness—not servants of Satan, but servants of Christ. That is the difference between the old life and the new life, **for sin shall not have dominion over you,**

for you are not under law but under grace (v. 14). That is a promise. The phrase is written in the indicative, not the imperative. Earlier it was written in the imperative: "do not let sin reign" (v. 12). Now Paul is writing in the indicative. He is describing our state of affairs now. Sin's dominion is gone. It is history. We cannot be brought back again into absolute bondage to sin as we once were.

Application

This is a blessed reality that we enjoy as Christians. Sin no longer has dominion over us. Continue to remind yourself of this truth. To live it out practically, also remember that your war against sin is a Spirit-empowered endeavor. No longer under the condemnation of the law, we can live for righteousness' sake in the freedom of the Spirit.

3

Under Grace

ONE OF THE HARDEST THINGS TO understand about Paul is how he uses references to the law. He does not always refer to the law in the same way, which has vexed the best minds of Christendom for two thousand years. When Paul says, "You are not under law," some people take this as a license to sin, as if we are no longer under any obligation to keep the law of God. They believe that we passed from law to grace; the law was Moses but grace is Jesus, so we are free from the law. I do not think that is what Paul means here, nor do I think Paul is referring simply to the Law of Moses. Earlier, in Romans 5, he pointed out that the law was in the world even before Sinai. God reveals His law in nature and in the conscience of human beings. We cannot just restrict law to the laws of Moses. From the beginning of our sinfulness we have been under the dreadful burden of the law, because the law condemns us. The law reveals our disobedience, and the law cannot possibly be the means by which we will be saved because, as debtors to the law, we can never pay our debt.

I think he means that we are no longer under the law in the sense of being underneath the awesome, weighty burden of the law. Paul says that we are no longer in the condition of being crushed under the weight of the law, no longer oppressed by its burden of guilt and judgment. We are now under grace. "For by grace you have been saved through faith, and that not of yourselves; it is the gift of God" (Eph. 2:8)—a truth of which Paul was continually reminding Christians. Now that we have been freed from the burden of the law, are we going to go back? Now that we know that we have been justified by faith alone, are we going to try to return to justifying ourselves through our works? No. We move from grace to grace, from faith to faith. Grace does not end at our justification; grace is ever present in the process and progress. We are as much sanctified by grace as we are justified by grace.

The only way that we can have any assurance of salvation is by looking at grace, not at our performance or achievements. That is why we have to get justification by faith in our bloodstream every minute of every day. We must continually return to the ground of our justification, which is Christ's righteousness alone. It is grace. It is *sola gratia*, by grace alone. The law slays us. It is a mirror of our sin, so it drives us to the cross. That is what Paul is talking about here. We are not under law; we are under grace.

Application

In Romans 12:12, Paul calls us to be "continuing steadfastly in prayer." How might we also "get justification by faith in our bloodstream every minute of every day"? We need to train our hearts and minds to keep Christ at the forefront of our lives so that our thoughts about Him, His person and work, and the grace that we have because of Him are a constant for us. Get into God's Word daily. Surround yourself with fellow believers who remind you of these truths. Make these truths the source of your praise in your constant prayer.

4

Slaves of Righteousness, Part 1

BUT GOD BE THANKED THAT THOUGH YOU WERE slaves of sin, yet you obeyed from the heart that form of doctrine to which you were delivered. And having been set free from sin, you became slaves of righteousness (vv. 17–18). Paul uses a word here that has almost disappeared from Christian vocabulary—"righteousness." If I give a seminar on spiritual growth, people will flock to it. If I give them five keys to spirituality, they will sign up. If I give a seminar on how to become righteous, no one will come because righteousness is no longer the goal of many professing Christians. Many of today's professing Christians want to be spiritual or pious or moral, but not righteous. Righteousness is so closely linked to the idea of self-righteousness that we sometimes want to distance ourselves as far as we can from the very idea.

We know that we cannot be saved by our righteousness, so we do not think that righteousness has any part in our quest for sanctification. Remember that Jesus said, "Seek first the kingdom of God and His righteousness, and all these things shall be added to you" (Matt. 6:33). The primary business of the Christian life is the quest for righteousness. Jesus also said, "Unless your righteousness exceeds the righteousness of the scribes and Pharisees, you will by no means enter the kingdom of heaven" (5:20). Jesus might simply have been saying that the only righteousness that will get someone into the kingdom of God is a righteousness greater than that of the Pharisees, namely, His own. Jesus might have been giving a cryptic, thinly veiled lesson on justification by faith alone, but I do not think so. I think He really meant what He said—that unless our righteousness exceeds the righteousness of the Pharisees, we will never make it. We are not going to make it on the basis of our righteousness, but only on the basis of faith. If the faith is genuine, the fruit of that faith will be real righteousness.

Application

Another key word in Romans 6:17–18 is "doctrine." Throughout Romans 6, Paul has been calling us to righteousness but also stressing the indicative reality that we are set free from sin. This is a doctrine of the Christian life. We must arm ourselves with doctrine—with truth—if we are truly to live the Christian life. Doctrine and practical Christian living cannot be separated.

5

Slaves of Righteousness, Part 2

WE MIGHT NOT THINK THAT EXCEEDING the Pharisees is very difficult. After all, those Pharisees who had Jesus killed were the worst criminals of all time. They were the hypocrites, the ones who provoked Jesus' wrath. "Woe to you, scribes and Pharisees, hypocrites," Jesus said (Matt. 23:13; Luke 11:44).

Although Jesus roundly and soundly condemned them, He threw them a bone from time to time: "You tithe mint and rue and all manner of herbs, and pass by justice and the love of God. These you ought to have done, without leaving the others undone" (Luke 11:42). They did not care about justice or mercy, but at least they tithed. Some polls show that 4 percent of professing evangelical Christians tithe their goods and services to the Lord; the other 96 percent systematically, routinely, day after day rob God of what He calls us to give Him for the building of His kingdom. That is a very serious matter. At least the Pharisees were tithers.

Jesus said to the Pharisees: "You search the Scriptures, for in them you think you have eternal life; and these are they which testify of Me. But you are not willing to come to Me that you may have life" (John 5:39–40). They did search the Scriptures, but they did not have life.

The majority of those who have been Christians for at least ten years have never read the whole Bible, so the Pharisees beat us there. Their prayers were motivated by pomp and outward displays of piety when they prayed in the marketplace, but at least they prayed.

Jesus said to them: "Woe to you, scribes and Pharisees, hypocrites! For you travel land and sea to win one proselyte, and when he is won, you make him twice as much a son of hell as yourselves" (Matt. 23:15). Calling them "[children] of hell" was not complimentary, but they were committed to evangelism and missions. They went over land and sea for one convert. It was hard to travel in those days. When I am asked to travel somewhere to speak, I have a speaking committee to make those decisions for me; they are not going to send me over land and sea to make one convert. The scribes and Pharisees beat us like drums on many points. Jesus says that unless our righteousness exceeds their righteousness, we will never enter into the kingdom of God.

Application

It is sobering to think of what we often fail to do in the Christian life. The Pharisees excelled in tithing, searching the Scriptures, and prayer. We ought to excel in these too. But we must do so from the heart and not hypocritically seeking after the applause of others. Let us also not be self-righteous. Though we seek after righteousness, we must remember that the righteousness we cling to is not our own but Christ's.

6

The Gift of God

I SPEAK IN HUMAN TERMS BECAUSE OF the weakness of your flesh. For just as you presented your members as slaves of uncleanness, and of lawlessness leading to more lawlessness, so now present your members as slaves of righteousness for holiness. For when you were slaves of sin, you were free in regard to righteousness (vv. 19–20). Formerly, we did not have any righteousness. When we were under slavery to the dominion of sin, we were completely free from righteousness. What fruit did you have then in the things of which you are now ashamed? For the end of those things is death. But now having been set free from sin, and having become slaves of God, you have your fruit to holiness, and the end, everlasting life (vv. 21–22). Freedom from sin means freedom for righteousness, freedom for eternal life.

Paul closes this section with a well-known passage: For the wages of sin is death, but the gift of God is eternal life in Christ Jesus our Lord (v. 23). The wages of sin—what does sin earn? What is its basic wage? The more we sin, the more we earn, and what we earn is death. There is always a payoff. Remember what God said: "'Vengeance is Mine, I will repay,' says the Lord" (12:19). If we are slaves to sin, we earn demerits; we earn wrath. If God did not pay what we earn, He would be unjust. "The wages of sin is death."

In stark contrast to that is the good news, the gift of God. Wages are something that we earn; a gift is something that we cannot possibly earn. Wages are something that we merit; the gift, on the other hand, is free. It is gratuitous. The wages of sin is death; the gift of God is eternal life in Christ Jesus our Lord. All the way through this section, Paul has been dealing with contrasts: slavery to sin versus slavery to righteousness; wages of death versus the gift of eternal life. We now have experienced grace.

G.C. Berkouwer once said, "The essence of Christian theology is grace, and the essence of Christian ethics is gratitude." What draws us to obedience and righteousness is not duty but love. It is gratitude. Once we have received this grace of eternal life in Jesus Christ, we should be willing to crawl over broken glass to honor and praise Him for that grace.

Application

A heart of thankfulness should characterize every Christian. One of the greatest ways that we show our gratitude to God is by worshiping Him. Worship is not optional, and it flows from a heart of gratitude. Continue to commit Hebrews 12:28–29 to memory: "Therefore, since we are receiving a kingdom which cannot be shaken, let us have grace, by which we may serve God acceptably with reverence and godly fear. For our God is a consuming fire."

Romans 7

OR DO YOU NOT KNOW, BRETHREN *(for I speak to those who know the law), that the law has dominion over a man as long as he lives? For the woman who has a husband is bound by the law to her husband as long as he lives. But if the husband dies, she is released from the law of her husband. So then if, while her husband lives, she marries another man, she will be called an adulteress; but if her husband dies, she is free from that law, so that she is no adulteress, though she has married another man. Therefore, my brethren, you also have become dead to the law through the body of Christ, that you may be married to another—to Him who was raised from the dead, that we should bear fruit to God. For when we were in the flesh, the sinful passions which were aroused by the law were at work in our members to bear fruit to death. But now we have been delivered from the law, having died to what we were held by, so that we should serve in the newness of the Spirit and not in the oldness of the letter.*

What shall we say then? Is the law sin? Certainly not! On the contrary, I would not have known sin except through the law. For I would not have known covetousness unless the law had said, "You shall not covet." But sin, taking opportunity by the commandment, produced in me all manner of evil desire. For apart from the law sin was dead. I was alive once without the law, but when the commandment came, sin revived and I died. And the commandment, which was to bring life, I found to bring death. For sin, taking occasion by the commandment, deceived me, and by it killed me. Therefore the law is holy, and the commandment holy and just and good.

Has then what is good become death to me? Certainly not! But sin, that it might appear sin, was producing death in me through what is good, so that sin through the commandment might become exceedingly sinful. For we know that the law is spiritual, but I am carnal, sold under sin. For what I am doing, I do not understand. For what I will to do, that I do not practice; but what I hate, that I do. If, then, I do what I will not to do, I agree with the law that it is good. But now, it is no longer I who do it, but sin that dwells in me. For I know that in me (that is, in my flesh) nothing good dwells; for to will is present with me, but how to perform what is good I do not find. For the good that I will to do, I do not do; but the evil I will not to do, that I practice. Now if I do what I will not to do, it is no longer I who do it, but sin that dwells in me.

I find then a law, that evil is present with me, the one who wills to do good. For I delight in the law of God according to the inward man. But I see another law in my members, warring against the law of my mind, and bringing me into captivity to the law of sin which is in my members. O wretched man that I am! Who will deliver me from this body of death? I thank God—through Jesus Christ our Lord!

So then, with the mind I myself serve the law of God, but with the flesh the law of sin.

WEEK 19

1

Married to Another

WE HAVE COME TO ROMANS 7, which means that we are sailing into uncharted waters. Before we look at the beginning of chapter 7, we do well to recall that when Paul wrote this epistle, he did not divide it into chapters or verses. Such divisions are advantageous, however, because they facilitate our study. The disadvantage is the tendency they create to look at each chapter as a self-standing unit and to forget its interconnectedness to what has gone before and what comes after. There is no great break in subject matter between the end of Romans 6 and the beginning of Romans 7, just as everything we looked at in Romans 6 was an extension of what Paul had written before it on the gospel and its consequences.

Paul continues the application of our having been crucified with Christ: **Or do you not know, brethren (for I speak to those who know the law), that the law has dominion over a man as long as he lives? For the woman who has a husband is bound by the law to her husband as long as he lives** (vv. 1–2a). Here Paul gives an extended analogy from marriage. It is very simple: we get married; we take our vows. We promise to honor and cherish each other as long as we both shall live. We understand that if one partner in the marriage covenant should die, then all the obligations incumbent upon the one remaining are now set aside, and the widow or widower is completely free in the eyes of God to be married again. The law that binds us and regulates our marriage is in effect only as long as our partner remains alive.

Therefore, my brethren, you also have become dead to the law through the body of Christ, that you may be married to another

(v. 4a). There is a shift here: our spouse has not died, but we have died. Paul does not say that the law has died. We have died, and therefore our marriage to the law is over. The law no longer has dominion over us the way it did before we died. We died in Christ, and in Christ the law was fulfilled.

From the very beginning, the law of God has had dominion over us. Since the fall, the consequences of God's law have issued in our death. The law of God has exposed us to the judgment and condemnation of the holiness of God. Since the fall, we have been under the relentless burden of the law that weighs us down and exposes us moment by moment to the full curse of that law. The law has not been removed, but in Christ we have died, and Christ has taken the full weight of the curse of the law upon Himself so that we no longer carry that burden on our backs.

Application

Paul is focusing on the moral law of God in this passage. While it is true that dimensions of the ceremonial and civil law have passed away, having been fulfilled in Christ and the wall of hostility having been torn down between Jew and Gentile in the church, the moral law is forever binding. Yet Christ also fulfilled the demands of God's moral law for us perfectly. In this sense, we are dead to the law because of Christ's work, but in our being conformed to Christ, God gives us a desire to live it out.

2

The Covenants of Works and Grace

THE ORIGINAL COVENANT THAT GOD MADE with man is sometimes called the *creation covenant*. In it Adam and Eve were on probation. They were made good, in the image of God, and God set before them a test and told them that they were not to eat the fruit of a particular tree. If they did, they would die. If they were obedient, the tree of life was theirs. We know how things fell apart. The original relationship that human beings had with God is what Reformed theologians call the *covenant of works*. Of course, the very fact that God entered into any kind of covenant with His creatures is pure grace. The gracious covenant He entered into with Adam and Eve is called a *covenant of works* because the terms and conditions for blessedness are related to obedience.

We saw earlier the stark contrast between the first Adam—the calamitous response to the whole race because of his disobedience (see Rom. 5:18)—and the Second Adam, the Lord Jesus Christ, who, like the first Adam, was put to the test and subjected to a probation. He was exposed to the complete, unbridled assault of Satan in the wilderness for forty days, and yet He resisted to the end, saying that His meat and drink was to do the will of the Father (John 4:34) and that He lived by every word that proceeds from the mouth of God (Matt. 4:4; Luke 4:4).

His perfection endured not simply for forty days in the wilderness; it endured from the day He was born until the moment He expired on the cross. At no time in that interim did Christ violate the law of God. His perfect act of obedience is as much the grounds of our salvation as is His punishment on the cross as He satisfied the wrath of God for our guilt. He died for our sin; He lived for our righteousness. As the new Adam, Jesus kept the covenant of works. He did what no other human being has ever accomplished. He remained absolutely faithful and obedient to every law of God from the beginning.

The *covenant of grace* refers to the promise God gave immediately after the fall of Adam and Eve. He did not annihilate the human race but promised redemption that would come through the Seed of the woman. The promise of the covenant of grace is that we will be redeemed not because we keep the law. We cannot keep the law. We will be redeemed through the ministry of the One who does keep the law. In the final analysis, as much as we talk about justification by faith alone, it is really just shorthand for justification by Christ alone, because our justification is ultimately through works alone. The only way that anyone can be justified in the sight of God is through real righteousness, and real righteousness is achieved only through real obedience to the law of God.

We are justified through the works of Jesus alone, who alone kept the terms of the covenant of works. Since He died for us as our substitute in a vicarious manner, the Apostle sees that, in a very real sense, we died with Him, and because we died with Him, we died to the law as a way of salvation. As Paul will say later, this does not mean that we have a license to sin. Additionally, just because we have been freed from the dominion and curse of the law does not mean that the law is a bad thing, something to be despised.

Application

The law was formally given to God's people at Mount Sinai in the Mosaic covenant. This covenant was part of the one covenant of grace. God never intended His people to be justified by the law, which is why the sacrificial system was in place, that His people might look in faith to His provision of forgiveness. While old covenant believers looked forward in faith to Christ, we look back to Christ in faith. Take a moment to pray to God, praising Him for your place in redemptive history, that you have seen the finished work of Christ in full assurance of your forgiveness.

3

Luther and the Law

A PSYCHOLOGICAL THEOLOGIAN, ERIK H. ERIKSON, once attempted an analysis of Martin Luther—five hundred years after Luther lived—and he came to the conclusion that Luther was at least seriously neurotic and probably psychotic.

Luther's father, who owned mines in Germany, was very pleased to send his son to the best law school. He wanted to be able to boast about his son the attorney. Luther went to the university and distinguished himself and was considered by many to be the most brilliant young student of jurisprudence in all of Germany. On his way home for a school break, Luther encountered a severe thunderstorm and a lightning bolt struck right next to him. He fell to the ground and in utter terror cried out, "Help me, St. Anne! I'll become a monk."

To his father's unvarnished chagrin, Luther entered the monastery in Erfurt and sought to become a monk of the Augustinian order. If anybody ever tried to get to heaven through monkery, it was Martin Luther. He would come into the confessional and spend an hour or two (or more) confessing his sins from the preceding twenty-four hours. He would receive absolution, and peace would flood his soul, but on the walk back to the cell he would think of a sin he had failed to confess, and he would be in misery once again. All he could see was Christ the angry Judge and the Law of Moses hanging over his head. "You ask me if I love God," said Luther; "sometimes I hate him."

That is why Erikson looked at the life of Luther and said that he was crazy. Maybe he was. They say that there is a thin line between genius and insanity. It may be that Luther was skating back and forth across that line through his entire life. I would not be surprised, because it would take someone like that to stand against the whole world the way Luther did at the Diet of Worms. But I do not think we can understand Luther's misery simply in terms of defective psychology. We have to look deeper. Whatever else we say about Luther, we must say that he transferred his training in the law to the law of God.

What is the worst sin that a person could commit? The logic is simple. If the greatest commandment is to love the Lord your God with all our heart, strength, and soul and our neighbor as ourselves, it would seem to me that breaking that commandment is the worst thing we could do. Yet have we ever lost sleep because we failed to keep the Great Commandment? I have not. Luther would examine himself and say in his prayers, "God, I did not love You with my whole heart today. How can I get relief from Your judgment?" That does not bother us, but it was devastating Luther. If he was crazy, I thank God that He gave us a crazy man to open our eyes to the gospel. The craziest thing we could ever do is to try to work our way into heaven.

Application

Before we came to see God's holiness, we likely underestimated the extent of God's demands in the law and overestimated our performance. Remember that if you are ever engaging with someone who thinks like this, it is a perfect opportunity to explain why the cross was necessary. We could never have fulfilled the law's demands. Communicate the beauty of God's grace in providing His Son to keep the law on our behalf.

4

The Function of the Law, Part 1

THE GREAT SIXTEENTH-CENTURY REFORMERS Martin Luther and John Calvin tended to have different emphases when it came to the use of the law in the life of the Christian. Luther stressed what he called the *elenchticus* use of the law, the *usus elenchticus*, which simply means the teaching or pedagogical purpose of the law. The law's main function, according to Luther, is to serve as the schoolmaster to drive us to Christ. The law exposes our sinful condition and strips away all pretense to our moral ability to reach heaven by our works.

Luther emphasized the law's basic function in leading us to Christ, whereas Calvin more heavily stressed the use of the law in revealing the character of God. That is what we have to understand first: whose law it is. The moral law is not simply a list of abstract duties, a list of do's and don'ts. The law first reveals the lawgiver. In the final analysis, laws are not grounded in the nature of things; the law is grounded in the character of God. It flows from His very being. As the Author of human life and the Creator of our souls, God has every right to impose upon us whatever obligations He wants.

God has the right to say, "Thou shalt do this" and "Thou shalt not do that." Who are we to defy the Lord God omnipotent, to say that He does not have any right to tell us what to do and what not to do? "I'm a woman, and I have an inalienable right over my own body." No, you do not. The God who made our bodies rules our bodies, and He tells us what we may do with them. Therefore, the first use of the law is to express the character of God. It reveals His holiness. That is why we distance ourselves from it. We are not zealous to pursue a deeper knowledge of the law. When we get involved with the study of the knowledge of God, we are irresistibly drawn close to that ultimate standard of righteousness found in God's character. At the same instant that the law reveals the holiness of God, it reveals to us our unholiness. The law is a mirror, and when I look in that mirror, it never lies; it drives me to my knees because the law of God reveals my pollution. As Calvin once said, the law reveals to us our corruption. As Luther said, it serves as the pedagogue that teaches us of the gospel and drives us to Christ.

Application

The law isn't just a superficial checklist. It extends right down to the heart. Jesus taught this explicitly in Matthew 5, that our unjust anger and our lusts are violations of the sixth and seventh commandments, respectively. You must point people to the beauty of the cross when sharing the gospel, and an essential way to stress its beauty of the cross is by driving home a person's need for it. Winsomely hold up the law and its full requirements, that the Spirit might use it.

5

The Function of the Law, Part 2

THE LAW DIRECTS US TO CHRIST, but there are two other functions or uses of the law as well. The law serves as a restraint upon our sin. We live in a lawless culture, and yet some sociologists are saying that we are an over-governed culture. Every year Congress adds hundreds of new laws—new ways to make us guilty before the state and to get into trouble. We have to have law enforcement to keep a civil society because every day people violate the law and other people. Can we imagine what society would be like if we did not have any law? We have laws that post the speed limit at 65 mph, but we go 75 or 80 mph. If speed limits were removed, we would be driving 90 or 95 mph. There is some restraint, which is why no government is worse than bad government. The worst of all possible societies are those marked by anarchy, because law, as much as we may hate it, still exercises some restraint upon us. As sinful as we are, we would be even more sinful if the restraints were removed.

The third use of the law, which in Latin is called the *tertius usus* of the law, is one of the most important insights of Swiss theology. Even though we are freed from the burden and destruction of the law, it continues to reveal to us what is pleasing to God.

A long time ago, I was invited to give a series of lectures on the holiness of God at a large church in New York State. I gave the first lecture, and afterward about twenty attendees went to a mansion of great grandeur for dessert and prayer. Once at the house, the group turned out the lights, got down on their knees, and began to pray. To my utter shock, they began to pray to their departed relatives. I was in the middle of a séance.

I said, "Do you know what the Word of God says about this? In the old covenant God made this activity a capital offense. He considers it an abomination. What in the history of redemption has changed so that an activity that was utterly repugnant to God is now all of a sudden pleasing to Him?"

The law, in its continual revelatory value, made it very clear to me that no Christian should ever be involved with such an activity. In that case, the law served as a guide for me. It likewise serves as a guide for all believers. We are not under its curse or weight, but the beauty of the law is still available to us, as Paul begins to deal with the subject in verse 7.

We have become dead to the law through Christ. We have been married to another—**to Him who was raised from the dead, that we should bear fruit to God. For when we were in the flesh, the sinful passions which were aroused by the law were at work in our members to bear fruit to death. But now we have been delivered from the law, having died to what we were held by, so that we should serve in the newness of the Spirit and not in the oldness of the letter** (vv. 4b–6).

Application

The civil law of Israel can give us insight into how to apply the moral law of God in our lives and culture. Even though the laws given to govern the Israelites as a nation are not all binding on us, we can learn from what the Westminster Confession of Faith calls their "general equity." Every part of God's law was given by Him, so all of it can be useful for our instruction and guidance.

6

The Function of the Law, Part 3

WHAT SHALL WE SAY THEN? **Is the law sin? Certainly not!** (v. 7a). The law in itself is always good and holy. Our sinful hearts may respond with hostile feelings toward God's righteous law when we hear or read it; by hearing and understanding the law we may be provoked to greater sinning than we would have been had we not known the law. Nevertheless, we cannot come to the conclusion that something is wrong with the law, that it is evil or sinful. Paul is saying that we need to keep in front of our eyes a clear distinction between the righteousness of the law and the sinfulness of our response to it. The law is not the culprit; it is our fallen corruption.

Is the law sin? **On the contrary, I would not have known sin except through the law. For I would not have known covetousness unless the law had said, "You shall not covet"** (v. 7b). Paul is again making the point that the revelatory character of God's law is a mirror by which we see not only the glory and radiance of God's perfection but also ourselves, warts and all. The law is not sin, but the law makes known to us our sin. We will not come to the gospel or beg for the mercy of God until the Holy Spirit convicts us of sin, and the instrument that the Spirit uses to bring us to the cross is the revelation of law.

We are at ease in Zion. We are inured to the power of the law. The pagan is virtually oblivious to the radical disobedience he exhibits every hour of his life. He may be willing to admit that he is not perfect, but he does not feel the weight of that. He just takes for granted that we are doing what comes naturally. To err is human; to forgive is divine, so the fact that we covet and lust is no major matter. Even as Christians, we are too often comfortable in our sin.

Paul uses repeatedly the image of someone spiritually dead to any awareness of the gravity of sin. It is the testimony of the greatest saints in the history of the church that the more deeply they have come to know the character of God, the more acutely conscious they have become of the severity of their sin. One of the sweet characteristics of God's mercy is that He does not reveal all our sin to us at once or in all its fullness. If God were to reveal to me this moment the degree of abiding sin that continues in my life, even since I have come to the cross, I could not bear it, nor could you. The downside is that when

God withholds His judgment from us and the anguish of conviction, we can begin to think that He does not care. The world has lost its fear of God. There is no sense of judgment.

Application

We often see this with children. A command is issued, and it almost seems that they go out of their way to rebel against it. We, too, have a sinful response to God's law, and until He awakens our hearts to its goodness as His holy standard, we may lack the conviction of sin. Being convicted of our sin isn't a pleasant experience, but it can lead us to repentance.

WEEK 20

1

The Law and Sin

BUT SIN, TAKING OPPORTUNITY BY **the commandment, produced in me all manner of evil desire** (v. 8a). Rather than the commandment's turning us from sin, restraining us from covetousness, our sin, in response to the law of God, was stirred to even greater sinfulness and covetousness. Sin took opportunity by the commandment, and it produced in us all manner of evil desire.

The little phrase "evil desire" is translated in a variety of ways. The Latin text uses the word from which the English term *concupiscence* comes. This word was involved in one of the great disputes between the Reformers of the sixteenth century and the Roman Catholic Church. Rome said that man was created with concupiscence, not with evil. They defined concupiscence as being *of* sin; it *inclines* to sin, but it is not sin. The Reformers replied that an evil desire that gives birth to evil action is already sin. Our sinful deeds flow out of our sinful desires, so we cannot excuse those evil desires as being less than sin. The Greek word used here is *epathumia*, which is the word for "passion" or "desire" with a prefix that intensifies it. Our specific sins make plain the root of those sins, which is our fallen nature. Actual sin, specific violations of the law of God, is rooted in a passion of sin, a sinful inclination or disposition. We have to understand that there is something wrong with the root of the tree, and nothing can change it short of the divine and supernatural intervention of the Holy Spirit.

For apart from the law sin was dead (v. 8b). Throughout chapter 6 and into chapter 7, Paul uses images of death and life. Until the law came, sin was dead. It was not active. It was dormant until it was awakened by the presence of the law.

In 1970, the film *Tora! Tora! Tora!* portrayed the events surrounding the attack on Pearl Harbor. The film was based on archives from the imperial navy in Japan and the American military headquarters. After the attack was successfully made, Admiral Yamamoto of the Japanese imperial navy said, "I am afraid that all we have accomplished here was to awaken a sleeping giant and fill him with a terrible resolve." That is what Paul is talking about. Sin, for the most part, was sleeping until the law came along and awoke that sleeping giant and filled us with the horrible resolve of wickedness.

Apart from the law, sin was dead. **I was alive once without the law, but when the commandment came, sin revived and I died** (v. 9). If we think back to our pre-Christian days, were we overburdened by a sense of sin and guilt? Not until the Holy Spirit brought His conviction on us, quickened our consciences, and made us alive to the law did we feel for the first time the weight of our guilt. That is what drove us to Christ and gave us a new life.

Take a moment to reflect on your pre-Christian experience or a time when you were straying from the Lord. What was it like? How did you feel about your sin? Now search your heart to see whether any area of your life isn't fully being given to the Lord, and map out some practical ways to repent

2

The Deceit of Sin

AND THE COMMANDMENT, **which was to bring life, I found to bring death. For sin, taking occasion by the commandment, deceived me, and by it killed me** (vv. 10–11). In the Scriptures, Satan is called "the great deceiver" or "the slanderer." What is so attractive about sin? Why would any creature made in the image of God be tempted by sin? Why would we be inclined to steal what belongs to somebody else? Why would we bear false witness against our neighbor? We are tempted because in the temptation is the offer of happiness, and the pursuit of happiness is given to us as a constitutional guarantee. The devil never says, "Do this and suffer" or "Do this and die." The passions are so excited by sin that we come to believe that unless we act on our passion, we will be denying ourselves fundamental happiness.

Sin is attractive because it brings us pleasure. It brings pleasure but never happiness. That is the monstrous lie of the father of lies: "Do this, and you will be happy." It is impossible for sin to bring happiness to a child of God, yet we do not believe it. "I will not be happy unless I do this" and "I will not be happy unless I have that"—this is how sin deceives us. The serpent told Eve, "You will not surely die. For God knows that in the day you eat of it your eyes will be opened, and you will be like God, knowing good and evil" (Gen. 3:4–5). In other words,

"You do not know what happiness is, Adam, and you do not know what pleasure is, Eve, until you taste the fruit." Satan tells us that God is withholding happiness and that we have a right to be happy.

The biggest moral justification in the secular culture for all kinds of monstrous evil is that we have the right. "I have the right to do what I prefer to do. I have the right to destroy my baby." Where did you get that right? "I have a right over my own body." Says who? Does God give us the right to do those things? We know better. Every person in the world knows better than that, but they say, "If I do not do this, I will not be happy." If we do evil things, we destroy all hope of happiness. We cannot get in our minds the difference between pleasure and happiness.

Application

A beautiful illustration of the true nature of sin can be found in Proverbs: "By transgression an evil man is snared, but the righteous sings and rejoices" (29:6). Sin is a trap; it quickly entangles us. But the reason the righteous can sing and rejoice is because they are not ensnared by it.

3

The Holiness of the Law

PAUL GIVES HIS CONCLUSION TO THIS SECTION: **Therefore the law is holy** (v. 12a). A woman I know left her husband and five children to live with another man. Another minister and I went to talk to her, understanding the fear and trembling involved in Jesus' words, "Where two or three are gathered together in My name, I am there in the midst of them" (Matt. 18:20). There, Jesus was promising to be in the midst of those gathered to fulfill the biblical mandate of calling a brother or sister back from sin, what we call church discipline. If there is ever a time when we need to know the presence of Christ, it is when we are calling someone back from sin.

During our visit, we were not angry or harsh. We pleaded with her, "You are a Christian, a married woman, and the mother of five children. You have to end this relationship and come home."

She responded, "I do not have to listen to legalism."

I said to her, "Legalism has many faces. We invent laws where God has left us free, we major in minors, and we obey the letter and destroy the spirit. You have to understand that it is never legalism to obey the law of God, because God's law is holy, and what you are doing is unholy."

Thanks be to God, she did repent and come back, but it does not always work out that way. People harden their hearts and make all manner of excuses.

So the law is holy, **and the commandment holy and just and good** (v. 12b). The law of God is holy, just, and good, but what happens when a holy and just law is delivered to unholy creatures? They do not think it is very just. When God puts a restraint upon our desires, we say that it is not fair, as if there were some hint of injustice in the character of God, but the law of God is good because He is good. The law of God was designed to bring life, but we turn it into an occasion of death.

Application

We need to guard ourselves from legalism. Desiring obedience to God's law, gratefully responding to His grace, is not legalism, but adding to His law is. The Puritan Thomas Watson said: "Satan tempts to sin under a pretense of religion. He is most to be feared when he transforms himself into an angel of light. He came to Christ with Scripture in his mouth: 'It is written.' The devil baits his hook with religion."

4

The Great Battle

WE NOW COME TO ONE OF THE MOST controversial sections in the entire epistle. If the teaching of predestination were not so strong in chapter 9, then chapter 7 would be the most controversial. What follows from here is Paul's description of the battle that goes on between the spirit and the flesh, between obedience and disobedience. A large portion of Christendom believes that what Paul describes is his own pre-conversion era; in other words, he is describing the struggles he had with sin before his conversion. Not for one minute do I believe that. When the Apostle speaks autobiographically in Romans 7 of the struggle that continues between the flesh and the spirit, he is talking about the struggle that characterizes every Christian's life. This dashes to the dust all false doctrines of sanctification that promise perfection this side of heaven. It debunks the idea of some kind of higher Christian life that only an elite group can experience.

Has then what is good become death to me? Certainly not! (v. 13a). Again, God forbid. **But sin, that it might appear sin, was producing death in me through what is good, so that sin through the commandment might become exceedingly sinful** (v. 13b). Paul cannot get loose from the idea of the weight of our sin, yet we just do not feel it.

I once read an essay by a psychiatrist about a patient with agoraphobia, the fear of going outside. A case in point was Howard Hughes. He lived as a recluse and let his fingernails grow several inches long. He lived out his days as a madman, using antiseptic on his doorknob, forbidding visitors entry to his home for fear that they would bring in germs. Those who have this phobia are afraid of all the dangers that lurk outside. They will not go on a picnic because they might be bitten by a poisonous snake. They will not go to the store or down the street because they might get hit by a car. They will not go visit their children because the airplane might crash. Such people justify their fears by pointing to the newspapers, which contain daily reports of snakebites, fatal automobile accidents, and plane crashes. These things do happen; there are clear and present dangers. In his essay, the psychiatrist wrote that agoraphobics have a neurotic response to real dangers, which moves to the level of psychosis. It happens to those who have lost their capacity to shield themselves from real danger. He explained that a normal human being is aware of dangers, but he sublimates that awareness; normal people are able to function in a world because they deaden their awareness to the perils of life in this world.

That is what happens to us with respect to sin, but the law breaks down the calluses. The law breaks down the normal defense mechanisms we use to deny our guilt. Every time we sin and know that we sin, we try to rationalize it. We do not say, "I sinned." We say, "I made a mistake, a bad choice." We do not acknowledge that we have offended the holiness of God.

Application

When you sin, free yourself from rationalizing it away, even in prayer before God. We often rationalize like this when we repent before others, placing the blame on them, saying things like this: "Forgive me, but if you hadn't acted like that, then I wouldn't have sinned." We need to openly acknowledge our sin to openly approach the throne of grace for forgiveness, and this is true also when we repent to others against whom we've sinned.

5

An Ongoing Struggle

PAUL TAKES IT TO THE NEXT LEVEL: **For we know that the law is spiritual, but I am carnal, sold under sin** (v. 14). This is the biblical basis, the biblical proof-text, for the doctrine of the carnal Christian. The idea of the carnal Christian was invented to deal with the problems inherent with mass evangelism, when many come forward and make a decision for Christ but live just as they were the day before. Rather than attribute this to a false profession of faith, some say, "Oh, they were converted. It just has not taken yet. They are carnal Christians." A true Christian believer, one born again of the Holy Spirit, cannot permanently have self on the throne of his or her life. It is an impossibility, as we noted previously. Defining a carnal Christian as someone still in the flesh altogether is a contradiction in terms. There is no such thing as a carnal Christian by that definition.

Someone I knew who had made a profession of faith in Christ was cohabiting with his girlfriend. The couple was involved with both the use and sale of drugs. He was happy as a clam. His life was not going to change. He believed that he did not need to change so long as he simply believed. He felt safe in the arms of Jesus while living in abject sin.

When we are born again of the Spirit, the carnal disposition of our original nature is not destroyed. We have to fight against it from the day we are converted until the day we enter the gates of heaven. We all have a residual force of the flesh, the *sarx*, and we have to fight against it. In that sense, every Christian is a carnal Christian, but there is no such thing as a completely carnal Christian. The completely carnal are not Christians. On the other hand, there is no such thing as a Christian who is carnal-less, one who is so Spirit-filled that he does not have to struggle with the remnants of his own carnality. Such is the Christian life. Paul does not make all this clear here in his initial affirmation, but the remainder of chapter 7 will make it as clear as it could possibly be.

Application

One of the most surprising experiences of Christians as they grow in grace is a deeper awareness of sin. Sometimes we may even feel defeated, as though growth weren't occurring. But God's transformation is taking place. Often, He starts with the outward, symptomatic expressions of our sin, and then begins working on our heart, on the things that we weren't even able to see to begin with. Take heart when God exposes you to your sin, and bring it to Him with a thankful heart.

6

Perfectionism

I MENTIONED BEFORE THAT ROMANS 7 HAS BEEN the focal point of very serious theological controversy. The focus of that controversy has to do with whether it is possible—and, indeed, important—for the Christian to achieve a state of moral perfection in this life before entering into glory. Several movements throughout church history have taught the idea that in addition to the singular moment of regeneration, there is a second work of grace that effects instant, complete sanctification.

The most important biblical text that speaks against this doctrine of a second work of grace is the text before us now, Romans 7:14–25. The Apostle Paul, writing in the present tense, talks of a painful, ongoing struggle in his life, which is that between walking according to the Spirit and surrendering to the vestigial remnants of the flesh.

The advocates of the perfectionist view have argued that although Paul writes in the present tense, he is not referring to his present situation but is recollecting the state in which he lived before his regeneration. This passage has been worked over by the best Greek interpreters of history. I can say dogmatically that I find absolutely no justification whatsoever for seeing here anything other than the contemporary struggle that the Apostle was having with respect to his own progress in sanctification.

In the nineteenth century, several churches, particularly in America, following some ideas set forth by John Wesley, developed Holiness churches. Contained in their doctrine is the idea of a second work of grace available to all Christians by which they can experience instantaneous holiness. The beginnings of modern Pentecostalism were also tied in with this perfectionist idea. Speaking in tongues was considered to be evidence of this second work of grace. Only in recent times with the advent of neo-Pentecostalism have adjustments been made to that doctrine. Now the thinking is that the baptism of the Holy Spirit empowers Christians for ministry but does not necessarily produce in them an immediate victory over all sin.

The conviction of the Holy Spirit is powerful enough to destroy such illusions and visions of grandeur. The testimony of the greatest saints in history is that the longer they are Christians and the more deeply immersed they become in the Word of God, the more acutely conscious they become of their shortcomings. As we grow in grace, we grow in our understanding of our ongoing need for that grace.

Application

Perfectionism is deadly. Even the Apostle Paul wrote about his painful struggle against sin, and when we look at the disciples who were with Christ, we see that they were never perfect and often failed, even denying Him. Imperfect Apostles such as Peter and Paul can be great encouragements to us in our present struggle. We must rest in the sufficiency of God's grace and trust that it can work in the areas of our lives even if we may feel hopeless.

WEEK 21

1

No Shortcuts

WITHIN THE FIRST FEW MONTHS OF MY CONVERSION, I remember sitting in the local college grill, smoking, and our math professor, a Christian, was sitting across from me. He took a straw and held it as if it were a cigarette and put it to his lips and pretended to inhale and exhale. He said, "Let me tell you about my experiences with the Holy Spirit." Of course, that was his way of rebuking me for my failure to clean up my life as a new Christian. Because of my smoking, I was on the lookout for instant sanctification. I tried everything.

It took twenty-five years from the day I became a Christian till the first time I went twenty-four hours without smoking, and it took another ten years to go a month without smoking, and it was at least another ten years after that to get rid of it altogether. All that time I listened to the accusation of Satan. I struggled with my spiritual state because I had an addiction to the flesh that I simply could not get rid of. I know I am not alone. In a sense, although it should not be the case, it becomes a normal dimension of the Christian life. We all are faced with some besetting sin that we bring before God and seek to get rid of. Sooner or later we have to hear the words, "My grace is sufficient for you" (2 Cor. 12:9).

I can feel the anguish. I do not mean to cheapen that oft-used expression, "I feel your pain," but I can feel the anguish of the Apostle in this text and elsewhere in his letters as he talks about the war that goes on in the soul of the Christian between the spirit and the flesh, between the old man, who does not want to die, and the new man, who is working for inward renewal and maturity in Christ. I cannot tell you why sometimes the Lord allows us to struggle for years before liberation comes, but He does. At every moment, however, the grace is there to overcome, no matter what the sin problem is.

Application

Although smoking might be a matter of Christian liberty, we are also called not to be overcome by even those things in which we have liberty (1 Cor. 6:12). Perhaps a sin that you've struggled with over the years has immediately come to mind. Remember that God's grace is sufficient and go to the Lord, asking for the Spirit's assistance in this area. The truth is that we need the Spirit's work in every part of the Christian life. If you ever hear the accusations of Satan, remember also that "salvation, and strength, and the kingdom of our God, and the power of His Christ have come, for the accuser of our brethren, who accused them before our God day and night, has been cast down" (Rev. 12:10).

2

The Spirit-Filled Life

JOHN WESLEY FIRST SUCCESSFULLY TAUGHT the idea that the Spirit does a work of grace that, while not rendering someone morally perfect, nevertheless enables him to achieve a "perfect love." For Wesley, this was the second work of grace. Out of that has come broad attention to the idea of a higher sanctification that results in two tiers of Christians. First is the ordinary Christian. He seeks spiritual growth by reading his Bible and going to church, and he is diligent about using the means of grace; nevertheless, he never reaches that plateau called the *higher life* or the *deeper life*. The Christian in the second tier has supposedly reached a greater level of victory. At the end of the nineteenth century and into the twentieth in England and the United States, Deeper Life movements were spawned that taught this higher plateau of spiritual victory.

In more recent times, similar movements have advocated what is called the *Spirit-filled life*. Here again are two levels of Christians. First are those regenerated by the power of the Holy Spirit and assisted in their quest for sanctification by the Spirit's help but who have not yet been filled with the Spirit to the level of the second plateau. Advocates of the Spirit-filled life do not claim total perfection but a much greater level of sanctification than that achieved by other Christians.

I once heard a leader in this movement say, "From time to time I will pray a prayer of confession for my sins, if I have any." Time would not allow me to confess all the transgressions I have been guilty of in the last twenty-four hours. If I were to think I could go without sin for an hour, I would have to pull God down or raise myself up. The Apostle Paul tells us that the law is spiritual, and when we look at ourselves through the lens of the law, we do not have to look very far or very long to find out that there is no *if* about the abiding sins that mar our lives.

Application

The reality of our sin is ever humbling, but humility before God and honesty about our sin is exactly what we need. Taking spiritual stock of our sin helps us know where we particularly need God's grace in our lives. Don't be afraid to acknowledge your sin and bring it before God in repentance, for "if we confess our sins, He is faithful and just to forgive us our sins and to cleanse us from all unrighteousness" (1 John 1:9).

3

Duality

IN CHRISTIAN CIRCLES IS ALSO A VIEW of anthropology called *trichotomy*, which teaches that we are made up of a triune nature—body, soul, and spirit. We see such wording in Paul's Thessalonican bene-diction: "Now may the God of peace Himself sanctify you completely; and may your whole spirit, soul, and body be preserved blameless at the coming of our Lord Jesus Christ" (1 Thess. 5:23). Elsewhere Paul talks about the bowels, the mind, the heart, and at least three or four other elements of the constituent makeup of man without setting forth an actual anthropology. Trichotomy holds that ordi-nary Christians have the Holy Spirit in body and soul but not yet in spirit. Average Christians are two-thirds of the way along in Chris-tian growth, but if they want the higher, Spirit-filled life, then the Spirit of God has to affect them not only in body and soul but also in spirit. Throughout church history, trichotomy has always carried some other heresy in its wake.

The Bible makes the clear distinction between the physical and nonphysical aspects of our humanity; according to Scripture, we are composed of body and soul. Only the Holy Spirit can distinguish between mind, soul, spirit, will, and the other designations we make. Fundamentally, Scripture sees us as a duality; we have a physical aspect and a nonphysical aspect. We are body and soul. Nowhere in Scripture do we find the idea that the Spirit will get to two of the three but not to the other.

That is but a brief theological preface to what Paul is setting forth here in Romans 7. In my estimation, the most acute and comprehensive refutation, both theologically and biblically, of all types of perfec-tionism was penned by the late great Princeton theologian Benjamin Breckinridge Warfield. He wrote a volume titled *Perfectionism*, which will prove helpful to anyone wanting to look more deeply at the Holi-ness movement or the Deeper Life movements I mentioned.

Application
God made us body and soul, and God saves us body and soul. When God saves, He saves all of us—that is, body and soul. The fact that God

saves us body and soul teaches us that fundamentally we are His. This ought to lead us to glorify God in our bodies and flee from all manner of sin, particularly sexual sin. Paul teaches in 1 Corinthians that "your body is the temple of the Holy Spirit who is in you" and that "you are not your own[,] for you were bought at a price" (6:19–20).

4

Perplexity and Progress

FOR WHAT I AM DOING, I DO NOT UNDERSTAND (v. 15a). Paul expresses some confusion. He is perplexed, but not by some abstract theological mystery. He is perplexed by his own behavior. *I don't understand myself. I just don't know why I do the things that I do.* He goes on to describe a conflict that is rooted in the will: **For what I will to do, that I do not practice; but what I hate, that I do** (v. 15b). Paul is not engaging in a philosophical discussion of how the will functions; he is speaking in concrete language that we can all relate to.

We would all like to lead a life of perfect obedience to Christ, but we do not because there is conflict in our hearts between our general desire for obedience and the specific acts of obedience that confront us. There is also the strength of the temptation toward disobedience. That is why we cry, "The spirit is willing, but the flesh is weak." We are people of mixed desires, which is why life does not really become complicated until we are born again. Before we were born again, we had only one principle—the flesh. We walked willingly and happily submitting to the temptations of Satan. Once the Holy Spirit has raised us from spiritual death, our lives become a battle between two jockeys, to use Augustine's analogy. Satan does not give up easily. The flesh does not die instantly. Life becomes complicated because we are involved in a war that penetrates the very deepest recesses of our souls and lasts until our glorification in heaven. This is the universal experience among Christians, and it is what the Apostle Paul is talking about.

We could stop right there and say, "Why not just eat, drink, and be merry, and not be so earnest about sanctification, since we cannot reach the goal anyway?" We must remember that elsewhere Paul wrote, "Forgetting those things which are behind and reaching forward to those things which are ahead, I press toward the goal for the prize of the upward call of God in Christ Jesus" (Phil. 3:13–14). We pummel our body to subdue it. We enter into and engage in a fight, and we are admonished by the Scriptures not to yield so easily to the sin that besets us, for we have not yet resisted to the point of shedding our blood (Heb. 12:4). The very fact that we read books like this one indicates that we take our Christian life seriously. We want to dig deeper into the Scriptures because we know that through the teaching of the truth of God's Word, we will be helped in the struggle. We make use of the means of God's grace to progress in our sanctification. The fact that no one makes it to the finish line in this lifetime does not mean that we are supposed to stop running. We are never allowed to be at ease in Zion and say, "This far I have progressed and no farther." We are to be diligent in every way to feed the new man and kill the old man.

Application

A sobering truth is that we likely don't acknowledge all the ways that we struggle with sin. There are sins of omission and commission, sins that we commit because we do not do what's right and sins that we commit because we do what's wrong. We likely get vexed about our sins of commission and fail to see our missed opportunities in serving others. Be mindful of sins of omission, too, that we might glorify God more greatly in obedient acts of justice and mercy.

5

The Danger of Victory

AS WE PROGRESS THROUGH OUR STUDY OF ROMANS, I hope to provide some very practical suggestions on how to increase our sanctification. I am not going to give secrets for a spiritual life, because I do not believe in those. But I do believe that one Christian will progress further than another, not because there are two distinct levels of Christian living—Spirit-filled and non-Spirit-filled—but because each of us is at a different place in our Christian pilgrimage. Many have never struggled to quit smoking, as I did, but they have struggled with something else. We come with different baggage, and therefore our progress in sanctification is different.

One of the worst sins we can commit is that of establishing our achievements as the norm by which all Christians are to be judged; however, doing so is tempting. If we have success or victory in an area of life, our tendency is to elevate it as the test of true spirituality so that we find ourselves thinking critically of those who do not measure up in that regard.

I struggled with that for many years. From the day I was born again, I had a hunger and thirst for the Scriptures. Nobody had to twist my arm and say, "You have to set aside time every day to read the Bible." I cannot remember a time that I picked up the Bible from a sense of duty, but I used to wonder about my Christian friends. *I never see them reading the Scriptures. What is the matter with them?* In keeping with my vocation, God had planted a desire in my heart that made it easier to do that particular thing. Even so, I have wasted more time not studying the Scriptures than others not so called.

If we are gifted with evangelism, we want to establish evangelism as the supreme gift. If gifted in teaching, we see it as the most important gift. If gifted with generosity, then giving becomes the real touchstone of spirituality. That is why Paul had to write to the Corinthians and explain that believers have different gifts. Part of our growth as Christians is to develop an understanding that things of little difficulty to us may be very difficult for other people, and that things we struggle with may never cause others to struggle. We are in this together—sharing in the Spirit and the Word, encouraging and praying for one another, and covering one another with charity.

Application

As God's people, we are called to manifest love, a charity that covers a multitude of sins. This certainly does not mean that we are to be soft on gross and heinous sin. The New Testament makes clear that we are not to give each other license for sin, but the average, run-of-the-mill, everyday struggles that all Christians have are to be covered by charity. We are to be forbearing and patient and encouraging toward one another.

6

Views of the World

WE ARE ALWAYS SUSCEPTIBLE AS CHRISTIANS to ideas that are quite contrary to the truth of God. They tend to slip in unnoticed. We do not plan to embrace pagan notions, which are incompatible with the truth of God, but it has been said that if a lie is repeated often enough, people begin to believe it. Such information sneaks into the crevices of our brains, and we are unaware of it, particularly during childhood. We are taught that certain truths are self-evident and well attested by contemporary science and that to question them is to risk the charge of being insane.

One such idea is what we call a *mechanistic* view of the universe. Although somewhat passé in contemporary paradigms of natural science, it is nevertheless still pervasive at the common level. This view holds that the universe works like a machine and functions according to fixed laws within nature. From infancy we have been told that the universe operates according to the laws of nature, and these laws are presented as if they are immutable, fixed, autonomous powers. Such thinking is on a collision course with everything the Scriptures teach us about the nature of God, which is that the world is His creation and He rules it. He governs the motion of every atom and subatomic particle in the universe, not as an absentee landlord or a cosmic spectator but through His providence. Gravity cannot function for a second apart from God's providential rule and permission. What we call the *laws of nature* are merely descriptive terms for how God ordinarily governs His creation, but we are seeing now a declaration of independence from the sovereign providence of God; the assumption is that the universe operates itself.

The idea of an independent, autonomous universe is the second most pervasive pagan idea that creeps into our thinking. Overwhelmingly, the most widespread pervasive pagan idea is the humanistic, secular view of the human will, which is far removed from the biblical view. So deeply entrenched is this pagan notion that when we preach the sovereignty of God in His ministry of redemption, people immediately protest, often vociferously, that it violates the free will of man. When we begin to probe what is meant by the *free will of man*, usually expounded is the widespread, pagan understanding of the will.

Application

God is good. He rules over every facet of creation and providentially provides for all His creatures. Jesus teaches us this principle when He calls us not to be anxious about seeking the kingdom first, for just as God provides for the birds of the air and adorns the flowers of the field,

He will certainly care for us as His children (Luke 12:22–34). Here, the doctrine of God's sovereign providence gives us great confidence to pursue His glory in advancing Christ's kingdom as our highest priority in life.

WEEK 22

1

The Will in Conflict

FOR THE GOOD THAT I WILL TO DO, **I do not do; but the evil I will not to do, that I practice** (v. 19). Paul is describing a conflict between rival goods. The most difficult decisions are not just those between good and evil but those between two goods. Such decisions can paralyze us. The desire to be perfectly obedient Christians is an inclination in our wills. The new man in our heart has the desire to please God, but there still lives in our members the vestigial remnants of the old man of the flesh, which has declared war on the leanings of the spirit. When the conflict comes, many times we would rather follow the old man than the new man. In the moment, it is more desirable to sin than to obey Christ. Part of us wants to obey Christ, but not all. We have evil inclinations and desires that bump up against our good intentions.

Once we understand how the will functions and that we are involved in the conflict that the Apostle sets forth in Romans 7, we can discover the way out—the means of grace. The means of grace are the instruments God gives to help us overcome the weaknesses of the flesh. Since we will always choose what we are most inclined to choose at the moment of decision, we can make use of the means of grace by programming ourselves with worship, prayer, and Scripture so that our desires become sanctified.

If we know how much God hates our sin, and if we have affection for Him, we will not want to displease Him by sinning. We are, however, constantly bombarded with opposing ideas. The Scriptures set before us what God delights in; we read it and say, "I want my life to be like that," but the rest of the week we hear voices from every side that lead us to lose sight of what is pleasing to God. As we take in what is pleasing to our friends and to the culture, our delight in God begins to lose its passion. We have to have the doctrine of justification by faith in our bloodstream, because there is enough continuing sin in our lives to remind us that without the righteousness of Christ, we have no hope whatsoever.

In our fallen condition, we have no disposition toward Christ, which is why Jesus said, "No one can come to Me unless the Father who sent Me draws him" (John 6:44a). We are in jail without bail, in bondage to sin. Augustine understood that, and so did Martin Luther, John Calvin, Jonathan Edwards, and Charles Spurgeon. Unless the Holy Spirit changes the disposition of our hearts through regeneration, we will never be inclined to come to Jesus.

If we have come to Christ, we have done so because we wanted to. We were inclined to, but not by nature. We were inclined to Christ by super-nature. God reached down and with His grace changed our desire. He changed our hearts from stone to hearts that beat with affection for Him and set us free.

Application

Have you ever thought about worship as your greatest means for victory in the Christian life? The Spirit of God is ultimately the One who sanctifies us, but we can avail ourselves of the ordinary means of grace. The Spirit moves as He wills, but we know that He ordinarily uses the Word.

Worship is the one place where we hear it read, prayed, and proclaimed, even seeing it visibly in the sacraments.

2

Indwelling Sin

PAUL HAS BEEN EXPLAINING HIS ONGOING STRUGGLE between his spirit and his flesh. He desires to be obedient to Christ, yet that desire often gives way to failure, and he continues to struggle with the sinful inclinations of his heart. We looked at the struggle exegetically and expositionally, and then we looked at it theologically and philosophically.

The things that Paul wants to do are the things that he does not do, and the things that he does not want to do are the very things that he does (7:19). **Now if I do what I will not to do, it is no longer I who do it, but sin that dwells in me** (v. 20). Paul is not trying to absolve himself from responsibility for his sin. His point is that he does what he does not want to do because of sin. He recognizes where that sin dwells—within him. Even though he is involved in this conflict, the new man is still what defines his personality. Despite the ongoing struggle and the failures of sin that mark his Christian life, Paul knows that he is a new creature. What God has done with him can be seen not in the remnants of his old man but in the triumph that God gives him through His Holy Spirit in the new man.

Earlier on, Paul said that we are to consider the old man dead; he has been crucified with Christ (6:11). Therefore, Paul says, he is not going to relate to the old man anymore. The real Paul, the Paul who has been redeemed from bondage to sin, is the Paul who is destined for glorification.

Regeneration accomplishes our rescue and release from the total bondage of sin that marks our fallen condition, the inherent corruption with which we are born that causes us to walk according to the course of the world and according to the prince of the power of the air (Eph. 2:2). When we are born of the Spirit, that bondage is broken. We are set free. We experience a liberty that man has not had since the fall, but even with the renewal by which we are dramatically changed inside, that change does not instantaneously eradicate all the impulses of sin. As we have seen repeatedly now, that struggle goes on until heaven. Paul says that although sin still dwells in him, that indwelling sin lacks the same captivating power that it had before his conversion.

Application

We might not always feel like it, but we are not waging a losing battle against sin. That is because, in Christ, the battle has already been won, and the Spirit is at work in us. God promises to bring His good work to completion in you (Phil. 1:6). Wage your war against sin in humble dependence on the Spirit, but also be confident that the Spirit is at work in you. This way, you can guard yourself from feeling defeated.

3

Delighting in God's Law

I FIND THEN A LAW, **that evil is present with me, the one who wills to do good** (v. 21). Paul is not talking about the Mosaic law or even about the moral law. He has discovered a fundamental truth that describes his current situation. His phrasing is a bit awkward, but we can still see the principle. He then identifies himself not with the one who wills to do evil but with the one who wants to do right: **For I delight in the law of God according to the inward man** (v. 22). If there is any question whether Paul is talking about his pre-conversion state or his ongoing struggle after his regeneration, this one text should put that to rest forever, because no unregenerate person delights in the law of God in the inward person. Psalm 1 makes sharp distinctions between the godly man and the ungodly man:

> Blessed is the man
>> Who walks not in the counsel of the ungodly,
>> Nor stands in the path of sinners,
>> Nor sits in the seat of the scornful;
> But his delight is in the law of the LORD,
>> And in His law he meditates day and night.
> He shall be like a tree
>> Planted by the rivers of water,
>> That brings forth its fruit in its season,
>> Whose leaf also shall not wither;
> And whatever he does shall prosper.
>
> The ungodly are not so,
> But are like the chaff which the wind drives away.
> Therefore the ungodly shall not stand in the judgment,
> Nor sinners in the congregation of the righteous.
>
> For the LORD knows the way of the righteous,
> But the way of the ungodly shall perish.

The godly man delights in the law of God and is therefore like a tree planted by the rivers of water, bringing forth its fruit in season. In contrast, the ungodly man is weightless, without substance, like the chaff that the wind drives away. In that portrait of the godly man, we see that his godliness is defined by his delight. The godly man is the one who delights in the law of the Lord and meditates on it day and night, which is how Paul is describing his condition. Paul uses a set of words that jump right off the page. He talks about the new man, the old man, the inward man, the outer man, the sinful man, and the spiritually inclined man. This language describes the difference between pre-conversion and post-conversion humanity.

Application

If you delight in the law of God, take comfort that your struggle with sin indicates that you, like Paul, have changed desires. Take a moment to pray to God and praise Him for changing you, but also give voice to your desire for the day when you will sin no more. Ask God for more of that future reality of glorification even now, that you may desire it even more strongly.

4

Body and Flesh, Part 1

IN THESE LAST FEW VERSES OF CHAPTER 7, I want to look closely at the ongoing war that the Apostle describes between the mind and the flesh. **I see another law in my members, warring against the law of my mind, and bringing me into captivity to the law of sin which is in my members. O wretched man that I am! Who will deliver me from this body of death? I thank God—through Jesus Christ our Lord! So then, with the mind I myself serve the law of God, but with the flesh the law of sin** (vv. 23–25). If we look closely at the text, we will see again two distinct Greek words. One, *sōma*, is translated by the English word *body*. We find it in the English word *psychosomatic*. The second Greek word, *sarx*, is translated *flesh*. In Latin the words are translated in the first instance by the word *corporeal*, from which we get *corporal*, and in the second instance by a word from which we get the English word *carnal*. So we have *corporal* and *carnal*, *sōma* and *sarx*, *body* and *flesh*.

This distinction between body and flesh has caused no small amount of confusion. Part of the confusion is linguistic, and part is philosophical or theological. The term *sarx* is used repeatedly in the New Testament, particularly by the Apostle Paul, to refer not to our physical nature but to our fallen nature. The *sarkical* nature is that which is controlled by original sin. The *sarx* describes the old man, the one that has no inclination toward the things of God and is a slave to sin, dead in sin and trespasses. That condition of radical corruption Paul describes by the term *sarx*. When Paul uses the term *sōma*, he is almost always describing the physical aspect of our humanity. Paul also uses the term *sarx* from time to time to refer to our physical humanity (see 2 Cor. 5:16). Therein lies the linguistic problem. Not every time the word *sarx* appears in the Bible does it refer to sinful corruption, nor does the word *sōma* always refer to the physical.

There is a linguistic key that helps us over the hurdle. Almost any-time we see in the New Testament a contrast between spirit and flesh or mind and flesh, the term *sarx* is being used to describe not the phys-ical body but the corrupt nature of the whole person. The corruption of *sarx* is not just a sinful corruption of physical appetites. Every part of an unregenerate person is in a state of flesh. By nature we have a mind of flesh, a soul of flesh, and a spirit of flesh, but anytime we see Paul contrasting flesh with spirit or flesh with mind, he is talking about the distinction between the old man, the flesh, and the new man, the inner man, which has been made alive by the Holy Spirit.

Application

We must always look for deliverance to our Lord Jesus Christ. While we do work with God for our sanctification in a way that we do not for our justification, we must always look to Christ, for just as our justification is because of His work, our sanctification is ultimately His work through the Spirit along with ours. Strive for holiness, first by never taking your eyes off Him.

5

Body and Flesh, Part 2

THERE IS ALSO A THEOLOGICAL PROBLEM when it comes to distinguishing between the meanings of *sōma* and *sarx*, which is the influence of ancient Hellenistic philosophy and oriental dualism into early Christian thinking. Plato saw the highest dimension of human experience as being in the mind, and he saw the flesh, the body, as the prison house of the soul. Plato said that the physical aspect of our humanity blocks the mind's ability to penetrate ultimate truth, but the mind, or the soul, is eternal and free and in touch with ultimate reality. The obstruction to a vision of truth is found in the body, and therefore the body is something from which we need to be redeemed.

Plato put forth that anything physical is at best an imperfect copy of the ultimate idea. His view of the body is quite different from the biblical view, which puts forth salvation *of* the body. The Greeks believed in salvation *from* the body. The physical came to be seen as inherently imperfect or evil. Plato's view heavily penetrated the thinking of the early Christian fathers, who began to teach that the way to salvation is through denying the body all physical pleasure. Food, drink, sex—anything that involved the body—was considered inherently evil, and the method of gaining sanctification was subduing bodily appetites.

We know that physical appetites can be the occasion for human sin, but not because the physical is inherently evil. It was God who made our bodies, and when He made them He pronounced His benediction upon them, calling them good. It was God who made marriage and the means of sexual procreation, which also received His benediction, but from the days of the early church down through the centuries, the idea has persisted that the kingdom of God is in eating and drinking; it has to do with physical appetites. The misuse of physical appetites is an occasion for sin, but we radically oversimplify when we claim that the struggle that Paul is talking about here is the struggle between the mind and the body. It is between the *sarx* and the *pneuma*, the flesh and the spirit. It is between the old man and the new man, between a fallen, corrupt nature and the renewed inner person.

Application

Our bodies are not inherently sinful. Not only did God make us body and soul, but we will exist body and soul eternally in the new heavens and new earth. When Christ redeems us, He redeems all of us. This is the power of the resurrection and why Paul looks forward to it to be delivered "from this body of death" (v. 24). When you wrestle with besetting sins that particularly relate to the body, do not hesitate to cry out like Paul in assurance that, despite the wretchedness of sin, you have a Deliverer in Christ.

6

Amazing Grace

"O WRETCHED MAN THAT I AM!" (v. 24a). Here we have an exclamation that declares a condition of misery. Paul cries out in anguish after just relating his ongoing struggle with the weighty burden of sin pressing against the inclinations he has toward obedience. Paul uses language that is as politically incorrect as language can be in the contemporary church. In today's church, we have become so narcissistic, so preoccupied with self-esteem and self-worth, that preachers must be careful never to engender feelings of guilt or worthlessness in people.

There is a sense in which we can so wallow in our guilt and be so preoccupied with our failure that we almost take delight in it, like some form of masochism, but that is not the real problem we face in the church today. The problem we face is a denial of the radical character of sin. We do not hate sin the way we should. We do not abhor the disobedience that we manifest in our lives.

Because Paul was a new man, he was able to say, "I delight in the law of God according to the inward man" (v. 22). The sin that indwelt him was not his identity, in the final analysis. "O wretched man that I am!" He is expressing an Apostolic state of misery. The Latin text sheds some light on this. It speaks of being in a state of infelicity, a state without happiness or blessedness. When Paul looked at his sin, he saw his wretchedness, and he was threatened and overwhelmed by the power of this misery. He could see nothing in himself in which to put his delight.

"Who will deliver me from this body of death?" (v. 24b). He knows in whom he has believed, and he knows who his Deliverer is: "I thank God—through Jesus Christ our Lord!" (v. 25c). Who will deliver us? God. How will He deliver us? Through Jesus Christ our Lord. We have a Redeemer. We have a Deliverer who promises to deliver us fully and finally from the body of death, from this awful, substantive burden that plagues us all our lives.

After pouring out his heart, Paul concludes this section by saying that if we have problems walking in the Christian life, inconsistencies in our pilgrimage, we can look at him. He has the same problems. No triumphalism flows from the pen of the Apostle. He was keenly in touch with who he was in his fallen condition, but he was also keenly in touch with who he was in Christ Jesus, who had rescued him from the principle that resides in the flesh.

Application

When we sing "Amazing Grace," we sing "Amazing grace!—how sweet the sound—that saved a *wretch* like me!" Whenever we sin, we ought to reflect on whether it brought about the power or pleasure it promised. Paul teaches that it actually never brings about a state of happiness or blessedness. Be quick to acknowledge this in repentance when you sin, that you might fully savor the extent of God's amazing grace toward you.

Romans 8

THERE IS THEREFORE NOW NO CONDEMNATION *to those who are in Christ Jesus, who do not walk according to the flesh, but according to the Spirit. For the law of the Spirit of life in Christ Jesus has made me free from the law of sin and death. For what the law could not do in that it was weak through the flesh, God did by sending His own Son in the likeness of sinful flesh, on account of sin: He condemned sin in the flesh, that the righteous requirement of the law might be fulfilled in us who do not walk according to the flesh but according to the Spirit. For those who live according to the flesh set their minds on the things of the flesh, but those who live according to the Spirit, the things of the Spirit. For to be carnally minded is death, but to be spiritually minded is life and peace. Because the carnal mind is enmity against God; for it is not subject to the law of God, nor indeed can be. So then, those who are in the flesh cannot please God.*

But you are not in the flesh but in the Spirit, if indeed the Spirit of God dwells in you. Now if anyone does not have the Spirit of Christ, he is not His. And if Christ is in you, the body is dead because of sin, but the Spirit is life because of righteousness. But if the Spirit of Him who raised Jesus from the dead dwells in you, He who raised Christ from the dead will also give life to your mortal bodies through His Spirit who dwells in you.

Therefore, brethren, we are debtors—not to the flesh, to live according to the flesh. For if you live according to the flesh you will die; but if by the Spirit you put to death the deeds of the body, you will live. For as many as are led by the Spirit of God, these are sons of God. For you did not receive the spirit of bondage again to fear, but you received the Spirit of adoption by whom we cry out, "Abba, Father." The Spirit Himself bears witness with our spirit that we are children of God, and if children, then heirs—heirs of God and joint heirs with Christ, if indeed we suffer with Him, that we may also be glorified together.

For I consider that the sufferings of this present time are not worthy to be compared with the glory which shall be revealed in us. For the earnest expectation of the creation eagerly waits for the revealing of the sons of God. For the creation was subjected to futility, not willingly, but because of Him who subjected it in hope; because the creation itself also will be delivered from the bondage of corruption into the glorious liberty of the children of God. For we know that the whole creation groans and labors with birth pangs together until now. Not only that, but we also who have the firstfruits of the Spirit, even we ourselves groan within ourselves, eagerly waiting for the adoption, the redemption of our body. For we were saved in this hope, but hope that is seen is not hope; for why does one still hope for what he sees? But if we hope for what we do not see, we eagerly wait for it with perseverance.

Likewise the Spirit also helps in our weaknesses. For we do not know what we should pray for as we ought, but the Spirit Himself makes intercession for us with groanings which cannot be uttered. Now He who searches the hearts knows what the mind of the Spirit is, because He makes intercession for the saints according to the will of God.

And we know that all things work together for good to those who love God, to those who are the called according to His purpose. For whom He foreknew, He also predestined to be conformed to the image of His Son, that He might be the firstborn among many brethren. Moreover whom He predestined, these He also called; whom He called, these He also justified; and whom He justified, these He also glorified.

What then shall we say to these things? If God is for us, who can be against us? He who did not spare His own Son, but delivered Him up for us all, how shall He not with Him also freely give us all things? Who shall bring a charge against God's elect? It is God who justifies. Who is he who condemns? It is Christ who died, and furthermore is also risen, who is even at the right hand of God, who also makes intercession for us. Who shall separate us from the love of Christ? Shall tribulation, or distress, or persecution, or famine, or nakedness, or peril, or sword? As it is written:

> *"For Your sake we are killed all day long;*
> *We are accounted as sheep for the slaughter."*

Yet in all these things we are more than conquerors through Him who loved us. For I am persuaded that neither death nor life, nor angels nor principalities nor powers, nor things present nor things to come, nor height nor depth, nor any other created thing, shall be able to separate us from the love of God which is in Christ Jesus our Lord.

WEEK 23

1

No Condemnation

CHAPTER 8 IS INSEPARABLY LINKED TO WHAT has just been articulated. We know this because it begins with the word *therefore*, which signifies a conclusion from what has come before: **There is therefore now no condemnation** (8:1a). When Paul uses "therefore now," he is referring not just to the last section but to everything he has laid out up to this point. He calls attention to everything he has set forth about the redemption that is ours in Jesus Christ and concludes that there is no condemnation. He does not mean that God will never judge the world but rather that there is an end of condemnation specifically and particularly to a designated group.

If we are Christians, not only is there no condemnation for the sins we have committed, but also we have moved beyond condemnation for whatever we are going to do tomorrow or the day after tomorrow or the day after that. This is one of the most beautiful texts in Scripture for the assurance of salvation. The threat of condemnation is removed forever if we are in Christ Jesus. It is unthinkable that after the cross, God will visit more wrath upon His Son. He drank the cup of the condemnation of the Father for His sheep forever. There is no condemnation left anymore for His Son, and if we are in the Son, we are in the cleft of the rock. We are in the shelter of the Rock of Ages. We are covered and hidden, safe now and forevermore.

Only Paul's words can take us from the wretched misery of the ongoing struggle and failure with temptation and sin to the glorious conclusion that, despite the struggle, we have passed beyond the threat of death and judgment. There is no condemnation left for us. Even though we still stumble, our lives are described as those **who do not walk according to the flesh, but according to the Spirit** (v. 1b). We are not enslaved by the flesh anymore. Who will rescue us from this body of death? God will, through Jesus Christ our Lord.

Application

Remember the *therefores* in your life. If you have been born again through faith in Jesus Christ, all the *therefores* of the Christian life are yours. As it relates especially to Paul's thought in Romans 6–8, being born again in Christ, you therefore are dead to sin and alive to righteousness, are being delivered from the body of death, and are free from all present or future condemnation to walk in the new life of the Spirit. Rejoice!

2

"Neither Do I Condemn You"

JOHN TELLS A STORY OF A WOMAN caught in adultery:

> But Jesus went to the Mount of Olives.
>
> Now early in the morning He came again into the temple, and all the people came to Him; and He sat down and taught them. Then the scribes and Pharisees brought to Him a woman caught in adultery. And when they had set her in the midst, they said to Him, "Teacher, this woman was caught in adultery, in the very act. Now Moses, in the law, commanded us that such should be stoned. But what do You say?" This they said, testing Him, that they might have something of which to accuse Him. But Jesus stooped down and wrote on the ground with His finger, as though He did not hear.

So when they continued asking Him, He raised Himself up and said to them, "He who is without sin among you, let him throw a stone at her first." And again He stooped down and wrote on the ground. Then those who heard it, being convicted by their conscience, went out one by one, beginning with the oldest even to the last. And Jesus was left alone, and the woman standing in the midst. When Jesus had raised Himself up and saw no one but the woman, He said to her, "Woman, where are those accusers of yours? Has no one condemned you?"

She said, "No one, Lord."

And Jesus said to her, "Neither do I condemn you; go and sin no more." (John 8:1–11)

She was dragged in her shame by the Pharisees to the feet of Jesus. In the midst of her public humiliation, the Pharisees began to test Jesus to see whether He would fully enforce the Law of Moses, which required the death penalty. Jesus knelt down in the sand and began to write. This is the only record we have of Jesus' writing anything. We do not know what He wrote, but we can guess. Maybe He wrote in the sand *embezzler* while He looked at one of the men, who then dropped his stone and walked away. One by one the accusers dropped their stones and walked away, leaving Jesus alone with the woman. Was there anybody in that group without sin? Jesus was without sin, so He had every right to pick up a stone and execute her, but He did not have a stone in His hand. He looked at her and gave her the most comforting words that the woman had ever heard in her life and was ever to hear again: "Neither do I condemn you; go and sin no more" (v. 11).

How much would it mean if Jesus looked at us and spoke those words? "From this day forward I will not condemn you; you never have to fear condemnation from Me. The world may condemn you—even the church might condemn you—but if you are in Me, you are safe."

Application

Jesus teaches us in the Sermon on the Mount not to be quick in judging others for their sins when we haven't acknowledged and addressed our own sins (see Matt. 7:1–5). After pronouncing the woman who was caught in adultery free of condemnation, Jesus also called her to "sin no more." Let us not magnify the sins of others without searching ourselves, but just as we call ourselves to repentance, let us graciously do so with others.

3

Who Is Safe?

WE LIVE AT A TIME WHEN PEOPLE LOOK ASKANCE at any idea of a wrathful God. People believe that there is no room for damnation whatsoever, but damnation is certain to come. The Greek translated in English as *condemnation* is translated in Latin as *damnationus*, from which we get the word *damnation*. Therefore, we could render the text this way: "There is therefore now no damnation for those who are in Christ Jesus." At the end of that clause is a comma, and what follows the comma might raise in our minds a question, at least for a moment. There's no condemnation (damnation) to those who are in Christ Jesus, "who do not walk according to the flesh, but according to the Spirit" (v. 1b). Concerning the punctuation, the terms could be restrictive. In other words, Paul could be saying that condemnation has been removed from all Christians who are not "carnal Christians," a false teaching that we examined earlier. The idea, then, would be that condemnation has been removed from the Spirit-filled Christian but not from the carnal Christian. The carnal Christian, even though he is in Christ, is still exposed to the threat of condemnation. That is not what the Apostle is teaching. He is saying that there is no condemnation to those who are in Christ Jesus because those who are in Christ Jesus do not walk according to the flesh but according to the Spirit.

For the law of the Spirit of life in Christ Jesus has made me free from the law of sin and death (v. 2). Here again is a confusing use of the term *law*. Sometimes in the epistle, Paul uses the term *law* to mean "principle"; other times, he uses the term to refer to the moral standards by which God judges us. Here, the first instance of the word *law* refers to principle and the second instance refers to moral standards. The principle of life in Jesus Christ is what makes us free from the principle of sin and death. When we are not in Christ, we operate by the principle of sin. Outside Christ, sin defines our existence, and the natural consequence of that sin is death.

Application

Focus your heart and prayers today on the reality that you have been set free from all condemnation in Christ. Your freedom, though it was not purchased by you, came at an infinite price, the death of the Lord Jesus Christ, and in God's abundant grace, He even lavished you with the Holy Spirit to walk in a manner pleasing to Him. Thank the Lord for so great a salvation.

4

The Impotency of the Law

PAUL SWITCHES HIS MEANING OF THE WORD *LAW*: **For what the law could not do in that it was weak through the flesh, God did by sending His own Son in the likeness of sinful flesh, on account of sin** (v. 3a). Paul is speaking of the impotency of the moral law, its failure, at a certain place and point. The law does not save because it cannot save, which is what Paul has been arguing throughout the letter. The Holy

Spirit knows how weak we are in our grasp of the gospel, and like dogs that keep returning to their vomit, we keep falling back to the idea that somehow we can justify ourselves by our behavior, good deeds, and morality. Paul has come at this from every angle to get rid of that idea and to brush off the spot where that idea once stood, reiterating that the law cannot do it.

The law is impotent. Not only does the law not save us, but it cannot. It does not have the power. Paul is not being critical of the law. This weakness is not the law's fault. The law cannot redeem us because it is incapable of redeeming those in the flesh. People in the flesh are incapable of obeying the law, so when they look to the law as a means of salvation, they exercise futility and reach for an impossible dream. "For what the law could not do [see the contrast here] . . . , God did." There in a nutshell is the gospel. What our morality can never achieve, God can achieve. What our behavior and performance are incapable of attaining, God can attain for us. That is the gospel. We cannot; He can. It is that simple.

God did it by sending His own Son in the likeness of sinful flesh, on account of sin. What the law could not do, God could do, and He did it by sending His Son. Later in this chapter, Paul is going to talk about a different kind of sonship, that which comes by adoption. He introduces the concept of sonship here, but it pertains to God's only begotten Son, the *monogenēs*. What the law could not do is to give us Christ; God gives us Christ. Paul does not say that God did it by sending His Son in the *sarx*, in the condition of corruption, as a sinner to replace us. Notice how careful Paul is to say that God sent "His own Son in the *likeness* of sinful flesh," not in the *identity* of sinful flesh. Jesus Christ is like us, the author of Hebrews tells us, in all respects except one—He is without sin (Heb. 4:15). In the incarnation, all that is proper to humanity was given to the human nature of our Redeemer except for sin, because sin was not part of human nature as originally created. Jesus was born without original sin. Jesus was born as Adam was before the fall. Jesus was not in bondage to a corrupt nature. Christ came in the flesh as a human being, and He condemned the sin that binds us by taking it upon Himself.

Application

Jesus has accomplished what was impossible for the law to do and what was impossible for us to accomplish by the law. The law was never meant to be a means of attaining our salvation, and even if it were, we would not ever be able to attain salvation on account of our fallen natures and sin. But having been given new natures by the Spirit, we look to the moral law to know what is pleasing to God. Take a moment and read the section of Exodus 20 or Deuteronomy 5 that contains the Ten Commandments to meditate on God's law.

5

Sin Condemned

HE CONDEMNED SIN IN THE FLESH, **that the righteous requirement of the law might be fulfilled in us who do not walk according to the flesh but according to the Spirit** (vv. 3b–4). Here Paul is describing the cross, the work of Christ in expiation. When Christ went to the cross in our place, sin was condemned. The cup that He wrestled with at Gethsemane was filled with the wrath of God—wrath that was directed against sin—and Jesus drank it. He accepted to Himself the imputation of my sin and your sin. When He went to the cross, the last thing He worried about was the punitive treatment at the hands of the Romans. He went to the cross to receive the punishment for sin by the Father in order to remove our sins.

In justification God pronounces us just in Jesus Christ, and with that pronouncement He removes our sin. He takes our sin away and puts it in the sea of forgetfulness. As far as the east is from the west, He removes our transgressions from us. God does this; the law cannot. The law exposes and defines our sin and imposes the burden of the curse upon it. But the law can never remove it from us. There is no earthly power to make us clean. The blot is indelible. Only God can remove our sin, which is what the gospel is. In His Son there is no condemnation for His people. There is condemnation for their sin, but it is condemned in Christ and removed. God has taken it out of the books and transferred to us the righteousness of His Son. Our only hope is the righteousness of Christ. If that righteousness is taken away from us, all we are left with is our own. If that happens, not only can condemnation reach us, but it most certainly will. We must be willing to shed our blood if necessary for the sake of the gospel.

Application

Fidelity to the gospel is a life-or-death matter. Let us thank God this day for the faithfulness of the martyrs of the early church who were willing even to die for the sake of the gospel. Let us also give thanks to God for the many who put their lives on the line to see its light shine in the darkest places on earth. May we do all that we can to learn the gospel well, that we may proclaim it with passion. We are all called to live for it and to be willing to die for it if that proves necessary.

6

The Carnal Mindset

PAUL CONTINUES TO SET FORTH THE contrast between life in the flesh and life in the Spirit, between the old man and the new man, giving us more characteristics of each state. **For those who live according to the flesh set their minds on the things of the flesh** (v. 5a). The unregenerate person is described by a mindset. If we question whether we are in the kingdom of God, the first place to look is our mindset. What is the focus of our life? What do we think about all the time? Are we preoccupied with goals and ambitions and the desires and appetites of this world? I am not asking whether we simply think about such things but rather what our minds are set on. What is our focus?

We do not know where we are going to be a year from now or ten years from now. What really matters is where we are going to be one hundred years from now. If our minds are set on the things of the flesh, then one hundred years from now we will be in perdition, but if our minds are concerned about the things of God—the Spirit of God, the truth of God, the sweetness of God—then one hundred years from now we will be enjoying the brightness of God's glory without interruption. It is easy to fix our minds on the things of this world so that we go through our lives missing the things of eternity. Where is our mind set? Where is our heart set? Where is our treasure? Those who live according to the flesh set their minds on the things of the flesh, **but those who live according to the Spirit, the things of the Spirit** (v. 5b).

Here is the second thing that marks carnality: **to be carnally minded is death** (v. 6a). If we set our minds on the things of this world, there is an inescapable consequence, which is death. We would do anything in our power to escape death, but it is the only possible consequence if our mind is fixed on the things of this world.

Application

Set before yourself regularly the heavenly hope of enjoying the brightness of God's glory without interruption. By doing this, we might be more profitable with the use of our time in this world with so many distractions. The things of this world often call for our attention and prompt us to fixate on the things of the flesh. Setting before us our heavenly hope is a great remedy for befriending the things of this fallen world.

WEEK 24

1

Enmity against God

TO BE CARNALLY MINDED, PAUL SAID, IS DEATH, **but to be spiritually minded is life and peace. Because the carnal mind is enmity against God** (vv. 6b–7a).

If you repeat a lie often enough, people will begin to believe it, and not only will they believe it, but they will also defend it as a truism. Our culture is permeated with the idea that there is no war between man and God. We hear, "God hates the sin but loves the sinner." We hear that God loves everybody unconditionally, but that is the biggest lie of our day, because He does not. At the last judgment, God will not send sins to hell; He will send sinners to hell. Even though sinners enjoy the blessings of God's providential love, His filial love is not their dessert.

The Scriptures are graphic in describing God's attitude toward impenitent, carnally minded people. God abhors them. Nobody talks that way anymore—except for God in His Word. To set our minds on the things of this world is death. God is the supreme obstacle to people's finding happiness in their desires of the flesh. God is always standing in the way. The life of the flesh is lived not in neutrality but in opposition to God, which is Paul's point. To be carnally minded is to be at enmity with God.

People will never admit to that, **for it is not subject to the law of God** (v. 7b). Why, since the fall, do we hate God by nature? Why, in our state of corruption, do we have a fleshly mindset? Why do we have what Paul earlier called "debased mind[s]" (1:28)? The reason is God's law. We are at war with God because we do not want to be subject to the law of God. The media covers every ethical controversy facing mankind today, yet Christianity is held at bay in the discussion. The majority do not want the church involved in ethics because they want the right to do what they want to do. Who gave them that right? Certainly not the law of God. Every time we want to do our will, express our appetites, and live out our preferences, we run right into the wall of the law of God.

Application

Here, Romans 8 provides us with a way to rightly view the sin that we see in the world. When you tune in to your news feed, remember to be asking whether what you're seeing is subject to the law of God or in rebellion to it. If it is in rebellion to it, it is at enmity against God. Like God, we must abhor sin and call others to saving faith and repentance, which will bear the fruit of obedience to God's law. This is a loving way to call others to Him, lest they perish.

2

Unable, But . . .

WE ARE AT ENMITY WITH GOD BECAUSE our carnal mind is not subject to the law of God. The carnal mind is not subject to the law of God because it cannot be. **So then, those who are in the flesh cannot please God** (v. 8). They cannot obey the law of God or do the will of God, and the worst verdict is that they cannot do anything to please God. Those who are not Christians can do nothing to please God. So long as we are in the flesh, the only response we will have from God is a response of His displeasure, which is a euphemism for wrath.

I once made the comment that my favorite word in the Bible is *but*. It is the word that gives me relief when my life is set against the law of God, when I see myself being measured by the standard of God's righteousness, and I slip deeper and deeper into despair because I cannot begin to measure up. Relief comes with that word *but*. Paul writes to the Ephesians, "But God, who is rich in mercy . . ." (Eph. 2:4). The defining thing for the Christian is that at one point God said, "But wait a minute; there is something else."

Paul explains that we are not in the flesh, in the painful condition that he has just described: **But you are not in the flesh but in the Spirit, if indeed the Spirit of God dwells in you** (v. 9a). That is the only necessary condition Paul gives. Paul does not say that we are in the Spirit if we have the victorious Christian life. We are in the Spirit if one condition is met—the Spirit of God dwells in us. This is where an understanding of the work of the Holy Spirit in our lives is so vitally necessary to a biblical understanding of what Christianity is all about. We cannot be Christians unless the Holy Spirit regenerates us and changes our hearts of stone into hearts of flesh. As Jesus said to Nicodemus, unless a man is born of the Spirit, he cannot even see the kingdom of God, let alone enter it. The Spirit enters and indwells every person whom He regenerates, and everyone He indwells He gives the guarantee of future redemption. He seals the redeemed against the day of judgment. When we are born of the Spirit, we are signed, sealed, and delivered. We still fight with ongoing sin, but if the Spirit is in us, we are not in the flesh. We are in the Spirit, in Christ, and these blessed promises apply to us.

Application

All Christians are born again because all Christians have been reborn and indwelt by the Spirit of God. There is not a condition that we must meet to have the Spirit's work in our lives—the Spirit indwells us at the moment of our regeneration by God's grace—but Paul does call us in the sanctified life now to walk according to the Spirit in ways that we could not before.

3

Indwelt by the Spirit

NOW IF ANYONE DOES NOT HAVE THE SPIRIT OF CHRIST, **he is not His** (v. 9b). If we are not indwelt by the Holy Spirit, if we have not been reborn, we do not belong to Christ. If we do belong to Christ, however, we have been born of the Spirit. We have been set free to live not according to the flesh but according to the Spirit.

Some years ago, a stunning novel was made into a major Hollywood motion picture starring Dustin Hoffman. *The Marathon Man* involved great intrigue and concerned a person trying to escape the clutches of a secret Nazi war criminal who was living in the United States. When the hero met with his friends in the underground, he asked, "Is it safe?" Over and over again the inquiry came: "Is it safe?" The unifying theme of this entire section of Romans addresses a similar question for those who wonder if they are safe from the wrath of God. Can we be assured that indeed there is no condemnation because we are in Christ Jesus?

We looked at the distinction that the Apostle makes between the carnal life of the fallen flesh and the spiritual life of the Christian and came to this conclusion: "So then, those who are in the flesh cannot please God" (v. 8). Those who remain unconverted, those still defined by the corrupt nature—the *sarx* or flesh—are in such a state that nothing they do can please God. Even an unbeliever's prayers are displeasing to God because those prayers do not come from the heart. Such prayers come from some peril that the one praying is facing. The Scripture warns us that while we remain in the flesh, there is nothing we can do that will please God.

"But you are not in the flesh but in the Spirit, if indeed the Spirit of God dwells in you" (v. 9a). Previously I labored the point that what marks the life of the true believer is that he is indwelt by the Holy Spirit. Every person indwelt by the Spirit is safe. Every person indwelt by the Spirit is a new creature in Christ and enjoys all the fruits that flow from justification.

Application

The Westminster Shorter Catechism helpfully teaches us that justification is accompanied by our adoption and sanctification (Q&A 32) and that what flows from these is "assurance of God's love, peace of conscience, joy in the Holy Ghost, increase of grace, and perseverance therein to the end" (Q&A 36). If you have trusted in Jesus Christ, the Spirit of God indwells you. Go to God's throne of grace and ask for fuller manifestations of the benefits that are yours because of this reality.

4

The Spirit Is Life

"NOW IF ANYONE DOES NOT HAVE the Spirit of Christ, he is not His" (v. 9b). Our safety in the kingdom of God is not determined by our church membership or whatever good deeds we have managed to perform. Rather, our safety consists of being in Christ and Christ in us. We can offer all our labors to God and belong to a church and have perfect Sunday school attendance, but if the Spirit of Christ does not dwell in us, we do not belong to Him. The most terrifying warning from the lips of Jesus comes to us at the conclusion of the Sermon on the Mount: "Many will say to Me in that day, 'Lord, Lord, have we not prophesied in Your name, cast out demons in Your name, and done many wonders in Your name?' And then I will declare to them, 'I never knew you; depart from Me, you who practice lawlessness!'" (Matt. 7:22–23). That is why Paul reminds us that if we do not have the Spirit of Christ, then we do not belong to Christ.

And if Christ is in you, the body is dead because of sin, but the

Spirit is life because of righteousness (v. 10). There is a bit of difficulty here in this text, a conundrum of interpretation. Translators have a close call to make. We have repeatedly seen in this section of the epistle the contrast between the spirit and the flesh. Whenever we see that contrast, the flesh refers to the fallen, corrupt nature that we inherit from Adam, and the spirit refers to the new man, the person reborn by the Holy Spirit. When the Bible speaks of the Holy Spirit, there is no doubt as to who is in view—the third person of the Trinity. But when the word *spirit, pneuma,* occurs by itself without that adjective *holy,* we question whether the passage is speaking of the Spirit of God or of Christ or whether it is simply the human spirit. The Bible teaches that we have a spirit, or *soul,* as it is sometimes called. In my Bible (NKJV), the word *spirit* in this verse is capitalized, which means that the translators became convinced that this must be the Holy Spirit. They may be right, but if the word *holy* is not there, the only way we can distinguish between the Holy Spirit and the human spirit is by the context. I disagree with the translators in this case because the contrast is between the body and the spirit. We are talking about the human body, which is contrasted here with the human spirit. What is the result of Christ's being in us? "The body is dead because of sin, but the spirit [our human spirit] is life because of righteousness." If the destiny of our human spirit is different from that of our bodies, it is only because the divine Spirit is dwelling within us.

Application

It is strange to think about an aspect of our person's being "dead," as in the body's being dead because of sin in today's passage. But thinking this way, we might come to see the appetites of the body that so often lead us into sin with greater suspicion, realizing that the temptation that comes with them is the way of death. In Christ, you have been made alive in the Spirit, and He will one day also redeem your body at the resurrection.

5

Assurance

BUT IF THE SPIRIT OF HIM WHO RAISED JESUS **from the dead dwells in you, He who raised Christ from the dead will also give life to your mortal bodies through His Spirit who dwells in you** (v. 11). We are safe because we are indwelt by the Holy Spirit. All through this text, the question of safety is connected to the question of the assurance of salvation. Are we really in a state of grace?

With respect to the assurance of salvation, there are four types of people. (1) Some are not saved, and they know that they are not saved. They are not in a state of grace. They are unregenerate. (2) Some are saved and have the full assurance of their state of redemption. They are saved, and they know that they are saved. (3) Some are saved, but they are not sure of their state. Their souls are restless. It is quite easy to understand those three categories. It is the fourth that muddies the water. (4) Some are not saved but think they are saved. They have assurance of salvation, which they most assuredly do not possess; their assurance is a false assurance.

There are two basic reasons why people can have a false sense of assurance of salvation. The most common is a false understanding of what is necessary for salvation. If people are told that everybody goes to heaven when they die, the reasoning of the unbeliever can be very simple: "Everybody is saved; I am a body; therefore, I am saved." The false premise is that everybody who dies goes to heaven. Another false understanding is that people who live a good life will most assuredly go to heaven when they die: "I have tried to live a good life; ergo, I can be sure that I am going to heaven."

The second reason for false assurance has to do with the evaluation of ourselves. We may have a correct understanding of what is required for going to heaven. We understand that salvation requires personal trust in Christ alone for salvation, but we may deceive ourselves with respect to the profession of faith that we think we have made. In other words, we may think that we profess true faith when, in fact, we do not. We may think that we believe in justification by faith alone because we understand the doctrine intellectually and can pass a test on it in theology class, but in our heart and soul we are not trusting in Christ alone for salvation. We deceive ourselves concerning our state of grace.

That is why Romans 7 and 8 are so important. Paul is showing us a picture of a true believer. We know that being converted and in a state of grace does not guarantee the end of temptation or falling into momentary lapses of disobedience, but such a person is not controlled by the flesh. He is indwelt by the Spirit of God. If we are indwelt by the Spirit of God, it has to make a difference in how we live.

Application

Our good works do not save us. We are saved by Christ alone through our personal trust in Him for our salvation. We add nothing to His work, not even our faith, which is a gift from God (Eph. 2:8–10). Good works, however, "done in obedience to God's commandments, are the fruits and evidences of a true and lively faith; and by them believers manifest their thankfulness [and] strengthen their assurance" (WCF 16.2).

6

Sonship

SONSHIP IS DEFINED BIBLICALLY IN TERMS of those whose lead we follow. It is not a question of biology but of obedience. We are children of the one whom we obey, and if we obey the lusts of the flesh, if we obey the inclinations of Satan, then we are children of the Devil, not of Abraham or God (see John 8:31–47). That is why Paul says that those whose lives are directed by the Spirit of God are sons of God; they follow and obey the One leading them in the way of God.

For you did not receive the spirit of bondage again to fear, but you received the Spirit of adoption by whom we cry out, "Abba, Father" (v. 15). There is a contrast here between two kinds of spirits. One is the spirit of bondage, which is produced by the flesh. It is the spirit of the unregenerate person. Such people remain in prison. They are incarcerated by their old nature. They are slaves to the sinful impulses of their recalcitrant hearts. If we have the Spirit within us, however, we no longer have the spirit of bondage. We are no longer shaking and quaking in servile fear before the Lord God. We now have the Spirit of adoption.

It is interesting that the concept of adoption is generally not found among Jewish theologians from antiquity. Adoption is a Roman idea, and Paul uses the metaphor to describe believers' relationship to God. We do not think this is such a big deal because we have been told, as a result of nineteenth-century comparative-religion theology, that all roads go to heaven. That is as far away from the biblical view as we can get. In the Bible, we see that God has one child, the *monogenēs*, the only begotten, even Jesus Christ. All the rest of His children are not naturally born children; they are adopted. We cannot get into the family of God by biological birth. The only way we can enter in is if God adopts us, and the only way we are adopted is if we are united by the Holy Spirit to the Son of God, Jesus Christ.

Application

Are you a child of God? Scripture teaches us that we become children of God by believing in Jesus Christ: "As many as received Him, to them He gave the right to become children of God, to those who believe in His name" (John 1:12). With faith in Jesus Christ and adoption by the Spirit, you have a legal standing as a child of God. Rejoice this day that you can go to the Lord in prayer as "Father" in the freedom of the Spirit.

WEEK 25

1

Abba, Father

ONE OF THE GREAT CONSEQUENCES OF justification is that all who are justified are immediately adopted into the family of God and now have the unspeakable privilege of addressing God as Father. It is by the Holy Spirit shed abroad in our hearts that we have the authority to cry, "Abba, Father." We have likely heard that the word *Abba* is the common familial term of endearment translated *Daddy*. There is truth in that, but it is a dangerous truth. We are invited to use that term, *Abba*, when we enter into the inner circle of the family of God. There is no closer relationship. I do not want to disparage the idea that we do have the privilege of using this close term of affection with our heavenly Father, but I want to stress that the term *Daddy* can be used in a childish or frivolous way. The fact that we can address God now as *Father* and say *Abba* to Him does not give us the right to enter into His presence presumptuously or arrogantly.

One of the most radical things we find in Jesus is the claim He makes over and over again during His earthly ministry of the special intimacy that He had with the Father:

> Most assuredly, I say to you, the Son can do nothing of Himself, but what He sees the Father do. (John 5:19)

> I do nothing of Myself; but as My Father taught Me, I speak these things. (John 8:28)

> All that the Father gives Me will come to Me. (John 6:37)

Again and again Jesus referred to God as His Father, which enraged the Pharisees. It is so common to us that we read over it and miss its significance. We miss how radical it was in Jesus' day that any Jewish person would pray and address God as *Father*, but Jesus did it almost every time He prayed. When His disciples asked Him to teach them how to pray, He said, "In this manner, therefore, pray: 'Our Father in heaven . . .'" (Matt. 6:9a). Jesus gave to us the unique privilege that He alone held to address the God of heaven and earth as *Father*. When we pray, we can call God *Father* because He is now our Father. We have been adopted into His family. It is an unbelievable privilege that we should never take for granted. Jesus never took it for granted. It is so integral to the life of Christian prayer that we would not think of addressing God without the term, but it is a privilege given only to those who have been adopted and have received the Spirit of adoption.

Application

As Christians, we grow accustomed to approaching God in prayer by calling Him "Our Father," especially because of the model prayer that Jesus taught us to pray, the Lord's Prayer. When you pray to God, don't lose the significance of what you are saying in approaching Him as your Father even though it might seem so common and familiar. This is a truth that should never cease to astound us and is a rich source for fitting praise to God.

2

Witness of the Spirit

FINALLY, WE COME TO THE DEEPEST and highest level of assurance of salvation that we can achieve in this world: **The Spirit Himself bears witness with our spirit** (v. 16a). Here again, we see that word *spirit* used to refer to both the Holy Spirit and our spirit. There is a spiritual conversation here, a spiritual communication that comes from the Holy Spirit to the human spirit, which indicates **that we are children of God** (v. 16b). In the final analysis, our assurance of salvation is not a logical deduction springing from our theology. Our assurance is certainly not based on a careful analysis of our behavior. Our final assurance comes by the testimony of God the Holy Spirit, who bears witness with and through our spirits that we are children of God.

This is wonderful but also dangerous. Paul is not falling into some kind of gnostic mysticism here, a special revelation or secret pipeline through which the Holy Spirit talks to us and gives a private revelation. Paul is talking about how the Spirit of the Lord confirms a truth to our human spirit. The Spirit does not come and whisper into our ear when we are driving down the highway, "Relax, you are one of Mine." We need to understand that when the Spirit communicates to God's people, He communicates to them by the Word, with the Word, through the Word, and never against the Word. There are millions who claim to be led by the Spirit into sin and disobedience. The testimony we receive from the Holy Spirit comes in and through the Word.

It is so important that we understand that. If we lack assurance and want our hearts to be at peace, we must go to the Word. The Spirit confirms His truth to us in and through the Word. If we want to be led by the Spirit of God, we must immerse ourselves in the Spirit-inspired Word. We are called to test the spirits to make sure that the spirit who is leading us is the Holy Spirit, and the only test we can apply is the test of the Word itself.

The Spirit bears witness with our spirit that we are children of God, **and if children, then heirs** (v. 17a), because all of God's children participate in His estate. They are all His promised beneficiaries. If we are children, we are **heirs of God and joint heirs with Christ, if indeed we suffer with Him, that we may also be glorified together** (v. 17b).

Application

In Christ, we are children of God and heirs with Him, but we do not yet have our full inheritance. The Spirit, however, has been given to us as a guarantee of our inheritance (Eph. 1:13–14). This is why the Spirit is the ultimate source of our assurance. If you ever begin to doubt, run to the Word of God. Feast on God's promises to you, that the Spirit might bear witness with your spirit that these promises are yours.

3

The Problem of Evil

WE HAVE JUST CONSIDERED THE EXTRAORDINARY grace and blessedness that comes with our having been adopted by the Father into the family of God as heirs of God and joint heirs with Christ. All the Father gives to the Son is shared with all those united to the Son by faith. Now Paul considers once more the afflictions, trials, tribulation, pain, and suffering that are such an integral part of the vale of tears through which we walk in this world. Through too much television exposure, we have become jaded by scenes of upheaval and violence all around the world, yet the news leaves us asking, has the world gone crazy? Violence upon violence, hostility upon hostility, suffering, blood, and death all around us—when we look at the reality of all that and see the suffering that comes in its wake, we pause at times and wonder, where is God in all this?

A philosopher, John Stuart Mill, considered the manifest presence in the world of pain, suffering, violence, and wickedness, and he concluded that what we encounter on a daily basis belies any hope of a good and loving God. In skepticism he said that if God is a God of love yet He allows such pain and suffering, then He is powerless to prevent it and is nothing more than a divine weakling incapable of administering peace and justice. If, on the other hand, He has the power to prevent evil but chooses not to, standing by and allowing it, then He may be powerful but He is not good or loving. The complaint that Mill raised against historical Christianity is that either God is good but not all-powerful, or He is all-powerful but not good.

What is missing from Mill's oversimplified equation concerning the economy of grief and pain in the world is the reality of sin. God not only tolerates violence and suffering, but also—even more so—actually ordains it, yet we cannot leave sin out of the equation. It is not that God lacks in goodness; it is that we lack in goodness.

Application

The problem of evil is a perennial problem in philosophy. Often, we can feel it experientially too. Sin and suffering exist in this life, but they should never lead us to question the power, wisdom, or goodness of God. Look instead to the cross and marvel that despite our sin and even when it was at its greatest, the goodness of God was on display in working out our salvation. Trust Him.

4

Present Suffering, Future Glory

THE ENTRANCE OF HUMAN SIN INTO the world plunged the whole creation into ruin. When the Bible rehearses the repercussions of the fall, it does so in cosmic terms. The effects of the fall on the human species and the ruination of the whole creation are laid at our doorstep. This reflects God's judgment upon us, which spills over into the domain in which we were created to be God's vice-regents in exercising dominion over the earth, the animals, and the ground. When we were ruined, everything under our dominion was affected by it.

That is what Paul is concerned to reflect in the passage before us, but first he sets a contrast between the present and the future, between the present sufferings and the future glory that God has prepared for His people. Paul is quick to point out that this is not a simple formula of ratio and proportionality. There is no analogy between the present climate of pain and the future climate of blessedness. The comparative here is in terms of *how much more*. The usually articulate Paul cannot seem to find words, even under the inspiration of the Holy Spirit, to describe the radical difference between the now and the then: **For I consider that the sufferings of this present time are not worthy to be compared with the glory which shall be revealed in us** (v. 18). The difference between the present degree of pain we experience and the blessedness to which God has appointed His people is so immensely different that there is no way to compare them. Any comparison we come up with falls short.

Notice that Paul considers the sufferings of this *present* time; in other words, suffering is real, not just an illusion. Paul was not a practitioner of Christian Science. He understood in a visceral way, in a way that few of us have experienced, the stark reality of human suffering. One of the most persecuted, afflicted men ever to grace this fallen planet was the Apostle Paul. Indeed, his Savior was even more acquainted with grief and sorrow; nevertheless, there are few who have approached Paul's personal experience of suffering. He shook off that suffering in light of the hope that God has given in Jesus Christ. He said that it is not even worthy to talk about the suffering in comparison to what God has laid up for us in the future.

Application

Earlier in Romans 8, Paul connects our suffering with the suffering of Christ (v. 17). The church is the body of Christ, and as Paul learned in his conversion, when the church is persecuted, in a real sense, Christ is persecuted. This is why the resurrected Lord said to Paul, "Saul, Saul, why are you persecuting *Me*?" (Acts 9:4, emphasis added). Suffering as the church for the sake of the gospel is a suffering with Christ. Remember that we are never alone in our suffering and that we will one day experience glory in a manner like Christ. Our present suffering will be incomparable to what we will enjoy on that day.

5

Future Promise

CHRISTIANS HAVE BEEN RIDICULED FOR their hope of heaven and future redemption. We are told that this is pie in the sky. Karl Marx believed that religion was invented for economic reasons. He said that in a society dominated by class, the owners are always in the minority to the workers, and if ever the majority—the laborers—understood the strength inherent in their number, they would rise up in revolt against the owners. Therefore, the owners gave the workers religion and the promise of a future benefit. In the meantime, workers lived in chains and in sweat and toil while the owners, according to Marx, laughed all the way to the bank.

Consider that in the American experiment with slavery. If we look carefully at some of the songs that enrich our hymnody, we hear the motif of the slave who sings:

Swing low, sweet chariot,
Comin' for to carry me home;
Swing low, sweet chariot,
Comin' for to carry me home.

I looked over Jordan,
And what did I see,

Comin' for to carry me home,
A band of angels comin' after me,
Comin' for to carry me home.

A slave's only hope lay in another world, in heaven. Marx said that religion is "the opiate of the people." Opium is a narcotic given to dull the senses, to minister to pain, to give people hope when there is no hope.

I do not believe what Marx said. I believe that God's promises are eternal, immutable, and unbreakable. Again and again God says to His people, "Yes, the pain now is real, but wait. We are not finished yet. I have a plan for My people, and that plan is glorious. I have established My Son upon His throne, and I have called a people to Myself that I have given as a gift to My Son, and together with Him they will reign forever." That redemption will extend far beyond the realm of the human; the whole world, which has been plunged into ruin, will be redeemed. There will be a renovation—a new heaven and a new earth. This is our Father's world. It is His property, and He may dispose of it however He sees fit, and He has seen fit to appoint it for glory for those who love His coming. Paul is eloquent here, rhapsodic, in considering this future promise.

Application

People may dismiss Christianity as a "crutch," thinking that they do not need it, that it is for the weak. If someone you meet ever responds this way, take heart and do not be ashamed to reply, "I couldn't live without it." The reality is that that Christianity is for the broken, for the sinful. Those who see this as a problem do not recognize their own sinfulness. Remember that Jesus said, "Those who are well have no need of a physician, but those who are sick. I did not come to call the righteous, but sinners, to repentance" (Mark 2:17).

6

Expectation

FOR THE EARNEST EXPECTATION OF THE CREATION eagerly waits for **the revealing of the sons of God** (v. 19). We find here a personification. Even the impersonal forces of nature are brought into the arena of celebrating God's redemption:

> Let the rivers clap their hands;
> Let the hills be joyful together before the LORD,
> For He is coming to judge the earth.
> With righteousness He shall judge the world,
> And the peoples with equity. (Ps. 98:8–9)

> The mountains and the hills
> Shall break forth into singing before you,
> And all the trees of the field shall clap their hands. (Isa. 55:12)

All creation rejoices in the expectation of what lies in the future.

There is something I always notice when I walk into the woods to go hunting: the absolute silence. I hear no birds singing. I hear only my footsteps as I make my way to the tree stand from which I wait and watch. Once I have been up in the tree stand for fifteen or twenty minutes, however, I begin to hear the chatter of squirrels, the songs of birds, and the gobbling of turkeys. The woods come alive. I have sat in tree stands and looked down from my perch and seen wild boar, turkeys, and deer feeding—a variety of beasts coexisting in the wild in a spirit of peace—but as soon as they realize that man is present, a pall of fear falls over the bird, the squirrel, the deer, and the turkey. It was not supposed to be like that. God intended that the animals rejoice in the presence of those who had been given dominion over them, but now the animals suffer because of us, and they are no longer comfortable when we intrude into their domain. Nevertheless, these dumb brutes, as they are called, have an earnest expectation, a conviction of hope, for the day when that will all change, when the glory of God will be revealed in us.

Application

Sin did not affect us only; it had consequences for all creation. But the destiny of this creation is also caught up with the destiny of our redemption. When God finishes the work of calling His elect, the full restoration of creation is near. The revealing of the sons of God, their full acknowledgment and acquittal, brings with it the new heavens and earth. Creation will rejoice before God at the salvation of His people. Next time you see a beautiful sunset, think on this.

WEEK 26

1

Subjected in Hope

FOR THE CREATION WAS SUBJECTED TO FUTILITY, **not willingly, but because of Him who subjected it in hope** (v. 20). The word *futility* is one of the ugliest words in the English language. Nothing can drive the human being to despair more quickly or deeply than the idea that our pain and labor are mere exercises in futility and utterly meaningless. What could be worse than the sentence given to Sisyphus in the Greek myth? Sisyphus uses all his energy to push a gigantic rock to the top of a mountain, but as soon as he gets it to the top, the rock falls back to the bottom, and he has to push it back to the top again and again, forever. He was sentenced to vain labor. Paul's words to the Corinthians stand in contrast to what happens in the myth: "Therefore, my beloved brethren, be steadfast, immovable, always abounding in the work of the Lord, knowing that your labor is not in vain in the Lord" (1 Cor. 15:58). That is the hope of the gospel, that our pain is not meaningless. Our toil is not futile. Every ounce of effort we expend in this world, every tear that falls across our cheek, is not meaningless.

For the present time, the whole creation has been subjected to the appearance of futility, something that did not occur by vote. It was set by divine decree. This world is filled with pain and suffering, not because God is not good but because He is good and will not tolerate evil. God has subjected the entire creation to pain and affliction because of our sin. The next time we hurt and become angry with God and shake our fist in His face and ask, "Why me?" we must listen for the reply: "Why not you?" The real question is why God in His grace should store up for us in heaven a glory and blessedness so great that the suffering we endure now is not worthy to be compared with it.

Application

We may become discouraged by the seeming lack of fruit of our labors for the Lord. Sharing the gospel with a coworker just doesn't seem to be getting anywhere, or our children seem to be straying from the Lord. We never know, however, the way that the Lord may be using us. We may be planting seeds that another person may water, or we may be watering where someone else has planted, but no matter our labor, the Lord sees, and He is the One who gives the growth. Let us not grow discouraged.

2

Creation Delivered

THE CREATION ITSELF ALSO WILL BE DELIVERED from the bondage of corruption into the glorious liberty of the children of God (v. 21). We have seen what the gospel has done to deliver us. By nature we are people in bondage, but Paul has just explained that through the power of the Holy Spirit, we have been set free. We are no longer under those bonds of sin. We have been released from that incarceration. We have been set free, and that release from bondage does not end with us. The goal of the finished work of Christ is to rescue the entire creation so that even the land will stop mourning and the animals will no longer be afraid. Though nature may be red in tooth and fang, the bloody crimson violence will be done away with in the new heavens and the new earth, where the lion will lie down with the lamb. Paul says that the creation itself will be delivered from the bondage of corruption into glorious liberty.

Just as the created world has suffered because of our sin, the whole creation will participate in the liberation from the consequences of sin at the time of the manifestation of the children of God. **We know that the whole creation groans and labors with birth pangs together until now** (v. 22). Here we see the metaphor of a woman in labor, at that threshold of pain before the delivery. It is excruciating. She cries; she groans. Paul says that the whole creation is like that, crying and groaning in birth pangs, but the pain of that labor is not worthy to be compared with the joy that follows when the child is born.

Not only that, but we also who have the firstfruits of the Spirit, even we ourselves groan within ourselves, eagerly waiting for the adoption, the redemption of our body (v. 23). We have already been adopted, so there is a present sense in which we experience the adoption into the family of God, but there is still a *not yet* dimension of what it means to be adopted, which will be revealed when we receive the inheritance stored up for us in heaven. How wonderful it is to hear the promise of what God will say: "Come, My beloved. Inherit the kingdom that I have prepared for you from the foundation of the world." That is our expectation and hope.

Application

The tension of the *already/not yet* in the Christian life can sometimes be palpable. We want to see more growth and maturity in Christ, and not seeing it, we can groan like the Apostle Paul for deliverance. May our eagerness not get the best of us in leading us to despair but lead us only to greater measures of desire. This groaning is part of the Spirit's sanctifying work as He conforms us to be more and more like Christ.

3

The Help of the Spirit

FOR WE WERE SAVED IN THIS HOPE, **but hope that is seen is not hope; for why does one still hope for what he sees?** (v. 24). Paul talks constantly about hope. As I noted earlier, he does not use the term *hope* the way that we commonly use it. We use the term *hope* to express our desire for some future result that is at present uncertain, but the concept of hope in the New Testament indicates a situation in which the future is absolutely certain. It is faith looking forward. It is faith being certain and receiving the assurance of what God promises for tomorrow. Our hope is the anchor for our souls. It is what gives stability to our faith. When we stumble and trip today, when we become uncertain in our faith because of afflictions, hope kicks in. We are reminded of God's promise for tomorrow. Paul says that hope in what is seen is not hope, **but if we hope for what we do not see, we eagerly wait for it**

with perseverance (v. 25). Paul has linked perseverance and character many times in this epistle. It is hope that keeps us going.

One of the most important passages in the Bible that instruct us about the nature of godly prayer is this one: **Likewise the Spirit also helps in our weaknesses. For we do not know what we should pray for as we ought, but the Spirit Himself makes intercession for us with groanings which cannot be uttered. Now He who searches the hearts knows what the mind of the Spirit is, because He makes intercession for the saints according to the will of God** (vv. 26–27). Prayer is a Trinitarian activity; it is more than simply praying to the Father through the Son. In this text we see that our great Helper, the Holy Spirit, assists in the articulation of our prayers addressed to Christ and the Father.

When we pray, we must remember to ask the Holy Spirit to assist us because so often we do not pray rightly. If we really want to see answers to prayer that will put strength in our souls, we pray according to the leading of the Holy Spirit. The Spirit helps us pray according to the will of God rather than according to the will of our flesh. We will see prayers answered when they correspond to the will of the Father. If we ask God to do something against His will, we are going to be frustrated. He will answer those prayers—He will say no. When the Spirit, who searches the deep things of God and knows our souls and the mind of the Father, helps us to pray as we ought, we begin to pray according to the will of God.

Application

Perhaps one reason that we do not pray as often as we would like to is that we do not know what to pray for. When we do not know what to pray, we do not come quickly to God. If you experience this tendency, then be sure also to ask the Spirit's assistance to bring you more often before the throne of grace. We need not only His intercessory work in prayer but also His work to bring us to our knees in prayer.

4

Good versus Evil

WE KNOW FROM THE TEACHING OF SCRIPTURE that our ultimate destiny as Christians is to enter into heaven, a place, we are told in the book of Revelation, where there will be no night, no death, and no tears. In heaven we will live forever without affliction and pain. The environment of heaven will never be marred by the presence of evil or sin. Heaven is a place where nothing goes wrong and no evil takes place.

What about now? We are not in heaven. We are still in a vale of tears. How would we feel if Jesus walked in the door and spoke directly to us, saying, "I have good news for you: I promise that nothing bad will ever happen to you again"? In a very real sense, He has already said that, although He does so in a sideways manner. It is basically the affirmation that we are given here in Romans 8:28. Paul says with assurance, **And we know . . .** He is not speaking with the editorial *we* or the magisterial *we*; he is speaking inclusively of all who are in the faith. The one thing that all true believers know for sure is **that all things work together for good to those who love God, to those who are the called according to His purpose** (v. 28). Paul gives us an astonishing affirmation when he says with certainty that all things are working together for good for those of us who love the Lord and who are the called according to His purpose.

One of the most fundamental principles of biblical Christianity is that we are never to call good evil or evil good. That is essentially the lie of Satan, which has been spread abroad through every generation. The great seduction of the enemy is to convince us that sin is really not so bad. In fact, it is actually good. If we are to experience the best that life has to offer, the Devil says, we must indulge ourselves in things that God prohibits. Because Satan lies, he calls evil good and good evil.

When certain actions take place, they are simply evil; nevertheless, under the providence of God, under His sovereignty over human events, He has the power to bring good out of them, which is a glorious thing that we can experience as Christians. Everything that we are called upon to suffer, even things that are truly bad, are nevertheless being used by God for our ultimate good. Viewed from a proximate perspective, such actions are indeed bad, and there is no redemptive virtue in them, but from the ultimate perspective it is good that they are happening because God is using them for His ultimate purpose. That is a critical point to grasp if we are to understand anything of the providence of God.

Application

"All things work together for good . . ." Do you believe it? Let us remember this truth in our daily lives moment by moment, but especially when we encounter suffering. We can know that all things work together for good because God is good. Holding fast to this truth, we protect ourselves from ever casting even the smallest shadow of doubt on the goodness of God, and we get to experience His goodness as He brings us through suffering with deeper measures of trust and humility.

5

Concurrence

THE FACT THAT EVIL IS REDEEMED FOR GOOD is based on what theologians call, under the heading of providence, the *doctrine of concurrence* or *confluence*. The doctrine of concurrence holds that certain actions in which humans exercise their will to do what they wish, even to making diabolical choices, are nevertheless under the providence of God, who is at work in them. He has the power to trump our evil inclinations and desires and bring good to pass.

The best illustration in the Bible of the doctrine of concurrence occurs at the end of the book of Genesis. Joseph suffered greatly at the hands of his treacherous and envious brothers. He was separated from his family and countrymen, sold into slavery, falsely accused, and thrown into prison. Finally, through the providence of God, Joseph was rescued and elevated to the right hand of Pharaoh, becoming the prime minister of Egypt. Then famine came to Joseph's homeland of Canaan, and Jacob, Joseph's father, sent his other sons as emissaries down to Egypt to seek relief. In the process, they met Joseph. They did not recognize him, but Joseph recognized them. What follows is one of the most poignant narratives in the entire Old Testament. The moment of truth came when Joseph revealed his identity to his brothers. They were terrified of his wrath and begged for his forgiveness. Joseph said, "As for you, you meant evil against me; but God meant it for good" (Gen. 50:20). What an incredible, incomprehensible biblical revelation that is.

God orders His providences so as not to cancel out secondary causes. He does not annihilate the actions of the human will, which are undertaken freely. In the Genesis text, we see that Joseph was aware that his brothers had not only sinned against him and committed something that was really evil, but also sinned with intent, with malice aforethought. They had conspired and schemed to get rid of their brother of whom they were so envious. We have in this text the appearance of what we call *intentionality*. As rational beings, the brothers of Joseph had fully intended to bring harm to him, so their sin was intentional. But Joseph said that despite their intentions and their efforts to bring them about, God was involved in the whole thing. God was acting, and His intention was purely righteous; there was no mixture of evil in it. His sovereign providence in it was altogether good.

Application

Today, actively reflect on a particular circumstance in your life that seemed evil or was even meant by someone for your harm but really worked out for your good. After you've had time to identify this moment, take time to amply praise the Lord, who works good out of evil. There is no other place where this reality is seen more clearly than at the cross.

6

The Sovereignty of God

THE WESTMINSTER CONFESSION SAYS that God ordains whatsoever comes to pass, but it is quick to add that this does not occur in such a way as to eliminate secondary causes or to make of no significance the will of the creature. God does not do violence to the will of the creature. Nevertheless, God's sovereignty prevails in every instance.

Some have said, "God's sovereignty ends where human freedom begins," but it is blasphemy, and a moment's thought will reveal it to be so. The sovereignty of God is not in any way limited by, conditioned on, or dependent on man's authority. Our freedom is a gift from God. It is real. We exercise and enjoy freedom, but it is everywhere limited by God's sovereignty. That is what we mean by *sovereignty*. God is sovereign; we are not. Even the fall of the human race was in some sense ordained by God.

God knew before the fall that Adam and Eve were going to fall. God also had the power and authority to intervene to crush the head of the serpent before the serpent opened his mouth. God could have prevented the fall from occurring, but He did not. Yet He did not force Adam and Eve to sin. If He chose not to stop them from sinning, then in some sense He ordained that they not be stopped. If He ordained that they not be stopped, then it means that He ordained that they would, in fact, sin. If the Lord God omnipotent permitted the fall for His purposes, He must have had a good reason for it. Even though evil is in the world, the fact that it is here has to be good, or it could not possibly be here. Whatever God ordains should come to pass according to His inscrutable and eternal purpose must be ultimately for good.

Evil is evil, but it is within the broader, eternal purpose of God and ultimately for His glory. We have that affirmation here in Romans 8:28. Not all things are good. Paul is not an illusionist who says that there is no such thing as evil, but he does say that all things are working together for good; that is, the ultimate purpose for why evil afflicts us is a good purpose.

Application

We must both affirm God's sovereignty and recognize the great gift that He has given us, that we are free moral creatures. God has indeed foreordained whatsoever will come to pass. Though we do not know all that God has willed for our lives, we do know that He desires us to be holy. Let us use our freedom for His glory in striving after the holiness "without which no one will see the Lord" (Heb. 12:14).

WEEK 27

1

Good for Whom?

NOTICE THE LIMITATION THAT PAUL GIVES HERE: God's working all things together for good is not for the benefit of everybody. Rather, all things are working together for good "to those who love God, to those who are the called according to His purpose." The drama of concurrence of synergy, whereby God is making all things work together for good, is simply for those who love Him. Obviously, that does not include everybody because the vast majority of mankind lives and dies at enmity with God. But if we are Christians and the love of God has been shed abroad in our hearts, we have nothing to fear.

Paul's statement is part of Romans 8, where we are still dealing with the question, Is it safe? Are we in a place where we now have no condemnation to fear? If so, we have nothing to fear for eternity. We have nothing to fear from the afflictions we have to endure in this present life, because all these things are every moment working together under the sovereignty of God for good. If we love Him, good is working for the believer.

Those who love God are "those who are the called according to His purpose" (v. 28b). Debates ensue constantly about election and predestination. Every generation of Christians has to fight this battle, as if election were some esoteric doctrine that only elite intellectuals and professional theologians could grasp, though the doctrine is on every page in the Bible. Even if the doctrine were backed up only by the verse before us in Romans, it would be enough to establish the doctrine of election forever. In this verse, Romans 8:28, assurance is given to those who love God, and those who love God are identified as the ones who are the called according to His purpose. Some say that "those who are the called" is referring to those who respond positively to the preaching of the gospel. It is a nice theory, but it is not what the Apostle is saying. Paul is defining those who love God as the ones "who are the called according to [God's] purpose."

Application

Some wrestle with the doctrine of election. It may raise numerous questions, but Scripture's teaching about its reality is plain. If you or someone you know struggles with this doctrine, a good place to go to see the beauty of it is Romans 8:28. The ultimate good that awaits those who have been elected by God is eternal glory, and since election is by God's sovereign choice, election is a rich source of assurance for all those who believe that this glory will be theirs, never to be lost.

2

Effectual Calling

IN ALMOST EVERY INSTANCE WHERE THE BIBLE SPEAKS of the call of God, it is speaking of what we call the *effectual call. Effectual calling* is a term that describes the fact that what God calls forth occurs; what He purposes to effect by His call is effected. It started with creation. When God called the world into existence *ex nihilo,* it was not an invitation. God did not plead with the darkness to produce light. He did not woo the universe to come into being. When God in His omnipotent power said, "Let there be light" (Gen. 1:3), that call was always and everywhere effectual. What God purposes in whatever call He gives, that purpose can never be frustrated because God is God. He is not a president elected by majority vote. He rules sovereignly from all eternity because He is the Lord God omnipotent who reigns. Nothing—no darkness, emptiness, threat of chaos, or sinful disposition—can ultimately resist the power of His call because His grace in the call is irresistible.

It is not that we lack the capacity to resist. Our whole lives demonstrate that we can and do resist grace. *Irresistible grace* means that even though we resist with all our might, God's grace trumps our resistance and brings to pass what His eternal plan has been and is. When God and Christ called Paul to be an Apostle, it was no mere summons. Paul explained that he was called to be an Apostle not by men but by the will of God (Gal. 1:1). He was referring to that divine purpose, which is effected by the call itself.

When we talk about the *called* or the *elect*, we mean those who have been summoned not only outwardly but also inwardly by the Spirit, who changes the disposition of their hearts and effects the transformation of their souls—the resurrection from spiritual death to spiritual life. If we are believers today, it is not because we made God's call effectual in our lives; it is because God did. We were called according to His purpose.

Application

The Westminster Shorter Catechism teaches us that a dimension of the Spirit's work in effectual calling is to "persuade and enable us to embrace Jesus Christ" (Q&A 31). When the Spirit renews our hearts, we can't not embrace Christ because we have come to see His beauty and the answer to our sin and misery. The Spirit makes us willing to come for life. Praise God for the Spirit's work in your life today, and ask for His continued work in your heart.

3

God's Purpose

WHAT IS A PURPOSE? A PURPOSE IS A DESIRED END, a planned consequence. When we set forth our goals and articulate our purposes, our plans are fallible at best. We know that the best-laid plans of mice and men can go astray. Fortunately, the poet Robert Burns was talking only about the plans of mice and men; he did not include God in that category, because the best-laid plans of God never come to naught. A pervasive doctrine in the Christian world today strips God of His sovereignty and, in effect, of His very deity. According to this doctrine, a poor, impoverished deity wrings His hands in heaven, hoping, at times against hope, that somebody will take seriously the sacrifice that His

Son made and bring His plan of salvation to fruition. That is not God, nor is a deity like that worthy to be given the title *God*.

God is the Lord God, the God who says to Pharaoh, "Let My people go" (Ex. 10:3). Pharaoh's heart was hardened, which is attributed in Scripture both to God and to Pharaoh himself. Paul will explore that in Romans 9. For now, we need only keep in mind that even Pharaoh, the most powerful man in the universe at that time, was clay in the hands of our Creator and our Redeemer, who had a purpose for His people, and through those people He had a purpose for the whole world: exodus, liberation, redemption, and salvation.

It is not as if God considered the exodus only after hearing the cries of the Israelites as they groaned about the burdens laid on them by Pharaoh. It is not as if God noticed the calamitous situation and said, "I had better do something about it." God spoke to the children of Israel through Joseph, whom the enslaving Pharaoh did not know, saying, "You meant evil against me; but God meant it for good, in order to bring it about as it is this day, to save many people alive" (Gen. 50:20). God planned the bondage of Israel. He planned the exodus from Egypt just as much as He planned the betrayal of Joseph and his imprisonment to demonstrate that all the afflictions and suffering that Joseph endured were working together not only for Joseph's good but for Israel's good and the good of all saints of every age.

Application

God did not look down the corridors of time for foreseen faith in order to know whom to elect to salvation. He *planned* whom He would sovereignly save. Westminster Confession of Faith 3.2 tells us, "Although God knows whatsoever may or can come to pass upon all supposed conditions, yet hath he not decreed anything because he foresaw it as future, or as that which would come to pass upon such conditions." God's foreordination is active and not reactive. When it comes to our salvation, God plans, and God executes.

4

No Tragedies

IMMEDIATELY FOLLOWING PAUL'S dramatic affirmation that all things work together for good to those who love the Lord, Paul launches into the Golden Chain: **For whom He foreknew, He also predestined to be conformed to the image of His Son, that He might be the firstborn among many brethren. Moreover whom He predestined, these He also called; whom He called, these He also justified; and whom He justified, these He also glorified** (vv. 29–30).

What we get from Romans 8:28 is this: in the short run, each of us is visited at some point by tragedy. We are actors in the theater of the tragic. Tragedies are on our minds every day, but what Romans 8:28 teaches is that ultimately—not proximately but ultimately—there are no tragedies for the Christian. Tragedy now is blessing later. In every tragedy we experience, God is working with it, molding it and shaping it, for our eternal blessedness. The tragic is ephemeral and temporary. It is in the world but never permanent.

The other side of the coin is this: for the unbeliever who persists in his unbelief, every blessing he receives from the hand of God in this life is ultimately working for his damnation. Every blessing that the impenitent person ungratefully receives from the hands of God adds more sin to that depository of sin that Paul mentioned earlier: "In accordance with your hardness and your impenitent heart you are treasuring up for yourself wrath in the day of wrath and revelation of the righteous judgment of God, who will render to each one according to his deeds" (2:5–6). Every blessing that goes unthanked, unacknowledged, and unappreciated by the pagan will end up as a tragedy for the ungrateful one.

We live in a topsy-turvy world in which the tragedy for the Christian is a blessing for eternity, but the blessing for the pagan is a tragedy for eternity. God works all things together for good for those who love Him.

Application

Gratitude ought to fill the heart of every believer. We have been given life and breath, and even more than that, we have been given eternal life in Jesus Christ. We might not know why God is bringing us through a particularly difficult season, but we do know that He has saved us, and we do know that He is working all things together for our good, and for that, we ought to be grateful.

5

TULIP

ALL THROUGH ROMANS 8, PAUL IS DEALING WITH the position of safety we have in our state of salvation in Jesus Christ. After we are justified, there is no more condemnation. The entire chapter is filled with encouragement to those who are in Jesus Christ. The acme of that encouragement comes in verse 28: "We know that all things work together for good to those who love God, to those who are the called according to His purpose." The idea that God effectually calls certain people according to His good pleasure and purpose introduces the so-called Golden Chain in the verses before us now.

In terms of the theological significance of the Golden Chain, let me introduce it by reviewing some background that we covered earlier in our study of Romans. In seventeenth-century Holland, a group of theologians rose up from the Dutch Reformed Church to protest against historic Reformation theology, and with Jacobus Arminius and his friends they entered into what was called *Remonstration*, that is, a protest against some of the sixteenth-century Calvinist doctrines. Five doctrines in particular were given the weight of their theological criticism: (1) the doctrine of man's total moral inability as the result of the fall; (2) the idea of a predestination that is rooted in God's sovereign decrees from all eternity in which the number of the elect is fixed; (3) the idea that the atonement of Christ was designed by the Father as the sole means by which He would bring His elect to salvation; (4) the doctrine of effectual calling; that is, when the Holy Spirit calls people and effects their regeneration, that work of divine grace is so powerful that no human resistance can overcome it; and (5) the idea of eternal security, which holds that once a person is in a state of grace, he will remain in that state forever.

These five points of remonstration provoked the judgment of the senate of Dordrecht, and the protesters were labeled as heretics and disciplined for their errors. As a result of the controversy, these five issues became known as the five points of Calvinism and fell under the rubric of the acrostic TULIP: T for *total depravity*; U for *unconditional election*; L for *limited atonement*; I for *irresistible grace*; and P for *perseverance of the saints*.

Application

The five points of Calvinism are a helpful teaching tool and summary of why and how God saves. If you do not have the acrostic TULIP memorized, take a moment to memorize what each of its letters means. Use it to reflect on your own conversion, as an encouragement in your Christian life now, or as preparation for sharing the good news of God's salvation with someone else.

6

Unconditional Election

WHAT WE ARE CONCERNED ABOUT HERE is the U in TULIP, the doctrine of unconditional election. The phrase *unconditional election* simply means that from all eternity God chose, or elected, a definite number of fallen human beings to be redeemed and to be conformed to the image of His Son. This election was unconditional in the sense that it was not based upon some foreseen conditions of the creature.

At the time of the Reformation and the recovery of biblical soteriology (the doctrine of salvation), the magisterial Reformers were of one mind on the issue of election. The Reformed doctrine of predestination is so often identified with the Swiss theologian John Calvin, but that is a little bit of a distortion historically, because there is nothing in Calvin's doctrine of predestination that was not first in Martin Luther's doctrine. Luther defended this doctrine vigorously against the diatribe of Desiderius Erasmus of Rotterdam. There was nothing in Luther's doctrine of predestination that was not first articulated by the great Augustine, and nothing in Augustine's doctrine of predestination that was not first in the mind and teaching of the Apostle Paul. Additionally, there was nothing in Paul's doctrine of predestination that was not first articulated by our Lord Himself, and there was nothing in Jesus' doctrine of predestination that was not first articulated by Moses in the Old Testament.

As convinced as Luther was of the supreme doctrine of God's electing grace, his chief lieutenant, Philip Melanchthon, a brilliant theologian in his own right, modified Luther's view when Luther died. Melanchthon's modification became the view that was embraced by later Lutheranism, a doctrine of predestination called the *prescient* view of predestination.

The word *prescience* comes from a prefix and a root. The prefix *pre-* means "beforehand" and the root word *science* means "knowledge," so *prescience* is a kind of prior knowledge. We often use the term *foreknowledge* to describe the same idea. Melanchthon's view, which has become the majority report in modern evangelical Christianity, is this: God knows in advance which people will render a positive response to the gospel and choose by their free will to come to Jesus Christ. On the basis of that prior knowledge, God chooses them to be saved. I mention it because the text before us now is the standard proof-text for the prescient view of predestination, and it is important that we understand the parameters of the controversy as we look at Romans 8:29–30.

Application

The prescient view of predestination is problematic because it moves God's decision to save outside Himself, placing His electing purposes in us, which calls into question certain attributes of God, such as His sovereignty and aseity. We should instead content ourselves with reasons such as God's "eternal and immutable purpose," "the secret counsel and good pleasure of his will," and "his mere free grace and love" for our election (WCF 3.5). Not to us, but to God alone be the glory.

WEEK 28

1

Foreknowledge, Part 1

IMMEDIATELY AFTER PAUL SAYS THAT "ALL things work together for good to those who love God, to those who are the called according to His purpose" (v. 28), he introduces the idea of foreknowledge: "For whom He foreknew, He also predestined to be conformed to the image of His Son" (v. 29a). The first link in the Golden Chain is the link of foreknowledge. It is important to understand that *predestination* is not a concept or a word invented by John Calvin or Martin Luther or Augustine. It is a biblical word, one that we find here in Romans and in Ephesians also. The idea of predestination unto eternal life is found throughout the whole of Scripture. The question is not whether we are going to have a doctrine of predestination; as we have seen, predestination is a biblical concept. The question is, what is the correct understanding of the doctrine of predestination? If we want to be submissive to the Word of God, we have to wrestle with what Scripture teaches concerning the doctrine of predestination.

I am convinced that the prescient view of predestination that relegates it simply to an act of God's omniscient foreknowledge is not an explanation of the biblical doctrine but is precisely a denial of the biblical doctrine. Because Paul starts with foreknowledge, those who hold to the prescient view say, "That is what predestination is about—foreknowledge." The idea is that God knows the future, sees which people will choose Christ, and then chooses them based on His knowledge of what they will choose. According to this view, since foreknowledge comes before predestination in the Golden Chain, obviously what the Apostle is teaching here is that predestination is based upon foreknowledge. Nowhere does Scripture say that; it is an inference read into the text by virtue of the order of the words. The fact that foreknowledge comes before predestination leads people to the conclusion that predestination is based upon God's prior knowledge of a condition that people will meet, but those who come to that conclusion about Romans 8 have not read Romans 9.

The mere fact that the word *foreknowledge* comes before the word *predestination* does not necessitate that predestination is based upon a foreknowledge of human actions. If we are debating predestination and someone says that the basis of it is God's prior knowledge of our human behavior, we respond that God cannot predestine anyone from all eternity that He does not first know from all eternity. God does not predestine a nameless, faceless group of elect people. Obviously, if He predestines a people from the foundation of the world, He has to know what people He is predestinating. In that sense, before He acts in the decree of election with respect to certain people, He has to know what He is doing.

Application

If the prescient view of predestination were true, it would still not be able to explain the reality of God's gift of faith. All saving faith is a gift of God (Eph. 2:8), so God would still have to foreknow all those to whom He would give this gift. Being dead in sin, no one could have believed if it were not for God's electing grace. Let us empty ourselves of any presumption that things could have been otherwise.

2

Foreknowledge, Part 2

THE WORD USED HERE BY THE APOSTLE PAUL in Romans 8:29, which is translated *foreknew*, is the word *prŏginō*. It comes from a form of the noun *gnosis*, which is the Greek word for "knowledge." When we are sick and go to the doctor, he offers a diagnosis. When we ask, "Am I going to get better?" he may offer a prognosis. Both have to do with *gnosis*, or knowledge.

The word for "knowledge" in New Testament Greek is used in two distinct ways. We have seen that by God's self-revelation in and through nature, people know that He exists (Rom. 1:18–20). Knowing God, we refuse to acknowledge Him as God; neither are we grateful. We don't honor God as God. Paul declares in Romans 1 that by general revelation everybody in the world has some *gnosis*, some knowledge of God, yet when Paul writes his first epistle to the Corinthians, he says that the unregenerate person, the pagan, does not know God. We could get away from this seeming contradiction if Paul had used different words for "knowledge" in each of those instances, but that escape hatch will not work, because he uses the same word in both letters.

To clear up the apparent discrepancy between Paul's teaching in Romans and his teaching in 1 Corinthians, we can say that general revelation gives to all men an inescapable cognitive knowledge of God, and that though we seek to destroy it and do not want to have it in our minds, we cannot eliminate it altogether. Therefore, we are left without excuse. On judgment day, we can never say with impunity that we did not know that God was there. We do have that *gnosis* as a result of revelation. At the same time, that *gnosis* never rises to a redemptive level of spiritual apprehension and personal knowledge of God. Personal, redemptive, spiritual knowledge of God comes only as a result of the work of the Holy Spirit within our hearts and minds.

Now, why labor this when we are talking about a particular text in Romans 8? We do so because it is the root of the term that starts the Golden Chain: "For whom He foreknew [*prŏginō*], He also predestined." The full import of the word includes not mere cognition on God's part but a redemptive knowledge that is spiritual and affective—not *e*ffective in this case, but *a*ffective. Therefore, we could reasonably translate this text, "Those whom He foreloved [those whom He knew in a personal, intimate, redemptive sense from all eternity], He predestined."

Application

In our relationships, we long for unconditional love. Often, we sin most against those we love the most. That they are gracious to forgive us and receive us in love is one of the sweetest experiences in life. God placed His unconditional electing love on us in Jesus Christ. He not only foreknew us but foreloved us.

3

Predestined to Be Conformed

THE LANGUAGE THAT PAUL USES with respect to the goal of predestination is not immediately linked to redemption or salvation. Paul does not say, "Those whom He foreknew, He also predestined unto salvation." The concept is certainly there, but it is not the language that Paul uses. "Whom He foreknew, He also predestined," but predestined to what? What are people predestined to? They are "predestined to be conformed to the image of His Son" (v. 29a). The purpose of predestination is that the elect may be brought, by God's grace, into a relationship with the Son of God. When Paul—and all the New Testament—writes about predestination, the focus is always and everywhere related to Christ. Predestination is never discussed in the abstract; it is always related to our relationship with Christ.

Why does God, from all eternity, predestinate certain people to be in conformity to Jesus? We come next to a subjunctive clause, which indicates purpose. The Apostle is setting forth very clearly the purpose of predestination: "that He might be the firstborn among many brethren" (v. 29b). Predestination is for Christ's sake. It is that Christ may see the travail of His soul and be satisfied.

It is not, as so many today say, that Christ provided a potential atonement and offered a potential redemption for a potential number of people. The God of Scripture is One who, from all eternity, had a sovereign purpose of salvation in mind, and He sovereignly sent His Son into the world to effect the atonement for His people, that they may be adopted into the family of God. We are heirs of God, joint heirs with Jesus, because God sovereignly decreed that people would come to Christ. The only reason we find anywhere in Scripture as to why anyone is saved is for Christ's sake.

In Jesus' prayer in the upper room, He thanked the Father for giving people to Him, and "as You have given Him authority over all flesh, that He should give eternal life to as many as You have given Him" (John 17:2). Arminians reverse that to read, "All who come to Me, the Father will give to Me." No, those whom the Father gives to the Son come to the Son. We who have come to Christ have done so because we are gifts of love that the Father has given to His Son. That is the *why* of predestination.

Application

We quickly associate predestination with our eternal state. Understood this way, predestination can be a great source of encouragement. All who believe are predestinated to eternal glory in Christ, and nothing can take that away. But predestination isn't merely about the future. It is also a great source of motivation in the Christian life. In all your reflection on God's predestinating love in Christ, make sure to connect it to the practicalities of striving after greater Christlikeness right now.

4

The Good Pleasure of God's Will

ELSEWHERE THE APOSTLE SAYS THAT GOD chooses people "according to the good pleasure of His will" (Eph. 1:5). That "according to" tells us the basis upon which God chooses or determines the elect. As we will see in Romans 9, "it is not of him who wills, nor of him who runs, but of God who shows mercy" (v. 16). In Romans 9, Paul uses Jacob and Esau to show that before they were born, before they had done anything good or bad, God decreed that the elder would serve the younger. "Jacob I have loved, but Esau I have hated" (v. 13). We will wait until we get to Romans 9 to look more deeply at it, but in Ephesians and elsewhere Paul speaks about God's choosing or predestinating according to the good pleasure of His will.

If God's choosing us is not based on some foreseen thing that we have done or will do, if His election is unconditional, then on what basis does God make His choice? At first glance it might seem completely arbitrary, as if God just closed His eyes and said, "I will take some of these and some of those." God does not do anything by chance. The fact that our election is not in us does not mean that there is not a reason for it, and the reason we are given is that God's electing is according to the good pleasure of His will. Paul describes the pleasure of God's will as the *good pleasure* of His will. The only pleasure that God takes in His will is good pleasure, not bad pleasure. Whatever He pleases and wills to do always flows from His character, which is altogether righteous.

"Moreover whom He predestined, these He also called; whom He called, these He also justified; and whom He justified, these He also glorified" (Rom. 8:30). This is called the *Golden Chain* because several links are bound together. First is foreknowledge, which is followed by predestination. We find calling next, then justification, and finally glorification. The Golden Chain is also referred to as the *ordo salutis*, which we will study further next time.

Application

People often think that God is unfair when they hear the doctrine of election. Perhaps you can identify with others who have wrestled with it. An important piece in seeing God's goodness in election is understanding whom God has elected. God elects fallen sinners.

5

The Ordo Salutis

IN THEOLOGY WE TALK ABOUT SOMETHING called the *ordo salutis*, which is Latin for "the order of salvation." There are several aspects to the *ordo salutis*, but Paul does not mention all of them here. He does not mention sanctification, which follows justification. Justification, sanctification, and glorification occur in a certain logical order in the plan of salvation. The order that Paul gives us here in Romans 8 begins with foreknowledge and then moves to predestination. The ones whom God has predestined are also called, and these same ones are also justified and glorified. Tacit here in the text is the concept *all*. All whom God foreknows, in the way that Paul is speaking of here, are predestined, and all those in the category of the predestined are also in the category of the called.

Is the calling that Paul describes in verse 28 an external call, a general call, or the internal, effectual call of the Holy Spirit? God called the world into existence; He did not invite it but commanded it, and it came. When Christ called Paul to be an Apostle, Paul became an Apostle. When Jesus called Lazarus out of the tomb, it was no mere external call that He hoped Lazarus would respond to; it was a sovereign call, an effectual call, one that brought to pass what God had designed. So which kind of call is Paul writing about here in the Golden Chain? Paul writes that those whom God calls, He justifies. Not all who are outwardly called are justified, because many who receive an outward call say no. All who are called inwardly, effectually, come to faith by the power of the Holy Spirit, and they are justified. We see in the Golden Chain a doctrine of predestination that is completely removed from the Arminian view. Paul says that those whom God foreknew, He predestined, and all whom He predestined, He called, and all whom He called, He justified, and all the justified He glorified.

Remember the context: are we safe in our salvation? Once we are justified, can we lose our salvation? We cannot if the Golden Chain is true. It tells us that all the justified will be glorified, so if we are saved now, we are saved forever. That is the Golden Chain. It is not a rusty chain, but one made of the precious truth of the gospel.

Application

The Puritan Stephen Charnock said, "As soon might Satan pull God out of heaven, undermine the security of Christ, and tear him from the bosom of the Father, as deprive the believer of his spiritual life, or destroy that principle of grace which God has implanted in him." This is how certain it is that the Golden Chain will hold together. If you trust in Jesus Christ, your salvation is secure.

6

Our Response

AFTER DECLARING THE GOLDEN CHAIN IN all its links, Paul asks a question of his readers: **What then shall we say to these things?** (v. 31a). In other words, what should the response be? I read a book in which the author described a woman whose husband became convinced of the doctrines of grace and the Reformed faith, a conviction that nearly broke up the marriage. The man's wife said that she could not believe in a God who elects some people to salvation but passes over the rest so that they will perish forever. Her answer to the Apostle's question, "What then shall we say to these things?" was that she did not want anything to do with a God who elects people in that manner. That is not how Paul answers his own question. His answer is this: **If God is for us, who can be against us?** (v. 31b).

One of the greatest Latin phrases in church history is *Deus pro nobis*, "God for us." The famous twentieth-century theologian Karl Barth said that the most important word in the Greek language is *huper*, which means "in behalf of." What should our response be to the Golden Chain? What should our response be to the fact that we have been rooted and grounded in the eternal purposes of God? The response is this: "If God is for us, who can be against us?" I will tell you who can be against us: everybody in the world. Paul is not suggesting that if God is for us, nobody will ever stand to oppose us. The import of his declaration is simple: all the human opposition that rises against us is meaningless in the final analysis, because all the opposition in the world cannot overthrow the glory that God has laid up for His saints from the foundation of the world.

If God is with us from all eternity, and if God is for us in His decree of election, in effectual calling, and in justifying us by His grace, and if God is for us by glorifying every one of His people, then whose opposition can mean anything? It is amazing that people kick and scream against the doctrine of sovereign grace and election. It is one of the most comforting doctrines we will ever learn from sacred Scripture.

Application

Remember when you face opposition that God is for you. Even when the opposition you face isn't from some external source and you become your own worst enemy in your doubts, God is for you. Pray this day that God would give you great comfort in His eternal decree especially when you lack assurance, that you might know that your faith in Christ is not in vain but eternally secured.

WEEK 29

1

God for Us

ATHANASIUS, AN IMPORTANT EARLY CHURCH FATHER, was driven into exile countless times. His tombstone reads, *Athanasius contra mundum*—that is, "Athanasius against the world." *Deus pro nobis*, Athanasius; God was for you though the whole world was against you. My mother taught me to say, "Sticks and stones can break my bones, but words will never hurt me." The first time I tried it, I discovered that words can hurt. Slanderous accusations can be more painful than sticks and stones, but they bounce off the skin of the Christian in the presence of God, because God has declared us righteous in His sight. The verdict is in. There is no higher court of appeal than the verdict rendered by the sovereign Judge of all the earth.

"If God is for us, who can be against us?" (v. 31b). Paul sets forth that phrase in a conditional sense; in other words, the language suggests a kind of uncertainty. The Apostle says, "*If* God is for us," as if it were a matter open to some doubt or further speculation, but Paul is not indicating uncertainty about God's being for us. He has labored thus far through the epistle to demonstrate how deeply God is for His elect. Paul is speaking in the language of logic, even of a syllogism, which gives a first premise and then a second premise and then rushes toward a conclusion. The conclusion of a syllogism is one that follows inexorably from the premises, if the premises are sound. If A and B are true, then C must of necessity follow. So when Paul asks, "If God is for us," he is writing syllogistically, not with respect to uncertainty. We could just as easily translate it with the word *since*: "Since God is for us, who can be against us?"

Obviously, if God is for us, the whole world can be against us, because man in his revolt against God protests not only against his Creator but against all the redeemed. Implicit in the Apostle's statement is not just who *can* be against us, but who *could possibly* stand against us. This is, of course, a rhetorical question; the answer is obvious. No one can stand against us if God is standing with us. An aphorism that has since become something of a cliché goes like this: one person with God on his side is in a majority against all the rest of the human race.

Application

We are familiar with conditions in this life. We have responsibilities that, if not met, can have drastic consequences. We can rest assured, however, when it comes to salvation. The conditions for our salvation have been met in Jesus Christ. Even our faith, which meets the condition that we must ourselves believe on the Lord Jesus Christ to be saved, is the result of God's work in our hearts. Praise the Lord today that from start to finish, from eternity past to eternity future, your salvation is unassailable in Christ.

2

Spared

HE WHO DID NOT SPARE HIS OWN SON, **but delivered Him up for us all, how shall He not with Him also freely give us all things?** (v. 32). We notice first the idea of sparing. When people are rescued from an almost certain doom at the last second, we say that they have been spared a disaster that was about to befall them. When we read such language in Romans 8, how can we not think back to Genesis 22, where God commanded Abraham to offer his son Isaac, the son whom he loved, on the altar at Mount Moriah? In obedience Abraham took his son on an arduous journey and placed him on the altar, bound in ropes, and he lifted up the knife to slay him, but at the last second God stopped him: "Do not lay your hand on the lad, or do anything to him" (Gen. 22:12). God commanded Abraham to spare his son.

It was on Mount Moriah, later named Mount Calvary, just outside the city of Jerusalem, where, one thousand years after Abraham's experience, our Savior on the night before His death went into the garden of Gethsemane and sweated drops of blood, pleading with the Father to allow the cup to pass from Him. "Nevertheless," Jesus said, "not what I will, but what You will" (Mark 14:36). In that moment of the grand passion of Christ, the Father said no. The Father would not spare His Son.

How can we not understand the posture of God toward His people after He has gone to such lengths to effect our redemption? God spared nothing, not even His Son, so that we might be saved. Therefore, Paul says that He "delivered Him up for us all." I don't believe for a moment that God did this for all mankind. God gave His Son to redeem His elect, those who are a part of the Golden Chain.

Because of Christ's perfect obedience for us, the Father bestows every conceivable blessing upon Him. His inheritance is the world and everything in it. Paul says that because the Son died for us and the Father did not spare Him, He will also give us everything that He gives His Son. Here Paul adds to the idea of our adoption, which he developed earlier in Romans 8. We are heirs of God and joint heirs with Christ; the Father is pleased to give all things to His Son, whom He did not spare, and not only to His Son but to all those whom He had given to His Son for His Son's glory.

Application

When we consider that God did not spare His own Son for us, we might think, *How can we ask for anything more?* But the astounding thing here is that Paul promises that God will "also freely give us all things." God is so gracious to us; He knows our needs, and He hears our prayers. Trust in this when you meet with adversity for the sake of Christ, and remember your blessedness: "Blessed are you when they revile and persecute you, and say all kinds of evil against you falsely for My sake. Rejoice and be exceedingly glad, for great is your reward in heaven" (Matt. 5:11–12).

3

No Charge

PAUL CONTINUES WITH HIS LIST OF QUESTIONS. **Who shall bring a charge against God's elect?** (v. 33a). Satan works to bring every conceivable slanderous charge against God's elect. Satan never ceases accusing the brethren. He never stops harassing us and getting at our consciences, telling us how wicked we are and that we do not deserve to be in fellowship with Christ. The principal work of Satan in the life of the believer is not temptation, though he is engaged in that; his chief work is accusation. He accuses us in order to take away our assurance and joy and the consolation that is ours in Christ. He keeps reminding us of our sin. He keeps telling us of our shortcomings. He lays against God's elect every conceivable charge that he can bring; yet there is no work more futile, which is why Paul mocks Satan with this question. What can be sillier than to bring accusations against those who have been redeemed through the blood of the Lamb? The One who justifies is the Judge of all, and He has declared us just by the imputation of the perfect righteousness of Christ.

Who can rightly bring any charge against Jesus? He said to His contemporaries, "Which of you convicts Me of sin?" (John 8:46). He is sinless, so any attempt to charge Jesus with sin is an exercise in futility. It is a waste of time and breath because the Father knows that Christ is without sin. Christ's perfect obedience is transferred to the account of all who put their faith in Him. It is just as futile for anyone to lay a charge against us as it is to lay a charge against Christ, because we are clothed in His righteousness. We are justified by His merit. God has not pardoned or exonerated us, but having clothed us with the righteousness of Christ, He has pronounced His verdict of righteous. Once the supreme, sovereign Judge declares us righteous in His sight, all the slander in the world can make no impact on God's assured, final judgment. There is now no condemnation for those who are in Christ Jesus because the Judge has declared us just.

Justification is not just an abstract doctrine, and we must never negotiate it. It is the very heart and soul of the gospel. Because of our justification in Jesus Christ, we need fear no slander from Satan or from the world.

Application

Next time God gives you an open door to share the gospel with someone, bring His perfect law to bear on the conscience of that person, but also be sure to explain that because of the sacrifice of His righteous Son, our Judge also justifies. That is our only hope under the condemnation of the law.

4

No Condemnation

IT IS GOD WHO JUSTIFIES. **Who is he who condemns?** (vv. 33b–34a). Once God has justified us, who can condemn us? Condemnation is gone. **It is Christ who died, and furthermore is also risen, who is even at the right hand of God, who also makes intercession for us** (v. 34b). It is Christ who died; it is Christ who was raised for our justification; it is Christ who ascended to the right hand of God, where He is seated in the position of cosmic authority. He is the King of kings and Lord of lords. The highest tribunal in the cosmos is the One who died for us. When Stephen's enemies stoned him, they acted with great fury, gnashing their teeth in hatred. They threw rocks that opened gashes on that saint, yet while his blood poured from his veins and life drained from him, he looked up, and God gave him a vision into heaven. He saw the Son of Man standing at the right hand of God (Acts 7:54–60). The earthly court condemned him to death, but at that very moment in the heavenly court, the Judge of all the earth was Stephen's defense counsel. What matters is where the court sits, and it sits at the right hand of God.

Not only is our Savior our Judge and defense attorney, but He is also our intercessor. He is our Great High Priest, pleading our case before God every minute. It is foolish, therefore, to worry about the slander of men. Who shall lay any charge against God's elect? God is the One who justifies. Christ is the One who died and was raised for our justification. Christ is the One sitting at the right hand of the Father, and Christ is the One who intercedes for us every day. **Who shall separate us from the love of Christ?** (v. 35a). Those who live a life of uncertainty, thinking that they can lose their salvation if they fail to persevere to the end, need only remember that God preserves without fail all those whom He has redeemed.

Paul explores things that have the potential to drive a wedge between us and our Savior: **Shall tribulation, or distress, or persecution, or famine, or nakedness, or peril, or sword?** (v. 35b). In these very things we have assurance of Jesus' presence with us. If anything seals His love for us, it is His promise to be with us in the midst of persecution and peril and sword and famine and everything that the world, the flesh, and the Devil can throw against us. The things that Paul anticipates here are not exhaustive; this list is representative. Paul could go on forever, naming things that try to separate us from the love of Christ.

Application

When you pray, do you consider that Jesus is also interceding for you? Reflect on this the next time you go to the Lord in prayer. For all our requests, Jesus is asking the Father to give us all that we need. We can be certain that we are kept secure in our faith, knowing that the Father is pleased to grant what we need because of His Son. That His Son has died for us is all the evidence we need that He has been raised for us.

5

Conquerors

IN THE NINETEENTH CENTURY, some of the most cynical attacks ever written against Christianity came from the pen of Friedrich Nietzsche. He declared the death of God. According to Nietzsche, God died of pity. Nietzsche was convinced that Western civilization, particularly Western Europe, had become completely decadent by his day, primarily due to the baleful influence of Christianity. He could not stand that Christianity exalted virtues like mercy, love, and pity. He believed that such virtues strip human beings of their natural humanity. Nietzsche argued that what most defines humanness is the will to power. Every human being has a drive to dominate, conquer, and rise to the top. Nietzsche said that Christianity with its false piety takes away the strength of humanity, leaving a race of impotent men. Nietzsche called for a new humanity, the dawn of a new superman, the *Übermensch*.

The chief characteristic of this superman, according to Nietzsche, is that of conqueror. He is the man, Nietzsche said, who sails his ship into uncharted waters. He is the Ernest Hemingway of his day who grabs the bull by the horns. He will bow to no opposition and show fear before no power of nature, such as a volcano. He is defiant to the end. He is *Übermensch*, the superman, in contradistinction to the weak, pitiable Christian who turns the other cheek.

I always think of Nietzsche when I read Paul's words about our being more than conquerors in pestilence, tribulation, peril, and sword and in being led as sheep to the slaughter. The Greek word that Paul uses for "conquerors" comes from the term *hupernikaō*. We are hyper-conquerors. The Latin is even better—*super vincēmus*: in all these things we are supermen through Him who loved us.

We have a superman, an *Übermensch*, in Christ. He has conquered the world. Nietzsche believed that dialectical courage would mark the superman; dialectical courage is irrational courage. Nietzsche also declared that life is meaningless and that there are no real values. Since life is meaningless, he said, people can be of good cheer. There is no reason for rational courage because it only leaves people at the bottom of the sea. How different that is from Jesus' charge to His people: "Be of good cheer, I have overcome the world" (John 16:33). There is reason for our cheer and joy—the Lord Jesus Christ has conquered powers, principalities, and every wickedness in the cosmos.

Application

Nietzsche claimed that virtues such as mercy, love, and pity are weak. Yet Jesus displayed God's power and might in overcoming the world through His weakness. What may have appeared as weakness in His death was the greatest display of strength ever seen. All the powers of darkness were unleashed to do their worst to the Son of God, and He defeated them through weakness. When something attempts to separate you from the love of Christ, remember that everything that comes against Christ and His church has been and will be openly shamed (Col. 2:15).

6

No Separation

FOR I AM PERSUADED THAT NEITHER DEATH NOR LIFE, **nor angels nor principalities nor powers, nor things present nor things to come, nor height nor depth, nor any other created thing, shall be able to separate us from the love of God which is in Christ Jesus our Lord** (vv. 38–39). We may feel at times that God has departed from us, but that is when we have to believe His Word rather than our feelings. The Word of God promises and guarantees that death cannot separate us from Christ's love, nor can life or earthly governments. Men could throw Joseph in prison for years, but they could not separate Joseph from the love of his God. Principalities in the demonic world or Satan and his angels cannot separate us from the love of Christ, nor can anything that happens today or tomorrow. What about height? What about depth? Paul is giving us selective examples of what might separate us from the love of Christ. His point is that nothing—height, depth, life, death, powers, principalities, or any creature—can separate us from the love of God that is in Christ Jesus.

Is it safe? That has been the theme of our study of Romans 8. If we have been saved, we are safe from anything that this world can put against us because God from all eternity has loved and redeemed us.

We are His elect. We have been chosen by God to be conformed to the image of Christ and to be Christ's possession—not for a day or a week but for eternity. If we do not like the idea of God's sovereign grace, if we are still kicking against it, why? It is our guarantee that nothing can separate us from the great love wherewith He loves us.

Application

If you or someone you know struggles with assurance of salvation, here is some comforting counsel: Search your heart for any affection toward Jesus Christ as He is presented in Scripture. Such affection would not be there without the work of the Spirit in your life. Read Romans 8:38–39 again and remember that you are also a part of creation. Nothing can separate us from the love of God in Jesus Christ—not even ourselves. This is why your salvation is safe.

Romans 9

I TELL THE TRUTH IN CHRIST, *I am not lying, my conscience also bearing me witness in the Holy Spirit, that I have great sorrow and continual grief in my heart. For I could wish that I myself were accursed from Christ for my brethren, my countrymen according to the flesh, who are Israelites, to whom pertain the adoption, the glory, the covenants, the giving of the law, the service of God, and the promises; of whom are the fathers and from whom, according to the flesh, Christ came, who is over all, the eternally blessed God. Amen.*

But it is not that the word of God has taken no effect. For they are not all Israel who are of Israel, nor are they all children because they are the seed of Abraham; but, "In Isaac your seed shall be called." That is, those who are the children of the flesh, these are not the children of God; but the children of the promise are counted as the seed. For this is the word of promise: "At this time I will come and Sarah shall have a son."

And not only this, but when Rebecca also had conceived by one man, even by our father Isaac (for the children not yet being born, nor having done any good or evil, that the purpose of God according to election might stand, not of works but of Him who calls), it was said to her, "The older shall serve the younger." As it is written, "Jacob I have loved, but Esau I have hated."

What shall we say then? Is there unrighteousness with God? Certainly not! For He says to Moses, "I will have mercy on whomever I will have mercy, and I will have compassion on whomever I will have compassion." So then it is not of him who wills, nor of him who runs, but of God who shows mercy. For the Scripture says to the Pharaoh, "For this very purpose I have raised you up, that I may show My power in you, and that My name may be declared in all the earth." Therefore He has mercy on whom He wills, and whom He wills He hardens.

You will say to me then, "Why does He still find fault? For who has resisted His will?" But indeed, O man, who are you to reply against God? Will the thing formed say to him who formed it, "Why have you made me like this?" Does not the potter have power over the clay, from the same lump to make one vessel for honor and another for dishonor?

What if God, wanting to show His wrath and to make His power known, endured with much longsuffering the vessels of wrath prepared for destruction, and that He might make known the riches of His glory on the vessels of mercy, which He had prepared beforehand for glory, even us whom He called, not of the Jews only, but also of the Gentiles?

As He says also in Hosea:

"I will call them My people, who were not My people,
And her beloved, who was not beloved."
"And it shall come to pass in the place where it was said to them,
'You are not My people,'
There they shall be called sons of the living God."

Isaiah also cries out concerning Israel:

"Though the number of the children of Israel be as the sand of
*   the sea,*
The remnant will be saved.
For He will finish the work and cut it short in righteousness,
Because the Lord will make a short work upon the earth."

And as Isaiah said before:

"Unless the Lord of Sabaoth had left us a seed,
We would have become like Sodom,
And we would have been made like Gomorrah."

What shall we say then? That Gentiles, who did not pursue righteousness, have attained to righteousness, even the righteousness of faith; but Israel, pursuing the law of righteousness, has not attained to the law of righteousness. Why? Because they did not seek it by faith, but as it were, by the works of the law. For they stumbled at that stumbling stone. As it is written:

> *"Behold, I lay in Zion a stumbling stone and rock of offense,
> And whoever believes on Him will not be put to shame."*

WEEK 30

1

The Doctrine of Election

THE DOCTRINE OF GOD'S SOVEREIGN ELECTION is not an arcane item found rarely in obscure passages of Scripture, nor does it require the pursuit of a diligent scholar to uncover it. The doctrine of election appears on virtually every page of the Bible, from Genesis to Revelation. No section of Scripture sets it forth, however, more definitively and persuasively than Romans 9.

I struggled with the doctrine for at least five years after my conversion, despite my godly and able professors who tried to explain the Scriptures. When I was a seminary student, I had a card on my desk on which I had written these words: *It is your duty to believe and to teach what the Bible teaches, not what you would like it to teach.* That bothered my conscience because I did not like Romans 9, but the sheer force of the text overwhelmed me, and afterward it became my lot in life to teach and defend the doctrine of election against those who hold the position I formerly held. Although the doctrine set forth in Romans 9 is absolutely clear, people use three basic ways to get around it.

(1) The easiest and most common way of getting around the doctrine of election is to ignore or avoid it. People direct the discussion to other portions of Scripture, staying studiously away from Romans 9. This tends to happen with those who know enough to realize the force of it.

(2) Others say that Paul in Romans 9 is not writing about God's sovereign election of individuals but about God's sovereign election of nations to a particular historic destiny, specifically Israel as distinguished from Syria, Babylonia, Greece, Rome, or other nations of antiquity. The grace that the Apostle is expounding here, they argue, is not saving grace but

the promise of earthly benefits, such as the inheritance of a piece of real estate, which is still very much contested, even with violence.

(3) The doctrine of election is also gotten around by a method that we have repeatedly considered during our study of Romans—God's foreknowledge. Supposedly, God looks down the corridor of time and knows in advance how people will respond when they hear the gospel. He chooses for salvation those who He knows will say yes to Christ, but He rejects those who He knows will reject Him. We have called this the prescient view of election.

Application

We must guard against twisting Scripture to align with our own ideas of what it ought to teach. There is a danger to handling God's Word in this manner, but there is a remedy to it when we approach Scripture for what it is—God's Word. Go to the Lord in prayer and ask Him for the Spirit's help in understanding Scripture in accord with His intended meaning. If you struggle with a particular teaching or passage of Scripture, pray about it specifically.

2

Sober Beginnings

FOR DECADES, I UNDERSTOOD THE OPENING of Romans 9 to be Paul's declaring a formal oath, the taking of a vow. **I tell the truth in Christ, I am not lying, my conscience also bearing me witness in the Holy Spirit** (v. 1). In times past, I pointed to this passage as an example of the sort of lawful vow or oath that Scripture permits. I reasoned that if Paul takes an oath in his writing, then such oaths are indeed permissible. I learned, however, that I was mistaken in my understanding of this text. Paul uses the preposition *en* instead of *pros*: "I tell the truth in Christ [*en Christos*]." Historically, when people swore in the name of Christ, they used the preposition *pros* ("by") rather than *en*. So in all likelihood, Paul was not swearing an oath here or giving a sacred vow.

Although Paul's opening statement falls short of a vow or oath, Paul is giving a declaration with the deepest solemnity he can muster. He is about to deal with issues that are problematic for the Jews. Before Paul looks at how God has taken the gospel from the Jews to the Gentile community, grafting Gentiles in the place of Israel (Romans 9–11), he wants to make sure that the Jewish community in Rome might read his epistle through his tears. He is not angry or hostile toward his kinsmen—quite the contrary. He speaks as a Christian who embraces and loves truth, *alētheia*, which is embodied in Christ.

Paul is speaking in Christ, in the Holy Spirit, from the depths of his conscience. In other words, Paul's conscience witnesses to him that he speaks the truth. There is no deceit or malice. He is speaking the sober, unvarnished truth to those in Christ, and he is doing so by the Holy Spirit.

Application

We know that God's Word is true because of its source. God cannot lie (Num. 23:19; Titus 1:2; Heb. 6:18). Jesus also said concerning Himself, "I am the way, the truth, and the life" (John 14:6), and He promised His disciples the "Spirit of truth" (John 14:17). God Himself—Father, Son, and Holy Spirit—is the profound reason that we contend to speak the truth in all things.

3

Acquainted with Grief

PAUL IS DECLARING A SOLEMN TRUTH: **I have great sorrow and continual grief in my heart** (v. 2). He is going through what the text calls *dolor*, a Latin term that we find in the name of an ancient street in Jerusalem, *Via Dolorosa*, which means "the way of grief or pain." Paul's grief is not passing. It attends his life and perturbs his heart continually.

When Jesus approached Jerusalem, He considered how the people of the city had hardened themselves against the Word of God. He cried out in a lament, "O Jerusalem, Jerusalem, the one who kills the prophets and stones those who are sent to her! How often I wanted to gather your children together, as a hen gathers her chicks under her wings, but you were not willing!" (Matt. 23:37). That is why Jesus is known as a man of sorrows, acquainted with grief.

Some time ago, I was given the assignment of writing an article about grief for *Tabletalk* magazine. The editors asked me to write from personal experience. As I contemplated the assignment, I thought of the loss of my father when I was seventeen years old. I was stricken with grief, which has never completely left my soul. I think also of the loss of my friend James Montgomery Boice. Upon his death, I lost a friend and a comrade. Yet as I searched my heart, I discovered that most of my grief experiences have involved departures from biblical truth. In that sense, I relate to the Apostle Paul. He loved his fellow Jews and cared about their well-being. When they did not respond to Christ as the Messiah, Paul was grieved in his heart.

I dearly love many non-Christian friends in my hometown and all over the country. I hurt that they do not know the Savior. The same feeling is revealed about Paul as he begins this important chapter. He has a great sorrow, a continual grief, in his heart.

Application

Do you hurt for your lost loved ones? This question is one that we should always be asking ourselves, that we not become callous as though God were not able to work in their hearts. It can be difficult to bear the sorrow that we feel when our loved ones are resistant to the gospel year after year. Continue to pray for those you love who do not know Christ. God can and often does surprise us.

4

Accursed

PAUL ESCALATES THE DESCRIPTION OF HIS PAIN to a degree unprecedented in his writings: **For I could wish that I myself were accursed from Christ for my brethren, my countrymen according to the flesh, who are Israelites** (vv. 3–4a). Paul loves his people so much that he would be willing to give up his salvation for his brothers and sisters, his fellow Jews. I cannot imagine too many things that I would be unwilling to do to see my friends come to Christ, but I have never said that I would be willing to trade my salvation for theirs. I do not think I have that much love for anybody, but the Apostle did.

The word that Paul uses is *anathema*, which means that he would willingly place himself under the very curse of God and be delivered to total destruction if by doing so his people would know Christ. *Anathema* is the word that Paul uses when he writes to the Galatians as they are being seduced away from the true gospel: "But even if we, or an angel from heaven, preach any other gospel to you than what we have preached to you, let him be *anathema*" (Gal. 1:8). Let him be damned. Any threat to the gospel provoked the wrath of the Apostle. To the false teachers Paul would say, "Damn you for destroying the gospel," the worst kind of curse against a human being. It goes back deeply into the Old Testament. At the time of the conquest of Canaan, God put the Canaanites under the ban, which meant that He forbade the people of Israel to spare Canaanite lives or to take their goods. God delivered them to absolute destruction. That is the meaning of *anathema*, and Paul was willing to know it personally if that would save his kinsmen.

Application

The heart of the Apostle Paul is on display in these verses at the opening of Romans 9. It might be hard for us to imagine such zeal and think that it must be something peculiar to the Apostle. But let us remember that Paul calls us to be imitators of him, as he is of Christ (1 Cor. 11:1). Be bold in defending the gospel, but also in your profound desire to see the salvation of the lost.

5

Missed Privileges

PAUL'S NATURAL KINSMEN ARE THOSE **to whom pertain the adoption, the glory, the covenants, the giving of the law, the service of God, and the promises** (v. 4b). First, the adoption pertains to the Israelites. We think of adoption almost exclusively in New Testament categories; it is the great benefit received by all who are justified and welcomed into God's family. The idea of God's adopted children, however, goes back into the pages of the Old Testament. Israel was the adopted son of God.

In his Gospel, Matthew makes application from Old Testament prophecy. After Jesus was born and Herod issued the threat of infant slaughter, an angel warned Joseph in a dream to flee from Bethlehem and not return to Nazareth but to go into Egypt until the threat had passed. Matthew tells us that Joseph took Mary and the babe and fled to Egypt. When the Herodian persecution was over, Joseph returned to Israel, thereby fulfilling the Old Testament prophecy, "Out of Egypt I called My Son" (Matt. 2:15). The original reference to adoption is found at the exodus, when God redeemed His people from the yoke of slavery under Pharaoh, calling the nation His son (Hos. 11:1). The

Israelites were those who had been called to enjoy adoption, and it pains Paul that they had missed their privilege.

Glory is also on Paul's list of Israelite privileges. In high school I had a friend who was a tremendous athlete. He excelled in several sports, but his best was ice hockey, and we played together on the team. After scoring a goal, he would raise his stick high and yell to the fans, "My people, my people." I asked him why he did that, and he replied, "I'm basking in the glory." After hockey we played golf together, but eventually we lost touch. Several years later, when I was living in Pittsburgh, I got a call from him. "R.C., I'm coming to Pittsburgh. Let's get together and play golf. I want to recover the glory." We have such a superficial understanding of glory.

Application

We often hear phrases such as *the glory days*, referring to bygone years or seasons of our lives that seem to be gone forever, never to return. The glory of God is not something that fades away. It neither increases nor decreases but is perfect in every way. May we never trade the imperishable glory of God that is ours in Christ for the things of this world, which is fading away.

6

Glory

I'VE MENTIONED BEFORE THAT THE GREEK WORD for "glory" is *doxa*. From it we get *doxology*. When we sing the Doxology on Sunday mornings, we are giving glory to God. The Latin equivalent is the word *gloria,* from which we get the Gloria Patri:

Glory be to the Father, and to the Son, and to the Holy Ghost.
As it was in the beginning, is now, and ever shall be. Amen.

Glory attributes supernatural majesty to God. His glory is so brilliant that human eyes are not permitted to behold it, yet God allowed His glory to dwell in the midst of His people Israel. The Old Testament glory hovered over the mercy seat and the ark of the covenant in the Holy of Holies.

Glory in Israel was connected to the *shekinah,* a blazing light that manifested God's glory and made Him a consuming fire. Ezekiel saw the glory of God rising from the city of Jerusalem and departing (Ezekiel 10). At the birth of Jesus, the glory of God flooded the landscape (Luke 2:8–9). That *doxa* or *gloria* pertained to Israel. God first manifested His glory in the community He formed from the slaves in Egypt.

Israel had been given the covenants—with Adam, with Noah, with Abraham, Isaac, and Jacob, with Moses, and with David. The Israelites had also been given the law and the service of God. Paul uses the word *latreia,* which actually refers to the worship of God. Our instructions about how to bring praise sacrifices to God in corporate worship did not come to us from the Greeks or the Romans. The principles of worship that shape our devotion were born in Israel. God delivered to Israel the principles by which He is to be worshiped, adored, and sanctified.

Those promises we stand on did not come *de novo* from the mind of Paul or John or Peter in the New Testament era. The promises of God came through centuries of prophetic utterances going all the way back to the *protoevangel* in Genesis 3, where God promised that the Seed of the woman would crush the head of the serpent (v. 15). The thousands of promises of the One to come out of Israel from the root of Jesse pertained to the Israelites.

All these things—the adoption, the glory, the covenants, the giving of the law, the worship of God, and God's promises—came through Paul's kinsmen, Israel. Do we wonder, then, at the weight of Paul's tears?

Application

The realities that were Israel's in the old covenant are also the church's in the new covenant. Paul will explain in Romans 9–11 that Israel had not been rejected but had been enlarged to include all manner of people. As the church, we have the adoption, the glory, the covenants, the law, the worship, and the promises in the person and work of Christ. Take some time to reflect on what is yours in Him, and go to the Lord in praise for His matchless grace.

WEEK 31

1

Christ over All

PAUL ADDS MORE ABOUT HIS KINSMEN: **of whom are the fathers and from whom, according to the flesh, Christ came, who is over all, the eternally blessed God. Amen** (v. 5). What primarily pertains to the Israelites is Jesus, a Jew, from the seed of David.

Paul notes that Christ came from the seed of David "according to the flesh," *kata sarka*; Paul affirms Jesus' Jewish ancestry, but he does not stop there. He gives one of the clearest and most decisive affirmations of the deity of Christ that we find anywhere in Scripture. Christ is over all things, the entire universe. The Jews used this expression to refer to God's dominion over the entire creation; He is the Most High God. Here Paul says that Christ is over all. Some attack the biblical concept of Christ's deity by trying to change the syntax of the verse, translating it "Christ who is blessed eternally by God." In other words, Jesus' lordship was God's gift to Him, a manifestation of divine blessing rather than a mark of divinity. That is a tortuous approach to the syntax of this particular passage because the same could be said of any Christian—that he or she is blessed of God. The Apostle is referring to Jesus as *the* eternally blessed God.

After Paul makes this profound affirmation of the full deity of Christ, he interjects "Amen," which is the word that the Jews used to affirm the truth of a statement. In some churches, people respond to the preaching of the Word with a shout of "Amen," but it is rarely heard in our more staid assemblies. The shout "Amen" is an affirmation of the truth they are hearing. "Amen" is the term that Jesus used when prefacing His teaching to the disciples: "Amen, amen, I say to you." We translate "Truly, truly, I say to you" or "Verily, verily, I say unto you." The word *amen* comes from *emut*, which means "truth." Paul punctuates his profound affirmation of the divine nature of Christ with this word, which every Jew understood to be a clear affirmation of truth. Here Paul says "amen" about his own words: "Christ came, who is over all, the eternally blessed God. Amen."

Application

The doctrine of the divinity of Jesus Christ is not some tertiary matter. The Jesus in whom we place our faith is the Son of God who became flesh to live and die for us, and He has been raised and rules over everything at the Father's right hand. Placing our faith in anyone else but Him would be foolish, so rest in Him alone and call others to do the same.

2

God's Work through His Word

I WANT YOU TO FOLLOW CLOSELY the reasoning of the Apostle Paul. He has lamented the fate of his fellow Jews. Although his kinsmen had been given the covenants and promises, they had missed out on the redemption brought to them by the Messiah; therefore, it seemed that the promises and covenants that God had made with His people in antiquity were to no avail. Jesus "came to His own, and His own did not receive Him" (John 1:11). His very people had turned against Him.

Does this mean that all the promises of salvation that God made through the centuries have come to naught? Does this mean that because the Jews have failed to understand those promises and have missed their Messiah, God's plan of redemption has ended? Paul says no: **But it is not that the word of God has taken no effect** (v. 6a).

I once jokingly asked my congregation, "What am I doing here? Why do I bother to expound the Word of God to people who can't remember the sermon three weeks later?" In a real sense, that doesn't bother me, because my job is to open the Scriptures and expound them as carefully, accurately, and persuasively as I know how. The efficacy of that preaching, the power of the exposition, never lies with me. I am not responsible for the effect that the Word of God has upon the hearer. God takes His Word and applies it to people.

The Spirit of God works with the Word of God to pierce our souls. It is impossible for the Word of God to be without effect. If my congregation forgets something I say or even the whole sermon, I know that the Holy Spirit is going to take that Word where He wants to take it, and He will hide it in our hearts. We may not know that it's hidden there; we may not be able to remember, but we have been affected. That is the power of the Word. That is why Paul says that although the

Jews of his generation along with those who heard the prophets earlier have rejected God's Word, that rejection has not nullified the Word of God. God will not permit His Word to return to Him void (Isa. 55:11).

Application

We live in a time when we can hear sermons from gifted preachers all around the world. Yet God calls us to be a part of a local church and there to receive our primary instruction in the Word. Since God is pleased to work through His Word and works effectually by His Spirit, then we ought to listen to our pastor as he preaches the Scriptures and anticipate in faith that God will work through the faithful preaching of His Word.

3

True Israel

PAUL REMINDS HIS READERS THAT **they are not all Israel who are of Israel, nor are they all children because they are the seed of Abraham** (vv. 6b–7a). He has to work against the idea that salvation is passed on biologically or through the visible nation of Israel. Following Augustine, we distinguish between the visible church and the invisible church. The point of the distinction is that not all members of a visible church are redeemed. Not everybody in the visible church is numbered among the elect, but only those in the invisible church. It's called *invisible* because we cannot read the hearts of the congregation. I don't know who has made a true profession of faith. Some might have made a profession with their lips but their hearts remain far from God. I cannot read people's hearts, but I can hear their words. People cannot read my heart, but God can. The invisible church is absolutely manifest to the scrutiny of Almighty God. He knows His own, and though we may seek to fool our fellow citizens about our state of grace, nobody has ever fooled God about the state of his or her heart.

Paul makes that same distinction. Just because somebody is an ethnic Jew, a member of the commonwealth of Israel, does not mean that he is saved. The Pharisees fell into that trap. They said, "Abraham is our father" (John 8:39), as if that automatically guaranteed them entrance into the kingdom of God. Not every Jew is a child of promise. Looking to the Old Testament, Paul says that belonging to the seed of Abraham is no guarantee of entry into the kingdom of God. Ishmael was a child of Abraham, but Ishmael was not the child of promise. Paul reminds his readers that in Isaac the seed was called; that is, the children of the flesh are not the children of God. The children of promise are counted as the seed. **For this is the word of promise: "At this time I will come and Sarah shall have a son"** (v. 9).

Application

We ought to serve the children in our churches diligently so that we might see them, by God's good pleasure, embrace the promise of salvation by faith. In many churches, congregations make vows to assist parents as they raise their children in the nurture and admonition of the Lord. Whether it is teaching children, worshiping cheerfully beside them, or supporting their parents, look for opportunities to serve those whom Jesus was pleased to receive (see Mark 10:13–16).

4

The Denial of the Doctrine

THERE IS MUCH AT STAKE IN the reading of Romans 8 and 9, so something I said earlier bears repeating. In my opinion and in the opinion of church history, there is no portion of Scripture that teaches the unconditional election of God in His sovereign grace more persuasively than Romans 9. Despite the perspicuity of the text, the majority of professing evangelicals in our day deny the doctrine of unconditional election. Earlier I noted three ways that people try to get around the doctrine. I repeat them here and, in our next study, add a fourth.

The first and most common way is a systematic avoidance of the text. I did a radio interview not too long ago in which the radio host was against anything regarding the sovereignty of God in election. Every time I tried to take him to Romans 9, he steadfastly refused to go there. Instead, he recited text after text from other portions of the Bible that tell us that people have to choose Christ and believe in Him. The one I hear most often is John 3:16: "God so loved the world that He gave His only begotten Son, that whoever believes in Him should not perish but have everlasting life." The radio host concluded, "Obviously, if all who believe will be saved, it must mean that everybody has the ability to believe." I told him, no, it does not necessarily mean that, particularly when in that same chapter our Lord had just told Nicodemus that unless a man is born again he cannot see the kingdom of God, let alone enter it. Unless the Holy Spirit opens our eyes and ears, we will never believe in or choose Jesus.

The second way in which people get around the doctrine of election is by arguing that Paul in Romans 9 is writing about nations, not individuals. But when Paul makes his point about election, he mentions *individuals*. He writes about Jacob and Esau. The reference to individuals cannot be ignored, so the argument falls by its own weight.

Closely related to that argument is a third one: in Romans 9, Paul is writing about God's election of individuals for temporal blessings. Some are elected to inherit land, possessions, herds, and goats, but not salvation. I cannot imagine a more astonishing interpretation of the text. In order to interpret Romans 9 in this manner, it has to be pulled away from its connection to Romans 1–8. Paul introduced the doctrine of predestination in 8:29–30. There, Paul clearly puts the idea of predestination in the context of personal salvation, a theme that he has been developing since chapter 1. To see the Apostle as describing in chapter 9 anything other than real salvation is to clutch at straws.

Application

As you study Romans 9, it is important to recognize its clear teaching about unconditional election and also to consider why many evangelicals struggle with the doctrine. When we try to understand others' concerns, we might better know how to speak the truth in love. If the doctrine of election is difficult for them, let us not provide greater difficulty but patiently and prayerfully search the Scripture with them.

5

The Fourth Denial

THE GREAT SWISS THEOLOGIAN ROGER NICOLE made tremendous contributions to the church in the twentieth century. He once made the observation that we are, by nature, Pelagian. We assume that we have the power to incline our hearts to Christ while we are yet in the flesh. Our natural hostility to the sovereignty of grace is not instantly cured by conversion, which is why a majority of Christians still effectively hold to semi-Pelagianism and seek to escape the full implications of the doctrine of election.

The fourth attempt to escape the teaching of Romans 9 connects to this mentality and is the most popular view, the doctrine of prescience, which I explained earlier. If you recall, this doctrine holds that God does elect individuals to ultimate salvation, but that the ground of that election is rooted in His prescience, His prior awareness of what people will do when they are given the gospel. Paul writes: **Not only this, but when Rebecca also had conceived by one man, even by our father**

Isaac (for the children not yet being born, nor having done any good or evil, that the purpose of God according to election might stand, not of works but of Him who calls), it was said to her, "The older shall serve the younger" (vv. 10–12). The doctrine of prescience is not only denied, dear friends, but demolished. The Apostle dusts off the spot where it stood, because he addresses unambiguously the very concept that lies at the heart of the prescient view of predestination. The Apostle guides us to look at the two unborn children Jacob and Esau. They were not only brothers; they were also twins. They had the same environmental background, the same mother, father, and birthday. Paul reminds the reader of God's decree that the elder should serve the younger and that this decree was made before either boy was born. It is manifestly obvious that if these two boys were the subjects of divine election, then their election had been settled before they were born.

Application

At the heart of the prescient view of predestination is the belief that we can believe the gospel in our own power. Along with belief in this prescient view often comes the denial of the doctrine of the perseverance of the saints, that all those whom God saves will surely persevere in faith until the end. Unconditional election is a comforting doctrine because our salvation is not determined by some foreseen act of faith or our performance as Christians. All this is lost in the prescient view. Let us praise God for His grace in predestining us to believe.

6

The Ground of Election

NOTICE PAUL'S USE OF THE WORDS *purpose* and *calls*—"that the purpose of God according to election might stand, not of works but of Him who calls" (v. 11b). In both instances, he is referring to the One who elects. The decree came before the boys were born, before they had done any good or evil, to make certain that the purpose of God according to election might stand. Their election was based not on what the boys would do but on what God does. The decree was issued according to the purpose of God so that His purpose would be exalted and established. His purpose is the ground of election.

Our election is never found in us. "So then it is not of him who wills, nor of him who runs, but of God who shows mercy" (v. 16). The prescient advocates say that in the final analysis our election is rooted in some work we do, but election would be conditional if we had to meet a condition in order for God to elect us. A conditional election flies in the face of the very point that the Apostle is laboring to make.

Inevitably, discussions of predestination come down to the free will of the creature, but bringing the notion of free will to this text is humanistic. The idea of a human will not enslaved by sin is an unbiblical understanding. At the heart of this text is indeed a profound affirmation of free will. It teaches that our salvation rests ultimately and eternally on free will, but it is not our free will; it is God's. It is the free will of the Creator, the Redeemer, who, in His sovereign grace, pours His mercy out upon those He chooses. In this case, God distinguishes between Jacob and Esau, the younger and the elder.

Application

The gospel does call people to faith and repentance, and as Christians, we are called to strive after holiness. This does not mean that we are saved because of the degree of our faith, repentance, or holiness. These do, however, flow out of the work of God's Spirit in our lives. Pray to the Lord that you would see increases in your faith, that it would be strengthened, and that through it the Spirit might work as you seek to be holy as God is holy.

WEEK 32

1

The Nature of God's Love

JEWISH CUSTOM HELD THAT THE ELDER received the inheritance and the blessing, but in the case of Jacob and Esau, God turned it upside down and declared that the elder would serve the younger. **"Jacob I have loved"**—Jacob, the supplanter, the liar, the one with very little to commend himself—**"but Esau I have hated"** (v. 13). Some say, "You are teaching that God hates people, and my minister told me that God loves everybody unconditionally."

How do we deal with Paul's words? I've written an entire book on just this verse, "Jacob I have loved, but Esau I have hated." We have to be careful to distinguish between the various ways that the Bible refers to the love of God. The Bible speaks of God's universal love, that is, the love He has for all people. The first has to do with God's *love of benevolence*. The word *benevolence* comes from the prefix *bene-*, which means "good" or "well," and the word *volēns*, "will," so *benevolence* means "goodwill." God has a basic attitude of goodwill to all His creatures, and that posture or attitude of good is shown by His love of beneficence. God's love of benevolence underlies God's giving good gifts to people indiscriminately.

There is, however, a special dimension of God's love, His *love of complacency*. It is a love that takes delight in the object of one's affection. This is the love that the Father has for the Son. Christ is the Beloved, but the Father, in pouring out His love of complacency upon His only begotten Son, extends that love to all who are in Christ Jesus.

Our adoption includes us in that special, redemptive love of God in a way that those outside the fellowship of Christ do not share.

The fact that God loved Jacob and hated Esau does not indicate that God had a malicious sense of odium within His being against Esau. God was not filled with loathing toward him, although there are times in the Old Testament when that kind of loathing is attributed to God against evildoers and impenitent people. Here we are seeing a love-hate contrast, which is intended to communicate the truth that those who receive only God's benevolent love might consider it hatred when compared to God's complacent love, because His benevolent love is such a lower degree of love.

Application

Jesus said to His disciples, "If anyone comes to Me and does not hate his father and mother, wife and children, brothers and sisters, yes, and his own life also, he cannot be My disciple" (Luke 14:26). Jesus was not advising His disciples to have an attitude of hostility toward their earthly parents. Jesus knew that people are called to honor their father and mother, something that they certainly are not doing if they despise them. Jesus was making a comparison. Those who want to love Him must love Him before all others. Jesus requires that the love we have for our friends, spouse, mother, father, or children be so much less than the love we have for Him that it could be seen as hatred.

2

The Righteousness of God

MY FIRST ASSIGNMENT AS A COLLEGE PROFESSOR was to teach the history of philosophy. Many students know that the study of philosophy can be exceedingly difficult. The ideas that are analyzed tend to be abstract and heavy. Otherwise excellent students stumble when they come into the arena of philosophy. It takes a certain kind of mind to track with philosophical inquiry. I tried to give my students some helpful hints on how to wade through the writings of David Hume or René Descartes or Immanuel Kant. I told them, "When you read these men, see if you can discover what problem they are trying to solve and what question they are trying to answer. If you can isolate the problem and clarify in your mind the question they are addressing, it will help you understand how they came to various conclusions."

In my early days of teaching, I disagreed with most of the content I taught on the history of philosophy, but integrity demanded that I try to be scrupulous in setting forth the ideas espoused by various philosophers. If I dared to offer a critique, I had to avoid setting up straw men. I stated my opponent's position with as much force as I knew how.

I discussed with my students how to argue over various ideas and for different positions when controversy arises. I advised that they try to think the way the opponent thinks and track with the opponent's process. I instructed them that when debating, they ought to state the opponent's position more cogently than even the opponent can so that he will know that his position is at least understood. I wanted my students to know that approaching debate that way provides opportunity to address the issues head-on.

I provide that background to aid our understanding Paul, the master teacher. Paul was the greatest theologian ever to walk the face of the earth. He had the equivalent of two PhDs by the time he was twenty-one years old. It has been argued that he was the most learned man in Palestine. Had Paul not become a Christian, we would likely know of him anyway due to his superior intellect. When we deal with a genius of the scope of the Apostle Paul and find ourselves struggling with what he is saying, we need to ask, what problem is he trying to solve and what question is he trying to answer?

Application

When we study the Bible, we must endeavor to understand it rightly. To do so will help us to also represent it accurately to others. Pray that God would use your study of His Word not only to provide the occasion for the Spirit's work in illuminating its meaning to you but also so that you might share that meaning for the salvation of those who are far from Christ and for the edification of those who are united to Him.

3

Paul's Questions

IN ROMANS 9, THE APOSTLE DOES WHAT any good teacher does, particularly one steeped in the rigors of debate: he anticipates the reaction of his students or opponents. Paul anticipates the point of tension, the argument, in what he is teaching about the sovereignty of God in election, and he raises a rhetorical question: **What shall we say then? Is there unrighteousness with God?** (v. 14a). The word translated *unrighteousness* comes from the Greek word *adikia*. When a word is prefaced with that simple letter, *a*, it is a negation of the root. (*Agnosticism* comes from the word *agnosis*, which means "without knowledge" or "non-knowledge.") The root of *adikia* is *dikaios*, which means "righteous" or "just." When you put that prefix, *a-*, in front of *dikaios*, it negates the root. Paul is using the term that defines injustice or unrighteousness. If we go to the Latin text, we find, "What do we say then? Is there iniquity, *iniquitos*, in God?" There is force behind Paul's rhetorical question.

Why would Paul raise a question like this one? Is there anything more fundamental than the clear manifestation that God is altogether righteous? It is unthinkable. It is blasphemous to attribute to God any smear of iniquity, any tinge of unrighteousness, or any hint of injustice.

Words like *injustice, unrighteousness,* and *iniquity* simply do not belong as predicates of God's character. Paul raises a rhetorical question with an unthinkable answer, but why does he raise it? He is anticipating a response to his teaching on the sovereignty of God in election, which he has been setting forth since chapter 8. As soon as Paul makes the radical statement about Jacob and Esau, he can hear the hisses and boos in the gallery: "That's not fair!" It certainly does seem unfair if, for nothing found in Jacob or Esau, God chooses one over the other. The fact that it seems unfair is a chief reason why Christians kick against this doctrine.

Paul's rhetorical question convinces me that the Reformed understanding of predestination is the biblical one and the one that Paul is teaching. In many contexts where I have defended the doctrine of unconditional election, I have heard the objection against predestination and election—that it represents God's unfairness—countless times. Every time I teach the doctrine, somebody objects and says, "That's not fair."

My Arminian friends and some of my Lutheran friends who borrow this prescient view of predestination have had to defend their position against various objections, but I trust that no one has accused them of calling God unrighteous. Why would anybody think of God as unjust, unrighteous, or iniquitous for choosing people on the basis of the decisions they make—either good or bad? What could be fairer than that? Here in Romans 9, Paul anticipates accusations because the doctrine provokes that kind of response from his audience.

Application

Paul's question anticipates certain objections, such as that God could be accused of unrighteousness in His choice of whom to save. This accusation cannot be raised against God, for He is righteous in every way. An important thing to remember is that we are the unrighteous, and that God in His rich mercy extended grace to us. May we never entertain the idea of God's being unrighteous for a single moment, and may we never forget our unrighteousness, that our praise for His grace might be never ceasing.

4

Sovereignty and Grace

PAUL ANSWERS HIS RHETORICAL QUESTION ABOUT divine justice and election: **Certainly not!** (v. 14b). Those strong words are translated in different ways, such as "By no means!" and "God forbid!" I think the most accurate translation is "May it never be!" In other words, no one can dispute the fact that in God is no unrighteousness, injustice, or iniquity, though indeed it may seem that way initially.

After answering his question with that demonstrative reply, Paul inserts a revelation from the Pentateuch: **For He says to Moses, "I will have mercy on whomever I will have mercy, and I will have compassion on whomever I will have compassion"** (v. 15). Paul reminds us of the absolute sovereignty of grace. Obviously, if God is not sovereign, then He is not God. To be God is to be sovereign. When we consider divine sovereignty, we generally look at it in three specific domains. The first domain of God's sovereignty is the universe, which He governs. God, who made the universe, called it into being from nothing by the sheer power of His command. He exercises His sovereign authority over the stars, the floods, and the rivers; He exercises it over history and all things.

The second domain in which God's sovereignty reigns is law. God has the sovereign right to legislate the manner of behavior and response that His creatures should render to Him. Do you believe that God has the right to impose obligations upon His creatures and to bind your conscience with His laws that command "you shall" and "you shall not"? Contrary to the moral relativism so pervasive in our culture, you certainly know, if you have the slightest understanding of the

Christian faith, that God has the authority to command you to do what He says is right.

Most Christians hold to God's sovereignty over nature and law, but when it comes to the third domain—the sovereignty of God's disposition of grace—90 percent get off the train. To them, God is not sovereign in His disposition of grace because if He were, He would show the same mercy to everyone. Scripture paints a different picture of God's exercise of grace: "I will have mercy on whomever I will have mercy, and I will have compassion on whomever I will have compassion."

How can God say that and still be just? He can, because He is exercising mercy upon sinners. No one can shake his fist at God justly, yet plenty do, saying, "That's not fair. You have given me a bad deal." No sinner has the right to say with impunity, "God, You owe me grace." If grace is owed, it is not grace. The very essence of grace is its voluntary character. God reserves to Himself the sovereign, absolute right to give grace to some and withhold that grace from others.

Application

If grace is something unmerited, and God's elect are those who receive His grace, then election is also unmerited. To abandon the doctrine of God's sovereign election fundamentally distorts our understanding of grace. Throughout the day, reflect on God's grace to you in Jesus Christ, and let it humble you. We serve a gracious God. Let us be grateful.

5

Non-Justice

WHEN WE COME TO THE CONCEPT OF JUSTICE, there is a circle of righteousness, or justice, and everything just or righteous fits in that circle. But when we consider the concept of non-justice, it gets confusing.

Non-justice points to and includes everything outside our circle of justice. We have justice inside the circle and non-justice outside the circle, but what about injustice? Injustice is outside the category of justice; it falls into the realm of non-justice. Injustice is a bad thing. It is evil to commit an injustice. Mercy is not bad, so is mercy inside the circle of justice? The answer is no; mercy is non-justice. There are two things outside the circle of justice: one is injustice, which is evil, and the other is mercy, which is not evil. So is there injustice in God? No. Is there unrighteousness in God? No. Is there iniquity in God? No. Is there non-justice in God? Yes, there is. There is mercy and grace, but grace is never inside the circle of justice. Over the years I have told my students, "Don't ever ask God for justice—you might get it."

Through the entire epistle, Paul has been laboring to show that all are sinful; none is just. We have no hope of standing before the judgment of a holy and righteous God, but the wonderful grace of the gospel is that God has provided for us a justice not our own. This justice is the righteousness of Christ, which is imputed to us. This is how Paul has explained the gospel all along. The fact that we are adopted into the family of God and receive the gift of the transfer of the righteousness of Christ to our account is, from beginning to end, the result of God's grace. "For by grace you have been saved through faith, and that not of yourselves; it is the gift of God" (Eph. 2:8).

God in His sovereign disposition of grace interrupts our life while we are alienated from Him, dead in sin and trespasses, and the Holy Spirit comes and quickens us from death to life and changes the disposition of our heart. Where formerly Christ seemed repugnant, now He is the sweetest thing in the world. We rush to Him, we choose Him, we embrace Him, and we trust Him, because God in His grace has given us the pearl of great price. If God does that for us, is He obligated to do it for everybody? If the president of the United States exercises executive clemency and pardons somebody in prison, is he then obligated to pardon everybody? No. What Jacob got was grace; what Esau got was not injustice. God withheld His mercy from Esau—mercy to which Esau had no claim—but the withholding was not an act of injustice on God's part. Jacob got mercy; Esau got justice. The elect get grace; the non-elect get justice. Nobody gets injustice.

Application

The objections to the doctrine of election that we have been looking at in Romans 9 are not uncommon. This is a doctrine with which many struggle, but there are a standard set of objections against it. Take a moment to look over today's study once again and rehearse the differences between God's justice and mercy to prepare for opportunities to provide an answer to someone who struggles with this doctrine.

6

God's Undeserved Mercy

GOD DOES NOT HAVE TO HAVE MERCY on everybody. God called Abraham out of paganism, out of Ur of the Chaldeans, and made him a covenant promise, not because Abraham had done any good thing but so that the purposes of God, according to His grace, might stand. God did not do that for Hammurabi or Nebuchadnezzar. Jesus intervened in the life of Paul in a way that He did not do for Pontius Pilate or Caiaphas or for the scribes and Pharisees.

If we read the Bible from Genesis to Revelation, we see that God does not treat everybody the same way. If He did, we would all have the same place in hell, but He exercises mercy to some so that the glory of His purposes may be known.

So then it is not of him who wills, nor of him who runs, but of God who shows mercy (v. 16). Paul sets forth the doctrine of election with such clarity in Romans 8 and 9 that he leaves us without excuse. How can we look at this text closely and still say, "It really is of him who wills and him who runs. My free will is the basis of my salvation." No, it is God's free will. Perhaps you have heard it said that God's sovereignty ends where human free will begins. Maybe you have even said it. It is blasphemy, of course, because if God's sovereignty is limited by our free will, then we are sovereign. We do have free will. We have the ability to choose what we want. That is true freedom, but it is always and everywhere limited by God's sovereignty. Anytime man's free will bumps up against God's free will, who wins? It is no contest. It is God's good pleasure to save His elect that He may show forth His grace in salvation.

Let me end with a rebuke. I do not want to be harsh—I understand how difficult this doctrine can be and how much baggage we carry into the discussion of it. If you are hanging on to your semi-Pelagian views of election, get rid of them. Your theology is undermining the sovereignty of God, His grace, and the sweetness of His mercy. We do that when we want to exalt our decisions above His, and it is the very essence of sin. We have to bow before Him and acquiesce not only to the sovereignty of His grace but to the *goodness* of the sovereignty of His grace.

Application

We must affirm God's sovereignty over all things, including our salvation. Since God is sovereign over all things, we can trust Him in the difficult times of our lives because we also affirm His sovereign *goodness*. Since God is sovereign over our salvation, we can trust Him to never let go of us, that we will one day meet Him face-to-face. Take a moment to reflect on your heavenly hope, and remember, as Peter tells us, that our inheritance there is "incorruptible and undefiled and . . . does not fade away" (1 Peter 1:4).

WEEK 33

1

Double Predestination

JOHN CALVIN SAID THAT THE DOCTRINE OF ELECTION is one of the most difficult doctrines of sacred Scripture and must be handled with care, caution, tenderness, but that it should not be neglected. The doctrine comes from the Word of God, and even though we may struggle with it, we must not sweep it under the rug; we must deal with it, albeit carefully.

Here is where we face what I have to call "double or nothing." If some of humanity is elect, then others are non-elect. The non-elect are those whom we call the *reprobate*. So as far as I'm concerned, unless we are universalists there is no way to avoid the idea of a double aspect to divine predestination. Of course predestination is double. There is election and reprobation. We cannot avoid that fact with mental gymnastics. Once we affirm double predestination, however, we have to ask what kind of double predestination we affirm.

One view, sometimes called *hyper-Calvinism*, teaches a symmetrical view of predestination, or equal ultimacy. A symmetrical view of double predestination holds that in the case of the elect, God decreed their election from eternity and in the fullness of time intervenes in their lives and creates saving faith in their hearts by His grace. God invades the souls of the elect and quickens them from spiritual death to spiritual life and brings them to faith in Christ. In a symmetrical manner, the reprobate are doomed from eternity, and God in the fullness of time intrudes into their lives and creates fresh evil in their souls, ensuring their ultimate reprobation and damnation. This symmetrical view believes that God works grace by direct intrusion and that He works hardening by creating evil in the reprobate in an equal manner.

But that is not the orthodox Reformed doctrine of double predestination, and I do not hold to that symmetrical view, or equal ultimacy. I hold to a positive-negative view of double predestination.

A positive-negative distinction in predestination is this: in the case of the elect, God positively intervenes in their lives to rescue them from their corrupt condition. The Holy Spirit changes their hearts of stone to hearts alive to the things of God. That is His positive intervention. In the case of the reprobate, God works negatively insofar as He passes over them. He leaves them to their own devices, but He does not intrude into their lives to create fresh evil. In the mass of fallen humanity, some receive the saving grace of God; God intervenes to rescue them from their sinful condition. He passes over the remainder. Those whom He passes over are not elect; they are reprobate. They are judged because of the evil already present in them, which is in view in this portion of Romans 9 that is dealing with Pharaoh's hardened heart.

Application

When it comes to God's decree of election, we have no way of knowing whether a person with whom we are sharing the gospel is elect. Charles Spurgeon said: "If God would have painted a yellow stripe on the backs of the elect I would go around lifting shirts. But since He didn't I must preach 'whosoever will' and when 'whosoever' believes I know that he is one of the elect." Our calling is to faithfully proclaim the gospel and not get caught up in the mysteries of God's decree.

2

God and Pharaoh

PAUL QUOTES WHAT GOD SAYS TO PHARAOH, **"For this very purpose I have raised you up"** (v. 17a). In this case, it is not enough to say that

God permits Pharaoh to sin. It is not enough to say that God's will is involved only so far as God stayed out of the picture altogether and left Pharaoh to his own devices. That is an attractive way to handle the text, but I do not think it is sufficient to deal with Paul's teaching. Not only has God allowed Pharaoh to continue in willful disobedience, but He also has raised him up. A better way to translate that text is this way: "I have appointed you to this task."

The eternal God Almighty raised up Pharaoh, sat him in the seat of power over the Egyptians, and gave him power to rule over his own people and the Israelite slaves. God put Pharaoh in a position of power for the purpose of showing His own power: **"that I may show My power in you, and that My name may be declared in all the earth"** (v. 17b). Martin Luther said that the people of Israel were *machtlos*, "without any might." All the power was invested in Pharaoh, and it was invested there by the Lord God omnipotent. In the face of God's power, Pharaoh's power was impotent. It is as if God said to Pharaoh, "I appointed you to this position not to show the world how much power you have, Pharaoh, but to show the world My power. That's why I appointed you to this task, so that My people, in their powerlessness, their *machtlos*, might know where the power of their salvation lies."

Therefore He has mercy on whom He wills, and whom He wills He hardens (v. 18). On the surface, it sounds once again as though there is a balance, a symmetry, in which God melts the hearts of the elect and calcifies the hearts of the reprobate. The Bible does say, not only here but throughout the exodus account, that God repeatedly hardens the heart of Pharaoh. How are we to understand that? First, both Pharaoh and God were involved, so in a very real sense God was actively involved in the hardening of the heart of a human being, but how exactly did God harden the heart of Pharaoh? How does He harden anybody's heart?

God deals with impenitent sinners by giving them over to their sin. In the book of Revelation, we find that the final disposition of the wicked is through this very means: "He who is unjust, let him be unjust still; he who is filthy, let him be filthy still" (22:11). God does not have to create any new evil in the human heart. To make someone more wicked than he already is, God need only remove His restraints. One of the great mercies that God gives us is keeping us from being as sinful as we could possibly be.

Application

Christians need not fear that God will hand us over to our sin. The Holy Spirit is truly at work in the hearts of those who are united to Christ and His death and resurrection by faith. We can be assured in the reality that we are new creatures in Christ. But the reality that God does deal with sinners by giving them over to their sin ought to make us all the more diligent in our pursuit of righteousness.

3

Removal of Divine Restraint

EARLIER IN OUR STUDY, I MENTIONED THAT Reformed theology uses the acronym TULIP to describe our situation of original sin. The T in the acronym stands for *total depravity*. I do not like the term *total depravity*; it is misleading. I prefer *radical corruption*. The term *total depravity* suggests that we are as bad as we could possibly be; that is, we are utterly depraved. Think, however, of all the sins you have committed in your lifetime. As bad as they have been, they could have been worse. You could have committed more sins, and the sins you have committed could have been more vicious. The same could be said of Ted Bundy, Charles Manson, and Adolf Hitler. No one has been as sinful as he could theoretically be—not because some island of righteousness holds him back from utter depravity, but because the restraining power of God is a bridle that keeps all in check. When we abuse God's patience and long-suffering, our hearts become harder and harder, and at any moment God can remove the restraints and give us over to our sin.

From Genesis to Revelation, we see that God's abandoning a sinner to wickedness is not an act of unrighteousness on His part; it is a manifestation of His perfect justice. It is as if He is saying, "Do you want to sin? I am not going to strive with you anymore. I am going to loosen the leash and let you do what you want, because I know that the desires of your heart are only wicked continually."

Being given over to sin is itself a judgment on sin—that is a biblical principle. It presupposes an existing sinful condition. God did not look around Egypt for somebody to appoint to resist Moses and in the process stumble upon the poor, innocent, righteous young man Pharaoh and say, "I will take this benevolent young fellow because he is an able administrator, and I will put him on the seat of power over the Egyptians and make him as evil as I can so that I can get My will done and show My power to the whole world." That would be sheer cosmic tyranny, and it is not what God did. He hardened a man who was already hard. Pharaoh could not say before God, "God, what's going on here? You are punishing me for the hardness of my heart while You have been making sure that my heart gets hardened. That is not fair." Yes, it is fair. It is perfect justice for God to give an evil one over to evil.

Application

God does not tempt anyone to sin (James 1:13). Moreover, for all those who have been purchased by Christ, God provides a way out of our temptations to sin. Remember the promise of 1 Corinthians 10:13 next time you are tempted to sin: "God is faithful, who will not allow you to be tempted beyond what you are able, but with the temptation will also make the way of escape, that you may be able to bear it."

4

Potter and Clay

AT THIS POINT IN THE TEXT, Paul is expecting another objection. He has already heard this one: "Is there unrighteousness with God?" (v. 14). Now, as soon as Paul mentions Pharaoh's hardening, he heads off the objection that he knows will follow: **You will say to me then, "Why does He still find fault? For who has resisted His will?"** (v. 19). Paul does not answer that question. He does not slip into Arminianism and say, "The reason He still finds fault is that all sin is found in man, so it is dependent on what people do with their choices." We find none of that here.

Paul's response to this anticipated objection is simply a moral rebuke: **But indeed, O man, who are you to reply against God?** (v. 20a). Before Paul begins to answer the question, he calls the objector to remember who he, the objector, is and who God is. He is basically saying to those who constantly carp against God's sovereignty, "Who do you think you are?"

Remember Job. He was the victim of much injustice at the hands of men and Satan; he suffered affliction without relief. Finally, he raised his fist against heaven and shook it in the face of God. God answered Job by means of a lengthy, relentless interrogation:

> Who is this who darkens counsel
> By words without knowledge?
> Now prepare yourself like a man;
> I will question you, and you shall answer Me. (Job 38:2–3)

God's interrogation of Job continues: "Can you bind the cluster of the Pleiades, or loose the belt of Orion?" (v. 31). Job answered no. "Can you draw out Leviathan with a hook, or snare his tongue with a line which you lower?" (41:1). The answer was no, chapter after chapter, and finally Job said, "I abhor myself, and repent in dust and ashes" (42:6). Even when we struggle, even when we do not fully comprehend the mystery of God's sovereign will, let that not lead us to blasphemy.

The absolute integrity and righteousness of Almighty God is not to be questioned. **Will the thing formed say to him who formed it, "Why have you made me like this?"** (v. 20b). Pharaoh could not shake his fist at God and ask, "Why have You hardened my heart?" God owed Pharaoh no explanation. Pharaoh's heart had no inherent righteousness. God used Pharaoh for His glorious, holy, merciful, and gracious plan of salvation.

Application

Sometimes we can look back on our lives and wonder why God allowed a particular tragedy or a particular sin on our part. We might be tempted in these moments to question God, but we ought not to be presumptuous, as though we knew His reasons or, worse, were questioning His wisdom. Instead, let us trust Him and continue along the path of faith and repentance, assured of His promise that He is working all things for our good.

5

Infralapsarianism

"BUT INDEED, O MAN, WHO ARE YOU TO reply against God? Will the thing formed say to him who formed it, 'Why have you made me like this?'" (v. 20). Does not the potter have power over the clay, from the same lump to make one vessel for honor and another for dishonor? (v. 21). I want to look at this passage more closely in light of a classic controversy within the Reformed tradition, that between *supralapsarianism* and *infralapsarianism*. This controversy has been labeled as an arcane principle of theology, but as difficult and controversial as the issue has been historically, it is not without significance. It makes a big difference which side we come down on, and I address it here because the controversy is provoked by the text before us.

The debate between supralapsarianism and infralapsarianism has to do with the relationship of God's decrees to election and the fall, particularly to the fall—the lapse of the human race into sin—hence, the root of both terms, *lapsarianism*. Both *supra* and *infra* deal with God's involvement with the fall and the order of God's decrees with respect to it and to election.

Some think that those who hold to the doctrine of infralapsarianism claim that God's decree of election came after the fall, and that those who hold to supralapsarianism claim that God's decree of election came before the fall. That is a false distinction. Both sides understand that God's decrees regarding election and reprobation are rooted in eternity. God did not issue a decree to save people as a plan B, as if His original purpose in creation had been ruined by Adam and Eve's sin. In other words, God did not have to remedy the mess of the fall by coming up with a plan of salvation. Both sides agree that God's sovereign plan of salvation was determined before the foundation of the world—before Adam and Eve existed. The question is not *when* the decrees were executed by God in His eternal plan, but rather the *order* of the decrees.

The infralapsarian position, held by the vast majority of historic Calvinists and Reformed theologians, claims that God's decree of election was made in view of the fall. When God makes from one batch of clay vessels fit for destruction and from another vessels fit for honor, it does not mean that He planned from eternity to make some people bad and other people redeemable. God applies His redeeming grace to a mass of humanity completely dead in sin and trespasses. The decree of electing grace is made in light of the fall. In fact, if it were not made in light of the fall, it would not be a decree of grace.

Application

As you consider this theological debate, read Ephesians 1:3–14 and especially note verses 4–6: "He chose us in Him before the foundation of the world, that we should be holy and without blame before Him in love, having predestined us for adoption as sons by Jesus Christ to Himself, according to the good pleasure of His will, to the praise of the glory of His grace, by which He made us accepted in the Beloved." Our election is explicitly connected to the person and work of Christ.

6

Supralapsarianism

ON THE OTHER SIDE OF THE COIN is the supralapsarian position, which teaches that God decreed the fall in light of His doctrine of election. God first elected certain people to salvation and others to reprobation, and in order to accomplish that eternal purpose, He decreed the fall of humanity. The purpose of the fall was to provide the necessary clay for God to choose some to salvation and others to reprobation. Supralapsarians say that God planned to save some and condemn others, and that in order to make that possible, He consigned the whole world to ruin. Therefore, the purpose of the fall was to provide the necessary condition through which God shows His grace and wrath. That is problematic because it violates what we call the biblical *a priori*— God is not the author or creator of sin. God does not choose to create people in a fallen condition so that He can condemn them to eternal damnation. It is not God's purpose to force people to sin and then punish them for that sin.

I do not believe that God creates people wicked and then punishes them for their wickedness, nor is Paul teaching that here in Romans 9. At the same time, as Augustine said, in some sense God did ordain the fall. Why do I say this? Because of God's sovereignty, power, and authority. God is sovereign over nature and human history. He rules all things by His power and authority. He is sovereign over the disposition of His grace. Nothing can happen apart from God's sovereign action. If I plan to steal a car tonight, my evil intentions might be a secret from the car's owner, but they are not hidden from God. He knows what I am going to do before I do it, and He knows what I am going to say before I say it. Before a word is even formed on my lips, He knows it altogether (Ps. 139:4). God knows my intentions, even though others do not unless I tell them.

God has the power to stop me from stealing a car, but does He have the *authority* to stop me? He does. God has the authority and power to prevent anything from happening that does, in fact, happen. God can exercise His authority and power and sovereignty by stopping something from happening or by not stopping it. Those are God's options always in every way. Since the fall happened, God knew that it was going to happen, and He could have prevented it, but He chose not to. His purpose in not stopping it, however, was not to provide Himself with a wicked batch of clay on which to exercise His sovereign decree of reprobation. Why God allowed it is something that we cannot fully know. The answer that Scripture gives is that somehow the lapse into sin, which produced a batch of fallen humanity and fragile, corrupt clay, was for His glory.

Application

The Canons of Dort are helpful in stating the infralapsarian position that magnifies God's grace:

> [God] graciously softens the hearts, however hard, of his chosen ones and inclines them to believe, but by his just judgment he leaves in their wickedness and hardness of heart those who have not been chosen. And in this especially is disclosed to us his act—unfathomable, and as merciful as it is just—of distinguishing between people equally lost. This is the well-known decision

of election and reprobation revealed in God's Word. This decision the wicked, impure, and unstable distort to their own ruin, but it provides holy and godly souls with comfort beyond words.

Rejoice in this comfort if you are in Christ.

WEEK 34

1

Wrath Made Known

PAUL ADDRESSES THIS QUESTION TO THE Roman Christians, but by extension he addresses it to us: **What if God, wanting to show His wrath and to make His power known, endured with much long-suffering the vessels of wrath prepared for destruction . . . ?** (v. 22). Would there be anything wrong with a just and holy God's displaying His power and wrath? We might struggle with that because we live in a culture that has rejected any idea of a wrathful God, but Paul refuted that back in Romans 1: "For the wrath of God is revealed from heaven against all ungodliness and unrighteousness of men" (v. 18).

When God was going to visit His wrath on Sodom and Gomorrah, Abraham asked Him, "Would You also destroy the righteous with the wicked? Suppose there were fifty righteous within the city; would You also destroy the place and not spare it for the fifty righteous that were in it?" (Gen. 18:23b–24). Abraham, the father of the faithful, fell into an abysmal heresy by suggesting even the possibility that God would punish innocent people. Abraham came to his senses and said to God, "Far be it from You to do such a thing as this, to slay the righteous with the wicked, so that the righteous should be as the wicked; far be it from You! Shall not the Judge of all the earth do right?" (v. 25). The distance between the likelihood of God's punishing the innocent with the guilty, the righteous with the wicked, is infinite. It is absolutely unthinkable.

When we see Paul talk about God's showing His power—His wrath for vessels fit for destruction and dishonor—we must not think that God punishes innocent people or that He finds fault with the faultless. "Shall not the Judge of all of the earth do right?" It is right for the Judge of the earth to show His wrath. We may not like His wrath; we may choke on the very idea of it. It should take us no more than five minutes to think about the justness of a holy God's displaying anger against sin. When Jesus made a rope from cords, went into the temple in Jerusalem, kicked over the tables, and drove out the money changers in a fit of rage, it was a demonstration of justifiable anger. Every time the New Testament mentions the last judgment, it shows everyone standing before the judgment seat of God with their mouths shut. The whole world is found guilty before Him.

Application

Death is a sobering reality, and it is especially difficult to process when unbelieving loved ones die. We might be tempted to question God as questions about our loved one's eternal destiny come into focus. We must remember that God is just. Even though it may be disturbing to reflect on His just judgment, it is exactly that—just.

2

Riches of Glory Made Known

GOD'S SOVEREIGNTY IN ELECTION IS REVEALED so that He might make known the riches of His glory on the vessels of mercy, which He

had prepared beforehand for glory (v. 23). The treasure of God's glory is likened to riches untold, riches that can never be counted. That is what the doctrine of election is about. We must never study the doctrine of predestination in the abstract. In the final analysis, although predestination certainly involves God's sovereignty—His omnipotence and omniscience—the doctrine is about the riches of God's glory. Paul cannot rehearse these things without soon breaking into doxology: "Oh, the depth of the riches both of the wisdom and knowledge of God!" (11:33a). I initially struggled to embrace the doctrine of election, but contemplating the riches of God's glory enabled me to see the sweetness of this doctrine. It screams not so much sovereignty as unfathomable grace and mercy.

That is why we talk about doctrines such as justification and election as the doctrines of grace. Grace is the idea here in the text we are considering. From a corrupt mass of clay God chose to make vessels of glory. If you are in Christ Jesus, that is what God has done for you in His mercy and grace. He has made you a vessel of mercy that He prepared before the foundation of the world for glory. We are bound from God's eternal plan for eternal glory in His family, **even us whom He called, not of the Jews only, but also of the Gentiles** (v. 24).

God will have mercy on whom He will have mercy and call a people who were not His people. Paul is talking about us. We who were no people now are His people by grace. We are the wild olive branch grafted into the root of the tree. We bring nothing to the table. Nothing in us could move God to include us in His kingdom. Our only hope is the riches of His glory and mercy. That is what election is all about.

Application

When it comes to the doctrines of election and reprobation, as John Calvin said, "A mystery which our minds cannot comprehend ought to be reverently adored." This is especially the case in that, while we don't have a complete understanding of God's eternal decree, we do know that what He is working out in human history ultimately displays His holiness and mercy for the sake of His own glory. As recipients of His mercy, we must praise Him all the more.

3

Not My People and My People

AS WE COME TO THE END OF CHAPTER 9, Paul looks to the past, to the pilgrimage of Old Testament Israel, and he reminds us that Hosea was required to marry an adulterous woman and that their children's names had symbolic significance. One child was called *Lo-Ammi*, which means in Hebrew "not my people." In that name God expressed His judgment against the ten tribes of Israel that had become apostate, but afterward: **"I will call them My people, who were not My people, and her beloved, who was not beloved"** (v. 25). The failure of one group became the occasion for God's expanding His mercy to those outside the community.

Mercy has been extended to the Gentiles. The Jewish people, who had been the stewards of the oracles of God, had missed the coming of the Messiah. When we are adopted into the family of God, we experience an affection from God that we have no claim upon. There is nothing lovely in us in the sight of God, but He has been pleased in His mercy to call us His people, to adopt us into His family where we have no birthright or entitlement. In Christ He calls us His beloved.

The culture in which we live endlessly repeats the myth that God loves everybody equally, so it is no big thing to be loved by God. "Of course God loves us. He is a loving God. God loves everybody." To the contrary, to be loved by God is a privilege, not a birthright. We have no claim on the love of God. Nothing in us would make Him desire us, yet He has, by His mercy, turned His affection to all who put their trust in Christ.

We must understand the mystery of the doctrine of election in terms of election being *in Christ*. We are not Christians because of any righteousness in us. We are Christians by the sheer grace of God alone. We might wonder why God redeems anyone. The only answer I can provide is the great love that the Father has for His Son. The Father will not allow the Son to see the travail of His soul and not be satisfied. Throughout John's Gospel, we see this taught from a different perspective. There, believers are a gift that the Father gives to the Son. Because the Father loves Christ, He gives Christ a people as His legacy, and by God's mercy we are included in that.

Application

Take a moment to prayerfully reflect on the truth that if you are one for whom Christ died, then you are a gift of the Father to the Son. This ought not to puff us up as though we were something special in ourselves; rather, it ought to cause us to feel the overwhelming love of God to us in Christ. It is unimaginable that the Father would take away a gift from His Son, so know this day that, having received the gift of faith and as a gift to Christ yourself, your salvation is sure.

4

Warnings to the Visible Church

PAUL CONTINUES CITING THE OLD TESTAMENT PROPHET: **"It shall come to pass in the place where it was said to them, 'You are not My people,' there they shall be called sons of the living God"** (v. 26). We participate in the family of God, but God has only one Son. Because God has placed us in Christ, we participate in that sonship. We have become sons of God who are not by nature children of God.

Isaiah also cries out concerning Israel: "Though the number of the children of Israel be as the sand of the sea, the remnant will be saved" (v. 27). Paul is looking back to the promise that God made to Abraham: "I will multiply your descendants as the stars of the heaven and as the sand which is on the seashore" (Gen. 22:17). There were countless descendants, yet out of that vast multitude only a remnant would actually be saved. Of all those whom God redeemed from the oppression of Pharaoh in Egypt, only a couple were permitted to enter the Promised Land; the vast majority did not make it. Jesus warned about this:

> Enter by the narrow gate; for wide is the gate and broad is the way that leads to destruction, and there are many who go in by it. Because narrow is the gate and difficult is the way which leads to life, and there are few who find it. (Matt. 7:13–14)

What about the Christian church? Are we safe by virtue of our membership in the visible church? We have learned that people outside the commonwealth of Israel were saved while people inside were not. Paul has already taught that one is not a Jew outwardly but inwardly. Receiving circumcision in an ecclesiastical ritual was not enough to get someone into the kingdom of God; circumcision of the heart was necessary. The same applies to the Christian community. Church membership or receiving baptism is no guarantee of redemption. A true Christian is a Christian internally, not just externally.

Jesus' warning was given to people in the visible church. That is why it is dangerous to seek assurance of our status before God by looking to church membership as proof of our inclusion in the kingdom. Augustine said that it is easy to count the people in the visible church, but that their souls cannot be seen. The state of our soul is invisible to man, but it is manifestly visible to God. The Bible tells us that "man looks at the outward appearance, but the LORD looks at the heart" (1 Sam. 16:7). God knows everyone within His adopted family in ways that we cannot possibly know. The invisible church is the true church; it is the full number of the redeemed.

Application

We must have a saving relationship with Jesus Christ through personal faith, experiencing the realities and benefits of redemption for ourselves. While church membership in the external, visible sense does not guarantee our salvation, we are eager to attend worship and fellowship with a local body of believers because of what is true about us internally.

5

God's Visible and *Invisible Remnant*

WHEN AUGUSTINE WAS ASKED WHERE THE invisible church is to be found, he replied that the invisible church is found almost totally within the visible church. It is remotely possible to be a true believer in Christ but not be involved in the visible church. Such a circumstance is one that I do not think can last for long. If we are truly in Christ, and if we are in the Word of God, we know that it is our duty to be part of the visible fellowship of God's people. If our hearts are really in tune with God, we will, sooner or later—in most cases sooner—unite ourselves with a visible church.

When some think of the thief on the cross who became a member of the invisible church before his death but had no opportunity to join the visible church, they are tempted to think that church membership does not matter. It does matter because the church is where the means of grace are concentrated. Where else can we go to hear an exposition of the Word of God? We are not going to hear it in the halls of Congress. We are going to find it only in the church. I realize that there are churches all over the world that have absolute hostility to the Word of God; we can go to such churches week after week and never experience the means of grace. It is, however, in the visible church that the means of grace are most heavily concentrated.

Augustine said, "He who does not have the church for his mother does not have God for his father." That is an overstatement, because you can be led to Christ outside the church. I was led to Christ outside the church, but I was nurtured by the church, in the church, through the ministry of the church. We must never despair of the church, because it is where the remnant is found.

And as Isaiah said before: "Unless the Lord of Sabaoth had left us a seed, we would have become like Sodom, and we would have been made like Gomorrah" (v. 29). If no remnant existed, if no seeds spilled out from the core of the flower or grain, then the harvest would end forever. Even as God brings His judgment upon Israel, there remains a seed that will bring forth its fruit in season. The prophet said that if God had not left a seed, they would have become like Sodom and Gomorrah, cities that God made short work of when He visited them in judgment.

Application

Being a part of the visible church in unity is essential in fulfilling one of Jesus' own prayers. In the High Priestly Prayer, Jesus prayed to the Father "that they all may be one, as You, Father, are in Me, and I in You, that they also may be one in Us, that the world may believe that You sent Me" (John 17:21). Jesus was praying not only for the disciples who were with Him "but also for those who will believe in [Him] through their word" (v. 20).

6

Whose Righteousness Matters?

PAUL GIVES US ANOTHER RHETORICAL QUESTION: **What shall we say then?** (v. 30a). In other words, what is our response to that grim history of Old Testament Israel? **The Gentiles, who did not pursue righteousness, have attained to righteousness, even the righteousness of faith** (v. 30b). We receive the benefits of the gospel even though we never sought them. It is not in our nature to pursue the things of God. The Gentiles, to whom Paul is writing here in Romans, had no clue about the history of redemption. They were not concerned with studying the Old Testament Scriptures. They did not care about the Law of Moses; they were not pursuing the righteousness of God. In God's mercy, they found what they had not pursued.

But Israel, pursuing the law of righteousness, has not attained to the law of righteousness (v. 31). How can it be, Paul asks, that those outside the redemptive-historical covenant community found the pearl of great price while those on the inside missed it? "He came to His own, and His own did not receive Him" (John 1:11). **Why? Because they did not seek it by faith, but as it were, by the works of the law. For they stumbled at that stumbling stone** (v. 32). The One whom God appointed as the cornerstone of His kingdom became a stumbling block, a stone of offense. Israel tripped over grace. They fell over their Messiah because they could not fathom receiving God's favor apart from their righteousness. The multitudes in Israel sought the righteousness of God through their endeavors and missed the kingdom of God, and that same error is deeply ingrained in churches all over the world. I venture to say that at least 80 percent of Christian church members in our country believe that they can get to heaven through their good works.

This has been the issue all the way through Romans. Whose righteousness matters? Whose righteousness justifies? Not ours. The tragedy for the Jewish nation is that they sought the kingdom of God on their righteousness, so they missed their Messiah. They did not seek it by faith but by the work of the law. They stumbled at that stumbling stone. Paul again quotes Isaiah: **As it is written: "Behold, I lay in Zion a stumbling stone and rock of offense, and whoever believes on Him will not be put to shame"** (v. 33). Israel was offended by the rock. They were ashamed of a suffering servant. Those who put their trust in that stumbling block and don't trip over it will not be put to shame.

Application

Romans 9 began with Paul's open heart for his kinsmen. He struggled with the unbelief of many in Israel's rejection of the Messiah. May this heartfelt burden also characterize us as we seek to share the gospel with those around us, so that they may not stumble to their condemnation. We ought to be saying also with Paul, "I am not ashamed of the gospel of Christ, for it is the power of God to salvation for everyone who believes" (Rom. 1:16).

Romans 10

BRETHREN, MY HEART'S DESIRE AND PRAYER *to God for Israel is that they may be saved. For I bear them witness that they have a zeal for God, but not according to knowledge. For they being ignorant of God's righteousness, and seeking to establish their own righteousness, have not submitted to the righteousness of God. For Christ is the end of the law for righteousness to everyone who believes.*

For Moses writes about the righteousness which is of the law, "The man who does those things shall live by them." But the righteousness of faith speaks in this way, "Do not say in your heart, 'Who will ascend into heaven?'" (that is, to bring Christ down from above) or, "'Who will descend into the abyss?'" (that is, to bring Christ up from the dead). But what does it say? "The word is near you, in your mouth and in your heart" (that is, the word of faith which we preach): that if you confess with your mouth the Lord Jesus and believe in your heart that God has raised Him from the dead, you will be saved. For with the heart one believes unto righteousness, and with the mouth confession is made unto salvation. For the Scripture says, "Whoever believes on Him will not be put to shame." For there is no distinction between Jew and Greek, for the same Lord over all is rich to all who call upon Him. For "whoever calls on the name of the LORD *shall be saved."*

How then shall they call on Him in whom they have not believed? And how shall they believe in Him of whom they have not heard? And how shall they hear without a preacher? And how shall they preach unless they are sent? As it is written:

> "How beautiful are the feet of those who preach the gospel of
>   peace,
> Who bring glad tidings of good things!"

But they have not all obeyed the gospel. For Isaiah says, "Lᴏʀᴅ, who has believed our report?" So then faith comes by hearing, and hearing by the word of God.

But I say, have they not heard? Yes indeed:

> "Their sound has gone out to all the earth,
> And their words to the ends of the world."

But I say, did Israel not know? First Moses says:

> "I will provoke you to jealousy by those who are not a nation,
> I will move you to anger by a foolish nation."

But Isaiah is very bold and says:

> "I was found by those who did not seek Me;
> I was made manifest to those who did not ask for Me."

But to Israel he says:

> "All day long I have stretched out My hands
> To a disobedient and contrary people."

WEEK 35

1

Zeal according to Knowledge

AT THE BEGINNING OF ROMANS 10, Paul reaffirms something that he stated earlier: **Brethren, my heart's desire and prayer to God for Israel is that they may be saved. For I bear them witness that they have a zeal for God, but not according to knowledge** (vv. 1–2). His heart was heavy because he loved his kinsmen, and his deepest desire was that they would all be saved. He recognized that they were zealous for religion; they never missed the meetings in the synagogue. They had a zeal for God, but their zeal was based on ignorance. A fanatic is somebody who loses sight of where he is going but redoubles his effort to get there. He is full of zeal, but he has no knowledge or understanding of that for which he is zealous.

Paul wrote in Romans 1 that God has revealed Himself clearly to everyone in creation, but people suppress that knowledge and exchange it for a lie. They serve and worship the creature rather than the Creator. Paul announced judgment on the human race, not because it is given to atheism but because of false religion. The judgment of God is provoked by religion in which the object of devotion is an idol, where the truth of God is swapped for the creature. God alone is worthy of our adoration, devotion, and service. It is not enough to be religious or to be a zealot.

When Jesus appeared on the scene, the most zealous people in Jerusalem were the Pharisees and scribes. They spent their lives pursuing righteousness. A Pharisee was "a separated one." Pharisees were consecrated to the pursuit of righteousness, but when true righteousness came into their midst to redeem them, they killed Him. They were looking for justification by works, so they stumbled over Jesus. They did not realize that they were required to give up any claim to merit and all boasting and say, "Nothing in my hand I bring, simply to Thy cross I cling." They were zealous, but not according to knowledge. **For they being ignorant of God's righteousness, and seeking to establish their own righteousness, have not submitted to the righteousness of God** (v. 3). Paul's kinsmen had sought to build their house upon the foundation of their merit and goodness. That is how they wanted to do it, and that is how we want to do it by nature, thinking that grace is for the weak.

Application

Israel had a zeal for God without knowledge. One danger for us is that we can pursue knowledge without any zeal. Theology is important and arguably the most important thing we can set our minds to in this life. We must study not only to acquire head knowledge but also so that what is in our heads will cascade down into our hearts, that our knowledge of theology would work toward its natural end—the love and worship of God.

2

End of the Law

A FRIEND OF MINE WENT TO GERMANY and asked if he could bring me some paperback copies of Perry Mason by Erle Stanley Gardner published in German. When he returned from Germany, he brought me a bag full of Perry Mason books. I asked him what I owed him for the purchase.

"You can't pay me; it's a gift," he replied.

He wanted to be gracious, but I wanted to pay my own way. It's hard to rely on grace alone, because it is the end of boasting. We have no bragging rights. The only thing that we can boast in is the perfection of the Redeemer.

The Jews have not submitted to the righteousness of God, Paul says, **for Christ is the end of the law for righteousness to everyone who believes** (v. 4). Almost every Sunday, we read one of the Ten Commandments in the liturgy of our worship service. We do so because if we do not listen to the law, we will never see our need for the gospel. The goal and purpose of the law is Christ. God did not give the law as a way for us to attain status in His family. The law was given to show us the righteousness of God. It was given so that we can see the perfect righteousness of God and by comparison see ourselves, warts and all, and despair of our own righteousness. The law sends us rushing to the cross and running for grace. The law exposes our sin, and anything that exposes our sin screams to our need for the Savior, whose righteousness alone can justify.

Paul said that this is the tragedy of the people he loved. They had missed it. They had sought the righteousness of God through their obedience to the law and had failed to see that the goal of the law is Christ and His righteousness, which can never be earned, bought, or deserved.

I hope that each of us has a heart on fire with zeal. Jesus warned those who were neither hot nor cold but lukewarm that He would vomit them out of His mouth (Rev. 3:16). He wanted His people to be filled with zeal, but a zeal according to knowledge, zeal that is informed by His Word. The fire in our hearts is not simply heat but also light, which comes from God's Word.

Application

Even though knowledge without zeal, light without heat, can be dangerous, heat without light is dangerous also. These are the ditches on both sides of the road and why knowledge and zeal must always go together. In your study of God's Word, look for the Spirit's working a deeper love for God in your heart, and in your growing love for Him, look for the Spirit's working a deeper longing to be in His Word.

3

The Word Is Near

PAUL BEGAN ROMANS 10 WITH A LAMENT that his kinsmen, Israel, had a zeal for the things of God, but not according to knowledge. They had failed to understand that the doctrine of justification was no novelty; it had been set forth early on in the Old Testament, particularly in the life of the patriarch Abraham. Justification before a holy God is by faith alone.

Paul follows up his lament: **For Moses writes about the righteousness which is of the law, "The man who does those things shall live by them." But the righteousness of faith speaks in this way, "Do not say in your heart, 'Who will ascend into heaven?'" (that is, to bring Christ down from above) or, "'Who will descend into the abyss?'" (that is, to bring Christ up from the dead)** (vv. 5–7). Paul's thoughts seem somewhat oblique at first glance. He is setting forth two ideas that represent manifest impossibilities. It is just as impossible for a person to be justified by the law or by his works as for a human being to ascend into the highest heaven and drag the Messiah from heaven to earth. The only way that the Messiah can descend from heaven is if God omnipotent sends Him, which is exactly what God the Father did in sending the Son into the world to be our Mediator.

It is also equally impossible for any human being by strength of his virtue or righteousness to descend into the pit of hell and bring Christ back from the dead. When Christ was executed, the disciples fled as sheep without a shepherd. They were in despair because they knew that it was totally beyond their power to bring Jesus back from the grave. Paul is saying that it is impossible for someone to be saved through the works of the law, just as it is impossible to bring Jesus back from the dead or to bring Him down from heaven.

In stark contrast to that manifest impossibility, Paul quotes Moses concerning God's Word: **But what does it say? "The word is near you, in your mouth and in your heart" (that is, the word of faith which we preach)** (v. 8). In other words, the central truth about justification is not so high or abstract or deep or profound as to be beyond our understanding. Understanding the gospel does not require a PhD in theology. We are not Gnostics, who believe that the gospel can be understood only by an elite group of scholars. The gospel is "near you," a Hebrew idiom meaning that it is within our grasp. It is right in front of us. The word of faith is simple. I have said to you throughout our study of Romans that to understand the doctrine of justification by faith alone—the very heart and soul of the gospel—is not a difficult thing. A child can understand it. To get it in the bloodstream, however, is something that requires a life of concentrated study of God's Word. Embracing what God has put in front of us requires hearing the Word of God day in and day out.

Application

Owning Bibles and having the ability to read God's Word is a privilege that is often neglected. People throughout church history would be astounded at the resources that we have available for our personal study—let alone Bibles—especially in the West. Remember this privilege and make the most of it as you, like a Berean, seek the Scriptures daily (see Acts 17:10–11).

4

The Righteousness of the Law

PAUL REMINDS US OF THE EASE with which we can understand the message, and he boils it down to this: **if you confess with your mouth the Lord Jesus and believe in your heart that God has raised Him from the dead, you will be saved** (v. 9). Paul conjoins two elements here. He does not just say that you must confess with your lips and profess with your mouth in order to be saved. Every Christian is called to profess his faith. We are to profess the faith, but the profession without authentic faith attending it will justify no one. I do not tire in repeating that, because one of the great perils of the church in our day is the way in which we do evangelism. We are so zealous to win people to Christ and to persuade them of the truth of the gospel that we are not satisfied with simply proclaiming the gospel and then allowing the Holy Spirit to take that truth and pierce human hearts with it. We want to give our assistance to make sure that our evangelistic statistics are good.

We have come up with various techniques for doing so. The technique employed at a crusade is the altar call. People are asked to respond to the gospel by coming to the front of the church or coliseum, or to raise their hand, pray a prayer, or sign a card. All these techniques are designed to urge people to take a step to finalize their commitment to Christ. Nothing is actually wrong with those things unless we think that walking down an aisle, raising our hand, signing a card, or saying the sinner's prayer will get us into the kingdom of God. If we think so, we are in trouble. We have to understand that a profession of faith alone will never justify us. The possession of faith, not the profession of it, is the necessary condition for our justification.

That is why Paul does not say that we will be saved if we confess with our mouth. He adds a condition: you must "believe in your heart." I used to get cantankerous with my seminary students when I would ask for their opinion about a particular issue and they would answer, "Well, Professor, I *feel* that such and such is the truth." I would reply, "I did not ask you how you feel about it; I am asking what you think." Conviction of truth is not a sensuous matter; it is primarily the assent of the mind. We live in such a sensuous culture that people intertwine feeling and thinking. Paul understood that it is impossible to possess a mental persuasion that never gets to the heart.

Application

If you have not already done so, memorize Romans 10:9: "If you confess with your mouth the Lord Jesus and believe in your heart that God has raised Him from the dead, you will be saved." Do not memorize it only for your own sake; seek to share it with someone else, even this week, that through the proclamation of this truth the Spirit might work in someone's heart unto faith and, ultimately, unto salvation.

5

The Ingredients of Faith, Part 1

WHEN THE REFORMERS WERE PROCLAIMING the doctrine of justification by faith alone, the great objection raised against it was its seeming implication of cheap grace or easy believism. Anyone can say that he believes in Jesus, but saying so is no manifestation of true godliness. What are the necessary ingredients of saving faith?

Martin Luther, following James' teaching that faith without works is dead (James 2:20), asked, "Can a dead faith justify anybody?" Luther answered emphatically in the negative. Luther said that the only kind of faith that justifies is a *fides viva*, a living faith, one that is manifested in a life of obedience to God. The first ingredient of faith is *notae*, which means that there is *content* to the faith we embrace. We have heard the cultural adage, "It does not matter what you believe as long as you are sincere," but let me suggest that it matters eternally and profoundly what we believe. People can put their trust and faith in the devil and be sincere about it. There is no comfort to be found from faith in a false object. Saving faith requires content, information, and knowledge.

The second ingredient of saving faith is *assensus*, intellectual assent to the truth of the data. We might understand and believe the facts of the resurrection of Jesus and the atonement, but that does no more than qualify us to be demons, because every demon from hell knows that this information is true. That is why Lutheran Reformers said that data and intellectual assent to the data are not enough. Intellectual affirmation of the truth claims of the gospel must be embraced with personal trust and affection for the truth, something that no demon will do. That is why Paul says that it is not enough to believe it in our heads; we have to believe in our hearts. The Old Testament teaches that as a man thinks in his heart, so is he (Prov. 23:7). The Old Testament writer has not confused organs of thinking with organs of feeling. The point is that we can say that we agree with something intellectually without its ever getting to the core of our being.

I study the text of Scripture in order to take the text from the Bible and communicate it to others, but every time I prepare a sermon, I have to prepare it for myself. At the end of the day, I have to look in the mirror and say, "R.C., do you believe what you proclaimed today?" Sometimes I find myself answering, "I believe it in my head." When that happens, I must ask myself, "Do you believe it with your life, or is this just an exercise in theology?" Ministers and teachers are in danger if the truth does not get down into the bloodstream of their hearts.

Application

Even, and perhaps especially, ministers and teachers need to test themselves as to whether their heart is in what they teach. Teaching theology and proclaiming the gospel, just as when it comes to believing the gospel, isn't merely an intellectual exercise. The gospel is a heart proclamation. May it be true of every one of us when we have an opportunity to teach God's people that we teach with conviction, and may we find joy in sitting under teaching that comes from a fully engaged heart.

6

The Ingredients of Faith, Part 2

THE THIRD INGREDIENT OF SAVING FAITH follows by resistless logic, as any syllogism yields its conclusion: we will be saved. Someone once asked me, "How can I know I'm saved if I have been elected?" I replied, "That is what you are elected to—salvation." Instead of worrying about the intricacies that attend the doctrine of election, we must get down to the simplest principle: if we confess with our mouths and believe with our hearts, we will be saved. We will not do that unless we are elect. Do you believe in your heart and trust in Christ alone? If so, then I can give you full assurance of your salvation. **For with the heart one believes unto righteousness, and with the mouth confession is made unto salvation. For the Scripture says, "Whoever believes on Him will not be put to shame"** (vv. 10–11). If you put your trust in Christ from the heart, you have no need of future embarrassment. You will not be put to shame for having held to a false hope or having devoted your life to a myth.

For there is no distinction between Jew and Greek, for the same Lord over all is rich to all who call upon Him. For "whoever calls on the name of the LORD shall be saved" (vv. 12–13). Paul makes that statement within a broader context. Even within the immediate context, he is not saying that anybody who calls for Jesus in a moment of trial will be saved. The Lord warns us that when He appears and God's wrath is manifest against the unrepentant, they will be screaming for the mountains to fall and the hills to cover them. People will say in that moment, "Jesus, help me! Save me!" It will be too late. Paul's statement applies to those who call upon the name of the Lord in the terms he has just used. A true call issues from the heart. It is an authentic reaching for the Savior. Anyone who calls truly will not be denied.

We may not be elect, but we cannot know for sure that we are not elect until we die. We may be like the thief on the cross and be brought to the Lord through the mysterious work of God through the Holy Spirit in our fleeting breath. We do not have to work through all the intricacies of doctrine so long as we understand that if we sincerely call upon the name of the Lord, we will be saved.

Application

Consider the significance of Paul's quoting from the Old Testament in Romans 10:12–13. His quotation is from Joel 2:32, where the "Lord" is in small caps, which indicates the use of God's divine, covenantal name. When we call on Jesus Christ for salvation, we proclaim nothing short of the reality that He is Lord of all, coeternal with the Father and Spirit and worthy of all our praise.

WEEK 36

1

The Privilege of Evangelism

PAUL GIVES A SERIES OF RELATED QUESTIONS, which are very important. The text bears heavily on the missions outreach of the church. **How then shall they call on Him in whom they have not believed?**

And how shall they believe in Him of whom they have not heard? And how shall they hear without a preacher? And how shall they preach unless they are sent? As it is written: "How beautiful are the feet of those who preach the gospel of peace, who bring glad tidings of good things!" (vv. 14–15).

When I was taught the doctrine of predestination years ago in one of my seminary classes, the professor seated the students in a semicircle. There were eighteen in the room. He asked us, "Gentlemen, if the doctrine of election is true, why should we be engaged in evangelism?" Nobody raised a hand, so he went around the semicircle, interrogating each student for a response. I breathed a sigh of relief because he had started on the left side of the semicircle; I was sitting on the extreme right end, so I had seventeen points of buffer between me and the relentless interrogation of the professor. He asked the first student, "If predestination is true, why should we be involved in evangelism?" The student did not know. The professor moved along to the second student, who also did not know. The third student answered, "Evangelism would be a Herculean waste of time if salvation has been settled by divine decree."

Those answers did not satisfy the professor, so he continued around the semicircle. My buffer disintegrated, and he finally got to me. "Well, Mr. Sproul, what do you think?"

Sheepishly I said, "I know that the answer has to be far more profound than this, but one of the reasons that we should be engaged in evangelism is that Jesus commanded us to do it."

The professor said, "Mr. Sproul, can you possibly think of a more significant reason to do evangelism than that Jesus Christ commands you to do it?"

The professor went on to say that engaging in evangelism must not be done from a sense of duty. Evangelism is one of the greatest privileges that God gives to the church. He explained that God could have preached His Word from the clouds without any human participation, but that He chose the means to accomplish it, chiefly, the foolishness of preaching. God gave us the unspeakable privilege of participating in His majestic program of redemption, which He planned from the foundation of the world.

No preacher is indispensable. Cemeteries are filled with indispensable people. God does not need preachers to accomplish His purposes of redemption. He did not need Isaiah, He did not need Jeremiah, and He did not need the Apostle Paul. God has given men the most sacred vocation possible—carrying this treasure in earthly vessels.

Application

Many of us may feel bashful in sharing the gospel with others. When we think of sharing the gospel primarily as a duty, we can begin to feel guilty for our failures. But when we begin to think of sharing the gospel as a privilege, we can often overcome our timidity. See it as your great privilege to be able to proclaim the truth to others, and do so in the confidence not in yourself but in God, who is pleased to work through it.

2

Election and Missions

PEOPLE ARE NOT GOING TO PUT THEIR TRUST in a Savior who they do not believe is capable of saving them. When I have a plumbing problem, I do not call the grocer, because I have no reason to believe that the grocer can fix my problem. Likewise, when I face the deepest problem of human existence—escaping from the wrath to come—why would I put any trust in or call upon somebody unless I first believed that He was able to redeem me? Belief is a precondition, a necessary condition, to calling upon Him.

"How then shall they call on Him in whom they have not believed? And how shall they believe in Him of whom they have not heard?"

(v. 14a). Millions have never heard the name of Jesus, and they are not going to put their trust in someone they know nothing about. They cannot possibly believe in Jesus because they know nothing about Him. I said earlier that saving faith requires information. That is why the church is commanded to go to every corner of the world and make that message plain to all people.

"How shall they hear without a preacher?" (v. 14b). The answer to Paul's question is that they will not. No one is going to hear about Jesus unless somebody tells him. Nobody is going to believe a gospel that he has never heard, and without a preacher he will never hear it.

"And how shall they preach unless they are sent?" (v. 15a). The Latin word for *send* is *missia,* from which we get the word *mission.* Missionaries are sent. We see throughout the pages of the Old Testament that God anointed prophets and sent them to people. Just so, missionaries cannot go unless somebody supports and sends them. Not everyone in the church is called to be a missionary, but every member of the church is responsible to make sure that the missionary activity gets done. We all have a part to play in that endeavor.

Paul quotes from Isaiah: "How beautiful are the feet of those who preach the gospel of peace, who bring glad tidings of good things!" (v. 15b). The full quote from the Old Testament reads, "How beautiful upon the mountains are the feet of him who brings good news, who proclaims peace, who brings glad tidings of good things, who proclaims salvation, who says to Zion, 'Your God reigns!'" (Isa. 52:7).

Paul gives the reason why, if election is true, we should preach. We preach not simply as a matter of duty but because God gives us the blessed privilege of having beautiful feet in the eyes of those who hear and respond to the gospel.

Application

Millions have never heard the name of Jesus, and millions more have made up their minds about Him presumptuously or because of some false notions about Him. Evangelism isn't only about telling someone about Jesus for the first time but can include engaging with others to clear up the confusion about who He is and how He saves. Arm yourself with the gospel—it's the answer in both scenarios—but also be prepared to ask questions to discover where someone's misapprehensions about the faith truly lie.

3

Faith Comes by Hearing

BUT THEY HAVE NOT ALL OBEYED THE GOSPEL (v. 16a). The gospel is being proclaimed widely, not only to Israel but also to the Gentile nations. Paul's point is that not everybody who hears the gospel obeys, or embraces, the gospel. At the beginning of the epistle, Paul established that the gospel is "the power of God to salvation" (1:16). Elsewhere, Paul writes that God has chosen the foolishness of preaching as His method to save the world (1 Cor. 1:21). When we considered the doctrine of election, or predestination, we saw that God ordains from all eternity not only the ends of people and nations but also the means to those ends. We saw that the primary means God uses to awaken faith in the hearts of the elect is the preaching of the gospel. Faith comes through the Word, specifically, the preaching of the Word.

For Isaiah says, "LORD, who has believed our report?" (v. 16b). The prophet was uttering a lament. There was a remnant who believed the report of the suffering servant of Israel, but Isaiah knew, as every prophet did, that the Word of God must be proclaimed over and over again. The gospel has been announced, but has anybody believed it?

So then faith comes by hearing, and hearing by the word of God. But I say, have they not heard? (vv. 17–18a). Of course they have heard:

"Their sound has gone out to all the earth, and their words to the ends of the world" (v. 18b). God had published His gospel throughout the borders of Israel and into the Gentile community. **But I say, did Israel not know? First Moses says: "I will provoke you to jealousy by those who are not a nation, I will move you to anger by a foolish nation"** (v. 19). In other words, why should anyone be surprised that the gospel is being proclaimed to the Gentiles? This was not a last-minute switch in God's plans. God had told the people of Israel that He would make them jealous by taking their proffered benefits across the border to all nations. Paul has in view here the universal proclamation of the gospel so that, as Paul said earlier, "whoever calls on the name of the Lord shall be saved" (v. 13).

Application

The doctrine of election is a great motivation for evangelism. It provides us with the assurance that our efforts will not be in vain. The doctrine of election also provides us with a great protection in our evangelism. Sometimes when we share the gospel, it is rejected. We are protected, however, from coming up with countless new strategies to supplement the gospel when we understand that God is ultimately the One who does the work of calling His elect, and He does so through the gospel. So let's proclaim it.

4

Who Is Saved?

WHEN WE TALK ABOUT THE DOCTRINE OF ELECTION, we are bound to be asked, "Isn't there something dishonest about offering salvation to all when, in fact, God never intended to save all people?" The question touches heavily on the controversy surrounding the doctrine of limited atonement—definite or particular redemption. The doctrine teaches that the atonement of Jesus was not designed by God to make salvation possible to all men. Looking at Paul's words—"Whoever calls on the name of the LORD shall be saved" (v. 13)—it certainly seems that Paul is making a universal offer, and if so, how can we talk about the atonement as being limited to certain people?

Unlike universalists, we understand that the benefits of the atonement are limited to those who believe. The New Testament does not claim that Jesus automatically saves everybody in the world. The condition for salvation is clear. To receive the benefits of the cross, people must put their trust in Christ. At the very least, we must say that the atonement is limited to believers. Jesus did not die for all indiscriminately; He died for believers.

So who are the believers? Paul answers that question: believers are the elect. Believers who are numbered among the elect will surely be brought to faith. The issue of limited atonement ultimately goes back to God's purpose in the covenant of redemption, where the Father covenanted with the Son and the Holy Spirit to bring about God's plan of salvation. Did God propose to send His Son into the world to die on the cross because He hoped that people would take advantage of that? Did He not know from all eternity the names of everyone who would embrace Jesus and those who would not? Did He send His Son to die to make salvation possible, or did He send His Son to die to make salvation certain? The doctrine of limited atonement holds that God knew what He was doing from all eternity. He constructed a plan of salvation, and in perfect agreement the Son came into the world to die for those whom the Father had given Him, knowing that those whom the Father had given Him would come and that His atonement would not be an exercise in futility or a hypothetical possibility. The Son knew that there would be a people saved as a result of His sacrifice, and the Holy Spirit knew all those to whom He would apply that work of the Son for salvation.

Application

The free offer of the gospel is not disingenuous. When we tell others about the good news of Jesus Christ, we also proclaim with integrity that all those who believe in this good news will be saved. All those who believe are indeed the elect of God and will be saved by grace alone through faith alone in Christ alone. It would be disingenuous, however, if limited atonement were not true because there would be no promise of salvation on offer—only a possibility.

5

No Universalism

THE LANGUAGE OF EVANGELISM IN OUR DAY IS: "God loves you and has a wonderful plan for your life." What if that promise had been made to Judas? "God loves you, Judas, and has a wonderful plan for your life—your destination is eternity in hell." That plan was not wonderful.

The Bible tells us that God loves everybody indiscriminately in terms of His love of beneficence, but the love that He gives to the redeemed is His love of complacency, which is limited only to believers. The Bible says that God abhors the wicked, but we tell people indiscriminately that God loves them unconditionally. That is considered the universal offer of the gospel, but the universal offer of the gospel is really to proclaim to every living creature the gospel of Jesus Christ.

You cannot know that you are not elect until you die, but you can know right now that you are not a believer. You may conclude that since you are not a believer, you are not among the elect, but you might yet believe. So we are called, as the Apostle tells us here, to go to the four corners of the world to preach the gospel. In that sense, there is to be a universal proclamation of the gospel.

To whom is the gospel offered? Is it offered to everyone indiscriminately, with no strings attached? No, the good news is offered only to those who believe. If you are not willing to put your faith in Christ, then the gospel is not offered to you. The gospel is proclaimed universally, but its benefits are offered only to believers, those who hear the Word and are brought to faith in and through the Word.

But Isaiah is very bold and says: "I was found by those who did not seek Me; I was made manifest to those who did not ask for Me" (v. 20). The overwhelming majority of churches in the United States, particularly evangelical churches, have embraced a seeker strategy for church growth, but the Bible says that apart from regeneration, no person seeks after God. Those who seek the kingdom of God—the main business of the Christian life—do not start seeking until they have been converted. Many unbelievers are desperately trying to find the benefits that only Christ can give them, but all the while they are actually fleeing from Jesus.

Paul, quoting Isaiah again, says, "I was found by those who did not seek Me." Was Paul looking for Jesus on the road to Damascus when the bright light knocked him down? No, he was looking for Christians to throw into prison and kill.

The last thing I was seeking was Jesus—until He found me. Once He found me, I wanted to know everything I could about Him. I wanted to go to church to learn more.

Application

The desire to learn more about Jesus Christ, and to attend church and search the Scriptures to do so, is not characteristic of the unregenerate. Doing these things out of a faith and love for Christ is a privilege only of those who have been given new hearts through the Spirit's ministry of regeneration. If you ever see your love of growing in your knowledge of Christ to be fading, run to Him with the faith and love that you had to begin with.

6

Manna

GOD WAS FOUND BECAUSE HIS WORD went out to all the earth, and He "was made manifest" because His character and plan were revealed through that word. **But to Israel he says: "All day long I have stretched out My hands to a disobedient and contrary people"** (v. 21). Earlier Paul said there is no difference between Jew and Gentile because both are under sin. Paul brought both before the tribunal of God, saying, "All have sinned and fall short of the glory of God" (see Rom. 3:9–23). A true Jew is one inwardly; nobody is saved by circumcision.

In Romans 2, Paul took his readers through all the failures of Israel, and then he asked, "What advantage then has the Jew, or what is the profit of circumcision?" (3:1). If circumcision does not save, what good is it being a Jew? "Much in every way," Paul replied, "chiefly because to them were committed the oracles of God" (3:2). The Jews had the Scriptures.

In the wilderness God provided food for His people through manna. He nurtured and fed His sheep by providing bread from heaven. He instructed the Israelites to take some manna out of the wilderness and preserve it so that future generations would know that the Lord God omnipotent had fed His people with bread from heaven (Ex. 16:33) until later when One would stand up and say, "I am the bread of life" (John 6:35). The Old Testament Scriptures pointed beyond the manna that was gathered from the dew of the earth to the manna that comes down from heaven.

There is a divine agreement within the Godhead—Father, Son, and Holy Spirit. They are working together in and through the Word. The Spirit does not divorce Himself from the Word. Many want to be led by the Spirit without the Word, but they cannot distinguish between the leading of God and indigestion, because they have nothing concrete against which to check their inclinations and hunches. The Holy Spirit leads and teaches in the Word and through the Word, but never against the Word. "So then faith comes by hearing, and hearing by the word of God" (Rom. 10:17).

Have you heard God through His Word? When the Bible is expounded, does it tickle your ears or inflame your soul? Does the Spirit of God take this Word and bother you with it? Does He pierce, comfort, strengthen, and encourage you with it? There is nothing else.

Revival would come to our country if every church member in America would say, "I am never again going to ask the minister to administrate the church or be responsible for its finances. I want somebody to feed me the Word of God." If every church member in America would ask that the Word of God be preached in an expository manner every Sunday, it would blow the lid off this country, because that is where the power is. It is not in our programs, buildings, or parking lots. It is in the Word.

Application

Take time to pray for revival in your country. True revival is a work of God's Spirit, and this work will never come if there is a famine of God's Word in the land. Pray that biblical preaching would begin to mark every church, that we would not be theologically ignorant of God's character and the great salvation that is only through Jesus Christ.

Romans 11

I SAY THEN, HAS GOD CAST AWAY HIS PEOPLE? *Certainly not! For I also am an Israelite, of the seed of Abraham, of the tribe of Benjamin. God has not cast away His people whom He foreknew. Or do you not know what the Scripture says of Elijah, how he pleads with God against Israel, saying, "Lᴏʀᴅ, they have killed Your prophets and torn down Your altars, and I alone am left, and they seek my life"? But what does the divine response say to him? "I have reserved for Myself seven thousand men who have not bowed the knee to Baal." Even so then, at this present time there is a remnant according to the election of grace. And if by grace, then it is no longer of works; otherwise grace is no longer grace. But if it is of works, it is no longer grace; otherwise work is no longer work.*

What then? Israel has not obtained what it seeks; but the elect have obtained it, and the rest were blinded. Just as it is written:

> *"God has given them a spirit of stupor,*
> *Eyes that they should not see*
> *And ears that they should not hear,*
> *To this very day."*

And David says:

> *"Let their table become a snare and a trap,*
> *A stumbling block and a recompense to them.*
> *Let their eyes be darkened, so that they do not see,*
> *And bow down their back always."*

I say then, have they stumbled that they should fall? Certainly not! But through their fall, to provoke them to jealousy, salvation has come to the Gentiles. Now if their fall is riches for the world, and their failure riches for the Gentiles, how much more their fullness!

For I speak to you Gentiles; inasmuch as I am an apostle to the Gentiles, I magnify my ministry, if by any means I may provoke to jealousy those who are my flesh and save some of them. For if their being cast away is the reconciling of the world, what will their acceptance be but life from the dead?

For if the firstfruit is holy, the lump is also holy; and if the root is holy, so are the branches. And if some of the branches were broken off, and you, being a wild olive tree, were grafted in among them, and with them became a partaker of the root and fatness of the olive tree, do not boast against the branches. But if you do boast, remember that you do not support the root, but the root supports you.

You will say then, "Branches were broken off that I might be grafted in." Well said. Because of unbelief they were broken off, and you stand by faith. Do not be haughty, but fear. For if God did not spare the natural branches, He may not spare you either. Therefore consider the goodness and severity of God: on those who fell, severity; but toward you, goodness, if you continue in His goodness. Otherwise you also will be cut off. And they also, if they do not continue in unbelief, will be grafted in, for God is able to graft them in again. For if you were cut out of the olive tree which is wild by nature, and were grafted contrary to nature into a cultivated olive tree, how much more will these, who are natural branches, be grafted into their own olive tree?

For I do not desire, brethren, that you should be ignorant of this mystery, lest you should be wise in your own opinion, that blindness in part has happened to Israel until the fullness of the Gentiles has come in. And so all Israel will be saved, as it is written:

> *"The Deliverer will come out of Zion,*
> *And He will turn away ungodliness from Jacob;*
> *For this is My covenant with them,*
> *When I take away their sins."*

Concerning the gospel they are enemies for your sake, but concerning the election they are beloved for the sake of the fathers. For the gifts and the calling of God are irrevocable. For as you were once disobedient to God, yet have now obtained mercy through their disobedience, even so these also have now been disobedient, that through the mercy shown you they also may obtain mercy. For God has committed them all to disobedience, that He might have mercy on all.

Oh, the depth of the riches both of the wisdom and knowledge of God! How unsearchable are His judgments and His ways past finding out!

> *"For who has known the mind of the Lord?*
> *Or who has become His counselor?"*
> *"Or who has first given to Him*
> *And it shall be repaid to him?"*

For of Him and through Him and to Him are all things, to whom be glory forever. Amen.

WEEK 37

1

A People Foreknown

PAUL BEGINS ROMANS 11, as he has done so often throughout this epistle, with a rhetorical question: **I say then, has God cast away His people?** (v. 1a). In Old Testament times, Israel was called out of paganism and set apart as a theocratic nation with God as its ultimate king. Israel was given a mandate and a destiny. It has been said by some historians, "How odd of God to choose the Jews." I believe it was George Bernard Shaw who once asked a theologian for certain proof of the existence of God, and the theologian replied to Shaw, "I can prove the existence of God with one or two words—the Jews." The history of Israel all the way back to Abraham up to the present day is a striking testimony of God's providential government of human history, especially redemptive history.

The history of ancient Israel is quite remarkable. After the Romans conquered Jerusalem in AD 70, the Jews were dispersed and sent out of their homeland. Despite two thousand years of exile, they have never lost their ethnic and national identity. Jews say to one another, "Next year in Jerusalem." For two thousand years this people has dreamed of returning to Mount Zion. They still have an unquenchable awareness of their ethnic and national identity. Paul lamented earlier the fact that Israel has missed the gospel by seeking salvation through the law, and now he poses a question about the consequences. Has God exercised a full and final rejection of the Jewish people? **Certainly not!** (v. 1b). God has not categorically rejected Old Testament Israel. Paul argues from the lesser to the greater. If God had rejected all the Jews, He would have rejected Paul, too, because Paul is one of them: **For I also am an Israelite, of the seed of Abraham, of the tribe of Benjamin** (v. 1c). Paul cites his pedigree, including a brief recounting of his genealogical background. He traces his roots to the tribe of Benjamin and all the way to Abraham.

God has not cast away His people whom He foreknew (v. 2a). God is incapable of rejecting a people whom He foreknew from the foundation of the world, the elect, of whom Paul has been writing since chapter 8. Here he brings the concept of election to the Jewish people. He wrote earlier, "For they are not all Israel who are of Israel" (9:6). He argued that the circumcised were not automatically saved, but only those circumcised in heart. Not all from the seed of Abraham were chosen from the foundation of the world. Ishmael was the seed of Abraham, but he remained a foreigner to God's redemptive purposes. "In Isaac your seed shall be called" (9:7). Paul does not want his readers to conclude from all the weighty things he has said about the Jews—their rejection of the Messiah and despising the gospel—that God has rejected them totally. Paul's readers cannot come to that conclusion because Paul himself is numbered among the Jews.

Application

Jesus was crucified by the Roman authorities. God did indeed have a special relation with the people of Israel, but the rejection of the Messiah is not something unique to the Jews. Were we to examine our own hearts before they were regenerated by the Holy Spirit, we would find that all of us in our fallen nature rejected the Messiah. That's what's so astounding in God's grace. He changes hearts that we might not reject Christ as Savior but receive Him.

2

The Elijah Syndrome

OR DO YOU NOT KNOW WHAT THE SCRIPTURE says of Elijah, how he pleads with God against Israel, saying, "LORD, they have killed Your prophets and torn down Your altars, and I alone am left, and they seek my life"? (vv. 2b–3). This cry from the prophet Elijah was uttered during a terrible time—perhaps the worst time—of apostasy in the history of Old Testament Israel. Elijah made this plea while Ahab was king. Ahab ruled with his consort Jezebel, a priestess of the cult of Baal. Using her influence with the king, Jezebel invited pagan idolaters into the royal house and persuaded Ahab to sanction the idolatrous religion in the high places of Israel. Under Ahab and Jezebel, a massive persecution was instituted against the classical religion of the Jews. In this iconoclastic movement of paganism, the sacred altars of the Jewish people were physically dismantled and burned while shrines were established to the pagan god Baal (see 1 Kings 16:29–34; 18:1–19:10).

Elijah challenged the prophets of the priests of Baal to use their power to bring down fire from heaven. An altar was placed on Mount Carmel, and Elijah told the prophets of Baal to ignite the fire of sacrifice on the altar. Those prophets prayed, wept, and called, but heaven was silent. Elijah mocked them, saying, "Cry aloud, for he is a god; either he is meditating, or he is busy, or he is on a journey, or perhaps he is sleeping and must be awakened" (18:27). Although the prophets called and performed their sacred rituals, cutting themselves, there was no response. Elijah ordered that the altar be doused with water. After it was saturated he prayed, and the Lord God omnipotent sent fire from heaven that consumed the altar (18:30–39).

In the midst of Israel's hellish reversion to paganism, the soul of

Elijah was tried to the uttermost. He experienced persecution daily and became a fugitive from the power of the throne. He was exhausted with living. In the midst of it, he cried out to God, "It is enough! Now, LORD, take my life, for I am no better than my fathers! . . . I have been very zealous for the LORD God of hosts; for the children of Israel have forsaken Your covenant, torn down Your altars, and killed Your prophets with the sword. I alone am left; and they seek to take my life" (19:4, 10). I call that the Elijah Syndrome; it is what true believers often experience when surrounded by apostasy.

Application
False teaching and idolatry are never tolerated among the true people of God. They were not tolerated among the remnant in Elijah's day, and they were not tolerated in the early church. Paul's stern warnings to the Galatians and the Corinthians are examples of this. Today, we must remain valiant in defense of the truth.

3

Apostasy

APOSTASY IS NOT THE SAME AS PAGANISM. An apostate is one who, at some point, professed the true God. Apostasy can take place only in the house of God. People become apostate by repudiating the faith they once professed. Whole churches can become apostate. When churches denounce essential truths of the Christian faith, they are apostate churches. Denominations—Protestant denominations—can become apostate. The church in which I grew up and was ordained is, I believe, part of an apostate denomination. It celebrates the imaging of pagan goddesses. It sanctions abortion on demand. Its official church councils have argued that to affirm the deity of Christ or His atonement is not a necessary qualification for pastors of the denomination. When a church does that, it is apostate.

True Christians might be in such churches, but they should not be. When a group becomes apostate, we have a moral obligation to leave and distance ourselves from it. We do not have to break fellowship over every difference of doctrine, but when real apostasy is manifested, it is time to shake the dust from our feet and get out. Not every Christian does that, however. Multitudes of Christians are still working, striving, laboring, and preaching within apostate bodies all over the world. Those who do might experience the Elijah Syndrome.

Paul tells his readers the response that Elijah received: **"I have reserved for Myself seven thousand men who have not bowed the knee to Baal"** (v. 4b). Not just one or five or even one hundred—God had kept for Himself seven thousand from within that godless nation. They had not kept themselves for God, but God had kept them. Some might have been found within the courts of Ahab and Jezebel; others were perhaps in areas that Elijah would not have guessed. Wherever they were, there were seven thousand preserved from apostasy by God Himself.

I believe I am not apostate, but the only reason I can give is that the Lord God in His sweet grace and mercy has preserved me. I believe in the perseverance of the saints only because I believe in the preservation of the saints. The Lord God in His grace preserves His people.

Application

The marks of the church are the faithful preaching of God's Word, the right administration of the sacraments, and—intimately connected to the administration of the sacraments—church discipline. We can be charitable over some differences, but when a church fails in the areas of preaching the gospel or calling people to repentance, then we have reason to seek another church.

4

A Remnant by Grace

EVEN SO THEN, AT THIS PRESENT TIME **there is a remnant according to the election of grace** (v. 5). Throughout the Old Testament, God speaks of preserving a remnant. If you go to a carpet store because it happened to be having a remnant sale, you are not going there to purchase whole rugs. You are buying what is left over after the rugs have been trimmed. Seed left after the field has been plowed, dregs found in the bottom of a cup, loose ends fit only for the trash barrel, and the stump left from a felled tree are all metaphors for the people of God. That is what we are—the dregs reserved by God in election. He has preserved His remnant, which He determined to redeem from the foundation of the world. That is why I know that the church of Jesus Christ will never be erased from the face of the earth. Parishes may fall and denominations may crumble, but God will preserve His elect in every generation. You will never be asked to stand alone in a dying world, because God has a people who cannot fail.

The church belongs to Christ. It is His bride, and the bride has been given to the Son by the Father. Before going to the cross, Jesus prayed in the upper room: "I do not pray for the world but for those whom You have given Me, for they are Yours. . . . Those whom You gave Me I have kept; and none of them is lost except the son of perdition [Judas], that the Scripture might be fulfilled" (John 17:9, 12).

The remnant is according to the election of grace. **And if by grace, then it is no longer of works** (v. 6a). Those two concepts—grace and works—are mutually exclusive, as we have seen throughout this epistle. Grace by definition is unmerited, unearned, and undeserved. Paul makes this simple—it is one or the other, grace or works. Our only hope is grace.

Application

Because the gates of hell will never prevail against the church (Matt. 16:18), we will never stand alone. Even if we were alone, God would never forsake us. When you worship this Lord's Day, shoulder to shoulder with fellow believers, remember that it is by God's grace that you stand and that it is by His grace that you stand together. We must not let anything come between that unity and must seek peace in the church insofar as it depends on us.

5

Spiritual Blindness

PAUL IS WRITING ABOUT THE JEWISH people as a whole, ethnic Israel, his kinsmen. **What then? Israel has not obtained what it seeks; but the elect have obtained it, and the rest were blinded** (v. 7). Paul quotes the Old Testament again: **Just as it is written: "God has given them a spirit of stupor, eyes that they should not see and ears that they should not hear, to this very day"** (v. 8). The people of Israel were blind because God had made them blind. Their blindness was punishment for their sin. They did not want to see the things of God, so, as He has done throughout redemptive history, He abandoned them to their sinful desire. This is God's poetic justice. If you do not want to hear the Word of God, be careful, because God will make you deaf, and then you will never hear it. If you do not want to see the kingdom of God, whatever you see even vaguely now will be taken away. If you are not alive and energetic to the things of the Spirit, be careful that God does not visit you with the spirit of lethargy, taking from you whatever weak zeal you have. When God works that way, it is always a punishment for evil inclinations.

Paul cites David, who was speaking about the enemies of God's kingdom: **"Let their table become a snare and a trap, a stumbling block and a recompense to them. Let their eyes be darkened, so that they do not see, and bow down their back always"** (vv. 9–10). Elsewhere, in Psalm 23, David writes: "You prepare a table before me in the presence of my enemies" (v. 5a). This is the table of the banquet feast, a table of blessing prepared by God made visible to the enemies of the kingdom. Concerning this imagery, Martin Luther said that ultimately this table, bestowed by the Lord God in His grace upon the nation of Israel, is the table of His Word. He has spread the banquet feast with the oracles of God.

David saw how his enemies hated the Word of God and the church in its Old Testament manifestation. Elsewhere David wrote, "Let their table become a snare before them, and their well-being a trap" (Ps. 69:22). When God's enemies come to that table and see the sumptuous food placed upon it, like a trap baited with meat that will spring when the animal pounces, the table will be a snare, a hammer on the heads of those who hate it.

Luther, looking at Psalm 69:22, said that it is like a flower in the field whose nectar is used to make honey for the bee, but the nectar is poison to the spider. To those who are being saved, the Word of God is sweetness and honey, but for those who are perishing, it is poison. May it be for you nothing but sweetness and honey so that you may feast on the table that God has prepared for you from the foundation of the world.

Application

We must keep a watch on our spiritual vitality. Any signs of lethargy when it comes to the things of God may be an indicator of spiritual trouble. If we notice a sluggishness in prayer, a disinterest in the study of God's Word, or a heartless resting in the formalities of worship and not true praise, then we ought to seek the Lord diligently to restore the vigor of our faith and thank Him that He showed us our emptiness without it.

6

Salvation for the Gentiles

IN THE GREEK LANGUAGE, UNLIKE ENGLISH, rhetorical questions have a specific structure that tells us conclusively whether the answer is yes or no. Once again Paul begins a section of the epistle with this literary device: **I say then, have they stumbled that they should fall?** (v. 11a). Paul has already told us that Israel had missed their calling. Holding to works-righteousness, they had become blind to the truth of redemption. They had tripped over the Messiah. He was a rock of offense and a stumbling block to His own people. Now Paul explores the purpose of their stumbling; in other words, what was God's design in it?

The result of stumbling is usually falling. When we trip, we fall, and when we fall, we often get hurt. Sometimes we fall and cannot get up. Did God want His people to fall, not just temporarily but fully and finally? Paul gives the same emphatic response that he has so often expressed in the epistle: **Certainly not!** (v. 11b). Other translations have "By no means!" or "God forbid!" We should not conclude that God's purpose in the stumbling of Israel was their permanent fall into destruction.

But through their fall, to provoke them to jealousy, salvation has come to the Gentiles (v. 11c). This passage reeks with irony. Later (v. 25), Paul will elaborate on this principle, calling it a "mystery." Paul refers to mystery frequently in his New Testament writings, particularly in his epistle to the Colossians, in which he writes of the *mustērion*. The Latin translation of the Greek *mustērion* is *sacramentum*, which is why some churches refer to the sacraments as the *sacred mysteries*. There is a linguistic connection between the Greek and the Latin words.

The New Testament understanding of the term *mystery* or *mustērion* is that of something that was at one time hidden but has now been revealed and made plain. The most important mystery with which the Apostle grapples time and again in his writing is this: "To them [the saints] God willed to make known what are the riches of the glory of this mystery among the Gentiles: which is Christ in you, the hope of glory" (Col. 1:27). The grand mystery so heavily veiled in the Old Testament is now made clear: the Gentiles are included in the people of God. God's intention to include the Gentiles in the covenant promise was not completely unknown in Old Testament Israel, but it was certainly vague and in shadows. The grand design of God, the mystery of the stumbling of Israel, is "to provoke them to jealousy."

Application

What had become of Israel in stumbling over Christ was something that God had planned for the salvation of the nations. Even in Israel's stumbling, God was working for good, that the nations might be saved and become a means for Israel's faith in the future. God is not finished with the Jewish people, so let us continue to be faithful in sharing the gospel with them.

WEEK 38

1

Gospel Jealousy

PAUL USES ANOTHER LITERARY DEVICE COMMON not only in his writings but also in the teaching technique of Jesus—the comparison. Jesus' comparisons were not simply between good and bad or good and better; His comparisons were in the nature of "how much more," a phrase that he used frequently. In the parable of the unjust judge (Luke 18:1–8), Jesus describes an unfortunate, disenfranchised widow. She sought her justice from a judge who had no regard for man or God. The judge would not hear the widow's case, but she persisted in her request. Finally the judge agreed to hear the case. He had no concern for the woman; he just wanted some peace. The judge heard her case and gave her a favorable verdict. Jesus said, "Hear what the unjust judge said. And shall God not avenge His own elect who cry out day and night to Him, though He bears long with them? I tell you that He will avenge them speedily" (vv. 6–8a). Jesus' point is that if an ungodly judge will render a just verdict, *how much more* will God, who is just, vindicate His people who cry unto Him day and night? Paul uses the same device here when he says, **Now if their fall is riches for the world, and their failure riches for the Gentiles, how much more their fullness!** (v. 12). If God brings a good thing out of the failure of Israel, how much more blessedness will He bring through their restoration?

Paul began this section of the epistle with the promise of his passionate concern for his kinsmen, ethnic Israel (9:1–5). **For I speak to you Gentiles; inasmuch as I am an apostle to the Gentiles** (v. 13a). Even though Paul was a Jew, he was called by Christ as a missionary and an Apostle to the Gentiles. Paul magnifies his ministry, not to magnify himself but to remind his Roman readers that Christ had chosen him for the work, of which they were a part. **I magnify my ministry, if by any means I may provoke to jealousy those who are my flesh and save some of them** (vv. 13b–14). He articulates passion for brothers and sisters of his own nation. He uses the term *jealousy*. The Jews were hostile, bitter in their opposition to the Christian church, but Paul hopes that as the glory of the church is continually made manifest, his kinsmen will see the greatness of the gospel. If that happens, his kinsmen will be jealous rather than angry and will try to pursue what believers enjoy.

Application

Many of us are surrounded by unbelieving family members, friends, and coworkers. When we identify ourselves as Christians, in some sense we direct a spotlight to ourselves, and our actions will often be judged in accordance with our profession. Paul magnified his ministry for the sake of others. Let us be like him as we press onward in pursuit of holiness, that others may see our good works and glorify the Father.

2

Life from the Dead

YEARS AGO I MINISTERED WITH THE founder of Jews for Jesus, Moishe Rosen. I do not know of any organization that has been more effective in leading people of Jewish ancestry to Christ. At the same time, I do not know of any missionary organization that has provoked more controversy or hostility than this one. It has particularly provoked the religious establishment of American Judaism, which is deeply resentful of Christian evangelism to its people. American Jews are profoundly opposed to any type of proselytism. I tell my Jewish friends that I am puzzled by that. I ask them, "Do you believe that Judaism is true and Christianity is false?"

"Yes," they reply.

"Do you believe that Jesus is the Messiah?"

"No," they reply.

They believe that our religion is false, that we are the ones stumbling in darkness. They think that we are guilty of idolatry because we worship a man and deny the monotheistic foundation of their Jewish faith, yet they have an antipathy toward evangelism. They do not evangelize Christians. If they believe that Judaism is the truth of God, why don't they crawl over glass to bring us into the true religion of

Abraham? When I ask, they have nothing to say. They mumble, "It is not for you; it is just for us."

Paul wants to break through those barriers. He wants to cut through the hostility and resistance by making the Jews jealous of what God has given to us. **For if their being cast away is the reconciling of the world, what will their acceptance be but life from the dead?** (v. 15). If their being rejected is God's plan for the reconciliation of the world, how much more would their acceptance bring blessedness to humanity? What would it be but life from the dead? This image has its roots in the Old Testament, where we find Ezekiel's vision of the valley of the dry bones:

> The hand of the LORD came upon me and brought me out in the Spirit of the LORD, and set me down in the midst of the valley; and it was full of bones. Then He caused me to pass by them all around, and behold, there were very many in the open valley; and indeed they were very dry. (Ezek. 37:1–2)

The bones had dried up in that arid environment into a state of hopeless death. God asked Ezekiel, "Son of man, can these bones live?" (v. 3). When God's word came over the valley of dry bones, suddenly there was a stirring and the bones began to rattle. They began to move together and were knit one to another, and then flesh came upon the bones, and then life began to course through the veins of those skeletons. From death in the valley came life, and this is the image that Paul has in view here when he declares that if rejection brings salvation, the acceptance will bring so much more.

Application

We must never assume a mentality that limits Christianity to any exclusive group. We must be as expansive as the new covenant is in our desire to the see the salvation of all people. God unveiled the mystery of the salvation of the nations in the gospel. May we never put up artificial boundaries that would inhibit the gospel's advance, but may we preach it indiscriminately.

3

Grafted In

FOR IF THE FIRSTFRUIT IS HOLY, the lump is also holy; and if the root is holy, so are the branches (v. 16). Paul mentions firstfruits, lumps, and roots. *Firstfruit* refers to the offerings that were brought into the temple in the Old Testament. The firstfruits were the initial blossomings, the best of the fruit, but the whole crop was consecrated as sacred unto the Lord. The *lump* is an analogy for bread leaven. A small amount of leaven introduced into dough makes the whole loaf rise. When the leavening agent was made sacred to God, holy and set apart, so, too, was the whole loaf. Paul also uses a tree metaphor: "If the root is holy, so are the branches." The branches are not made holy; only by their connection to the root are the branches considered sacred.

Paul presses the tree analogy further: **If some of the branches were broken off, and you, being a wild olive tree, were grafted in among them, and with them became a partaker of the root and fatness of the olive tree, do not boast against the branches** (vv. 17–18a). The broken-off branches are the disobedient, apostate Jews, the ones who stumbled and were cut off from the promises of God and thrown into the fire, just as Jesus said. The metaphor focuses on the olive tree, which was very important to the economy of Old Testament Israel. Olive oil was one of the most important, if not *the* most important, agrarian products in the land. The precious olive oil came from olives that grew on olive trees, which were very valuable in the land of Palestine. The olive tree is the most durable of all trees. The roots go deep, and the trees can live for three or four hundred years.

Other olive trees grew wild; they were not cultivated, so they bore no fruit. They were worthless, giant weeds, which is how Paul describes the Gentiles. God cut off the branches of the precious, durable, valuable olive tree and made a graft. The graft He put on the tree was taken from wild, worthless olive trees that could not be commended to God. "You . . . became a partaker of the root and fatness of the olive tree." These spindly, worthless, wild olive branches were plugged into the root from which they got the sap, the nutrients. The grafted branches drew everything valuable from the root of the cultivated olive tree. Salvation is of the Jews, and we must never forget that.

It should be the deathblow of anti-Semitism among Christian people. **But if you do boast, remember that you do not support the root, but the root supports you** (v. 18b). How could Paul be any more graphic? Remember where you came from, and remember the grace of God in bringing you where you are.

Application

Boasting in ourselves and the Christian faith do not go together. When Paul "boasted" in his second letter to the Corinthians, he boasted in his weakness (see 11:1–12:10). Our call is to boast in the Lord, and this requires an emptying of ourselves, that we might proclaim the excellencies of His grace. Nothing in us could merit our salvation. Neither does our faith merit our salvation, so let us not boast even over unbelievers on account of our faith.

4

Cut Off

YOU WILL SAY THEN, **"Branches were broken off that I might be grafted in." Well said. Because of unbelief they were broken off,**

and you stand by faith. Do not be haughty, but fear (vv. 19–20). Sometimes Christians read this text and say: "Shame on the Jews. They rejected the promises of God, but we have accepted them, so now we are God's chosen people." Paul warns us against that. We are not to get haughty.

Just as apostasy polluted Israel, it can pollute us. We have seen the unbelievable corruption of mainline churches that have become monuments of unbelief and apostasy. Just as God cuts off the branches of Israel, He will cut off the unproductive Gentile branches. **For if God did not spare the natural branches, He may not spare you either. Therefore consider the goodness and severity of God: on those who fell, severity; but toward you, goodness, if you continue in His goodness. Otherwise you also will be cut off** (vv. 21–22). We are to think about the goodness of God—it is an incredible and awesome goodness—yet while we are doing that, we are to consider the severity of God. Our God is an all-consuming fire, and when His judgment comes, when it falls upon wicked people, the judgment is severe.

The principle of cutting is deeply rooted in Old Testament faith. When covenants were made in the Old Testament, they were cut. Cutting rites were associated with the most important covenants of the Old Testament. The sign of the Old Testament covenant was circumcision. It may seem crude when you think about it, but cutting the foreskin of Jewish male children had a twofold symbolic significance. First, the Jewish males were cut to symbolize being cut out of the world, separated from the rest of lost humanity and consecrated to God through this covenant. Second, circumcision signified that failure to keep the terms of the covenant meant being cut off from God's blessing. That negative sanction was contained in the symbol that every Jewish boy carried on his body. The worst thing ever to befall a human being is being cut off from God.

When you join a church, you agree to submit to its discipline. If you become involved in gross sin or public scandal, the church is responsible to call you to account and plead with you to repent. If you refuse to repent, you are first suspended from the sacraments in hope that it will make you jealous to get back into the safety of the fold. If you persist in your impenitence, the final act of punishment is excommunication, which means that the church of Jesus Christ turns you over to Satan by cutting you out of its fellowship. We practice excommunication because Jesus commanded us to do so.

Many do not take church discipline seriously, but Jesus was speaking about the church when He said, "Assuredly, I say to you, whatever you bind on earth will be bound in heaven, and whatever you loose on earth will be loosed in heaven" (Matt. 18:18). We must take that seriously.

Application

Jesus alerts us to the reality that sin is fundamentally a matter of the heart (for example, see Matt. 5:21–30). The beauty of repentance before the sins in our hearts become actions is that God mercifully deals with them in a private manner. Let us be quick to repent of our sins at the level of the heart before we must deal with them publicly.

5

The Mystery Revealed

THE QUESTION BEFORE US IS WHETHER there is a future for ethnic Israel. Is God going to work again in history with the people who are Jewish *kata sarka*, according to the flesh? Thus far in Romans 11, Paul has addressed his concern for his kinsmen, Israel. In the course of redemptive history, the fall of ethnic Jews has led to our being incorporated into the family of God as wild olive branches grafted into the root. If the fall of the Jewish people redounded to the blessedness of the nations, how much more will their restoration? That is why we have to pay close attention to what he says here.

As Paul introduces the subject of Israel's blindness, he talks about a mystery, which, as we noted earlier, in Paul's vocabulary is something once hidden but now made manifest by God. He knows how destructive ignorance is to godliness. God has given us the Bible so that we might become mature in our understanding of the things in it and not seek comfort in ignorance. **For I do not desire, brethren, that you should be ignorant of this mystery, lest you should be wise in your own opinion** (v. 25a). Paul desires that his readers rest upon the revelation of God rather than their personal opinions, explaining **that blindness in part has happened to Israel until the fullness of the Gentiles has come in** (v. 25b).

The word *until* is a time-frame reference. It means "up to a certain point in time," and such a point in time has a terminal dimension to it. Beyond it something changes. When Paul says that blindness has happened to ethnic Israel, to the Jews, it has not happened forever. At the beginning of chapter 11, we saw that the state of apostasy into which the Jews had fallen was neither full nor final. Paul reminded us of his own Jewish ancestry as a way to show that not all the ethnic Jews had fallen away from the covenant. Here he points out that the fall of Israel is not only not full but also not final. It is not the end of the story. The blindness that has come upon them has a historical limit to it, which is "until the fullness of the Gentiles has come in."

The Greek word translated *fullness* is *plērōma*; the Latin word is *plentitude*, the plentitude of the Gentiles. Both words refer to something that reaches its saturation point. Presumably there is a point in history when God's extension of His salvific call to the Gentiles will reach its saturation point, after which God's relationship to ethnic Israel will change.

Application

In a very personal sense, we must wrestle with this word *until* in our own lives. We all have a limited time on this earth *until* we die. We must acknowledge this hard truth when it comes to our unbelieving loved ones. We have only a limited time to share the gospel with them *until* it's too late. Let us be sure to take the opportunities we have while we still can, and let us do so with much prayer and wisdom.

6

The Fullness of the Gentiles

I DO NOT HOLD TO THE VIEW of the full preterists. They say that all the prophecies about the return of Jesus and the fulfillment of the kingdom of God took place in AD 70 with the destruction of the temple. I do not believe that for a minute. I think something of dramatic significance took place in AD 70—the end of the Jewish age as they knew it. It was the end of the temple and of Jerusalem but not the end of God's economy of redemption for His people. I believe that Paul is saying here and throughout Romans 11 that God is not finished with the Jews.

It may be in the economy of redemption that God is going to bring Gentiles into His house for another five thousand years, but when I see what is happening in Jerusalem, I do not think so. We may be on the very cusp of the last roundup of Gentiles. We may be very close to the next step of redemptive history—God's work with ethnic Israel. No time since AD 70 has seen such a concentration of evangelism to ethnic Jews as that taking place in our day, nor has any time in church history mirrored the vast number of converts to Christianity from Judaism. I do not believe that God has two agendas, one for the Jew and one for the Gentile. He has one agenda that incorporates both the Jew and the Gentile in His kingdom.

So all Israel will be saved (v. 26a). If Paul is referring to spiritual Israel, he is departing from the way that he uses the term *Israel* here and in the preceding three chapters. Since chapter 8, Paul has been talking about ethnic Israel. Does he mean each and every Jew? The word *all* in Scripture does not function the way that we characteristically use it to indicate each and every. I believe Paul to be saying that the full complement of God's elect from Israel will be saved and that this will come in a new redemptive-historical visitation by the Holy Spirit when the time of the Gentiles is fulfilled.

The Apostle tells us that he does not want us to grope in the darkness; he wants to take away the mystery. He is telling us about the future of the kingdom of God, which we must take with great earnestness, joy, and consolation. I don't mean to suggest that God's work was finished in AD 70, but when He said, "This generation will by no means pass away" (Luke 21:32), He meant exactly what He said. That generation did not pass away until the temple and Jerusalem were destroyed and our Lord visited His people in the time of their wrath.

Application

The Bible is clear how we ought to live in light of the coming day of judgment. Peter echoes Jesus' teaching that the day of the Lord will come like a thief in the night, and when it does, judgment comes (2 Peter 3:10). Therefore, he calls us to holiness: "What manner of persons ought you to be in holy conduct and godliness, looking for and hastening the coming of the day of God . . . ?" (vv. 11–12a).

WEEK 39

1

The Future of Israel

AS IT IS WRITTEN: **"The Deliverer will come out of Zion, and He will turn away ungodliness from Jacob; for this is My covenant with them, when I take away their sins"** (vv. 26b–27). This is a compilation of more than one Old Testament text, but the Apostle Paul provides a summary that gets to the heart of all that he has been teaching to the people at Rome. Paul has labored to show his Roman readers—and us—that we, the Gentiles, are the wild branch grafted onto the root of the tree. We have no intrinsic claim to the promises God gave His people in the Old Testament because the Deliverer—the One who will redeem—came not from the Gentiles' lands; He came out of Zion.

One thing that the Messiah will accomplish is found in this Old Testament prophecy. The prophecy is referring to Israel. Israel had fallen into apostasy, into unspeakable sin against the Messiah Himself, and yet the redemptive work of the Messiah will provide the framework for the final redemption of Israel.

Paul gives a reason why the Deliverer will turn away ungodliness from Jacob. Jacob has rejected the covenant by saying no to God's yes in His promises of redemption. Jacob has turned away into consistent disobedience, but God is going to turn them back. Why will God do this? Does He owe them a second chance? He will turn them back because of His covenant promise and electing grace.

The reason why we can be absolutely certain that God is not finished with the Jews is that God predicted it. It is not as though God has a mysterious psychic sense about the future through which He peers down through the corridor of time and sees what we cannot see from our vantage point. God knows what is going to happen tomorrow before it happens because He has ordained it. His knowledge of future things is based upon His ordination of future things. God knows that the people of Israel will be restored in the last hour because it is His sovereign will that it should happen.

That is why the doctrine of election is so vitally important to Paul in the midst of his struggle about the future of his people. He knows that their future is in the hands of God, not in the hands of the Pharisees. God has the power, authority, and will to turn people away from their disobedience. Had God waited in heaven for us to turn from our sins and come to the cross, He would still be waiting. In His sovereign mercy and grace, God does not wait for us to turn or incline ourselves; God brings us away from our disobedience to respond to Him.

Application

God's work among the people of Israel is not finished. He has ordained that work, and whatever He has ordained will certainly come to pass. Today, God continues to call Jews to join themselves to the church, which Paul describes in Galatians 6:16 as "the Israel of God." The church is not the replacement of Israel but the expansive reality of what Israel has always been, for all those who have ever truly been of Israel have been children of faith. Is this faith yours?

2

Election for the Sake of the Fathers

CONCERNING THE GOSPEL THEY ARE ENEMIES **for your sake, but concerning the election they are beloved for the sake of the fathers** (v. 28). One of my favorite stories in the Old Testament is that of the lame son of Jonathan, Mephibosheth. When Saul and Jonathan were killed, a messenger came to David with that news, and David tore his garments because of his great love for Jonathan.

> Now David said, "Is there still anyone who is left of the house of Saul, that I may show him kindness for Jonathan's sake?" . . .
>
> And Ziba said to the king, "There is still a son of Jonathan who is lame in his feet." . . .
>
> Then King David sent and brought him out of the house of Machir the son of Ammiel, from Lo Debar.
>
> Now when Mephibosheth the son of Jonathan, the son of Saul, had come to David, he fell on his face and prostrated himself. Then David said, "Mephibosheth?"
>
> And he answered, "Here is your servant!"
>
> So David said to him, "Do not fear, for I will surely show you kindness for Jonathan your father's sake, and will restore to you all the land of Saul your grandfather; and you shall eat bread at my table continually."
>
> . . . So Mephibosheth dwelt in Jerusalem, for he ate continually at the king's table. And he was lame in both his feet. (2 Sam. 9:1, 3, 5–7, 13)

All of Saul's kin had fled for their lives. They assumed David wanted to get rid of them to prevent another uprising against his monarchy. Among Saul's relatives was a boy named Mephibosheth. He had been dropped by his nursemaid when he was a baby, and he became lame in both feet. He was whisked away into hiding. David sent his soldiers into the countryside to search for Saul's survivors, and they discovered Mephibosheth and brought him back to David. Mephibosheth was terrified, sure that he would be executed, but David brought him into his house and treated him as a son. David honored Mephibosheth, not because he had affection for the boy but for the sake of his love for Jonathan.

That story illustrates the history of redemption. The only reason that we are included in the kingdom of God is God's love for His Son. Our election, our adoption, is always in Christ Jesus. God will visit His mercy upon the seed of Abraham through the line of Isaac because of His promises to the fathers Abraham, Isaac, and Jacob. We have seen this theme woven throughout this epistle.

Application

David sought to show kindness to Mephibosheth on account of his love for another, which parallels God's love for us on account of His love for His Son. This should also inform us how we ought to love others. When we love imperfect fellow Christians, we love them ultimately for the sake of Christ, allowing love to cover a multitude of sins for our brothers and sisters united to Him (1 Peter 4:8). Furthermore, when we love even our enemies, we love them not because they are our enemies, for something in them, but for the sake of Christ, for it is to this that He has called us.

3

An Irrevocable Call

FOR THE GIFTS AND THE CALLING OF GOD **are irrevocable** (v. 29). That is one of the most comforting verses in Scripture as we struggle with our sins. When the Lord God exercises His redeeming call on someone, it is final; He never takes it back. The supreme gift that we have been given is grace, the gift of the mercy by which we have been called and brought into the kingdom and the fellowship of Christ and adopted into His household. God will never under any circumstances revoke it. Even our disobedience, which may displease Him and provoke Him to corrective wrath, will not cause Him to take that gift away. In like manner, God made promises to His people, to Abraham, Isaac, and Jacob.

He called them and gave gifts to them, and that, too, was without revocation. The sovereign election of God is always and ever final.

For as you were once disobedient to God, yet have now obtained mercy through their disobedience, even so these also have now been disobedient, that through the mercy shown you they also may obtain mercy (vv. 30–31). God gave gifts to the nation of Israel, but they became disobedient, and through their disobedience, our mercy was received. Through the mercy we receive, God is going to work to bring His mercy on those who were once disobedient. "He will turn away ungodliness from Jacob" (v. 26). He will say no to their sin and overcome it for the sake of His redemptive plan.

In Romans 3, Paul brought the Jew and the Gentile together before the judgment seat of God and said that both are guilty of sin: "All have sinned and fall short of the glory of God" (v. 23). Here Paul says, **God has committed them all to disobedience, that He might have mercy on all** (v. 32).

Application

This is true of every believer: we were all once disobedient to God. We might look around at our coworkers, friends, and loved ones and begin to worry about their unbelief. Their salvation may weigh heavily on us, but we ought not to despair. For just as we were once disobedient—as they are now—so God might bring them to obedience through His mercy in Christ. Let us never cease praying that this would be so in their lives.

4

The Unfathomable Riches of God

PAUL FOLLOWS HIS EXTRAORDINARY AFFIRMATION with a sigh, a holy groan, the first word of which is simply *Oh*: **Oh, the depth of the riches**

both of the wisdom and knowledge of God! (v. 33a). When we read this carefully, the text is almost palpable. Reading between the lines, we can see Paul's bare emotions as he pens these words, emotions that spring from his profound concern for his kinsmen, Israel. As Paul sets forth the promise of God for a final restoration of his people, his soul groans in passion, and what follows is a doxology.

My professor in Holland once said, "Gentlemen, all sound theology begins and ends with doxology." He was speaking of the fear of the Lord, reverence for God, a heartfelt sense of worship, which is the beginning of wisdom. The first lesson in systematic theology deals with the incomprehensibility of God. The fullness of the essence of God's glory so far transcends human ability to sound its depths that we are left in a state of awe before Him. I am not saying that we are involved in some sort of mystery religion where the things of God are unintelligible; what God reveals we can grasp, to a certain degree. Central to the teaching of John Calvin was the axiom *finitum non capax infinitum*: "the finite cannot contain or grasp the fullness of the infinite." Even after we are in heaven—when we are no longer looking through the glass darkly but basking in the refulgent glory of God—we will not have an exhaustive knowledge of the Creator.

Eternity is not long enough for the creature to come to a comprehensive knowledge of God, because even in eternity we will be creatures, and as creatures we are finite and will remain subject to Calvin's axiom. Never in this world or the next will the finite be able to fully contain or grasp the infinite, so as we stand in wonder and awe before what God has revealed of Himself in His Word, we are moved to doxology. The depth is so deep that we cannot plumb it.

Who can reach the depth of the riches of God's wisdom and knowledge? We are impressed by people who have advanced degrees, and yet the most brilliant human mind is filled with enormous gaps in knowledge. The mind of the brightest human being has more ignorance than knowledge, but in the mind of God there is no ignorance or folly. There is nothing but wisdom and knowledge.

Application

If it is so that we cannot fully comprehend God even in eternity, should we despair of learning more about Him now? May it never be so. The unfathomable depths of God's wisdom and knowledge are all the more reason to praise Him and learn about Him as much as we can. It is why our praise will never be exhausted in eternity. Recognize this and continue to dig into the deep things of God in your studies, so that all your theology might begin and end in doxology.

5

God Unchangeable

I AM OFTEN ASKED, "DOES PRAYER change God's mind?" To ask the question is to answer it. Nothing could be more absurd than to think our prayers would change the mind of God. Our prayers do change things—they change us. If God has determined to do something, what would possibly move Him to change His mind as a result of communion with us? Am I giving Him knowledge when I pray? "God, I know you intend to do this thing, but I don't think you have fully considered the consequences. Let me try to show you what will happen if you do it." No prayer has ever added a subatomic particle of knowledge to the mind of an infinite God.

Consider something even worse: when we think we can change God's mind, we are demonstrating that we think God's intentions are somehow foolish or, even worse, evil, apart from the benefit of our counsel. There is no folly in the mind of God. God does not need our prayers to gain more knowledge or wisdom. Through our prayers God gains our affection and reverence as we bow before Him. The first law of prayer is this: remember to whom we are speaking; and the second law of prayer is this: remember who we are. When we come with our prayers to God, we say, "Oh, the depth of the riches both of the wisdom and knowledge of God! **How unsearchable are His judgments and His ways past finding out!**" (v. 33b).

His judgments are unsearchable. In Paul's teaching to the Corinthians, he tells us of the Spirit, who searches all things of God. The Apostle's teaching there is easily misunderstood. Some think that even the Spirit is searching, groping in the darkness of the Father, trying to figure out what the Father is up to. No, when Paul speaks of the Spirit's searching the things of God, he is not implying that the Spirit is searching for information. Rather, the Spirit is putting the searchlight on the things of God to illumine them for our understanding. To us, the things of God are unsearchable, but thanks be to God that the Spirit searches them for us. That is why, when we come to the biblical text, we pray that God will condescend to our weakness and give us the assistance of the Holy Spirit to make His ways intelligible to us.

Application

We need God's Spirit, and praise be to God that He gives it to all His children. We approach God with all reverence in prayer, and because He has given us the Spirit of adoption, this reverence is magnified, for we approach Him as a Father. Jesus reminds us that even earthly fathers give their children good things when they ask, so let us not hesitate to ask for the Spirit's assistance when we pray to our Father (see Luke 11:1–13).

6

The Mind of the Lord

NOW WE COME TO ANOTHER QUOTATION from the Old Testament, this time from Isaiah, Jeremiah, and Joel. It begins this way: **"For who has known the mind of the LORD?"** (v. 34a). Has anybody ever questioned your motives? When people question my motives, I tell them that they could not possibly know why I do what I do unless I tell them, and even then I might not be telling the truth. Additionally, I might not be telling myself the truth, because I do not always know why I do what I do. Are you always in touch with your motives? I can never get inside the secret chambers of others' hearts, so how can I know their motives?

We cannot plumb the depths of someone else's mind, but that inability cannot be compared to our inability to know the mind of the Lord. "The secret things belong to the Lord our God, but those things which are revealed belong to us and to our children forever" (Deut. 29:29). The only way that we can know the mind of the Lord is if the Lord is pleased to reveal it. When He does, we can know for sure that what He reveals about His mind is not deceitful or inaccurate. That is why I love the Bible—it reveals the mind of God to us.

Paul continues the Old Testament quote: **"Who has become His counselor?"** (v. 34b). God does not have any counselors because He does not need any counselors. What would we counsel Him about? We do not go to God to give Him our advice; we go to God to hear His advice. During my formal education, there was an emphasis on learning the tools of critical analysis. When I come to the Scripture, I realize that it is criticizing me. My only analysis in that case is to examine what it says and then examine my heart for my nonconformity to it. We cannot improve on God. We are not qualified to be His counselor.

"Or who has first given to Him and it shall be repaid to him?" (v. 35). James writes, "Every good gift and every perfect gift is from above" (1:17). When God gives us a gift, He is not paying us back for something that we have given to Him. What can we give Him that He does not already have? That is the marvel of His grace in election. In electing us, He is not repaying a debt. The gift of His grace is given freely from the abundance of His mercy and love.

Application

Take a moment to reflect on and praise God for what you enjoy because of His good gift of the Spirit and things that He has prepared for you: "The Spirit searches all things, yes, the deep things of God. For what man knows the things of a man except the spirit of the man which is in him? Even so no one knows the things of God except the Spirit of God. Now we have received, not the spirit of the world, but the Spirit who is from God, that we might know the things that have been freely given to us by God" (1 Cor. 2:10b–12).

WEEK 40

1

All Things

WE HAVE COME TO THE END OF PAUL'S TREATMENT of the doctrines of grace that began in Romans 1 with the announcement of the gospel of God and justification by faith alone. The Apostle described the universal exposure of the human race to the wrath of God for repressing God's revelation. Man's repression led to manifold sins in the radical corruption of the race, sins both of the Jew and of the Greek. In Romans 3, Paul brought the whole of mankind before the tribunal of God, saying, "All have sinned and fall short of the glory of God" (v. 23).

What followed from that was the exposition of the doctrine of justification by faith alone, which, in turn, was followed by a treatment of sanctification—our growth in Christ after we are justified. Then came a magnificent statement of the providence of God over all things:

"All things work together for good to those who love God" (8:28). This introduced the Golden Chain of the doctrine of election, which Paul expounded in great detail in chapter 9. In chapter 10, Paul covered the great missionary enterprise of the church—we should be sending people throughout the world so that the gospel may be preached to all people.

Thus far in our study of chapter 11, we have seen Paul's profound treatment of the place of ethnic Israel in the future of God's redemption. That was brought to a close in a doxology: "Oh, the depth of the riches both of the wisdom and knowledge of God! How unsearchable are His judgments and His ways past finding out!" (v. 33).

Now we come to the last verse of chapter 11, which is also the last verse of Paul's unfolding of the gospel of God: **For of Him and through Him and to Him are all things, to whom be glory forever. Amen** (v. 36). In this single verse we find the sum and substance of the whole biblical revelation of the being and character of God. Paul sets it forth with a succinct use of three prepositions, each of which is virtually loaded with significance: "For *of* Him and *through* Him and *to* Him are all things." These three prepositions teach us about the nature of God. Through these three prepositions the Apostle is saying that God is the source and owner of everything that is. He is also the ultimate cause of everything that comes to pass, and everything that comes to pass occurs through the exercise of His sovereign will. God is not only the means of all things but also the end or the purpose of all things.

Application

The gospel leads to doxology. As you study Paul's doxology here at the end of Romans 11, take some time to scan what you've covered in Romans. It has all been leading to this point. As you do, may you also be led to deeper measures of praise and adoration to God for your salvation through Jesus Christ.

2

All Things Are of Him

ALL THINGS ARE *"OF HIM."* IN GREEK, the word *of* is a simple preposition that can be translated as either *of* or *from*. A distinction can be made between these two renditions. Both call attention to a profound truth about God. Everything is *of* God in the sense that it is His possession. God is not simply the owner of the gospel or the world. He owns everything in the world. The cattle on a thousand hills are His, and to that we add sheep, donkeys, camels, automobiles, homes, and the whole of creation. This is our Father's world.

Beyond this obvious element of God's ownership of all things, we also see that He is the *source* of everything. The first affirmation about God in Scripture is that He is the source of the universe: "In the beginning God created the heavens and the earth" (Gen. 1:1). In the New Testament, John's Gospel begins this way: "In the beginning was the Word, and the Word was with God, and the Word was God. He was in the beginning with God. All things were made through Him, and without Him nothing was made that was made. In Him was life, and the life was the light of men" (1:1–4). In the same chapter, John introduces the *Logos*, the second person of the Trinity, as the creative agent of the universe: "He was in the world, and the world was made through Him, and the world did not know Him" (v. 10).

Paul expands the cosmic work of Jesus in his letter to the Colossians, an epistle rich in affirmations of the dignity and glory of Christ:

> He is the image of the invisible God, the firstborn over all creation. For by Him all things were created that are in heaven and that are on earth, visible and invisible, whether thrones or dominions or principalities or powers. All things were created

through Him and for Him. And He is before all things, and in Him all things consist. (1:15–17)

The passages in John and in Colossians, which amplify what the Apostle says so briefly in Romans 11, are staggering in their assertions about the function of Christ as the cosmic substance, Creator, and Author of all things, for whom all things are made, and in whom all things consist.

Application

When Paul speaks about Jesus as "the firstborn over all creation" (Col. 1:15), we know that he is not speaking as though the Son of God were the first created being. Rather, His designation as the "firstborn" communicates His authority from the Father over all things. The preposition in the phrase "the firstborn *over* all creation" helps to clarify this. When you confess that Jesus is Lord, you confess nothing short of His being our Creator God, who with the Holy Spirit has eternally existed with the Father.

3

The Source of Truth

THE NEW TESTAMENT SPEAKS OF AT LEAST three dimensions of human experience of which God is the source.

First, God is the source of all truth. If we were to do a word study of the biblical concept of truth, *alētheia*, we would find in the theological dictionary of the New Testament, for example, a lengthy entry about it. We would see that the biblical concept of truth is defined as that which describes real states of affairs. In the eighteenth century, when philosophers were very much concerned about the science of episte-mology, of how we know anything, they wrestled at great length with the question that Pontius Pilate asked of Jesus. During Jesus' trial, Pilate asked Him, "What is truth?" (John 18:38).

John Locke became famous for introducing the correspon-dence theory of truth, which states, quite simply, that truth is what corresponds to reality. Locke was very close to the New Testament definition of truth as that which describes real states of affairs as dis-tinguished from fantasy, mirage, or imagination. No sooner had Locke laid the groundwork for the definition of the correspondence of truth, however, than the next generation of philosophers began to talk about the way in which our individual perceptions determine our under-standing of truth. So this question was raised: if truth is that which corresponds to reality, what if my perception of reality is different from yours?

The Christian response is this: truth is that which corresponds to reality as perceived by God. Only God has a comprehensive knowledge of all reality. God knows reality in its absolute fullness. There is no nuance or microscopic, subatomic particle of the universe unknown to the mind of God. What He knows, He knows perfectly, eternally, and exhaustively. The One who knows all things without error is the source of all truth.

That is why the battle for the Bible is so vital and why Christi-anity was founded upon the conviction that the Bible gives to us not the individual, existential, subjective insights of mortals, but the self-disclosure of truth that comes to us from the very fountainhead and source of all truth. God is the standard of all truth, which is what makes truth so sacred. When we are willing to play with the truth, to allow truth to be slain in the streets in order to maintain relationships, we are striking a blow against the very nature and character of God. No possession we have is more precious, more valuable, and more powerful than truth.

Application

Today, relativism runs rampant. Remember this as you engage with people about the gospel. They may dismiss it as "true for you but not for them." If you ever encounter this, affirm that if what you believe isn't true, your faith is in vain, just as Paul did with the Corinthians concerning the reality of the resurrection. Also clarify that if what they believe isn't true, they will be lost for all eternity, since dismissing objective reality isn't an option when it comes to the truth of God.

4

The Source of Goodness and Beauty

NOT ONLY IS GOD THE SOURCE OF TRUTH, but second, He is also the source of goodness. The ultimate norm for ethics and righteousness is the character of God Himself. Frequently we make distinctions between positive law and natural law or even biblical law. The primary meaning of the term *natural law* is laws that can be extrapolated from a study of nature or science. Theology also speaks of natural law as that which proceeds ultimately from the nature of God. How can we discern between good and evil? We look to the law of God to reveal to us the source of good and evil.

God's law is not some arbitrary legislation that God decided to impose on His creatures; rather, God's law flows from His very being. Theologians make a distinction between the internal and the external righteousness of God. External righteousness refers to what God does in His management of the universe. It refers to God's behavior in which there is no shadow of turning (James 1:17). His works are altogether righteous. God's external righteousness flows from His eternal being. God does what is right because He is the source of all righteousness, and when God behaves in a righteous way, He is simply working out His own being, which is altogether righteous. He is the source and standard of all that is good.

Third, God is also the source of beauty. Our church once produced a brochure that expressed our hopes for a building campaign, and the theme for the project was "for beauty and for holiness." We did not invent that theme; it is the theme that God gave to the people of Israel when He commanded that they build a house for Him. Anything we undertake must be driven by those twin concerns—God's glory and God's holiness.

We are told in the Old Testament to worship the Lord in the beauty of holiness (1 Chron. 16:29). If you look up every Old Testament passage that refers to beauty, you will see that God is the wellspring not only of the true and the good but also of the beautiful. Everything beautiful comes from Him and points back to Him. Pagans produce magnificent music or art, and their work points to the Author of everything beautiful even though they have no affection for God in their hearts. There is nothing virtuous in the ugly.

Application

The good, the true, and the beautiful are often referred to as the *transcendentals*. These qualities *transcend* any one thing in creation but can be traced back to God, who possesses them in His fullness and who bestows them on the things in creation. When you see them in the created order, may they stir up in you praise for our God, and wherever you notice their absence, strive to make that part of the world more like the goodness, truth, and beauty of God.

5

Through and To

"FOR OF HIM AND *THROUGH* HIM . . . are all things" (v. 36). If everyone believed that one phrase, the Arminian-Calvinistic debate would end forever because this text refers to the means by which God governs and orders His universe. The word *through* has to do with means, the instrument, by which things come to pass. Paul is simply reiterating here what he taught in Romans 8, that God in His providence exercises His sovereignty over, in, and through all things. All things that come to pass in this world ultimately come about through the sovereign agency of God Himself. We need to embrace this because the great joy of the Christian is to know that all things are in God's hand and are being used by Him for His purposes, regardless of the causal means He uses to bring about whatsoever He pleases. There are no accidents in a universe governed by God, in an ultimate sense. If God exists, sovereignty is an essential attribute of His very deity. If there were one maverick molecule in this universe running loose outside the scope of God's sovereign control, God would not be sovereign, and if He were not sovereign, He would not be God.

"For of Him and through Him and *to* Him are all things." The word *to* indicates the purpose toward which everything is moving. Where is everything going? What is the goal of the universe? What is the ultimate purpose of all history? In a word, the answer is God. He is the Alpha and the Omega, the beginning and the end. He is the source. All things are moving in history and in the universe to fulfill the purpose of God.

We observe many things that cause us to ask, "How can that possibly fit in with the purposes of God?" We see much evil and corruption, and we say that God cannot possibly have anything to do with it, but over against all that is wicked stands a mighty God who orders all things together for His glory.

Application

If salvation were left up to us and our natural ability to respond in faith to the gospel, then the glory of our salvation could in some sense be traced back to us. But since it is the case that all things are through God and all glory is His alone, we cannot claim any glory for ourselves, and it must be that God's gracious salvation is truly from Him alone. Praise Him as the One who regenerates hearts, enables faith, justifies sinners, and sustains to the end.

6

To Whom Be Glory Forever

ONE THEOLOGIAN SAID THAT THIS LAST verse of Romans 11 is Paul's version of the *non nobis Domine*—"Not unto us, O LORD, not unto us, but to Your name give glory" (Ps. 115:1). Your destiny has been appointed by God from the foundation of the world for His glory. The destiny of nations, history, and planets and the orbiting of the heavenly bodies have been created, designed, and ordained by God to display His glory. That is why the psalmist looked at the stars and was overcome with awe: "The heavens declare the glory of God; and the firmament shows His handiwork" (Ps. 19:1).

The Hebrew word for "glory," *kavod*, literally means "weightiness." It refers to God's significance or value. God's glory is His singular transcendent dignity, which no creature can possess in similar magnitude. God's glory is in a class by itself. In the Bible we see God's manifesting His glory through the shekinah cloud. The shekinah cloud is so excellent in its brilliance that human beings must shield their eyes from it, lest they go blind. That is the outward manifestation of the eternal inward dignity of God.

Revelation 21 and 22 describe the holy city coming down out of heaven. Strangely, it is described as a place where the sun does not shine. There are no candles nor moon nor artificial source of light. You would think that such a place would be bathed in perpetual darkness, but the author of Revelation tells us that there is no need of sun or artificial light in heaven because the glory of God and the radiance of

His Son bathe the holy city in light perpetually. The glow from the face of God—the manifestation of His glory—illuminates every inch of the kingdom of heaven. The light of the glory of God is never extinguished, which is why the Apostle says "to whom be glory forever" (Rom. 11:36). The glory of God began in eternity and will continue for eternity.

When we come into God's presence to worship Him, the only appropriate response is reverence, awe, humility, and submission. The contemporary church all too often displays a cavalier approach to worship. Many have no idea about the One they are dealing with, the One for whom the angels themselves have to cover their eyes when they sing of His glory. Our glory comes and goes, but the glory of God endures forever.

Application

For the Christian, the reality of life in a fallen world creates a yearning for God. It's fitting how this yearning is captured at the end of Revelation 22: "He who testifies to these things says, 'Surely I am coming quickly.' Amen. Even so, come, Lord Jesus!" (v. 20). Pray these words today, so that you would hold loosely to the things of this world as you await a glory that will last forever.

Romans 12

I BESEECH YOU THEREFORE, BRETHREN, *by the mercies of God, that you present your bodies a living sacrifice, holy, acceptable to God, which is your reasonable service. And do not be conformed to this world, but be transformed by the renewing of your mind, that you may prove what is that good and acceptable and perfect will of God.*

For I say, through the grace given to me, to everyone who is among you, not to think of himself more highly than he ought to think, but to think soberly, as God has dealt to each one a measure of faith. For as we have many members in one body, but all the members do not have the same function, so we, being many, are one body in Christ, and individually members of one another. Having then gifts differing according to the grace that is given to us, let us use them: if prophecy, let us prophesy in proportion to our faith; or ministry, let us use it in our ministering; he who teaches, in teaching; he who exhorts, in exhortation; he who gives, with liberality; he who leads, with diligence; he who shows mercy, with cheerfulness.

Let love be without hypocrisy. Abhor what is evil. Cling to what is good. Be kindly affectionate to one another with brotherly love, in honor giving preference to one another; not lagging in diligence, fervent in spirit, serving the Lord; rejoicing in hope, patient in tribulation, continuing steadfastly in prayer; distributing to the needs of the saints, given to hospitality.

Bless those who persecute you; bless and do not curse. Rejoice with those who rejoice, and weep with those who weep. Be of the same mind toward one another. Do not set your mind on high things, but associate with the humble. Do not be wise in your own opinion.

Repay no one evil for evil. Have regard for good things in the sight of all men. If it is possible, as much as depends on you, live peaceably with all men. Beloved, do not avenge yourselves, but rather give place to wrath; for it is written, "Vengeance is Mine, I will repay," says the Lord. Therefore

"If your enemy is hungry, feed him;
If he is thirsty, give him a drink;
For in so doing you will heap coals of fire on his head."

Do not be overcome by evil, but overcome evil with good.

WEEK 41

1

The Mercies of God

IN THE ENGLISH LANGUAGE, THERE IS A VARIETY of word forms—nouns, verbs, adverbs, adjectives, and prepositions—but there is also an abundance of symbols, such as the plus sign and the minus sign. One symbol with which you may not be familiar contains three dots in the form of a triangle. There is a dot at the top and another on either side. The triangle is the symbol for the word *ergo* or *therefore*. The symbol usually indicates the conclusion to an argument that has just been set forth; it indicates the *therefore*. As I have said before, anytime we see the word *therefore* in Scripture, our attention ought to perk up because we are coming to the sum of the matter.

As we come now to the beginning of Romans 12, we are immediately faced with a question. Concerning Paul's words, **I beseech you therefore, brethren** (v. 1a), does the *therefore* refer to the conclusion of Paul's doxology in chapter 11? That might be the case, but the majority of Pauline scholars would argue that the *therefore* is intended to follow the entire unfolding of Paul's argument for the gospel that began in chapter 1. At the beginning of Romans 12, Paul makes a clear transition from the doctrinal portion of the epistle to the application portion. In light of all that he has unfolded about the things of God, there is a practical conclusion that Paul wants his readers to reach. He is not simply making a logical argument, although he is certainly doing that; he is making an Apostolic plea. Now that his readers have been shown the true gospel—justification, sanctification, the doctrines of grace in election, perseverance, and the sweetness of God's providential care—Paul wants his readers to consider its implications and applications.

Paul pleads with the brethren **by the mercies of God** (v. 1b). Paul makes his plea in light of God's tender mercies, which he has just finished expounding in chapter 11, and those mercies are these: (1) we are justified by faith; (2) our sins are forgiven through the atonement of Christ; (3) God works all things together for our good; and (4) God calls people to Himself. Everything that Paul has expounded throughout the doctrinal section of the epistle, chapters 1–11, points back to God's mercy. The mercies of God lead us to the *therefore*.

Application

In the New Testament, indicatives are usually followed by imperatives, such that imperatives are always grounded by indicatives. Imperatives are commands, things that we ought to do, but our obedience is not an attempt to merit salvation. Imperatives are connected to gospel indicatives, statements that indicate something about the true state of affairs in light of the life, death, burial, resurrection, and ascension of Jesus Christ. All that we are called to do is always connected to gospel realities.

2

A Thank Offering

THE FIRST THING PAUL ASKS HIS READERS, by way of practical application, is to bring a thank offering to God: **present your bodies a living sacrifice, holy, acceptable to God, which is your reasonable service** (v. 1c). His request harks back to the Old Testament system of worship, which was established on the basis of sacrifice. The first sacrifice propagated by God in the Old Testament was the worship that He enjoined upon Adam and Eve and their sons. The sons came with their produce or livestock and offered a sacrifice on the altar. Such sacrifices were the very definition of early worship. The liturgical structure of the tabernacle and the temple in the Old Testament expanded on that mode of worship. Bulls, goats, lambs, turtledoves, and cereal offerings were brought into the sanctuary and sacrificed.

We think of *sacrifice* as the giving away of something of extreme value. There is an element of that in biblical sacrifice, but the primary point is not that we should lose something but that we should express something. The whole principle of giving to God is an expression of worship.

During Sunday morning worship services we hear, "Let us now worship God with the giving of our tithes and offerings." When that request comes, we are not asked to give something back to God from a sense of duty. We are asked to make an offering as an act of worship. Such giving is one way that we show our submission to the transcendent majesty of God. He is worthy of our praise, devotion, substance, and time—everything we have.

In the Old Testament, the animal sacrifices had to be killed before they could be offered. The lamb or goat or bull was slain, and its blood was poured on the altar. In stark contrast to that, in light of the gospel, we are to offer ourselves as living sacrifices—not our animals, vegetables, or cereal, but our bodies. We tend to think of worship as spiritual rather than physical, so we might wonder why Paul asks us to present our bodies rather than our souls. Actually, Paul is writing about the entire person. God wants us to give ourselves. Christ, in the ultimate sense, gave *Himself*, not His *self*. He gave Himself for us, and we are to respond by giving ourselves to Him. Of course, we cannot give ourselves to Christ the way that He gave Himself for us. He gave Himself to redeem us; we give ourselves to thank and serve Him.

Application

When are we to give ourselves to God as living sacrifices? We are to do so the minute we come to Christ. These sacrifices are not something offered on the Day of Atonement or on Sunday morning; they are offerings of our whole selves for our whole lives. The concept is easy to understand but hard to implement. Our lives are to be given over, body and soul, to the service of God. To be Christians is to present ourselves as living sacrifices.

3

A Holy Sacrifice

OUR SACRIFICE IS TO BE LIVING, and it is to be holy. The animals offered to God in the Old Testament economy were required to be the first-fruits of the flock, the animals without blemish, but Christ has already taken our sin. Therefore, when we give ourselves as living sacrifices to God, He wants that sacrifice sanctified or consecrated. In the words of the old hymn, "Give of your best to the Master." We are to give the most sanctified portion of our lives as an act of praise to God.

Paul is giving us a tough job. Remember that he starts out begging: "I beseech you . . ." We can sense the way in which the Old Testament economy is informing Paul's understanding of the metaphor of sacrifice. Not all the offerings that God received from His people in the Old Testament delighted Him. Offerings were brought to the Lord while the people were living in hypocrisy, offering Him false worship. Through the voice of the prophets, God would say to His people:

> I hate, I despise your feast days,
> And I do not savor your sacred assemblies.
> Though you offer Me burnt offerings and your grain offerings,
> I will not accept them,
> Nor will I regard your fattened peace offerings.
> Take away from Me the noise of your songs,

For I will not hear the melody of your stringed instruments.
But let justice run down like water,
And righteousness like a mighty stream. (Amos 5:21–24)

We often overlook the type of sacrifice that God requires of us. We think that any act of religion or spiritual sacrifice will necessarily be delightful to God. It will not. God requires that we offer ourselves in a way that is acceptable to Him. We are to offer ourselves in humility and repentance so that the sacrifice of our praise will provide a sweet aroma.

Application

The gospel is an antidote to false worship. One of the best ways to foster a sense of humility and repentance is by reflecting on the reality that Christ died for us while we were ungodly. He loved us while we were unlovable, so that we might love God with a proper sense of reverence and awe for the magnitude of His grace to us. This humility leads to repentance out of a heart of gratitude, through which we are able to offer a sacrifice of praise in our worship.

4

Reasonable Service

PAUL GROUNDS HIS APPEAL FOR LIVING, holy sacrifices: it is our "reasonable service." Other translations read "which is your spiritual worship." The Apostle actually says "logical worship." What could be more logical or reasonable than offering our whole selves to God in thanksgiving, praise, worship, and adoration with the saints behind the altar? We sing, "Worthy is the Lamb who was slain" (Rev. 5:12); that is our logical response. If we understand the gospel, then indifference and apathy are irrational responses. The worship that we are to offer God is not a mindless worship.

Many Christians today do not want to think. They do not want to grapple with the content of the Word of God. They want their religion to be one of feeling. "God calls us to have a childlike faith," they say. They are right about that, but it is not to be a childish faith. We are to be childlike in our morality and in our trust; we are not to be hardened professionals in sin. We are to be children in one sense, but we are called to be adults in our understanding. The Word of God repeatedly rebukes those who are satisfied with a diet of milk and pabulum in their Christian life. We are called to go for the meat of the gospel. We are called to grow up to the fullness of maturity in Jesus Christ. Our reasonable worship is one that, as we will see very soon in the text, involves the mind in an engaging way.

I host a daily radio program called *Renewing Your Mind*. The title is based on Paul's words in verse 2a: **Do not be conformed to this world, but be transformed by the renewing of your mind**. A contrast is presented in Romans 12:1–2 between what we are not to do and what we are to do. Both have to do with morphology, the study of forms. In English, the root words for *form* can either describe shape or indicate style. Paul is contrasting conformity with transformation; we are to flee from one to the other. To present our bodies as living sacrifices entails not being conformed to the world.

Application

We cannot be transformed without knowing what we are being transformed into. We cannot pursue nonconformity with the world if we do not know what conformity to God looks like. That is the importance of theological study, that we might know Him as He has revealed Himself. Let us be thoughtful Christians who are willing to grapple with God's Word, dependent on the Spirit, so that He might do a great work in our hearts.

5

Transformed

THE GREEK WORD THAT PAUL USES IN VERSE 2 for "transformed" is *metamorphosis*. We use that word to describe the transition that a caterpillar undergoes in order to become a butterfly. The word indicates a radical change of form. Therefore, the goal of the Christian life is not merely nonconformity, which is the easy part, but transformation. The prefix *trans-* added to the word *formed* means "above and beyond the forms of this world." Living as Christians means that we do not live by the drumbeat of this world but by a higher calling—the calling of God—and when we do that, the form of our life changes. We are not conformed to this dying age, but our lives are transformed by the power of God.

This transformation happens through mind renewal. If we want a transformed life, the most important thing is to get a new mind. The beginning of the Christian life is rooted in repentance. The Greek word for "repentance" is *metanoia*, which means "a change of mind." Before our initial repentance, we thought according to the precepts of this world. We thought just like our secular neighbors, who do everything in their power to bury their sin in their subconscious, but when the Holy Spirit awakened us to our absolute need for a Savior and we rushed to the cross, our minds and the direction of our lives were changed. The mind is central, because transformation comes from a renewed mind.

While a changed mind is a *necessary* condition for transformation, however, it is not a *sufficient* condition. People can study the Word of God and get a perfect score on every theological examination without that knowledge ever getting into the heart. No one is transformed apart from heart change. God has designed us in such a way that the avenue to the heart is through the mind. The book of Romans was given for our understanding, so that we would begin to think as Jesus thinks and begin to approve what He approves and despise what He despises. That is how our lives are changed. When we begin to think as Christians, we get a new mind. From that new mind our heart is changed, and when the heart is changed, our life is changed. That is how we become transformed people.

Application

Transformation is a reality that all Christians experience. It might not look the same for every Christian, but just as every Christian is born again and indwelt by the Holy Spirit, so every Christian is being transformed. Be eager to see this transformation in your life and work unto God, keeping in step with the Spirit, that it might be hastened for His glory.

6

The Purpose of Transformation

TRANSFORMATION HAPPENS FOR THIS PURPOSE: **that you may prove what is that good and acceptable and perfect will of God** (v. 2b). Many years before *Renewing Your Mind* was on the radio, Ligonier produced a five-minute radio program called *Ask R.C.* People contacted the program with questions and asked for theological comments and biblical references. The primary question we were asked was this: "How can I know the will of God for my life?" The answer is found not from a Ouija board or from signs or from fleeces—it is found by the renewing of the mind through feeding on the Word of God. A renewed mind begins to think God's thoughts after Him. When our minds are informed by the Word of God, we are able to certify, prove, and recognize what is that good, acceptable, and complete will of God.

When people ask me, "What's the will of God for my life?" I reply, "Are you asking me if you should be a lawyer or a baker, or whether you should marry Jane or Virginia?" We will address this subject more fully in our studies in days to come; here I tell you simply what the Bible says about it: "This is the will of God, your sanctification" (1 Thess. 4:3). If we are not growing in sanctification, seeking God's will about such things as our job, spouse, or place to live is worthless. God's will for each of us is that we grow into spiritual maturity, that our lives become more fully set apart and consecrated by the Holy Spirit, and that our minds are changed. After that, we will be able to tell what is pleasing to God. Then we will be able to know what He wants us to do—that good and acceptable and perfect will of God.

Application

The frightening thing about life is that we must still make decisions regarding things of which we are not certain daily even if we are not growing in our sanctification. This is all the more reason to pursue it— not because of the practical advantages that it might bring but because sanctification is one of the most certain things that we know about God's will for our lives. Pursuing sanctification, we can enjoy the freedom of making decisions about our lives from a position of faith.

WEEK 42

1

Sober Esteem

WE LIVE IN A CULTURE OBSESSED with self-esteem. Developing a good self-image has become almost cultic. Some years ago, an international test in mathematics was administered to children from ten nations, including the United States. The test had two parts. The first pertained to mathematical competency, and the second pertained to feelings of self-esteem with respect to the students' performance. Two ironies stood out. First, the Korean students were last in their estimation of their performance but first in actual competency. The reason is that along with the rigorous pursuit of academic excellence, Korean students are taught principles of humility. Conversely, and to our national shame, the American children scored last in mathematical competency but first in self-esteem. The American students had a high view of their competency in spite of their miserable performance. Self-esteem, as important as it is (we are not to brutalize people by tearing them apart with unnecessary criticisms and insults), can be damaging if we provide people with a higher opinion of themselves than they should have.

What does all that have to do with Romans? Paul writes, **For I say, through the grace given to me** (v. 3a). Paul is writing to them as one gifted and called by God, through no merit of his own, to the position of Apostle. Despite his calling, he considered himself the chief of sinners (1 Tim. 1:15). It is through the grace given to him that Paul writes an admonition **to everyone who is among you, not to think of himself more highly than he ought to think, but to think soberly** (v. 3b). Unfortunately, the English juxtaposes Paul's words "to think . . . more highly" with "to think soberly." The play on words present in the Greek cannot be translated into English. The Greek term for "to think soberly" is the same term used for "to think" but with a different prefix added to it. Therefore, Paul is not talking about an intellectual enterprise or analysis of our skills or ability or status; he is connecting the cognitive aspect, thinking, to the aspect of affection. He is not writing about estimation so much as about esteem. Simply, Paul is saying that we should not esteem ourselves too highly but rather think soberly and carefully about ourselves.

Application

The book of Proverbs teaches us that "pride goes before destruction, and a haughty spirit before a fall" (16:18). We must guard against esteeming ourselves so highly that it becomes sinful pride, leading to our destruction. The paradox of prideful self-esteem is that pride is often what leads us to tear down others. That is why it is so critical for us in the church, the body of Christ, to be united in humility.

2

Sobering Responsibilities

WHEN THE APOSTLE CALLS US TO a sober self-evaluation, particularly with respect to our abilities, he puts on us a tremendous responsibility. People come to me, asking, "How do I know if I am called to the ministry?" "How do I know if I should accept the office of deacon in the church?" "How do I know if I am qualified to be an elder?" We must remember that the church is the context in which Paul is giving this practical instruction. To those who are considering a vocation in the ministry, I say, "Before you think about the glory and drama of the ministry, you need to sit down and make a sober analysis of your gifts." I ask them to consider whether they really have what it takes to be a minister or a deacon or an elder or any other calling that they might consider pursuing.

I have seen in the course of seminary teaching many students with stars in their eyes about going into the ministry, but they lack the necessary gifts for the service of God in this particular vocation. Perhaps someone has flattered them or they have flattered themselves; along the way, the evaluation was not a sober one. When that happens, people are doomed to failure, frustration, disappointment, discouragement, and sometimes lifelong depression. Each year in the United States, sixteen thousand clergy demit the ministry, some for moral reasons but most because they deem their job to be a bad fit for their abilities. That is a dreadful experience for people, and it starts because they were intoxicated rather than sober in their self-esteem.

The closest follow-up to the instruction Paul gives here is found in his first letter to the Corinthians. The Corinthian community was torn apart with strife because everybody was elevating his own gifts and offices above everyone else's. There was an ongoing battle for power and status in that church. If that can happen in a first-century church, it can certainly happen in our churches today. To both the Corinthians and the Romans Paul uses one of his favorite metaphors for the church—a body. A body is made up of many parts, and each part needs the help of the other. Through unity in diversity, grace is given to everybody in the church, and everybody in the church has a role to play. We are not to despise the roles that other people play, nor are we to elevate our roles as the most important for the life of the church.

Application

Ordinarily, when people consider their future, whether they should go into a particular vocation, they take stock of their abilities and passion for the work. This ordinary way of setting a course in our lives also applies to the work of Christian ministry. With a proper assessment of one's gifts, a person can know in what ways God is equipping him or her to serve the church, but only with a true sense of this calling can one endure ministry's hardships.

3

One Body

HERE IS HOW PAUL SPELLS IT OUT to the Romans: they are not to think of themselves more highly than they ought but to think soberly, **as God has dealt to each one a measure of faith** (v. 3c). Paul wrote, "For by one Spirit we were all baptized into one body" (1 Cor. 12:13).

Persistent in the church today is the troubling idea that some believers are gifted by the Holy Spirit while others are not. In addition to the Spirit's work of regeneration in the life of the Christian, the Spirit also distributes gifts or abilities to every Christian. The church is to help believers find their particular gifts so that all work together for the good of the church.

For as we have many members in one body, but all the members do not have the same function, so we, being many, are one body in Christ, and individually members of one another (vv. 4–5). Years ago, I was approached about becoming the pastor of a church. I already had a full-time job, so I could not take on a full-time pastorate, but the request was persistent, so I gave it more thought. I was aware that something had been missing in my ministry, and that was a pulpit. After much discussion, prayer, and consideration, and, I hope, a sober analysis of my limitations, I agreed. That is how I came to serve at St. Andrew's Chapel. Since then, I have spent much time at conferences with pastors from all over the country, and now that I am a pastor, I have an ability to hear their cries in a way that I could not before. Pastors are expected to be jacks-of-all-trades and masters of none. They are expected to be administrators, statesmen, and psychological counselors. They are expected to be biblical experts, theologians, preachers, and teachers.

We need a reformation in the church in terms of what is expected from ministers. The primary task of the minister is the preaching of the Word of God, the feeding of the flock. I tell young pastors that 90 percent of their time should be taken up with preaching and teaching. God has not called them to be psychological counselors or brilliant administrators. He has called them to preach the Word and feed the sheep. The pastor should be free to spend his time preaching and teaching, because what Christians need above all is to be nurtured in the Word of God.

Application

One of the ways that you can support your pastor is to encourage his labor in God's Word. Take time to share with him how God is using his ministry of the Word positively in your life. Also take time to pray that he will be afforded sufficient time to prepare his preaching and teaching for the sake of your congregation. May God bring about such a reformation in our expectations that His people will be well fed.

4

Prophecy

EVERYONE HAS A TASK: **Having then gifts differing according to the grace that is given to us, let us use them** (v. 6a). God has given us gifts, and He has not given them to be wasted or set on a shelf or buried in the ground. God expects us to use them. Those with the gift of teaching should teach. Those gifted to preach must preach. Anyone with the gift of evangelism is called to evangelize.

Paul adds to the gifts list: **if prophecy, let us prophesy in proportion to our faith** (v. 6b). Some believe that the gift of prophecy is the immediate, supernatural, Spirit-given ability to interpret tongues and to make predictions for the future, just as prophets in the Old Testament did, and this is a struggle for those who believe that the supernatural gifts of the Apostolic age ceased with the death of the last Apostle. I believe that the gift of apostleship was intended for the first century only and did not pass on to the next generation. In one sense, the gift of prophecy that Paul is describing here applies only to the immediate time of the Apostolic age, but there are other problems involved.

In the Old Testament, the supreme agents of revelation were the prophets. The New Testament counterpart to the Old Testament prophet is not the New Testament prophet; it is the New Testament Apostle. There is parity between the Old Testament prophet and the New Testament Apostle—both are authoritative agents of revelation—but here

Paul distinguishes between the gift of prophecy and the gift of apostleship. One way that scholars deal with this is to make a distinction between the terms *Prophet* and *prophet* and *Apostle* and *apostle*. The term *Apostle*, with a capital *A*, refers to those selected by Christ and endowed with His authority, specific individuals such as Peter, Paul, and John. At the same time, all the church was involved in the Apostolic mission of spreading the Word of God to all nations. In that sense, every church member was an *apostle* (lowercase *a*). The same thing can be said about the office of prophet.

In New Testament terms, the prophet functioned as an interpreter of the Word of God. We like to think of the Old Testament prophets as those who predicted the future, what we call *foretelling*, yet their primary task was not predicting the future; it was *forthtelling*, communicating the word of God to the people. Old Testament prophets were God's prosecuting attorneys against a covenant community that had broken its vows. The Old Testament prophets were called upon to interpret God's word to the people. In like manner, the New Testament prophet was one gifted in interpreting or expositing the word of God. In contemporary terms, such a prophet is a preacher. Today it is the preacher who fulfills the task of interpreting and expositing the Word of God. What continues to this day from the role of the first-century prophet is interpreting the Word of God and expounding it to the people. Those are the primary tasks of the preacher.

Application

While not everyone is called to preach, everyone does play a part in the local church. It is curious to think how our omnipotent God could have accomplished His purposes without us, but it ought to be encouraging to us that He wants to work with, in, and through us. Think about your gifts in relation to how you might support of the ministry of the church, and be eager to use those gifts for the sake of the body of Christ. Remember that God desires to use your gifts.

5

Ministry

IF OUR GIFT IS MINISTRY, **let us use it in our ministering** (v. 7a). In view here principally is the ministry of the deacons, those who serve by taking care of the orphans, the widows, and the poor. Certain people with a servant's heart have been gifted by God to be deacons. It is a marvelous gift for the church. No church can be a healthy one without a heavy commitment to service—taking care of the oppressed, the poor, and the lonely. Ministry is not just preaching the Word of God. Deacons were appointed to serve the needs of the people so that the Apostles could preach without being encumbered with other tasks, but not all the deacons were content with being deacons. They sought to establish policy and rule the community; they wanted a higher status than that of servant.

King Uzziah came to the throne in Jerusalem when he was sixteen years old, and he reigned for fifty-two years (see 2 Kings 15:1–7; 2 Chronicles 26). His monarchy, for the most part, was marvelous because he did what was right in the sight of the Lord, but in his later years his status went to his head. He became dissatisfied with being the king. He wanted to be the priest, too, so he went into the temple and tried to offer the sacrifices. The priests were horrified, and when they tried to stop him, Uzziah went into a wild rage. At that moment, God struck Uzziah with leprosy. He died alone, cut off from the temple and the royal house in shame and disgrace. Uzziah was discontented with the office that God had given him.

The same thing happens in every church in every age in every part of the world, but we are not to let it happen. We are to identify our gifts and exercise them. We are not to be envious of others' gifts, and we are not to elevate our gifts over the gifts of others. During my forty-plus years of ministry, I have seen that happen repeatedly. People get passionate about the gift they have received and begin to think that others' gifts do not matter. The eye wants to say to the ear, "I do not need you," but ears do not help us see anything more clearly than we already see. The ear does not want to see; it wants to hear, so it says, "Who needs the eye?" How foolish.

Application

We might have a tendency to value our particular gifts over those of others, but on the other hand, we might have a tendency to think little of what we have to offer when we consider the enormous gifting of others. We ought to rejoice at the gifting of others. After all, their gifts are ultimately Christ's gifts to His church, so insofar as we rejoice in Christ, we ought also to rejoice in the gifts of others. What is true of them, however, is also true of us, so let us never become discouraged with our own gifts, for Christ is using them too.

6

Generosity, Leadership, and Mercy

EVERYBODY HAS AN OBLIGATION TO GIVE, but some really have the gift for it, and if so, this is how they must use it: **he who gives, with liberality** (v. 8b). There are people who not only give but do so generously. They give beyond what is required. Paul said elsewhere that God loves a cheerful giver (2 Cor. 9:7). Nobody wants to get a gift from a sourpuss who cannot stand to be separated from his money. God does not want such gifts.

Leadership is another gift to exercise: **he who leads, with diligence** (v. 8c). I once traveled to Germany with a group to tour the sites of the

Reformation. One day we went to examine the spot where the Diet of Worms had been assembled. We were given a lunch break and told to return afterward to where the buses were parked. We split up in different directions, and the group I joined had lunch near one of the town squares there. After lunch I could not remember how to get back to the bus, but a girl in our group said that she knew the way back. We all got in line behind her, and she started marching with great confidence toward the bus. I did not recognize anything that looked familiar, so I asked her, "Are you sure this is the right way to the bus?" She said, "Yes, R.C., I am sure." Finally, she stopped and said, "I am always sure but seldom right." She had not done due diligence; she should have spent some time with a map. If a gifted leader is going to be followed, he or she had better know the way to go.

The gift of mercy is to be shown this way: **he who shows mercy, with cheerfulness** (v. 8d). We receive God's mercy from a heart glad to give it. To be gifted in mercy is a wonderful thing, and it is as much needed among the people of God as the preaching of the Word. Scripture tells us that love covers a multitude of sins (1 Peter 4:8). There are disagreeable people in every congregation who make big issues of minor matters. They have no sense of charity or mercy—no sense of grace. We exist by grace. We cannot do anything apart from the tender mercy of God. Mercy is to be dispensed with cheerfulness.

Application

Mercy ought be a characteristic of every Christian, for it is characteristic of God. An Old Testament refrain about the nature of God comes from His revealing Himself to Moses in Exodus: "The LORD, the LORD God, *merciful* and gracious, longsuffering, and abounding in goodness and truth, keeping *mercy* for thousands, forgiving iniquity and transgression and sin" (34:6b–7a, emphasis added). Pray that God would give you a merciful spirit toward others.

WEEK 43

1

Love and Hate

PAUL HAS BEEN MAPPING OUT FOR us the communion of saints. The word *communion* comes from the prefix *com-*, which means "union" or "with oneness." In order for there to be a communion of saints, there first has to be a plurality. If we are Christians, we are supernaturally in Christ, and if we are in Christ, Christ is in us; however, the relationship we enjoy with Jesus is not simply a unilateral relationship. We have a supernatural bond, a union among ourselves, that flows from Christ. We are to like one another for Christ's sake, because we are in Him and we are with each other forever. That is the communion of saints, warts and all.

Throughout the epistle, Paul has given us lengthy, weighty concepts, and he has done so with long sentences and paragraphs. Here, however, Paul writes in staccato shots, giving us something almost like bullets in a PowerPoint presentation. In a terse manner, Paul sets out ethical injunctions, one after another, which we are to manifest in the Christian life. Paul was not present when Jesus gave His Sermon on the Mount, but much of the information communicated by our Lord there is recapitulated in brief form here. This section of the epistle is also reminiscent of the Apostle James' writings. He gave ethical injunctions in a similar manner to Paul's style here.

The first injunction is not just part of a loose list of virtues; rather, it is the thematic statement for all the responsibilities that follow. Paul begins with love: **Let love be without hypocrisy** (v. 9a). We are to manifest love that is genuine, sincere, and authentic. When Paul wrote to the Corinthians, he devoted an entire chapter to the meaning of love (1 Corinthians 13). We might consider this Romans passage as a similar exposition. God expects from us authentic love, that which is not mixed with hypocrisy or false sentiment.

Paul makes immediate application with two strong statements: **Abhor what is evil. Cling to what is good** (v. 9b). We are to hate one thing and to love something else. The hatred about which Paul writes is hatred of the highest dimension. He uses one of the strongest words for hatred found anywhere in the Bible. The word implies not mild displeasure or mere dislike; Paul is commanding in the name of the Lord that we loathe evil. We are to see evil as an unveiled assault on the character of God and on His sovereignty. As we seek to grow in grace, we seek to gain the mind of Christ, which is to think like Jesus, to love what Jesus loves, and to hate what Jesus hates.

Application

Reflect on the areas in which you would like to see your love grow in your life, using 1 Corinthians 13: "Love suffers long and is kind; love does not envy; love does not parade itself, is not puffed up; does not behave rudely, does not seek its own, is not provoked, thinks no evil; does not rejoice in iniquity, but rejoices in the truth; bears all things, believes all things, hopes all things, endures all things" (vv. 4–7).

2

The Evil of Abortion

HATRED IS ONE OF THE STRONGEST emotions that can inhabit the heart of a human being. Hatred is destructive and demeaning, but not when it is directed against evil.

I believe that the greatest ethical issue today is that of abortion. In recent years, many have come to see terrorism as more concerning than abortion. I am baffled by that, because more people were killed on September 10 in the womb of U.S. women than were killed on 9/11 in New York City. More babies were slaughtered on September 12 than adults were killed on 9/11. If we had a camera on the womb so that CNN could show us graphic videos of what actually happens in the slaughter of unborn children, abortion would be quickly abolished, but the reality of it is covered up. If there is one thing I know about God, it is that He hates abortion. The German ethicist Helmut Thielicke indicated something unusual in his massive mid-twentieth-century work on Christian ethics. The work appeared before *Roe v. Wade*, that is, before Western civilization had embraced abortion on demand. In his book, Thielicke wrote that abortion has always been considered a monolithic evil in Christian thought among both liberals and conservatives. That is clear from the very first century, in the Didache, which called abortion "murder." Abortion is an unspeakable evil that God abhors, one that the American church tolerates and winks at. That troubles me deeply, and I do not understand it.

As we are to despise what is evil, we are to cling to what is good. Paul uses intense language here. This term translated *cling* is the root of the Greek word *glue*. We are to hang on tightly to that which is good, allowing it to be cemented to our souls so that we do not drop or lose it with the next wind of cultural fantasy that comes our way.

Application

The Westminster Larger Catechism teaches us about the nature of God's law that "where a duty is commanded, the contrary sin is forbidden; and, where a sin is forbidden, the contrary duty is commanded" (Q&A 99). In considering the sixth commandment, it is clear that it forbids murder, but the duty to preserve life is commanded. Hating abortion is one of the ways that we reflect the character of our life-giving God and keep His commands.

3

Affection, Honor, and Diligence

PAUL'S NEXT COMMENTS ARE SPECIFICALLY ADDRESSED to the fellowship of believers, the household of faith: **Be kindly affectionate to one another with brotherly love** (v. 10a). We find here the idea of *philadelphia*, brotherly love. It is love among those who share a common family. The love we have for one another in the church is to be the same kind of love we experience in our families between parents and children and between siblings. We are to imitate that kind of love—brotherly affection—in a spirit of kindness toward one another. Kindness is one of the most important virtues in the Bible. It is a fruit of the Holy Spirit. A kind person is successful in the eyes of God.

In addition to affection and love, we are to live **in honor giving preference to one another** (v. 10b). There is some ambiguity in this statement, so it has been translated in various ways. The text is generally thought to be saying that we ought to prefer each other for honor. We are not to seek honor for ourselves but rather to reflect or deflect honor to others. In other words, it is a call to humility. Paul's basic thrust, however, is that believers are to be leaders in establishing the principle of honor among one another. Even if no one in the congregation is manifesting respect and honor, then we must demonstrate a spirit of humility. That is the heart of a servant, and it is to be the heart of the Christian.

My translation for the next phrase reads **not lagging in diligence** (v. 11a). An older translation reads "not slothful in business" (KJV). We are not to be lazy in business; however, Paul is not talking about commercial enterprise. The word *business* comes from the term *busy-ness*, which means that we should be busy people, busy with the things of God. Jonathan Edwards gave a sermon about pressing into the kingdom of God. "From the days of John the Baptist until now the kingdom of heaven suffers violence, and the violent take it by force" (Matt. 11:12). Edwards said that those who have come to Christ have been born again and given a spirit of zeal to pursue the things of God with a sense of urgency and with hunger and passion. Therefore, it is the duty of every Christian to press into the kingdom of God, making that the main business of life. The kingdom of God cannot be a secondary interest for a true Christian. We are to be diligent and active in the things of God.

Application

Do you have an unbelieving family member? In some sense, your connection to the church runs deeper, for all those united to Christ are united to one another. This is a reason that it can be so hard to see continued unbelief in our natural families, for we want to see them as part of our spiritual families. Pray earnestly today for the salvation of your unbelieving family members.

4

Hope, Patience, and Prayer

PAUL'S BULLETS CONTINUE: **rejoicing in hope, patient in tribulation, continuing steadfastly in prayer** (v. 12). Christianity can be reduced to three dimensions. First is the dimension of joy, which we should manifest at all times. We are called to rejoice in hope. I mentioned earlier in our studies that tribulation is inseparably related to hope, because when we are forced to suffer, the Holy Spirit uses those tribulations to work character in us and to provoke in our souls the virtue of hope. No matter how painful the present moment may be, we can still have joy because we know that the pain and suffering and tribulation we endure now is but for a moment. God has laid up for us such treasures in heaven that the brief moments of pain and suffering we have to endure now are not worthy to be compared to them. No matter how bad things are in this life, we can still be happy. We can still have joy because we have this hope of which we will never be ashamed.

The second dimension of the Christian life is patience. Although I had initially chosen Romans 12:12 as my life verse, I later abandoned it for a different verse because of my ongoing struggle with patience. I am impatient. I want to get past the finish line in order to get on to something else. I have never had the quiet spirit of patience that we are supposed to have, particularly in the midst of tribulation.

Paul is writing about patience here, the virtue of forbearance, of hanging on when things are tough. We are to remember the patience of Job, who cried out in the midst of his agony, "Though He slay me, yet will I trust Him" (Job 13:15). That is the kind of patience that gives perseverance and the ability to endure in the midst of difficulty.

The glue that brings those dimensions together is the third one: continuing steadfastly in prayer. The Christian life is one of prayer, but not simply prayer offered at certain hours or appointed times. There is to be an ongoing dialogue between our hearts and God all the time. We are to be always conscious of God's presence, relying on Him and communicating with the Father in our thoughts.

Application

The call to rejoice, be patient, and pray steadfastly might seem difficult to carry out, but when we understand that God is the source and sustainer of our spiritual life, we recognize how natural these things can be for the Christian life. We rejoice because of what God has done and is doing. We are patient, knowing that God is sovereignly at work. We are steadfast in prayer because adoration, confession, thanksgiving, and supplication become a constant part of our lives as Christians, for God is worthy, and He is able to deal with our sin and provide all that we need.

5

Blessing Others

REJOICING IN HOPE, PATIENT IN TRIBULATION, continuing steadfastly in prayer, **distributing to the needs of the saints, given to hospitality** (v. 13)—Paul is still explaining what it means to love without hypocrisy. We are to be those who meet the needs of our Christian brothers and sisters, and we are to be known for our hospitality. Hospitality has always been and continues to be an important virtue in the Middle East. It goes back to the Old Testament when the Jews were slaves in Egypt. They had no place to call their home. After God liberated them, they wandered for decades in the wilderness, and they longed for a place to call home. When God gave it to them, He admonished them not to forget where they had come from. They were to show hospitality to the stranger in their gates. They were to open their homes and hearts to those around them (for example, see Ex. 22:21; 23:9; Lev. 19:34; Deut. 10:18–19; Ps. 146:9; Jer. 7:6).

Verse 14 is also reminiscent of the Sermon on the Mount: **Bless those who persecute you; bless and do not curse** (v. 14). This is not simply a call to bless those who insult us occasionally. Paul was constantly attacked by people. His entire ministry was conducted under persecution, just as his Lord's ministry had been. Paul's response to persecution was to bless his enemies, not curse them. Refraining from cursing our enemies is not too difficult, but to bless them, to pray that God would bestow upon them His favor and grace, is much harder. Doing so is tough, but it is what love means.

A tremendous text follows: **Rejoice with those who rejoice, and weep with those who weep** (v. 15). Perhaps our brother or sister gets an award that we were hoping to get. Maybe our friends' team beats our team in the Super Bowl; can we rejoice with them? Can we participate in others' joy and forget about our sense of loss? That is how the body of Christ is knit together. If one rejoices, everybody rejoices. There are no politics of envy in the kingdom of God—none. If a brother prospers beyond how we prosper, we should delight in his prosperity and blessing rather than say, "He doesn't deserve that; why should he get this wonderful advantage?"

When one of us weeps, we all should weep. That is what the body of Christ is about. When Paul came to sorrowful people, he sorrowed with them. He stood beside them in their tribulation; he wept with those who wept. When Jesus came to the home of Lazarus, Mary, and Martha, the Bible tells us that He wept (John 11:35). He knew that He was going to raise Lazarus from the dead, but He wept because people around Him were weeping. Jesus wept with those who weep, and we are supposed to do that too.

Application

Sometimes when we are called to comfort those in mourning, we can feel inadequate. It may seem that our words don't come across right or even that they make too little of the situation and the pain of our loved ones. At such times, let us be present with them without feeling the urge to fix anything or make ourselves feel more at ease. We are called to weep with those who weep even when it is hard and we don't have any answers.

6

Affection and Ambition

IN OUR LAST STUDY, WE LOOKED AT Paul's injunction in verse 15: "Rejoice with those who rejoice, and weep with those who weep."

Paul adds something to that injunction, telling his readers to **be of**

the same mind toward one another (v. 16a). He is referring here to more than doctrinal unity. Certainly it is important for the people of God to believe the same things. After all, we have one Lord, one faith, and one baptism. We agree about the content of our faith, which is why churches produce confessions of faith, but intellectual agreement, such as we find in our creeds and doctrinal statements, is only a portion of what Paul is speaking about. In this context, being "of the same mind" has to do with affection. We are to have a certain kind of affection for one another as believers. We are not to reserve our love for a small group or clique within the church; we are to distribute our affections to the whole body of Christ.

Do not set your mind on high things, but associate with the humble (v. 16b). The second phrase amplifies—indeed, explains—the first. If we looked at just the first phrase, "Do not set your mind on high things," it would seem to contradict what the Apostle enjoins on many other occasions, telling us to set our mind on high things and to focus our attention on the lofty principles of the kingdom of God. Considering the first phrase together with the second phrase enables us to see that Paul is not talking about spiritually high things but about high positions in the world.

Paul is warning against a life driven by fleshly ambition. Such ambition can drive us to ruthlessness in our relationships so that we do not hesitate to step on others in our desire to reach the top of the ladder. Therefore, we are not to set our minds and hearts on the positions of esteem and exaltation in this world; rather, we are to associate with the humble. This is another example of how we are to imitate the life of Jesus. He associated with those of low esteem. Not many of the great and powerful have been called into the kingdom; God gives Himself to those of no reputation, to the lowly and meek (see Luke 1:46–48). Jesus, as the Son of God, practiced this same process. We, in turn, are called to follow His example of associating with the humble.

Application

It's easy to have a natural affinity for some people and not others. We may share the same interests or be at similar ages and stages of life. We can rejoice in these relationships in the church, but we also ought to seek out connections with those with whom we have less in common. This shows to the world the nature of the church, that we are all united and that our ties go beyond the ordinary ways of the world to a more substantial union in Christ.

WEEK 44

1

Wisdom and Personal Opinion

I STRUGGLE WITH PAUL'S NEXT POINT: **Do not be wise in your own opinion** (v. 16c). I have spent so much of my life working to understand matters of faith and theology that I often have more confidence in my judgment than I have in the judgment of others. Paul writes that I am not to rely solely on my opinion. I am not alone in this struggle. In the final analysis, everyone comes to his own conclusions. We give intellectual assent to whatever conclusion we come to after sifting through evidence. No one else can think for us; we have to think for ourselves. Although we are not to rely on our opinions, Paul is not denying the reality of human thought and conviction. We have to think for ourselves.

Sometimes as we listen to others, we find ourselves disagreeing with most of what we hear. Why do we come to such radically different conclusions about so many important things even though we believe in the same God, the same Lord, and the same Bible? When I find myself in disagreement with somebody, I try to find something that we can agree on, even if it is only the weather. At least that gives us something to work from. If we can start at a point of agreement and trace it to where we come to a fork in the road, we can better see why and where we went in different directions.

Along her journey, Alice in *Alice in Wonderland* came to a fork in the road. She did not know which way to go. In her confusion, she looked up and saw the Cheshire cat smiling at her, and she asked him which way she should go. The Cheshire cat said, "That depends. Where are you headed?" Alice said, "I don't know." The Cheshire cat said, "Then it doesn't matter." Again, however, we have to ask the question, why are we inclined to take one road over another? Answering that question involves an analysis of not only other people's thinking but also our own. In attempting to deal with differences of opinion, disagreements, and the frequent controversies that arise among Christians, we must take the guns we have aimed at our adversaries and turn them on ourselves. Why do we believe what we believe? Are we just opinionated? Are we fighting for an idea we inherited from the denomination or home or school in which we were raised? The next question to ask is, are our opinions consistent with the teaching of the Word of God? In the final analysis, our opinions do not mean anything; what matters is truth as God defines it. We are prone to error and given to delusion, so we ought never to trust merely in our own views.

Application

God's Word is our final authority in all things pertaining to faith and life. If we want a most certain ground for our knowledge, we must start with Scripture. But even our journey in coming to know the teachings of Scripture is not one that we navigate alone. As you study to understand God's Word, lean on the abundance of resources that are available to you in our day and seek wise counsel.

2

Evil for Evil

REPAY NO ONE EVIL FOR EVIL (v. 17a). The words *evil* and *sin* are not synonymous. All sin is evil, but not all evil is sin. Sin is one particular, although poignant, manifestation of evil. When the Scripture speaks of evil, it includes many things besides moral failure in human behavior. In the Old Testament, for example, the Hebrew word for *evil* has at least eight nuances. It can refer to any experience that we do not welcome as pleasant or good, an example of which we see in the prophet Isaiah: "I form the light and create darkness, I make peace and create calamity; I, the LORD, do all these things" (Isa. 45:7).

Another Old Testament nuance for *evil* is natural disasters, such as famines and earthquakes. Such catastrophes can bring upon us all kinds of bad consequences, but we do not go to the field that fails to yield its fruit and to the earthquake that destroys a town and accuse them of sin. Such occurrences are bad things, evil happenings, but they are natural evil as distinguished from moral evil.

Moral evil has to do with the behavior of moral agents, those whom God has created with the faculty of choosing and are therefore capable of obeying or disobeying the commandments of the Creator. Westminster Shorter Catechism 14 gives this definition of sin: "Sin is any want of conformity unto, or transgression of, the law of God." In other words, sin is defined as a failure to obey one of God's commands or prohibitions. Historically, the concept of evil has been defined by great minds of the church, such as Aquinas and Augustine, as a negation or a privation of good. Evil is *privatio*, a lack of the good. When a bumper crop is harvested, we call it a good crop, but when famine strikes and ruins the harvest, we call it evil. It is not, however, a moral evil. Moral evil has in common with other kinds of evil the idea of a lack, a negation, because sin lacks righteous obedience. Sin is defined in negative terms. It is unrighteousness, godlessness, and disobedience. The negative use of these terms indicates a lack of virtue.

When Paul writes, "Repay no one evil for evil," he is indicating the moral realm. Today when we are hurt or offended, we are prone to say, "It is payback time. What goes around comes around." We look for an opportunity to wound the one who has wounded us. We want to get even. In fact, we are very seldom satisfied with getting even. Getting even is simply tying the score. We do not want to get even; we want to get one up. If we are victims of someone's sin, the flesh wants to get even, and the payback involves us in sin. That is not the way that the Christian life is to be. We are not to return evil for evil.

Application

When we tell people that we are Christians, we must also act like Christians. We must practice what we preach. Even though the world sometimes calls what is evil "good," many people still recognize good and evil when they see it. Therefore, let us not return evil for evil, that Jesus' name may be glorified as we act in accordance with our profession.

3

Goodness and Peace

PEOPLE ARE WATCHING US; THEY KNOW who we are. Can unbelievers see something different about us that they cannot deny, even when they slander us? Do they see that we have tender hearts? Do they see that our word can be trusted? Do they see that we are not out to destroy them? **Have regard for good things in the sight of all men** (v. 17b). As hostile as unbelievers may be to Christians, they are not blind, and they can see certain virtues that they do not perhaps acknowledge but know are there.

If it is possible, as much as depends on you, live peaceably with all men (v. 18). Do we have any enemies? Do we have broken relationships? If we say yes to those questions, I suggest that we need to reevaluate our opinions. We all experience broken relationships and significant conflicts with others. Nevertheless, Paul says, we are to live peaceably with all men. Our Lord said, "Blessed are the peacemakers, for they shall be called sons of God" (Matt. 5:9). The making of peace should be part of our Christian character. We ought to endeavor to live peaceably with everybody.

We are warned in the Bible, however, to beware of the peacemakers of the flesh. There are the Neville Chamberlains of this world who think they have achieved peace for our time when they have not. There were the false prophets of Israel about whom Jeremiah complained, "They have also healed the hurt of My people slightly, saying, 'Peace, peace!' when there is no peace" (Jer. 6:14). Martin Luther described a fleshly peace, one based on falsehood rather than truth, a peace born of cowardice rather than courage. There is a wrong kind of peace, and because of that it is impossible to live at peace with all men.

Notice how Paul qualifies his admonition: "If it is possible, *as much as depends on you*, live peaceably with all men." Paul is addressing a problem that strains possibility to its limit. Our burden is to live peaceably with all men as much as doing so depends on us. When somebody offends us, we can have a spirit of retaliation, revenge, or vengeance, but that only exacerbates the tension and deepens the chasm that separates us from the offender. According to Paul, if somebody offends us, we are not to strike back. Instead, we are to seek peace. Doing so is hard, but it is what our Lord did throughout His earthly ministry.

Application

We must always keep ourselves in check, so that we do not harbor any animosity in our hearts that might spill over into hateful words and actions toward anyone. Jesus calls us to love our enemies (Matt. 5:43–48). As Christians, we must define *enemies* in a narrow sense. Our enemies may be those who desire our harm, but we ought not to desire the harm of anyone. Rather, we are called to pray for our enemies.

4

Vindication and Vengeance, Part 1

PAUL ESCALATES HIS WARNING, but he does so with a term of affection: **Beloved**. When in my preaching I come to something that may be hard for people to hear, I try to remind them that I love them, and I do so by prefacing the teaching with the term *beloved*. It is a signal to my congregation that a punch is coming. Paul was not flattering his readers; he loved them and understood their temptations, weaknesses, and struggles for Christian maturity and obedience. When he prefaces his admonition with a term of endearment, he is preparing them for something difficult: **do not avenge yourselves** (v. 19a).

When we are injured, we are not to seek revenge. Once we are wounded, our deepest natural desire is for revenge. One of the most important concepts we find in the New Testament is vindication. Vindication takes place when someone accused of a crime or an evil is found to be innocent of the charge, or when someone's labor is shown to be of great value after it was ridiculed or scorned. Vindication has to do with justice. Justice is served when innocent people are shown to be innocent and are exonerated of charges brought against them.

Our Lord gave a majestic parable about vindication. A widow brought her case to the court and sought justice, but the judge would not hear her; he had no regard for man or God. The widow persisted and eventually wore down the judge with her ceaseless entreaties.

Finally, just to get rid of her, he heard her case (Luke 18:1–7). The point of Jesus' parable is that if an unjust judge will from time to time execute justice, how much more will the heavenly Father be quick to bring justice? Jesus asks the question rhetorically: "Shall God not avenge His own elect who cry out day and night to Him, though He bears long with them?" (v. 7).

Application

Something fascinates us about vigilante justice. We see it everywhere in popular culture. It has been said that "the wheels of justice turn slowly," and sometimes when we see this in society and consider the evil in the world, we might think that merciless vengeance at our own hands is the answer. In truth, there is no perfect justice in this world, but God's justice is perfect, so let us never resort to evil, but let us trust in Him to enact justice in His perfect timing.

5

Vindication and Vengeance, Part 2

WHEN JONATHAN EDWARDS WAS UNJUSTLY ACCUSED of sin by a malicious man in his congregation, he was kicked out of his parish in Massachusetts, exiled into ministry to the Indians. When Edwards' friends heard the scandalous charges against him, they begged him to speak in his own defense, but he refused to do it. Although he wanted to be vindicated, he feared that if he sought to vindicate himself, his efforts, however successful, would still be less than the vindication that the Lord would eventually work on his behalf. His response may seem foolish because in many cases the Lord's vindications will not take place until we stand before the bar of justice in heaven. In Edwards' case, his accuser was so overcome by conscience that after ten years he confessed to the congregation that he had lied about Professor Edwards, and Edwards lived to see his vindication. We see the same thing with Job, who received vindication during his lifetime.

There is a difference between vindication and vengeance. Vindication reveals innocence, whereas vengeance is payback for harm. Vengeance is a desire for revenge. Actually, revenge is not inherently a bad thing. It is a good thing, because God takes revenge. Therefore, revenge in and of itself is not evil. What makes it evil is who undertakes it. Revenge belongs to God, who tells us that we ought not to avenge ourselves: **but rather give place to wrath; for it is written, "Vengeance is Mine, I will repay," says the Lord** (v. 19b). Revenge is God's prerogative to dispense, although He delegates to the civil magistrate the responsibility of vengeance, as we will see in Romans 13. In the final analysis, vengeance belongs to God. There will be payback. Our offenses will be avenged, but the One who is to do it is God. When God brings vengeance, He brings it perfectly. His justice never punishes more severely than the sin. If vengeance were left to us, our fallen condition is such that we would not be satisfied unless we could inflict more pain than the crime deserves. God never does that.

Application

Many things in life seem to go unresolved. If we start to add up all the hurtful words and unjust actions that we have suffered, we may be led into bitterness and spiteful unforgiveness. But when we reflect on God's perfect justice, we can often move beyond our pain. This is critical. Though we might have suffered injustice, chances are that we have been unjust ourselves, and if we aren't ready to forgive, we might not be able to rest fully in God's forgiveness.

6

Affection and Ambition

PAUL AGAIN HARKS BACK TO THE Sermon on the Mount: **"If your enemy is hungry, feed him; if he is thirsty, give him a drink"** (v. 20a). We are not to ask our enemy why he is hungry or thirsty. If somebody is high on drugs and falls into a ditch, we are not to ask him how he got into the ditch. Our job is to bind up his wounds, and if he is hungry and thirsty, we are to feed him and give him a drink, which is the ministry of mercy. If somebody suffers from a sexually transmitted disease, we minister to him in the midst of his suffering. Jesus did that, and we are to do likewise, **"for in so doing you will heap coals of fire on his head"** (v. 20b). We are to repay our enemy with good rather than evil. We are to repay him with kindness. When we respond to evil with good, we expose our enemy to God's wrath. If someone persists in treating us evilly while we persist in repaying him with good, we increase our enemy's guilt before God, although we certainly are not to repay evil with good in order to get evildoers into trouble. The point is that the burden is no longer on us. If we return good for evil, our hands are clean.

When I was a senior in seminary, I served as a student pastor in a Hungarian refugee church in a steel town in western Pennsylvania. The church had fewer than one hundred members. One lady in our congregation was somewhat vexing, and I once made a remark that she found offensive. Afterward she came to church on Sunday mornings and looked out the window during my sermon so that everybody could see her ignoring me. This created a real problem for me. I went to see her and apologized for my offensive remark. I apologized in tears and asked her forgiveness, but she would not forgive me. I went a second time and asked her forgiveness, but again she refused.

During that seminary assignment, I was required to meet monthly with my appointed mentor, an eighty-five-year-old retired missionary who had spent fifty years in China. During his time in China, he and his wife had been incarcerated in concentration camps for five years. I went with hat in hand and gave him the report about my trouble with the unforgiving woman. He told me: "It was a mistake to say what you said, but your biggest mistake was apologizing for it twice. Once you apologized sincerely and asked her forgiveness, the ball was placed in her court. Her refusal to forgive is far worse than the offense you caused in the first place. Do not keep pursuing it. The coals of fire are on her head."

Do not be overcome by evil, but overcome evil with good (v. 21)—that is the grand strategy of Jesus, the Apostolic church, and the Christian life.

Application

We are called to love even those who desire our harm. In the abstract, we as Christians heartily affirm that this is our calling, but when situations get concrete and insults start to fly, we may be tempted to sin. We cannot love our enemies in our own strength. Let us walk in dependence on the Holy Spirit, asking the Father to supply us with the supernatural love of Jesus Christ when we are most tempted to return evil for evil.

Romans 13

LET EVERY SOUL BE SUBJECT TO *the governing authorities. For there is no authority except from God, and the authorities that exist are appointed by God. Therefore whoever resists the authority resists the ordinance of God, and those who resist will bring judgment on themselves. For rulers are not a terror to good works, but to evil. Do you want to be unafraid of the authority? Do what is good, and you will have praise from the same. For he is God's minister to you for good. But if you do evil, be afraid; for he does not bear the sword in vain; for he is God's minister, an avenger to execute wrath on him who practices evil. Therefore you must be subject, not only because of wrath but also for conscience' sake. For because of this you also pay taxes, for they are God's ministers attending continually to this very thing. Render therefore to all their due: taxes to whom taxes are due, customs to whom customs, fear to whom fear, honor to whom honor.*

Owe no one anything except to love one another, for he who loves another has fulfilled the law. For the commandments, "You shall not commit adultery," "You shall not murder," "You shall not steal," "You shall not bear false witness," "You shall not covet," and if there is any other commandment, are all summed up in this saying, namely, "You shall love your neighbor as yourself." Love does no harm to a neighbor; therefore love is the fulfillment of the law.

And do this, knowing the time, that now it is high time to awake out of sleep; for now our salvation is nearer than when we first believed. The night is far spent, the day is at hand. Therefore let us cast off the works of darkness, and let us put on the armor of light. Let us walk properly, as in the day, not in revelry and drunkenness, not in lewdness and lust, not in strife and envy. But put on the Lord Jesus Christ, and make no provision for the flesh, to fulfill its lusts.

WEEK 45

1

Models of Civil Obedience

THE CIVIL MAGISTRATE DID NOT COME into being through the machinations of man; rather, civil government is an institution established
by God. God has established the church with its redemptive mission
and the government for the well-being of everyone. Government
might well be called a common-grace ministry. The church dispenses
the elements of special grace, that which has to do with our salvation,
whereas civil government attends to the common good of the human
race, not only for Christians but for all people.

It is the duty of every Christian, indeed of every person, to be subject
to the authorities: **Let every soul be subject to the governing authorities** (v. 1a). We struggle with this. In our sinful corruption, we kick
against the authorities placed over us. The universal call to submit to
authority touches the root of our corruption. Everyone is a sinner, and
every sin is an act of revolt against authority. If we respected the authority of God perfectly, we would never sin. Sin is a refusal to submit to the
governing authority of God Himself, and God knows that about us. If
we are not willing to submit to God, it is more difficult to submit to the
police department, the government, and other authorities that rule over
us. It is the duty of every Christian to be in subjection to the authorities.

From a theological perspective, the principle is that of civil obedience. Christians are called to be extraordinary models of civil
obedience. We are called to bend over backward to be submissive to
authorities. Throughout redemptive history there have been great
models of civil obedience, both men and women.

Jesus was born in Bethlehem, just as Micah had prophesied (Mic. 5:2). Certain events occurred that led Mary and Joseph to be in that prophesied location at the time of the birth: "It came to pass in those days that a decree went out from Caesar Augustus that all the world should be registered. This census first took place while Quirinius was governing Syria. So all went to be registered, everyone to his own city" (Luke 2:1–3). All people were required to be registered so that they could be taxed by a conquering emperor, one who had no regard for the cost to the people of doing so. The census required people to make an arduous journey to their birthplace to enroll for taxation, so Mary and Joseph made the journey. They risked their lives and that of the unborn child in obedience to the civil magistrate. That is an example of godliness.

Application

The call to be subject to governing authorities goes further than not breaking the law. Peter calls us even to "honor the king" (1 Peter 2:17), just as Paul calls us to pray for those in power over us (1 Tim. 2:1–2). If it is hard to be subject to governing authorities without being subject to God, it is even harder to honor and pray for those in power who champion policies we may abhor without affirming that their authority is from the One who can turn the hearts of kings (Prov. 21:1).

2

Civil Disobedience?

THE SECOND-CENTURY APOLOGIST JUSTIN MARTYR, who gave a defense of the faith to the emperor Antoninus Pius, argued that the emperor should examine the lives of Christians to see that they, above all other citizens in the empire, were the most scrupulous in paying their taxes and in their obedience to the civil magistrate. Throughout the New Testament, we find this strong motif of civil obedience.

But must we always obey the civil magistrate? When the Sanhedrin told the Apostles to preach no more in the name of Jesus, Peter said, "We ought to obey God rather than men" (Acts 5:29). Conflict arises when the civil magistrate commands or forbids something that conflicts with the commandments of God. In such cases, not only may we disobey the civil magistrate, but we must disobey. We are always and everywhere to obey the authorities over us—boss, police, governor, whatever that authority may be—unless that authority commands us to do something that God forbids, or forbids us from doing something that God commands. If the civil magistrate calls us to sin, we must say no. History is replete with examples of governments that have commanded the citizens to do evil. It can happen in any country, even our own.

Women have asked me about submission to their husbands: "I am trying to be submissive to my husband, but my husband will not allow me to go to church. What should I do?" I tell them to disobey their husbands in that instance because God commands us not to forsake the assembling together of the saints.

The principle is easy; the application is difficult. We are not free, however, to disobey the civil magistrate when we disagree with it or when authorities make us suffer or experience inconvenience. It is ironic that this master text on civil obedience was written to the Roman Christians, who were under the heavy hand of imperial Rome.

Application

The same Peter who understood that preaching the resurrection required obedience to God rather than men also counseled Christians to obey even when persecuted (see 1 Peter 2–3). Jesus is our great example of One who did not defy authority despite the injustices done to Him and the reality that He is the true ruler of heaven and earth. Let us model ourselves after Him in our submission to authority but never cower when obedience to Him requires otherwise.

3

All Authority Belongs to God

PAUL GIVES US THE THEOLOGICAL GROUNDS for the ethic: **For there is no authority except from God** (v. 1b). Ultimately, the only One who possesses inherent authority is God Himself, and the authority that God possesses is the eternal right to impose obligations upon His creatures. God has the inherent authority to command our obedience and submission to Him. "It is He who has made us, and not we ourselves" (Ps. 100:3). God's authority rests in His authorship and ownership of the entire world. All other authority we experience is not intrinsic but extrinsic. It has been delegated by God.

The Apostle Peter sounds the same message as Paul's: "Submit yourselves to every ordinance of man for the Lord's sake, whether to the king as supreme, or to governors, as to those who are sent by him for the punishment of evildoers and for the praise of those who do good" (1 Peter 2:13–14).

Is Jesus honored by our submission even to corrupt authorities? The universe is not structured as a democracy. It is a theocracy. The government of the universe is God, and He has appointed His only begotten Son as the King of kings and the Lord of lords. The Father has given to the Son all authority in heaven and on earth. At the end of his life, the president of the United States will have to stand before Jesus Christ and be held accountable for how he held his office. The Senate, the House of Representatives, and all such authorities will be answerable to the King of kings as to how they executed justice in their labors. We often overlook the fact that at the heart of the biblical message is a political message. We live in a kingdom where the supreme political authority is vested in Jesus Christ.

When we disobey lesser authorities, we are disobeying those whose authority rests on Christ and has come from Him and through Him. The president of the United States could not exercise his office for five minutes apart from the will of the King of kings. It is the God of providence who raises kingdoms and brings them down. Every king in the history of the world rules and has ruled only by the providential will of God. God casts the final ballot in every election.

Application

Take a moment today to pray for your local and national governing authorities in accord with Paul's instruction in 1 Timothy 2:1–2: "I exhort first of all that supplications, prayers, intercessions, and giving of thanks be made for all men, for kings and all who are in authority, that we may lead a quiet and peaceable life in all godliness and reverence."

4

Living under God's Authority

THE AUTHORITIES THAT EXIST ARE APPOINTED BY GOD (v. 1c). Every authority is established, in the final analysis, not by referendum or democratic vote but by the single appointment of the supreme ruler of heaven and earth; every authority is appointed by God. Paul is making clear that God appointed the Roman authorities. I wonder whether Paul, when his life was about to end by the sword, rued the day he wrote these words. He faced a vicious and unjust execution by the decree of Nero. More than likely, when Paul put his head on the block, his last thought was that Nero's authority to execute him came ultimately from God, and he died willingly.

Can we look past such authorities and see the authority that stands behind them? "Shall God not avenge His own elect who cry out day and night to Him . . . ?" (Luke 18:7). Will not God set the scales of justice right? When we are victimized by unjust, demonic governments that do everything but work for the glory and honor of Christ, God notices. Our Lord will vindicate His people who seek to be faithful to Him despite the injustice that comes their way from earthly authorities.

Therefore whoever resists the authority resists the ordinance of God (v. 2a). In the eighteenth century, Christians struggled over whether to pick up arms against the British government and declare their independence. One of the most heated discussions in Christian history occurred over how to understand Romans 13 in light of the War of Independence. The colonists were fighting for the maintenance of their governmental system, which the Parliament of England wanted to change. The colonists decided that British common law gave them the right to resist. That was a very complicated situation, which Christian scholars debate to this day, and the reason for the debate is this text in Romans 13. Whoever resists the authority resists the ordinance of God, **and those who resist will bring judgment on themselves** (v. 2b). That is a sober warning. If we resist the authorities that God has appointed, we might be regarded as heroes by some, but we can expect only the visitation of God's judgment.

Application

The great challenge of considering whether Christians are ever permitted to disobey governing authorities traces back to our understanding that all authority ultimately comes from God. We must be certain in exceedingly rare circumstances that disobeying lesser authorities is not actually disobeying the highest authority before we disobey. Let us prayerfully consider these things and seek His face as we continue studying our relationship as Christians to the state.

5

The Right to Govern

FOR RULERS ARE NOT A TERROR TO GOOD WORKS, **but to evil. Do you want to be unafraid of the authority? Do what is good, and you will have praise from the same** (v. 3). This is a proverbial point of wisdom. It is true in the main, but it is not true absolutely. Nobody did more good in the Roman Empire than the Apostle Paul, yet he did not, in the final analysis, receive praise from the civil magistrate. Instead, it gave him his death sentence. In general, even under corrupt governments, those who receive the harshest treatment are criminals, people involved in the worst forms of corruption. The whole point of civil government is to restrain evil, by force if necessary.

We hear that morality cannot be legislated. Every time an ethical issue comes up for political discussion, such as abortion or euthanasia, we hear that cry from every corner. It is true that we cannot change behavior just by changing the law, but that is not typically what people mean when they use that phrase. The phrase is used by those who claim that the government has no right to pass laws that have to do with moral matters. If we cannot legislate morality, however, what can we legislate?

Years ago, I was invited to give a message at the inaugural prayer breakfast for the Florida governor. Within hours of the breakfast, the governor-elect was set to be installed. He would take his oath and become the governor of the state. In my address, I explained that when we are consecrated to the ministry, set apart for the church, we are ordained. Ordination is a sacred occasion because we take vows to be faithful to God in the execution of our ministerial office. I told the governor, "Sir, today is your ordination day, because you are being ordained as God's minister of civil righteousness," and I talked about Romans 13. People told me afterward that they had never thought about government authority in such terms. Indeed, it was the governor's ordination day because civil magistrates are ordained by God. They are God's ministers, and they are called to serve God's good pleasure.

Application

Give thanks to God for His establishing of order in our society through civil government. Even if we consider the imperfection of order and justice in our society due to our sin, we only long all the more for the perfect rule that will be realized in the new heavens and new earth. Pray this day earnestly to God, "Your kingdom come" (Matt. 6:10), and "Come, Lord Jesus!" (Rev. 22:20).

6

The Sword and the Garden

FOR HE IS GOD'S MINISTER TO YOU FOR GOOD. **But if you do evil, be afraid; for he does not bear the sword in vain; for he is God's minister, an avenger to execute wrath on him who practices evil** (v. 4). Romans 13:4b is one of the most important verses in Scripture in terms of the development of historic, classic Christian ethics, especially with respect to two monumentally important issues. The first is capital punishment and the second is warfare and whether Christians can, in good conscience, engage in war. We see here that God Himself has given to the civil magistrate the power of the sword. "The power of the sword" is an idiomatic expression referring to capital punishment. God has given the civil magistrate the power to use a weapon to bring death in order to enforce the law.

The idea of the sword's being used to enforce the law of God was established exceedingly early in the biblical record. The third chapter of Genesis records the circumstances of the fall of the human race into sin, the seduction of Adam and Eve by the serpent in the garden:

> Then the LORD God said, "Behold, the man has become like one of Us, to know good and evil. And now, lest he put out his hand and take also of the tree of life, and eat, and live forever"—therefore the LORD God sent him out of the garden of Eden to till the ground from which he was taken. So He drove out the man; and He placed cherubim at the east of the garden of Eden, and a flaming sword which turned every way, to guard the way to the tree of life. (Gen. 3:22–24)

When Adam and Eve sinned, the curse for sin came upon them, the earth, and all things in it. Then God drove Adam and Eve out of the garden of Eden, and they were forced to live east of Eden, outside the presence of the Paradise in which they had been placed by their Creator. Human beings were forbidden to enter again into the garden, and God established a sentinel to block the way back in. He put angels at the gateway to the garden, armed with a flaming sword. We see here the first establishment of physical force as a governing restraint upon sinful people.

Application

It might sound strange to our modern ears to call our political leaders "God's ministers." But we must never lose this insight from Scripture, that civil authority is given by God. Life without it would be anarchy. Let us thank God for the restraining influence of His moral law on sin and for governing authorities who echo its eternal validity through punishing those who do evil. In this way, the state helps us to see that sin has deadly consequences, which is an essential element for understanding the gospel.

WEEK 46

1

The Institution of Capital Punishment

THE IMAGE OF THAT SWORD IS used throughout Scripture to indicate the authority given to those responsible for enforcing the law of God. In the Old Testament, several offenses were considered so heinous that for the commission of them, God, in the civil code of Israel, required the death penalty. In Genesis 9, we find another important text for understanding the power of the sword:

> So God blessed Noah and his sons, and said to them: "Be fruitful and multiply, and fill the earth. And the fear of you and the dread of you shall be on every beast of the earth, on every bird of the air, on all that move on the earth, and on all the fish of the sea. They are given into your hand. Every moving thing that lives shall be food for you. I have given you all things, even as the green herbs. But you shall not eat flesh with its life, that is, its blood. Surely for your lifeblood I will demand a reckoning; from the hand of every beast I will require it, and from the hand of man. From the hand of every man's brother I will require the life of man.
>
> > "Whoever sheds man's blood,
> > By man his blood shall be shed;
> > For in the image of God
> > He made man." (vv. 1–6)

We find there the biblical institution of capital punishment for murder. The way in which the text is expressed can be easily misunderstood.

"Whoever sheds man's blood, by man his blood shall be shed." We could misinterpret that to mean "he who lives by the sword dies by the sword," a sort of cryptic prophecy of the consequences of living a violent life, but the original text indicates not a prophetic prediction but an imperative: God is requiring the death penalty for murder. In the law code of the Old Testament, the offense of murder is carefully explained. Distinctions are made in Old Testament law that correspond to our distinctions between first- and second-degree murder, or murder and manslaughter. In the case of manslaughter, the penalty was not death but banishment to cities of refuge. When first-degree murder was committed, the civil magistrates of Israel were commanded to execute the guilty one.

Application

God's laws for Israel as a nation never conflicted with His moral law. The sixth commandment that forbids murder and calls us to protect and promote life does not conflict with the death penalty. The death penalty in Scripture shows the premium that is placed on life and why murder is such a heinous sin. As Jesus teaches in the Sermon on the Mount, we must guard our hearts from the sinful anger that leads to murder (Matt. 5:21–26).

2

Capital Punishment and the Creation Covenant

MANY CHRISTIANS HAVE BEEN STRONGLY MISINFORMED about this biblical position. When capital punishment was instituted by God, it was part of a renewal of the covenant of creation. There are many biblical covenants. God made a covenant with Abraham and with Isaac and

Jacob. God mediated a covenant through Moses. God made a covenant with David, and of course, we have the new covenant, which was instituted by Jesus. We call the original covenant the *covenant of creation*. The laws established at creation were not intended just for Jews or for Christians; the laws built into creation were given to every human being. Every person alive today is under the authority of the terms of the creation covenant.

Many do not believe in creation, so they do not think they have any covenant responsibility toward God, but unbelief and denial of the covenant do not eliminate the covenant. Every human being remains inescapably in a covenant relationship with God. Everyone is either a covenant keeper or a covenant breaker. The vast majority of the human race exists in a state of covenant rebellion.

After the creation covenant was established, sin spread throughout the world so rapidly that God decided to virtually wipe out the human race, saying that He would no longer strive with wicked people. Noah and his family were the exceptions. On one hand, the flood account is God's judgment on the mass of fallen humanity, and on the other hand, it is an account of God's grace toward Noah and his family and Noah's being the instrument of rescue of the world's wildlife. After the flood receded, the ark came to rest, and God reestablished a covenant with Noah, setting His bow in the sky and saying that He would never again destroy the world by flood. In that covenant, the Noahic covenant, we see the restitution and repetition of the ordinances and laws of the creation covenant (see Genesis 7–8).

The point is this: the law of capital punishment for murder is not restricted to the law code and civil penalties of Israel in the Old Testament, nor is it a portion of the jurisprudence of the New Testament; it is a law rooted and grounded in creation. So as long as creation lasts, the principle of capital punishment is in effect in cases of first-degree murder.

Application

When we consider the death penalty as it connects to creation, we truly see how ungodly murder is. God created a world full of life, so to murderously take a life is to be unlike Him in every way. It is a distortion of His image. As His image bearers, we are called to be about the business of life and not death. Therefore, let us protect the innocent, especially the unborn. Pray this day that abortion would be seen for what it is and that repentance would follow.

3

The Value of Human Life

YEARS AGO, I READ AN ARTICLE by Larry King in which he criticized the Christian community for its gross inconsistency. He complained that the Christian community protests against abortion on demand while arguing in favor of capital punishment. Larry King said that he would not support the Christian opposition to abortion until the church stops its support of capital punishment. I have never had the opportunity to tell Mr. King that there is no inconsistency here at all. There is a strong point of consistency behind both the church's opposition to abortion and its support of capital punishment—the sanctity of human life. The principle that resounds on virtually every page of Scripture and reiterated emphatically by Jesus in the Sermon on the Mount is that human life is so sacred that we must never take it with malice aforethought or for personal convenience.

Human life is sacred not because of some inherent value in humans that is lacking in whales, eagles, and turtles. Human life is so significant because of this: "Whoever sheds man's blood, by man his blood shall be shed; for in the image of God He made man" (Gen. 9:6). That is what makes us different from chickens and kangaroos; we have been stamped with the image of God. That is why, if somebody rises up as Cain did and kills his brother with malice aforethought, God sees it as an attack on Himself.

Human life is so sacred that if you rise up without just cause and kill your neighbor, you forfeit all rights and privileges to your own life. God gives the forfeited life not to the victim's relative for vengeance but to the civil authorities. God has given the government the sword, and government is to see to it that punishment is carried out. We hold to this in order to communicate to the world that we will not tolerate the murder of human beings.

That is the biblical rationale. We see it in the Old Testament and again in Romans 13. When God gives the power of the sword, He does not give it merely to see it rattled. The power of the sword is given to be used to enforce law and justice.

Application

One of the ways that we can keep the sixth commandment with respect to those who have committed murder and are serving life sentences or are awaiting execution is through service and prayer. We ought to be praying for people on death row, that they would come to know the Lord. Though we might not be the direct means that God uses to reach these men and women, God often uses prison chaplains to further the gospel in the darkest places. Let us support them.

4

Just-War Theory

ROMANS 13:4 ALSO SERVES AS THE *locus classicus* in historical Christian ethics concerning the just-war theory. The fundamental principle of the just-war theory is this: if a nation or a people aggressively invades or attacks another nation, the attacked nation is the victim of external aggression, so it has the right and the responsibility to protect itself from the invading aggressor. When Adolf Hitler invaded Poland, Czechoslovakia, and other nations, the local governments of those nations had the moral duty to try to stop the blitzkrieg from coming and enslaving their people.

The just-war theory has a long history. Augustine said that all wars are evil with the exception of the divinely ordained conquest of Canaan. Apart from that, he said, we do not have direct instructions from God to wage war, and we are left to make such decisions on the basis of human understanding and the application of principles drawn from sacred Scripture alone. He said, however, that not all involvement in war is evil. Thomas Aquinas seconded the motion, and in his moral theology he worked out the details of what is involved in a just war.

The sanctity-of-life principle lies behind the just-war theory. Human life is so sacred that the civil magistrate has been given the sword to protect the innocent from the evildoer, just as the policeman has been given arms and the right to use arms to stop rape, robbery, and murder. When the civil magistrate uses reasonable force to restrain the evildoer, he serves not only the community but also God. In terms of just war, those principles are simply elevated to the larger domain of national security.

In our day, we have the opportunity to invade without sending soldiers across borders. We send missiles across oceans. With the sophistication in modern weaponry, issues of just war become increasingly complex. The New Testament and the Christian church do not encourage a bellicose national posture or a militaristic style that exists by the threat of intimidation. The church has historically encouraged nations to be good neighbors to other nations and to use the sword as the last resort—when the defense of the people becomes a clear and present necessity.

Application

Just as God calls us as individuals to be at peace with all men insofar as it depends on us (Rom. 12:18), so, too, ought nations to strive for peace with one another. Peace in this fallen world is not guaranteed, however. Pray to God for peace in whatever wars or widespread persecutions are happening today, and thank Him that one day all nations will "beat their swords into plowshares" (see Isa. 2:1–4).

5

Responsibilities

TODAY THE CHRISTIAN IS DISCRIMINATED AGAINST if he believes that involvement in war is legitimate only if the cause is just. If I see my nation getting involved in an unjust war (even though I hold the position that there are just wars), I do not have legal recourse to say that I refuse to submit to that order. That is a very serious matter. As Christians, we must make sure that the cause is just before we pick up a gun or a sword and kill anybody. It is silly to assume that a government can be trusted to engage in only just military activity. I do not know of any nation in history that has not, at one point or another, used its power and authority in an unjust manner. That is why we have to be vigilant. When the nation is involved in the just defense of its borders, and the civil magistrate calls us to pick up the sword, it is our duty to use the sword. But if the nation conscripts us to engage in an unjust aggression or invasion of an innocent nation, I am equally obligated to say no.

No one ever said that living the Christian life is simple or that making ethical decisions is an easy matter. The principle is easy: we are always to obey the authorities over us unless those authorities command us to do something that God forbids, or forbids us from doing something that God commands. We cannot disobey the civil magistrate because it inconveniences us or burdens us with heavy taxation or because we disagree with its wisdom. Those are not just excuses for civil disobedience. At the same time, we are not to render slavish obedience to any authority, because authorities can work against the Word of God. We have to be careful to ensure that our decisions are motivated by an earnest desire to obey God in all He commands.

When we object to capital punishment or warfare in principle, we object to what God Himself has instituted and established. The sword is necessary because there is sin in the world, and the sword is given to work against and to restrain evildoers in order to protect the lives of the innocent. The primary responsibility of any civil government, whether in China, Russia, the United States, or Iran, is to protect, defend, and maintain human life. When any government turns its back on that primary responsibility, it is acting in utter defiance of the law of God and is exposing itself and the nation it governs to the judgment of God.

Application

We do well to remember that God is the One who raises up and brings down nations and will ultimately establish His own kingdom. Today, meditate on this major theme from the book of Daniel: "Blessed be the name of God forever and ever, for wisdom and might are His. And He changes the times and the seasons; He removes kings and raises up kings" (2:20–21); and from the mouth of the pagan king Nebuchadnezzar: "For His dominion is an everlasting dominion, and His kingdom is from generation to generation" (4:34b).

6

Rendering What Is Due

AT THE BEGINNING OF ROMANS 13, Paul set forth the role of civil government. He showed that the secular rulers of the world are God's ministers. The Apostle forges ahead: **Therefore you must be subject, not only because of wrath but also for conscience' sake** (v. 5). We are not to submit simply because we are afraid of the law-enforcement agencies of our nation. Rather, we have a responsibility to be submissive to the civil magistrates as a matter of conscience. If magistrates are oppressive, if we disagree radically with them, we are still to render obedience because our consciences are held captive by the Word of God. Since God authorizes our rulers and places them over us, we are to render obedience as a matter of principle unless they require us to do something that God forbids or forbid us from doing something that God commands. Living by principle lies at the heart of Christian ethics and the Christian life. We are not to live doing whatever our hearts desire; we are to be, in the main, submissive people—submissive ultimately to the law of God and to every other authority that God places over us.

Paul turns his attention to the payment of taxes: **For because of this you also pay taxes, for they are God's ministers attending continually to this very thing. Render therefore to all their due: taxes to whom taxes are due, customs to whom customs, fear to whom fear, honor to whom honor** (vv. 6–7). I admire the Apostle Paul for his faithfulness to Christ and his courage in telling the people of God to do their duty, even when that duty was something they despised.

The Roman government was, in terms of taxation and tribute policies, an oppressive government. The people who received Paul's admonition had been crushed by the burden of Roman taxation. Nevertheless, Paul said, they were to pay their taxes. Taxes might be unfair and oppressive, but God has given to the civil magistrate the right to levy taxes. The civil magistrate has to have his reign and rule financed. Since governments usually do not produce anything, most of their revenue, if not all, is dependent on the imposition of taxes rather than on voluntary contributions, and the government is allowed by God's decree to collect such taxes by the sword if necessary.

If we in the United States refuse to pay our taxes, we do not have to worry about the government coming after us with a sword. Our government's weapons are a bit more advanced. In any case, every government in every society throughout history has been involved in some form of levying taxes. It is the government's right to levy taxes, and it is our responsibility to pay them. There is a caveat, however. The government, to which God gives the right to levy taxes, has also received from God the responsibility to levy just and righteous taxes.

Application

As Christians, we are called to truth. This also means maintaining our integrity when it comes to our finances, especially when it comes to being forthright about our taxes. Let's use the paying of our taxes, however, as a reminder of our call to faithful living before God. Jesus calls us to "render . . . to Caesar the things that are Caesar's, and to God the things that are God's" (Matt. 22:21). May we be faithful in both.

WEEK 47

1

That Which Is Due

THE IDEA OF JUSTICE IS DEEPLY EMBEDDED in Paul's words, "Render therefore to all their due: taxes to whom taxes are due, customs to whom customs, fear to whom fear, honor to whom honor" (v. 7). Aristotle defined justice as giving people their due. Accordingly, in a beauty contest, the most beautiful contestant is due the prize. Even though there is no merit or virtue in being beautiful, the terms of the contest were defined by an aesthetic criterion, so whoever meets that criterion in its greatest dimension is due the prize. Righteousness and justice have a lot to do with *dueness*.

One of the great ethical debates in Christian ethics pertains to the sanctity of truth. Are we always in every circumstance obligated to give the unvarnished truth? Many Christian ethicists answer that question in the affirmative, saying that righteousness demands truth telling with no exception. The Bible gives us Rahab, however, who lied to protect Joshua and his people, and she made the roll call of the saints for her valorous action. The Bible also shows us the midwives of Egypt who were instructed by Pharaoh to kill every male born to a Hebrew woman. The midwives disobeyed and protected the newborn babies and then lied about it to the authorities. Scripture tells us, "Therefore God dealt well with the midwives" (Ex. 1:20). Because of that, many ethics students believe that there is a place for a righteous lie.

I had a landlady in Holland who, during World War II, had hollowed out a place under her living-room floor to hide her teenage son and a neighbor boy from the Gestapo. The police would arrive unannounced, looking for youngsters to send to the labor camps in Germany. Did my landlady have a moral obligation to tell the guards about the two young men hidden beneath the floorboards? The principle of giving truth to whom it is due—where righteousness and justice require it—would not only allow that woman to deceive the soldiers but require her to do so. The biblical principle is that we should always tell the truth when righteousness and justice require it, but righteousness and justice do not always require it. The principle that defines justice and righteousness is that which is due, owed, or obligatory.

Paul is telling the Roman Christians that we are obliged to pay our taxes. We must give the state what is due the state. Justice and righteousness require that we submit to taxation. Honor is due the king. Even if the king is not honorable, he is to be honored. It is his due.

We are to honor our father and mother even if they do not deserve it, because honor is due our parents. We cannot reduce Christian justice and righteousness to the simple formula of merit and demerit. People might not earn honor, but by God's decree it is their due, and I am to give honor to whom honor is due.

Application

In the Bible, the instances of God's people's misleading those who seek to do evil are rare. We should expect it to be even rarer for us to encounter such moral dilemmas in our own lives. When it comes to our taxes, we don't need to approve of everything that our money goes toward or to evaluate whether the government deserves our taxes. God calls us to pay taxes, and when we do so, we are ultimately being obedient to Him.

2

Debt

OWE NO ONE ANYTHING EXCEPT **to love one another, for he who loves another has fulfilled the law** (v. 8). Paul continues with an exposition of the way in which love fulfills the law. Many see this verse as a mandate against incurring any debt or borrowing money to build churches or homes or to buy an automobile. If we look at the scope of sacred Scripture, however, we will see that there are vast provisions for taking on debt as well as guidelines to protect people who are in debt.

There are strong biblical prohibitions against oppressive usury. Usury is an exploitatively high interest rate that bleeds people dry. If our culture were held up to the law of Israel, the interest rates routinely charged by credit card companies would clearly be seen as usurious and would come under the judgment of God. They are too high, and they exploit people and their weaknesses. Scripture provides a principle with respect to lending and rates of interest.

Scripture also sets out strong considerations for the poor who had to put up personal property as collateral for their indebtedness. If a person put up his garment, which he needed to keep warm at night, the creditor was allowed to keep that garment during the day but was required by law to give it back to its owner before the coldness of the evening (Deut. 24:12–13). Such scenarios in the Bible are all based upon a culture ordained by God that allowed borrowing and lending so long as the lending and borrowing were not exploitative and oppressive.

Every commentator I have examined on this subject says that Paul is instructing Christians to operate only under one perpetual debt or obligation, and that is to love our brothers. The application from the text concerning borrowing and lending is this: there is no sin in borrowing, but there is sin in borrowing something and not paying it back. We are required to fulfill our obligation. Many people take advantage of loans and do not fulfill their obligation, but when Christians incur debt, they, above all others, must move heaven and earth to honor their obligations as a matter of principle and conscience. If you owe somebody something, pay what you owe. Pay your bills and pay them on time. If you enter into a contract, fulfill the terms of the contract. That is basic integrity.

All of this is wrapped, as we will see, in the overarching principle of love. If we borrow our neighbor's rake and do not return it, we are failing to love our neighbor. All the practical applications of righteousness and justice that Paul gives us here are rooted and grounded in that overarching responsibility we have to love our neighbor as ourselves. The things that Paul sets forth are nothing more or less than practical applications of the Golden Rule.

Application

Worldly debt is incomparable to our spiritual debt to Christ. If we are to live out the principle that we ought to pay back what we owe and extend that principle to our relationship with Christ, our debt is eternal. Let us praise God for this, for He does not save us to be paid back, but He does give us the privilege to serve and worship Him forever, which itself only makes us further indebted to Him for His priceless grace to us in Jesus Christ.

3

Love and the Ten Commandments

WE CAN PAY OUR DEBT TO THE BANK, the store, and the credit card company, but our debt to love our neighbor is never discharged until we cross into heaven. Love is a perpetual obligation, an indebtedness given to us by Jesus: "'You shall love the LORD your God with all your heart, with all your soul, and with all your mind.' This is the first and great commandment. And the second is like it: 'You shall love your neighbor as yourself'" (Matt. 22:37–39).

In Romans 13, the Apostle links the obligation of love to some of the Ten Commandments. We are not to owe anyone anything except love: **For the commandments, "You shall not commit adultery," "You shall not murder," "You shall not steal," "You shall not bear false witness," "You shall not covet," and if there is any other commandment, all are summed up in this saying, namely, "You shall love your neighbor as yourself"** (v. 9). Paul mentions the commandments often described, particularly by our Lutheran friends, as coming from the second table of the law. Scripture refers to the Ten Commandments as being given on two tablets of stone. The first few commandments prescribe our duty and behavior with respect to God. We are to have no other gods before Him; we are not to make any graven images of Him, thereby keeping ourselves from idolatry; we are to make sure that God's name is not taken in vain; and we are to keep the Sabbath. The remainder of the Ten Commandments focuses on how we are to treat one another with respect to marriage, sanctity of life, possessions, truth telling, and the like. The first tablet of the law pertains to our obligations to God, and the second tablet, or table, pertains to our obligations to people, which is a very popular understanding of why the Ten Commandments were given on two tablets. I do not hold that position.

I think the commandments were given on two tablets due to the context in which they were given—the Mosaic covenant. In antiquity, when formal covenants were entered into, the agreement was made in duplicate. One copy was reserved for the sovereign; the other was given to the vassal. The stipulations of the Mosaic covenant were expressed in terms of the Ten Commandments, and therefore the two tablets might reflect the ancient practice of rendering two copies of the agreement. But neither I nor my Lutheran friends know for sure why the commandments were given this way. Wherever we come out on that question, the commandments that Paul mentions in Romans 13 are those that prescribe behavior on the horizontal plane—our behavior toward each other. Whoever loves another has fulfilled the law.

Application

The law of God gives us something concrete by which we can know whether we are truly loving our neighbors as ourselves. We define our love not by whether something feels right but by the righteous standards that God has revealed. Reflect on your relationship with fellow Christians at your local church. Are you seeing the fruit of love? Eagerly pursue this love with your brothers, sisters, fathers, and mothers in Christ.

4

Neighbor Love

THE RULE OF LOVE IS THIS: love God and do what the love of God requires in every human situation. Concerning the love of God, Paul wrote, "Fornication and all uncleanness or covetousness, let it not even be named among you, as is fitting for saints" (Eph. 5:3). Paul could not envision any situation that would justify disobedience to God's law of purity. When Paul writes about love in Romans 13, he is writing about the purpose and goal of the law—the love of neighbor.

Neighbor includes all people. Therefore, if we love our neighbor, we will not commit adultery because adultery is hatred of our neighbor. It is the destruction of our friends and family. Years ago, I counseled a woman who had entered into an ungodly relationship with someone else's husband. When I confronted the woman and her lover, she pushed me away, telling me to mind my own business. I counseled several people because of the trauma brought about by that adulterous relationship. Mothers and fathers, children, and best friends—adultery does not express love to one's neighbor.

"You shall not murder," "You shall not steal," "You shall not bear false witness." We do not love our neighbor by helping ourselves to his possessions, nor do we slander people we love or poison others against them. That kind of behavior violates a specific law of God, and most of all, it violates the law of love.

"You shall not covet." If we were given the responsibility of establishing a new nation and were allowed only ten basic laws in which to frame the charter, what laws would we include? Would we think to include a law against covetousness? God did because God knows what happens when someone is envious of another, and He knows how destructive envy can be. We can understand an impulse to steal that is fueled by an overwhelming desire to possess the stolen item, but it is something else to say, "If I cannot have it, you cannot either." Vandalism is the worst form of envy and covetousness. God understands what destroys human relationships and fractures love.

Paul sums up: **Love does no harm to a neighbor** (v. 10a). If we love our neighbor, we do not steal from him or slander him, nor do we allow ourselves to be jealous or envious or to bear false witness against him. If we love somebody, we do not want to harm him. That is the way we are to live as Christians; we are to be known by the love that we have for one another.

Therefore, Paul concludes, **love is the fulfillment of the law** (v. 10b).

Application

Our call to love our neighbor extends beyond the local church. Though the household of faith is the context in which we are particularly to do good, our goodness ought to know no bounds in the world. The world, after all, is the place where Jesus has called us to shine: "You are the light of the world. A city that is set on a hill cannot be hidden. Nor do they light a lamp and put it under a basket, but on a lampstand, and it gives light to all who are in the house. Let your light so shine before men, that they may see your good works and glorify your Father in heaven" (Matt. 5:14–16).

5

Time to Wake Up

AND DO THIS, KNOWING THE TIME, **that now it is high time to awake out of sleep; for now our salvation is nearer than when we first**

believed. The night is far spent, the day is at hand. Therefore let us cast off the works of darkness, and let us put on the armor of light (vv. 11–12). In this section, Paul enjoins a certain kind of behavior and prohibits another. He prefaces it by reminding the people of the time. The time requires vigilance, alertness, and diligence. Some say that Paul might have been referencing the destruction of Jerusalem. He might have been, but most commentators—rightly so, I think—say that Paul is talking about the consummation of our salvation when we pass into glory.

Do you ever wonder how long you are going to live? Whatever our age, it is time to wake up because the final day is approaching, and therefore our salvation is nearer than when we first believed. The verb that Paul uses here means "to save." The Greek word appears in the biblical text in every possible tense indicating a sense in which we were being saved and a sense in which we have been saved. The simple aorist tense is rendered "you are saved." The present tense is rendered "you are being saved," and the future tense reads "you shall be saved." The future perfect is rendered "you shall have been saved." Salvation is unfolded biblically in all those increments. Therefore, in the ultimate sense, we do not experience salvation the moment we were born again; that is just one aspect of salvation. The fullness of our salvation will not take place until our glorification when we enter into heaven.

Application

The time is now to place your trust in Jesus Christ if you haven't already. His return will be like a thief coming in the night. If you have trusted in Jesus Christ, you surely know some who have not. Pray earnestly for them this day, and continue to share with them the gospel of salvation in Jesus Christ alone before it is too late.

6

Night and Day

PAUL IS ADDRESSING BELIEVERS WHEN HE WRITES, "Our salvation is nearer than when we first believed" (v. 11b). That is not bad news. It is good news because it means that the fullness of our salvation comes closer to us with every passing hour. Paul uses a figure from the normal daily movement of the sun—the difference between night and day. The time already passed is the nighttime. We are now in the last watch of the night, and the dawn of the fullness of our salvation is about to break. This metaphor is used repeatedly in the Scriptures. By nature we are children of darkness. The metaphor is used to describe sin: "The light has come into the world, and men loved darkness rather than light, because their deeds were evil" (John 3:19).

Orlando is a beautiful city until the lights go out. Downtown Orlando in the wee hours of the night has been a bad crime center. Things happen in the darkness that do not happen in the light. People love darkness because it conceals them from exposure. When we are brought into the fullness of day, we are known for what we are.

Let us walk properly, as in the day, not in revelry and drunkenness, not in lewdness and lust, not in strife and envy. But put on the Lord Jesus Christ, and make no provision for the flesh, to fulfill its lusts (vv. 13–14). Paul's reference to rioting and drunkenness pertains to the pagan religious worship of the god Bacchus, the god of the grape and the vine. Bacchus was the sponsor of the ancient Bacchanalia, an orgiastic feast involving gluttony and unbridled sexual behavior. Participants set out to get drunk to silence pangs of conscience so that they could engage in unbridled sin. In contrast to that, we are to put on the Lord Jesus Christ and make no provision for our flesh. Paul means that we are not to make or provide opportunities for sin.

An old country preacher said that if we desire to overcome drunkenness, we had best not tie our horse to the post in front of the saloon. We are not to make provisions. We are not to make provisions for human sin and weakness. Martin Luther put it this way: "I cannot keep sparrows from flying about my head, but I can keep them from making a nest in my hair." We are not to make provision to accommodate our base desires. Instead, we are to provide for our soul by putting on Christ and walking in daylight.

Application

One of the reasons that Christians look forward to the return of Jesus Christ is that His return will be the end of our sinning. We strive now to live in that reality in light of our final salvation: "Denying ungodliness and worldly lusts, we should live soberly, righteously, and godly in the present age, looking for the blessed hope and glorious appearing of our great God and Savior Jesus Christ" (Titus 2:12–13).

Romans 14

RECEIVE ONE WHO IS WEAK IN *the faith, but not to disputes over doubtful things. For one believes he may eat all things, but he who is weak eats only vegetables. Let not him who eats despise him who does not eat, and let not him who does not eat judge him who eats; for God has received him. Who are you to judge another's servant? To his own master he stands or falls. Indeed, he will be made to stand, for God is able to make him stand.*

One person esteems one day above another; another esteems every day alike. Let each be fully convinced in his own mind. He who observes the day, observes it to the Lord; and he who does not observe the day, to the Lord he does not observe it. He who eats, eats to the Lord, for he gives God thanks; and he who does not eat, to the Lord he does not eat, and gives God thanks. For none of us lives to himself, and no one dies to himself. For if we live, we live to the Lord; and if we die, we die to the Lord. Therefore, whether we live or die, we are the Lord's. For to this end Christ died and rose and lived again, that He might be Lord of both the dead and the living. But why do you judge your brother? Or why do you show contempt for your brother? For we shall all stand before the judgment seat of Christ. For it is written:

> *"As I live, says the LORD,*
> *Every knee shall bow to Me,*
> *And every tongue shall confess to God."*

So then each of us shall give account of himself to God. Therefore let us not judge one another anymore, but rather resolve this, not to put a stumbling block or a cause to fall in our brother's way.

I know and am convinced by the Lord Jesus that there is nothing unclean of itself; but to him who considers anything to be unclean, to him it is unclean. Yet if your brother is grieved because of your food, you are no longer walking in love. Do not destroy with your food the one for whom Christ died. Therefore do not let your good be spoken of as evil; for the kingdom of God is not eating and drinking, but righteousness and peace and joy in the Holy Spirit. For he who serves Christ in these things is acceptable to God and approved by men.

Therefore let us pursue the things which make for peace and the things by which one may edify another. Do not destroy the work of God for the sake of food. All things indeed are pure, but it is evil for the man who eats with offense. It is good neither to eat meat nor drink wine nor do anything by which your brother stumbles or is offended or is made weak. Do you have faith? Have it to yourself before God. Happy is he who does not condemn himself in what he approves. But he who doubts is condemned if he eats, because he does not eat from faith; for whatever is not from faith is sin.

WEEK 48

1

Legalism

YEARS AGO, I WENT FOR DINNER to the home of Old Testament scholar Meredith Kline, north of Boston, Massachusetts. At the end of the visit, Dr. Kline prepared to drive me to my home, which was less than a mile away. As we left his house, a torrential downpour began. Neither of us had an umbrella, so we dashed the one hundred yards through the rain to the car and got drenched in the process. No sooner had we entered the car than Dr. Kline dashed back out into the rain. He had forgotten something. When he returned to the car, he explained. "I forgot my driver's license."

I was incredulous. "You ran through that rain just to get your driver's license? We are only going down the street!"

He replied, "It is a small thing, but the Lord said that if we cannot be faithful in little things, how will He trust us with the big things?"

As a matter of conscience and to submit himself to the civil magistrates, he made sure to have his license with him, as the law required. Without any great fanfare or demonstration of piety, he ran back to the house without revealing to me the reason until I interrogated him. Some might say that he was a man caught in the bonds of legalism, but I do not think that was the case. Obedience to God in small matters is never a matter of legalism.

Legalism is a most destructive distortion of Christianity. There are two major distortions that block our sanctification, flip sides of the same coin. One is the spirit of antinomianism, which abuses Christian freedom by willfully sinning in light of grace. The other is legalism, which binds the freedom that grace gives. Legalism makes mere externals the test of true spirituality. We have all encountered Christians who say that the essence of spirituality is to refrain from dancing and lipstick and going to movies. The creed becomes "touch not, taste not, handle not." People substitute mere externals for the fruit of the Spirit and use adherence to those mere externals as the test of righteousness. Either distortion can be very destructive to the Christian life.

Application

In disavowing legalism, we must be careful not to embrace antinomianism. Both misunderstand the place of God's law in the Christian life—legalism sees obedience to God's law and going beyond it as contributing to our justification, and antinomianism rejects the importance of obedience to God's law altogether. When you see these warring tendencies in your life, remember that grace is the remedy to both, keeping you looking at Christ alone for justification and striving to be like Him out of sheer gratitude in your sanctification.

2

Adiaphora

IN THE GARDEN OF EDEN, royal liberty was granted to humanity to eat freely from all the trees except those that God had clearly stated that we ought not to touch. This liberty was lost in the fall into sin. When Christ set His people free from the curse of the law, He restored this royal liberty. Yet we do not all have the same scruples. Some believe that dancing is a sin; others do not. I knew someone who became convinced that playing ping-pong was a sin because he had gotten so caught up in it. He was addicted to ping-pong, and his work and family began to suffer as a result. For him, ping-pong did become a sin, but that does not mean that everyone around him was called to set a prohibition against playing ping-pong. Ping-pong is not inherently evil.

We find in Scripture things about which God has said yes or no, but in between those matters of law there is a host of things that the New Testament describes as *adiaphorous*, morally neutral. In the early Christian church, some developed scruples about eating meat, which is *adiaphorous*.

We read in Paul's letter to the Corinthians about a scandal that emerged among the Christians there that concerned the issue of eating meat that had been used in pagan idol worship. Some of the Corinthian Christians wanted to distance themselves in every conceivable way from every act of idolatry. As a matter of conscience, they determined that they would never purchase such meat, and they began to look down on their brothers who did purchase it and consume it freely. Those who ate it believed that nothing was inherently wrong with consuming the meat. They ate it without any pangs of conscience. A rift developed in the church between the divided parties, and Paul had to mediate the dispute. Something similar was going on in the Roman community, so in this epistle Paul wants to teach the people a lesson about how to use their Christian liberty. Although Paul taught it to both the Romans and the Corinthians, the lesson must be taught afresh to each generation.

Application

We must be careful in our judgments against our fellow Christians. They are our brothers, sisters, fathers, and mothers in Christ. We ought not to let matters of indifference come between us and create disharmony in our church family. But in matters that the Bible clearly teaches are not *adiaphora*, we must lovingly call to repentance: "Brethren, if a man is overtaken in any trespass, you who are spiritual restore such a one in a spirit of gentleness, considering yourself lest you also be tempted" (Gal. 6:1).

3

The Weaker Brother

ROMANS 14 ADDRESSES THE ISSUE OF CHRISTIAN LIBERTY with respect to the weaker brother. The chapter cannot be considered in isolation from what went before it; this is a continuation of Paul's exposition of love of neighbor, what it means to have fellowship marked by *agape*, spiritual love. Building on that theme, Paul writes: **Receive one who is weak in the faith, but not to disputes over doubtful things. For one believes he may eat all things, but he who is weak eats only vegetables** (vv. 1–2).

Some in the early church were convinced that vegetarianism was the right road to follow. They believed that the spiritual measure was not only whether someone refrained from eating meat offered to idols but whether he refrained from meat altogether. The vegetarians thought that exercising such restraint moved them to a higher level of spirituality. Those vegetarians were the ones that Paul describes as weaker brothers. They did not understand the fullness of the biblical concept of Christian liberty. They were held captive to elemental principles of "taste not, touch not, handle not." They thought they were being devout when, in fact, they were being infantile and immature in their reasoning.

Some say that we should ridicule those who are weaker or have nothing to do with them, but Paul is emphatic that such an approach is wrong: **Let not him who eats despise him who does not eat, and let not him who does not eat judge him who eats; for God has received him** (v. 3). According to Paul, we are not to avoid one another when we differ on matters of *adiaphora*. Paul is not saying that we should be cavalier about heinous sin; he is referring to issues of indifference. The weaker brother has a misinformed understanding of what God allows or forbids, but the weaker one is still our brother and has been received by God. Since he has been welcomed into the family of God, the dispute is a family matter.

Application

As Christians, we are called to love one another, and as an outworking of love, patience must characterize our dealings with one another (see 1 Cor. 13:4). This is especially true with immature believers. Love is also not arrogant or rude, seeking after its own way (vv. 4–5), so if we find ourselves to be the immature ones, let us not insist that others conform to our standards when they are aligned with God's.

4

Another's Servant

AS GOD RECEIVES US BY GRACE, we must receive one another by grace. Love covers a multitude of sins as well as a multitude of misunderstandings and weak theology. One who is weak ought not to despise one who manifests liberty, and one who manifests liberty ought not to despise one with a scrupulous conscience.

Paul asks a rhetorical question: **Who are you to judge another's servant?** (v. 4a). Paul is using a marketplace analogy, but the point is that we are all servants of Christ, so who are we to despise another of Christ's servants? If a servant is acceptable to Jesus, how can he not be acceptable to us? The analogy is simple. The weak brother has his scruple unto the Lord; the strong brother has his freedom unto the Lord.

One person esteems one day above another (v. 5a). Paul is not writing about the Sabbath but about certain holy days that Jews observed. Some of the converted Jews had clung to their Jewish traditions and observations. Even though those traditions were no longer enjoined upon the Christian community, some of them, as a matter of conscience, continued those practices. Here Paul gives them freedom to do so.

There are other applications of Christian freedom. Someone I know sits on the board of trustees of a Christian institution, and as a member of that board, he is not allowed to drink wine. The organization has elevated a preference into a rule. They have legislated where God has given freedom. He explained to me that the board was concerned that its members stand out from the culture at large, and I replied, "Do you realize that Jesus and the Apostles could not serve on the board of your organization?" We can appreciate their concern to keep the institution unspotted from the world, but their position is one of weakness.

Application

Some things in the Christian life are nonnegotiable. Obedience to God's moral law is one of those things. Worshiping God on the Lord's Day is one of the ways that we fulfill the fourth commandment. Some matters have nothing to do with the Christian's liberty of conscience, so let us not neglect to meet with one another, and let us have peace with one another as we meet together.

5

Understanding Christian Liberty

THE CLASSICAL UNDERSTANDING OF CHRISTIAN LIBERTY is this: we are not to try to force somebody with a scruple against something, as uninformed as that scruple may be, to violate his conscience. The basic principle that unfolds here is one of loving sensitivity. Paul makes clear in his teaching that though we are to be sensitive, loving, and kind to the weaker brother, we ought never to allow him to exercise tyranny over the church.

We walk a very thin line. The weaker brother is not to destroy the freedom of all in the church. At the same time, we can forgo our freedom for a time out of consideration for our weaker brother. Paul is opposing a spirit of arrogance that leads us to insist on our rights to do whatever we please no matter what. That is the wrong approach. The stronger brother has to be willing to forgo his strength for the sake of the weaker brother, yet the church must never allow the weaker one to establish his weakness as law for the Christian community.

That is the essence of what the Apostle is setting forth here in Romans 14 and also in 1 Corinthians 8. We are to do what we do to the Lord. **For none of us lives to himself, and no one dies to himself. For if we live, we live to the Lord; and if we die, we die to the Lord. Therefore, whether we live or die, we are the Lord's. For to this end Christ died and rose and lived again, that He might be Lord of both the dead and the living. But why do you judge your brother? Or why do you show contempt for your brother? For we shall all stand before the judgment seat of Christ. For it is written: "As I live, says the LORD, every knee shall bow to Me, and every tongue shall confess to God." So then each of us shall give account of himself to God. Therefore let us not judge one another anymore, but rather resolve this, not to put a stumbling block or a cause to fall in our brother's way** (vv. 7–13). Simple human kindness and consideration have to go both ways. Again, the application is to things that have no inherent goodness or evil. No one can use this principle to participate in adultery or other sins. These precepts have to do with eating meat, drinking wine, observing certain days that have no direct bearing on the kingdom of God. The great danger is to allow these *adiaphorous* matters to become requirements for Christian spirituality and, even worse, the test for what is spiritual and righteous. Unfortunately, that is what happens again and again.

Application

We don't associate a critical attitude toward others with such emotions as joy and contentment and the sense of freedom that comes from them. We are set free from judging others who disagree with us over indifferent matters, and we are set free unto the Lord, to find the best ways to serve Him, for that is what we must give an account of when we one day stand before Him.

6

Christians and Alcohol

I RECALL A CERTAIN DINNER I ATE with a group at a restaurant. The waitress came to serve us and asked, "May I take your drink orders? Would anybody like a cocktail?" Our hostess cut her off, saying, "No, we are Christians." The smug self-righteousness of our hostess not only embarrassed the waitress, who was simply doing her job, but gave a wrong message about Christianity. Christianity is not about eating and drinking.

Drinking alcohol is a controversial topic in the Christian community. Many argue that Jesus never drank wine and that when the Pharisees called Jesus a winebibber, they were distorting the truth. They also argue that the wine Jesus made for the wedding in Cana was unfermented. Arguing that way, however, is a hopeless, tortuous treatment of the biblical text, but it happens when people come to the text with a cultural bias. Many are convinced that total abstinence is the only spiritual way, but we learn no such thing from the Scriptures—not from the Old Testament or from the celebration of the Passover. If we were to do a word study of the word *wine* in the Bible, we would see that it was the real thing. God sanctified it and warned against drinking too much of it, because getting drunk is a sin. God did not give that warning against drunkenness to people drinking grape juice.

This view is offensive to many people. To all such people who are convinced that they cannot drink wine, then they must never let wine touch their lips, because for them it is a sin. For others, it is not. Our brother ought not to judge us, and we ought not to judge our brother. If my brother believes that drinking a glass of wine is sin, I ought not to try to coax him into drinking a glass of wine. That would be an attempt to entice him to violate his conscience. The violation of one's conscience, even if it is a misinformed conscience, is a serious matter.

Application

When it comes to matters of Christian liberty, we must all search our own hearts to see whether we are causing others to stumble or are stumbling ourselves. Scripture plainly calls drunkenness a sin, but drinking alcohol in moderation is not. This means that we must know ourselves in these matters, so that we do not fall into sin.

WEEK 49

1

Nothing Unclean

I KNOW AND AM CONVINCED by the Lord Jesus that there is nothing unclean of itself (v. 14a). Paul is not giving an educated guess about what is clean or unclean. He writes from Apostolic conviction, a basis of certainty, which he grounds not in his own research but on what he received directly from Christ. Paul is passing on to the church what his Lord and Savior has revealed to him. Paul does not mean that there is no inherent evil in the world. Adultery and murder are inherently evil. Paul is still addressing the question about eating and drinking and the disputes that arose about them.

In the Old Testament, God called Israel from among the nations to be His chosen people so that they might be a light to the rest of the world. They were called to be different in many respects from the pagan world from which they had come. God had a unique relationship with the people of Israel, and He bound them to Himself at Mount Sinai by the giving of the law, the Ten Commandments. The commandments were the provisions of the covenant. To the laws governing His holy nation, God added ceremonial rites and responsibilities. There were great feasts to be celebrated, such as the Passover. He also gave to the children of Israel a list of dietary regulations that they were obliged to keep at all times, and the Israelites were scrupulous about trying to keep those dietary laws.

When the New Testament economy appeared, what had been considered unclean was declared clean. In the book of Acts, we read that Peter had a vision in which it was revealed to him that things previously deemed unclean were now clean (10:9–16). The whole issue provoked so much debate among the first generation of Jewish Christians that it was necessary to call the first great council of the church. This council, the Council of Jerusalem, addressed whether dietary laws should be imposed upon the Gentile community. After centuries of abstaining from certain foods, God suddenly annulled those laws. Nothing less than a specific revelation, such as Jesus gave to Peter, would have been sufficient to give them liberty of conscience to depart from that ancient tradition.

Application

Paul asserts that he is "convinced *by the Lord Jesus* that there is nothing unclean" (Rom. 14:14a, emphasis added). Christians, in adherence to the teaching of our Lord, ought then to grow into maturity concerning matters of moral indifference. We are not to bind other Christians or be bound ourselves in these matters because Christ has set all His servants free to serve Him alone.

2

Christian Practice and God's Law

TO WHAT EXTENT DOES THE OLD TESTAMENT LAW have any bearing upon our lives? Has the new covenant, with its accent on grace, completely freed us from obeying the Old Testament law? Many in the church today practice antinomianism, claiming that the Old Testament law has no claim whatsoever upon the New Testament Christian. Are we still to have our consciences influenced by the law of the Old Testament?

Reformed theology has historically divided Old Testament law into three parts: the moral law, the ceremonial law, and the dietary law. The church says that certain laws in the Old Testament are no longer applicable in the new covenant, including the dietary laws and the ceremonial laws. We do not slaughter animals and offer sacrifices. In fact, if we were to do that, we would be denying the perfect finished work of Jesus. The ceremonies of the Old Testament have been abrogated. They were fulfilled in Christ and, therefore, set aside. Likewise, the dietary laws are no longer binding on the New Testament Christian. But, it is argued, the third element, the moral law, remains intact; we are still bound by the moral law of God. I have a quibble with that, because obeying those ceremonial and dietary laws was a moral issue of the highest magnitude for Shadrach, Meshach, Abednego, and Daniel. For the Old Testament Jew, keeping every aspect of the law was a great ethical and moral concern. For that reason, we have to be careful when we categorize Old Testament laws.

The law of God reflects His holy character. The historical context in which He gave all His laws was this: "You shall therefore be holy, for I am holy" (Lev. 11:45; see also 19:2; 20:26; 21:8). Therefore, we are given to understand that God's laws are not arbitrary. He has a holy and sacred purpose for every law He legislates. The law comes from His character.

Application

We must guard ourselves against those who teach that Christians must return to dimensions of God's old covenant law with Israel. This issue is what vexed Paul so severely in his letter to the Galatians. Believing that adherence to the Mosaic law was required for justification was a denial of the gospel. Be aware of this if anyone begins to question why we do not adhere to the civil or ceremonial laws of the old covenant, and with a clean conscience strive to be holy as God is holy.

3

God's Unchanging Nature and the Law

THE NATURE OF GOD AND HIS CHARACTER are immutable. Those divine attributes can never be negotiated. He does not change. So then, since the law reflects God's character and His character never changes, how is it possible that any of the Old Testament laws could ever be abrogated? We see that the New Testament does in fact abrogate certain laws of the Old Testament and that it is God Himself who abrogates them. If God abrogates a law, it is abrogated. That leaves us asking a question about God's immutable character—does the abrogation of laws contradict God's immutability?

With respect to the moral law of God, we make a distinction

between two kinds of law: God's natural law and God's purposive law. God's law is *purposive* in that God has a sacred and holy purpose for every law He legislates. I use the term *natural law* in a different way from how it has been historically used in philosophy and juris-prudence. When I make a distinction between the natural law of God and the purposive law of God here, I am not really addressing some transcendent framework for laws enacted in various nations (as in philosophy and jurisprudence). Rather, here I am saying that God's natural laws are those that God gives based on His holy nature, and because they are based on His holy nature, those laws are immutable. For God to abrogate a law that comes from His nature, such as the law against idolatry, He would be compromising His character. God has given other laws for a particular redemptive purpose, which is not necessarily rooted in His eternal immutable being. For example, the dietary laws He gave to Israel were given for a particular reason for a particular time. When that time was fulfilled, God annulled those laws without doing any damage to His character.

God's character was in no way compromised when He put an end to the offering of bulls and goats in the ceremonial rites of the Old Testament. I hope we understand that distinction, because many people in the first century did not understand it. They struggled because they had spent their entire lives being careful not to eat certain foods or drink certain beverages.

Application

God's immutability is a comforting doctrine. He does not change, which means that the gospel of our salvation never changes. Our salvation in Christ, not being something that we earned, cannot be taken away from us. God's love for us does not change, and "Jesus Christ is the same yesterday, today, and forever" (Heb. 13:8), and through Him we have an "everlasting covenant" (v. 20). Praise Him for these truths today.

4

Kingdom Living

FOR THE KINGDOM OF GOD IS NOT **eating and drinking** (v. 17a). The disputes concerning trivial matters that tear churches apart would not happen if we would just grasp the principle that the kingdom of God is not about eating, drinking, lipstick, or any external thing. It is about **righteousness and peace and joy in the Holy Spirit** (v. 17b). We have here a triad of virtues that describes what the kingdom of God is about.

First, the kingdom is about righteousness. Righteousness is misunderstood in the church today, where the goal of so many is to be pious or spiritual. The goal of the kingdom is not spirituality. The goal of our Christian life is not spirituality. Spirituality is a good thing, but it is not the goal; it is a means to the goal. The goal of the Christian life is righteousness, and we are to seek it. We are to strive to be righteous people.

Second, the kingdom of God is about peace. Jeremiah decried those who proclaimed, "Peace, peace!" when there was no peace (Jer. 6:14; 8:11). There are so-called peacemakers in the church who say that since doctrine divides, we must not enter into debates about theological matters. Martin Luther called that *carnal* peace, because it is born of the flesh and comes from fear of conflict or cowardice. Of course, we are not to be bellicose people, looking for a fight and being contentious over every minor point, which happens when immature people major in minors.

Third, the kingdom of God is about joy. It does not consist of a company of sourpusses. We should be happy people. The kingdom of God is about the joy that has been shed abroad in our hearts because we have been redeemed by the Lord our God. Why should we be glum and fuss over who eats meat and drinks wine? Such things are not what the kingdom of God is about, according to Paul. Life in the kingdom is about loving the things of God and loving those for whom Christ died. That is the recipe for mature Christian unity.

Application

Matters of indifference ought never to rise to matters of first importance. Christian love is such a matter of first importance. When love is understood to be and practiced as our primary obligation to those for whom Christ died, then trivial matters will never steal away the peace and purity of the church. This is so even when it comes to the sins committed against us by fellow Christians, for "love will cover a multitude of sins" (1 Peter 4:8).

5

A Call to Action

HOW ARE WE TO TREAT WEAKER BROTHERS in terms of *adiaphorous* matters, that is, in things that are not inherently wrong but nevertheless bother the consciences of some? This is such a serious matter that Paul deals with it not only here in Romans but also in his correspondence to the Corinthian church and in his writing to the Galatians. The issue was also at the center of debate in the first-century church. The concern there was how the Jewish converts were to receive and deal with the Gentiles coming into the covenant community. It was a matter of great urgency to the Apostle.

Therefore let us pursue the things which make for peace and the things by which one may edify another. Do not destroy the work of God for the sake of food (vv. 19–20a). Here we find a conclusion that comes from Paul's previous reasoning. It is a call to action. When we pursue something, we chase after it not casually but with a degree of earnestness.

When I was three years old, the most exciting toy I received for Christmas was a metal plane in which I could sit and pedal around the streets. It was called a pursuit plane. That was the first time I heard the word *pursuit*. Not until much later did I understand that pursuit planes were designed to search out and destroy the enemy. That is the action to which Paul is calling us. We are to chase after and seek diligently the things that make for peace.

The opposite of peace is war; it is conflict. God's people are not to chase after fights and look for conflict. We are to search for things that make for peace, and the sort of peace we are to chase is peace that passes understanding. It is the peace that Jesus left as His legacy: "Peace I leave with you, My peace I give to you; not as the world gives do I give to you" (John 14:27). There is a reason why our Lord is called the Prince of Peace. In fact, His ultimate mission was to bring us peace with God, to reconcile us to Him.

Application

Peace among Christians is one of the greatest tools of evangelism and apologetics that the church has. With peace comes unity, and with unity comes peace; the two are inseparable. Jesus has given us His peace, that we may be one, in fulfillment of His prayer to the Father "that they may be made perfect in one, and that the world may know that You have sent Me" (John 17:23). Conflict between Christians goes against Christ's will for His church, so let us prayerfully guard against it.

6

Called to Build Up

THERE IS A SHARP CONTRAST BETWEEN two words in verses 19 and 20—*edify* and *destroy*. Many of us have a vivid mental picture of what happened in New York City on September 11, 2001. We saw video of the planes crashing into the World Trade Center towers, and we witnessed the implosion of those magnificent buildings. One thing we will never forget about the Twin Towers is how quickly they fell to the ground. It takes much longer to build a building than to destroy one. To edify, to produce an edifice, involves building, which is the stark opposite of destroying.

Paul is concerned about that when it comes to manifesting love in the body of Christ. He wants his readers to recognize that it is much easier to destroy our brother than to edify him. Christ came not to destroy us but to destroy the works of the devil. He came to build for Himself a people who will manifest His image. That is what we are to pursue in the church. We are not to be known for being critical, for attacking each other and gossiping. Slander is the principal work of Satan, which is why one of his titles is Slanderer. He is the destructive one who brings false claims to tear people apart. We are called in the name of Jesus to build up, not tear apart.

All things indeed are pure, but it is evil for the man who eats with offense. It is good neither to eat meat nor drink wine nor do anything by which your brother stumbles or is offended or is made weak (vv. 20b–21). Paul is repeating the principle of considering our weaker brothers and sisters. If we understand the freedom we have in Christ, we are not to flaunt our liberty before our weaker brothers who may not understand their freedom. We can eat our meat in private, before the Lord, who sees all things: **Have it to yourself before God. Happy is he who does not condemn himself in what he approves. But he who doubts is condemned if he eats, because he does not eat from faith; for whatever is not from faith is sin** (vv. 22b–23). It bears repeating that there is danger and impropriety in acting against conscience.

Application

The call to eat or drink privately does not mean that we must keep our exercise of Christian liberty completely to ourselves. The Lord Jesus Christ has declared all things clean, and one of the ways that immature believers learn to affirm this truth is through the testimony of good conscience of the mature in faith. The immature may stumble if we arrogantly flaunt our freedom, but may be built up in their own freedom if we speak openly about it in gentleness and patience.

Romans 15

WE THEN WHO ARE STRONG OUGHT *to bear with the scruples of the weak, and not to please ourselves. Let each of us please his neighbor for his good, leading to edification. For even Christ did not please Himself; but as it is written, "The reproaches of those who reproached You fell on Me." For whatever things were written before were written for our learning, that we through the patience and comfort of the Scriptures might have hope. Now may the God of patience and comfort grant you to be like-minded toward one another, according to Christ Jesus, that you may with one mind and one mouth glorify the God and Father of our Lord Jesus Christ.*

Therefore receive one another, just as Christ also received us, to the glory of God. Now I say that Jesus Christ has become a servant to the circumcision for the truth of God, to confirm the promises made to the fathers, and that the Gentiles might glorify God for His mercy, as it is written:

"For this reason I will confess to You among the Gentiles, And sing to Your name."

And again he says:

"Rejoice, O Gentiles, with His people!"

And again:

"Praise the LORD, all you Gentiles! Laud Him, all you peoples!"

And again, Isaiah says:

"There shall be a root of Jesse;
And He who shall rise to reign over the Gentiles,
In Him the Gentiles shall hope."

Now may the God of hope fill you with all joy and peace in believing, that you may abound in hope by the power of the Holy Spirit.

Now I myself am confident concerning you, my brethren, that you also are full of goodness, filled with all knowledge, able also to admonish one another. Nevertheless, brethren, I have written more boldly to you on some points, as reminding you, because of the grace given to me by God, that I might be a minister of Jesus Christ to the Gentiles, ministering the gospel of God, that the offering of the Gentiles might be acceptable, sanctified by the Holy Spirit. Therefore I have reason to glory in Christ Jesus in the things which pertain to God. For I will not dare to speak of any of those things which Christ has not accomplished through me, in word and deed, to make the Gentiles obedient—in mighty signs and wonders, by the power of the Spirit of God, so that from Jerusalem and round about to Illyricum I have fully preached the gospel of Christ. And so I have made it my aim to preach the gospel, not where Christ was named, lest I should build on another man's foundation, but as it is written:

"To whom He was not announced, they shall see;
And those who have not heard shall understand."

For this reason I also have been much hindered from coming to you. But now no longer having a place in these parts, and having a great desire these many years to come to you, whenever I journey to Spain, I shall come to you. For I hope to see you on my journey, and to be helped on my way there by you, if first I may enjoy your company for a while. But now I am going to Jerusalem to minister to the saints. For it pleased those from Macedonia and Achaia to make a certain contribution for the poor among the saints who are in Jerusalem. It pleased them indeed, and they are their debtors. For if the Gentiles have been partakers of their spiritual things, their duty is also to minister to them in material things. Therefore, when I have performed this and have sealed to them this fruit, I shall go by way of you to Spain. But I know that when I come to you, I shall come in the fullness of the blessing of the gospel of Christ.

Now I beg you, brethren, through the Lord Jesus Christ, and through the love of the Spirit, that you strive together with me in prayers to God for me, that I may be delivered from those in Judea who do not believe, and that my service for Jerusalem may be acceptable to the saints, that I may come to you with joy by the will of God, and may be refreshed together with you. Now the God of peace be with you all. Amen.

WEEK 50

1

Man-Pleasers

PAUL CONTINUES THAT LINE OF THOUGHT into chapter 15 with this admonition: **We then who are strong ought to bear with the scruples of the weak, and not to please ourselves. Let each of us please his neighbor for his good, leading to edification** (vv. 1–2). When the Galatians compromised the gospel, Paul wrote some of the strongest language we find anywhere in his epistles:

> I marvel that you are turning away so soon from Him who called you in the grace of Christ, to a different gospel, which is not another; but there are some who trouble you and want to pervert the gospel of Christ. But even if we, or an angel from heaven, preach any other gospel to you than what we have preached to you, let him be accursed. (Gal. 1:6–8)

Let him be *anathema*, let him be damned. Paul follows up those strong words with a sharp warning: "Do I now persuade men, or God? Or do I seek to please men? For if I still pleased men, I would not be a bondservant of Christ" (v. 10).

Paul's words to the Galatians seem to be a direct contradiction to what we just read from Romans, where he writes that we are not to please ourselves but to please our brother. To the Galatians he says that if he is pleasing man, he cannot be a disciple of God. He is talking about two different types of pleasing. In Galatians he is talking about a sin: compromising or distorting the gospel for the sake of man-pleasing, which has occurred repeatedly down through church history. The gospel is foolishness to those who are perishing. Human beings have a built-in hostility against the truth of God. If we seek the sort of carnal peace that attempts to avoid conflict at any cost, and if we seek to please men rather than God, we are enemies of the gospel.

In the context of the Galatians' struggle, Paul referred to man-pleasing as a dreadful vice, not a virtue, but it is not what Paul is talking about here in Romans. Here Paul is saying that we ought to bear with the scruples of the weak rather than please ourselves.

Application

To some degree, we all struggle with people-pleasing. A particular relationship in your own life might come to mind as a struggle in this area. Take a moment to pray to the Lord that you would live more fully before Him, seeking to please Him rather than others. If you struggle with putting yourself first before others, pray also that God would give you a servant heart for your fellow Christians.

2

The Zeal of Christ

WE DO NOT TRY TO PLEASE PEOPLE for the sake of personal gain. That is the principle underlying this discussion about being patient with one another. Paul gives the supreme model for doing so, quoting from Psalm 69: **For even Christ did not please Himself; but as it is written, "The reproaches of those who reproached You fell on Me"** (Rom. 15:3). Jesus did not find His pleasure in doing what He wanted to do. Later in that psalm we read:

> You know my reproach, my shame, and my dishonor;
> My adversaries are all before You.

Reproach has broken my heart,
And I am full of heaviness;
I looked for someone to take pity, but there was none;
And for comforters, but I found none.
They also gave me gall for my food,
And for my thirst they gave me vinegar to drink. (Ps. 69:19–21)

Psalm 69 is a psalm of messianic expectancy:

Because for Your sake I have borne reproach;
Shame has covered my face.
I have become a stranger to my brothers,
And an alien to my mother's children;
Because zeal for Your house has eaten me up,
And the reproaches of those who reproach You have fallen on
me. (vv. 7–9)

The Messiah was known for His singular zeal for His Father's house. Zeal for His Father's house consumed Him; it ate Him alive. Jesus is described that way in the Scriptures. He was so passionately committed to doing the will of the Father that He was consumed by it. His meat and drink was to please the Father, and as a result, the reproaches that were directed against God came upon Him. Paul directs the Romans to the supreme example of Jesus. He was willing to suffer the reproach of the world and not please Himself so that His people would be redeemed and edified, which is so unlike our natural selfishness. We want to please ourselves rather than others. Who among us has grace so sown in our soul that we are consumed by a passion to put others before ourselves?

Application
Our bearing with "the scruples of the weak" (Rom. 15:1) by forgoing our freedom as Christians cannot compare to the suffering of Jesus

Christ on our behalf. We ought eagerly to set aside our right to exercise freedom for the sake of others if it will result in their good. If you are ever called to put another person first in matters of Christian liberty, look to Christ's example for encouragement.

3

Formula for Joy

JOY IS A WELL-USED ACROSTIC: Jesus first, Others second, Yourself last. We do not need a PhD in theology to get that message. That is the formula for joy. When we do what the Apostle enjoins here, seeking to please others for their edification, the by-product for us is not loss but gain. We ourselves are edified in the process.

For whatever things were written before were written for our learning, that we through the patience and comfort of the Scriptures might have hope (v. 4). I know of nothing more comforting to the soul than the Word of God. When my soul is cast down (and it is cast down from time to time, as everyone's is), there is no greater panacea than to immerse myself in the Word of God.

When Simeon saw Jesus in the arms of His mother, he sang the Nunc Dimittis:

Lord, now You are letting Your servant depart in peace,
According to Your word;
For my eyes have seen Your salvation
Which You have prepared before the face of all peoples,
A light to bring revelation to the Gentiles,
And the glory of Your people Israel. (Luke 2:29–32)

Most think the Paraclete, the Comforter, the Helper is the third person of the Trinity, the Holy Spirit, but He is the other Paraclete, "another Helper" (John 14:16). The primary Paraclete is Jesus, and He bestows His comfort to His people through His Word. People have asked me why I fight tenaciously to maintain the integrity of Holy Scripture in an age of skeptical cynicism, and I ask in response, "Do you want to take away my comfort, which is here in the inspired Word of God?" When God speaks, even in judgment, there is comfort.

There is a difference between the accusations of Satan, when he calls attention to our sin, and the conviction of the Holy Spirit. When Satan comes to accuse us, he comes to destroy. There is no comfort in it. When the Spirit convicts us of sin, as painful as it may be, He never leaves us destroyed. Even in His conviction, He brings comfort and consolation, never leaving us without hope. Along with the conviction, He brings certainty of the forgiveness available to us.

Here Paul speaks of the comfort of the Scriptures in order that we might have hope. Without the patience and comfort that is delivered to our hearts by the Word of God, we would be like the rest of the world—without hope. The world is perishing before our very eyes. People parade in eloquent pride, presenting thin disguises of their sad hopelessness. Those without Christ are without hope; those in Christ are never without hope.

Application

All of Scripture is inspired by God. All of it has been given for our edification (2 Tim. 3:16–17). We cannot be merely New Testament Christians. In this passage, Paul has in mind the Old Testament, the things "written before," so let us study the whole counsel of God, knowing that the Spirit is pleased to use Scripture to build us up in hope, even when He uses it to convict us of sin.

4

Like-Minded in Hope

PAUL CONTINUES IN THE TERMS OF A BENEDICTION: Now may the God of patience and comfort grant you to be like-minded toward one another, according to Christ Jesus, that you may with one mind and one mouth glorify the God and Father of our Lord Jesus Christ (vv. 5–6). This is what heaven will be like. When we get to heaven, the saints will be of one mind and voice, singing together to the honor and glory of God, but that is also what the church in this world is supposed to look like.

We come to another conclusion: **Therefore receive one another, just as Christ also received us, to the glory of God** (v. 7). When we receive one another in our various weaknesses and strengths, we do it to the glory of God. It is not simply a matter of showing kindness; it is about glorifying Jesus.

Now I say that Jesus Christ has become a servant to the circumcision for the truth of God, to confirm the promises made to the fathers, and that the Gentiles might glorify God for His mercy (vv. 8–9a). Paul comes back to the place and function of the Gentiles in the kingdom of God in the new covenant. He then cites several passages from the Old Testament.

> **"For this reason I will confess to You among the Gentiles,**
> **And sing to Your name."** . . .
> **"Rejoice, O Gentiles, with His people!"** (vv. 9b–10)

Jew and Gentile come together with one voice, one mind, one Lord, one faith, and one baptism. Then:

> **"Praise the LORD, all you Gentiles!**
> **Laud Him, all you peoples!"** . . .

> "There shall be a root of Jesse;
> And He who shall rise to reign over the Gentiles,
> In Him the Gentiles shall hope." (vv. 11–12)

Someone from the family of Jesse, from the seed of David, would come centuries later and rise to reign over the Gentiles. That One was Christ, and in Him the Gentiles found hope. **Now may the God of hope fill you with all joy and peace in believing, that you may abound in hope by the power of the Holy Spirit** (v. 13). We are given the slightest hint here of what Paul will cover in great detail when he writes to the Corinthians and to the Galatians—the fruit of the Spirit. The Holy Spirit works in our hearts to shed love abroad and to produce the fruit of joy, peace, hope, forbearance, patience, kindness, goodness, and humility. That is what the God of all hope does when He fills us with His love in the power of the Holy Spirit.

Application

Our call to be united in Christ is grounded in Christ's person and work. He came to redeem all people from our bondage to sin—both Jew and Gentile. Christians from every nationality and walk of life must seek unity with one another. More than this, in truth, all Christians are already united to one another through their shared union with Christ. We receive one another because Christ received us.

5

A Minister's Burden

WE CAN TELL FROM PAUL'S TONE that he is gradually drawing the letter to a close. He expounded weighty theological matters in the first eleven chapters, and then he transitioned to practical application. Now

Paul begins to speak of his personal relationships with those who will receive the epistle. We tend to skip over the personal parts of the epistles, as if they contain no great weight of divine revelation.

Paul has just finished writing that the Christian life is to be characterized by a fullness of joy, a completeness of peace, and a dimension of hope worked in our soul by the power of the Holy Spirit. He continues: **Now I myself am confident concerning you, my brethren, that you also are full of goodness, filled with all knowledge, able also to admonish one another** (v. 14). This might well be viewed as a thinly veiled apology. Paul is aware that those who will receive this theological treatise—the weightiest epistle to come from the pen of the Apostle—already know all he is writing to them about. **Nevertheless, brethren, I have written more boldly to you on some points, as reminding you** (v. 15a).

From the beginning of his ministry to the very end, Paul was acutely conscious of the burden that Christ had put upon him as an Apostle of God's gospel. He knew that his duty was to communicate the full counsel of God. That burden has been shared by every earnest minister of the gospel ever since. The pulpit is not a place for the minister to orate or opine on his personal preferences or insights. The pulpit is where the Word of God is to be proclaimed, and the burden of everyone who stands in it is to make sure that the whole counsel of God is to be given to the people of God.

Application

Take a moment to pray for your pastor's ministry in the Word. Pray that he would have ample time to prepare for his weekly preaching and teaching duties and that he would be encouraged and supported in his labors by the church. Pray that just as he seeks to edify and feed the flock of God, he, too, would be edified and fed by the Chief Shepherd, Jesus Christ.

6

The Minister's Grace

PAUL UNDERSTOOD THAT HIS VERY ENGAGEMENT in ministry was a matter of grace: **because of the grace given to me by God, that I might be a minister of Jesus Christ to the Gentiles, ministering the gospel of God** (vv. 15b–16a). He had not earned his role as the Apostle to the Gentiles. Christ called him on the road to Damascus in the midst of the hatred and venom he was spewing out against the church of Jesus Christ. The only thing Paul had earned was the title he gave himself later—the chief of sinners (1 Tim. 1:15). He became an Apostle and spokesperson for Christ by grace, not merit. The same is true for all who dare to open the Bible and presume to preach or teach from it. Paul comes full circle from Romans 1, where he introduced himself as "Paul, a bondservant of Jesus Christ, called to be an apostle, separated to the gospel of God" (v. 1). Paul is an Apostle called to proclaim not his own message but the message that belongs to God and comes from God. Now he uses that very same language here toward the close of the epistle.

In the New Testament, those appointed to preach and teach are usually called elders or servants or pastors or shepherds; on rare occasions they are called ministers. *Minister* is the common term we use today, but it was not used frequently to describe the role of pastor in the early Christian community. Strikingly absent here is another word often used to describe those who minister to the people of God—*priest*. That word is almost completely absent from the New Testament, and yet it was regularly applied to those who stood between the people and God as intercessors to offer the sacrifice of worship in the Old Testament. The only reference to priesthood in the New Testament is Peter's mention of the royal priesthood to which Israel was called (1 Peter 2:9).

The office of *pastor* is not called the office of *priest*, because the function of the priest in the Old Testament had reached its fulfillment in the offering of the perfect sacrifice of Jesus on the cross. The entire sacrificial, or sacerdotal, system of the Old Testament was done away with once for all in Christ.

Application

Jesus Christ's sacrifice was perfect. We can do nothing to add to it. In fact, any attempt to add to it by our own efforts takes away from it. Like all other Christians, ministers are servants of Christ, and they are obligated to preach the pure gospel of grace. When your pastor faithfully preaches this message, encourage him in his faithful service to the Lord that rather than taking away from the glory of Christ's once-for-all sacrifice, he is magnifying it.

WEEK 51

1

The Minister's Offering

SOME CHURCHES TODAY STILL PRACTICE SACERDOTALISM. Salvation is mediated through the sacraments and, therefore, through the priesthood. In such cases, the church is seen as the instrument that brings people to salvation. This was a central issue in the sixteenth-century Reformation. The priesthood of Christ was fulfilled on the cross, so we are not priests. Paul does not consider himself a priest; he calls himself "a minister of Jesus Christ to the Gentiles, ministering the gospel of God" (v. 16a).

Although Paul does not call himself a priest, he borrows the language of the priesthood and uses it in a metaphorical way. Earlier in the letter, Paul had written, "I beseech you therefore, brethren, by the mercies of God, that you present your bodies a living sacrifice, holy, acceptable to God, which is your reasonable service" (12:1). We do not offer bulls and goats anymore, but we are called to make a sacrifice to Christ, an offering of our very lives, as our response to the gospel. In that sense, every Christian is a priest, but the offering is a sacrifice of praise, not of atonement. It is a sacrifice of worship, which is what we are called to do when we gather together as the Lord's people.

Here Paul uses the concept of the offering in a somewhat unusual way. He is ministering Jesus Christ to the Gentiles for this purpose: **that the offering of the Gentiles might be acceptable, sanctified by the Holy Spirit** (v. 16b). We can understand that sentence in two possible ways, but only one can be right. Some say that Paul is asking that the Gentiles' sacrifices of praise and worship would be acceptable to God as they are consecrated by the work of the Holy Spirit. I do not think the text should be interpreted that way. Paul is talking about his offering of the Gentiles to Christ.

Paul had been set apart to go to the Gentiles, and he had done that. As Paul had proclaimed the gospel of God to the Gentiles, the Holy Spirit had attached Himself to the proclamation of that word and worked to bring those Gentiles to conversion. That, Paul is saying, is his sacrifice, the fruit of his ministry. His sacrifice is the Gentile converts. Not for a minute was he claiming that he had the power to convert them. Paul knew that such power comes only through the Holy Spirit. Nevertheless, as a minister, he offers the fruit of his ministry to the Lord. In that sense, Paul exercises the office of priest.

Application

Every day, many of us are surrounded by unbelievers. We should not grow discouraged. Like the Apostle Paul, who labored for the sake of the Gentiles, offering them to God, so, too, we ought to be in continual prayer for our ministry to others. Let us pray that in our sharing of the gospel, God might work in the hearts of the unbelievers in our lives, receiving them as our offerings to Him.

2

The Minister's Glory

THEREFORE I HAVE REASON TO GLORY **in Christ Jesus in the things which pertain to God** (v. 17). Paul wrote to the Corinthians, quoting Jeremiah, "He who glories, let him glory in the LORD" (1 Cor. 1:31). Paul has reason to glory because all glory he has experienced is rooted and grounded in Christ Jesus. He understands that it is not of himself.

> I, brethren, when I came to you, did not come with excellence of speech or of wisdom declaring to you the testimony of God. For I determined not to know anything among you except Jesus Christ and Him crucified. I was with you in weakness, in fear, and in much trembling. And my speech and my preaching were not with persuasive words of human wisdom, but in demonstration of the Spirit and of power, that your faith should not be in the wisdom of men but in the power of God. (1 Cor. 2:1–5)

For I will not dare to speak of any of those things which Christ has not accomplished through me, in word and deed, to make the Gentiles obedient (v. 18). The only thing Paul has to talk about is what Christ has done. Paul is not just being humble; he is being truthful, accurate, and theologically sound.

Paul is looking at the results of his ministry, and he understands that those results have been wrought by God. Paul offers to God a return of the gifts that God Himself has given. That is all we can ever do. What can we give to God that we have not first received from His hand? We do not give God our money so that He will make us rich, give us something we want, or forgive us our sins. We acknowledge that God owns it all. Everything we possess belongs to Him, and He asks for just a small portion, a tenth. We all must be ready to give and be given at a moment's notice as an offering of praise to the Lord God.

Application

When God is pleased to use us in our ministry to others, we ought to be humbled, recognizing that we are only instruments in God's hands. The wonder is that God rewards our labors at all. Consider memorizing Psalm 116:12, and never stop asking its question: "What shall I render to the LORD for all His benefits toward me?"

3

Miracles

PAUL CALLS ATTENTION TO HIS MISSIONARY OUTREACH, which has been carried out **in mighty signs and wonders, by the power of the Spirit of God** (v. 19a). There is no word for *miracle* in the New Testament, but we find the words *signs*, *wonders*, and *powers*. We extrapolate from those words a concept that we call *miracle*. We use the word *miracle* in a generic sense, but there is a narrow, technical, theological definition of the word. In terms of general miracles, I believe that they do occur—all the time—but such "miracles" are not technically miracles. A miracle is a sign or power that signifies something. Such signs, or miracles, in the Apostolic age were meant to signify the breakthrough of God's kingdom and, most importantly, to signify the agents of that breakthrough. Moses, for example, was given power to perform miracles so that his credentials would authenticate his role as God's ambassador.

Nicodemus came to Jesus at night and said, "Rabbi, we know that You are a teacher come from God; for no one can do these signs that You do unless God is with him" (John 3:2). Nicodemus understood that the devil is a liar and that he can perform counterfeit signs such as those of the magicians of Egypt. Although Satan has more power than we do, he does not have the power of God. Satan cannot bring something out of nothing. Satan cannot bring life out of death. Only God can do that and those whom He empowers to do it, and He empowers them to authenticate them as agents of revelation.

Therefore, how can those who perform miracles be authenticated as God's agents if others, including Satan, can do the same things? God answers prayers and heals the sick today, but I do not expect that someone today can go to the house of Lazarus and raise him from the dead. I do not expect to see anybody today bringing something out of nothing—not until the Lord comes back. There was a purpose and set time in redemptive history for that special, tight category of miracles.

Paul gives his reason for mentioning the signs and wonders that the Holy Spirit has done through him: **so that from Jerusalem and round about to Illyricum I have fully preached the gospel of Christ** (v. 19b). Illyricum was in Asia Minor, far north of Jerusalem. Paul's ministry has extended far and wide. In every place he has traveled, the power of the Holy Spirit has been there to authenticate his ministry with signs and powers and wonders.

Application

The types of signs and wonders that accompanied the ministry of the Apostles as those specially sent by Christ have ceased. This does not mean that God is not at work in the world, but it does mean that we should no longer expect God's special working through an individual to confirm his ministry. That being the case, we have every right to be skeptical about such claims, for "God, who at various times and in various ways spoke in time past to the fathers by the prophets, has in these last days spoken to us by His Son" (Heb. 1:1–2).

4

Paul's Hope

AND SO I HAVE MADE IT MY AIM **to preach the gospel, not where Christ was named, lest I should build on another man's foundation, but as it is written: "To whom He was not announced, they shall see; and those who have not heard shall understand"** (vv. 20–21). There is nothing wrong with preaching on somebody else's foundation. Ministers build on the ministry of those who have gone before. Very rarely does a church begin and end with a single pastor, and it is customary in the ministry to build on another's foundation. Paul, however, was not a pastor; he was an Apostle and a missionary, and he was sent to places where the gospel had not been preached and where no one else had laid a foundation. That was his aim—to preach the gospel not where Christ was already named, lest he should build on another man's foundation.

Paul's travels have impacted his relationship with the Christians at Rome: **For this reason I also have been much hindered from coming to you. But now no longer having a place in these parts, and having a great desire these many years to come to you** (vv. 22–23). Whether Paul ever got to Spain we do not know. Scholars are divided on that point, but we have no certain evidence that his desire to get to Spain was fulfilled. He got to Rome, but he did not get there while traveling to Spain. He went to Rome in chains after getting in trouble with the Jews and then with the Romans, as we discover in the book of Acts.

Whenever I journey to Spain, I shall come to you. For I hope to see you on my journey, and to be helped on my way there by you, if

first I may enjoy your company for a while (v. 24). The fame of the church in Rome had gone into the whole world (1:8). Paul counts the Christians at Rome as his brothers and sisters in the Lord, and he longs to see them in person. He is optimistic about being able to do so in the near future.

Application

It is wise and good to look ahead to the future. Like Paul, let us make our plans out of godly desires, knowing that they are ultimately established by the Lord. Meditate today on these passages from the book of Proverbs: "A man's heart plans his way, but the Lord directs his steps" (16:9). "There are many plans in a man's heart, nevertheless the Lord's counsel—that will stand" (19:21).

5

Paul's Travels

BEFORE PAUL VISITS ROME, HE PLANS TO GO TO Jerusalem to minister to the saints. **For it pleased those from Macedonia and Achaia to make a certain contribution for the poor among the saints who are in Jerusalem** (v. 26). Paul has collected an offering from Gentile converts and plans to take it to Jerusalem and distribute it to the Jewish believers living in the midst of hostility and poverty.

It pleased them indeed, and they are their debtors. For if the Gentiles have been partakers of their spiritual things, their duty is also to minister to them in material things (v. 27). The Gentile converts had been supremely blessed to receive what they had received from Israel. They understood that they were the wild olive branch that had been grafted into the root of Israel. The Gentiles were the heirs of the spiritual promises brought to them by the Apostle Paul, and they see themselves as debtors to their Jewish brothers and sisters suffering in Jerusalem. The Gentiles were pleased to give a contribution for those saints. Since the Gentiles had been partakers of Israel's spiritual things, they saw it as a matter of duty to minister to the Jews in material things.

Therefore, when I have performed this and have sealed to them this fruit, I shall go by way of you to Spain (v. 28). After Paul goes to Jerusalem, he wants to visit Rome on his way to Spain. **But I know that when I come to you, I shall come in the fullness of the blessing of the gospel of Christ** (v. 29). Paul would arrive at Rome in chains and still rejoice that he was there because of the privilege of being a minister of the gospel.

Application

Paul's collecting money for the poor in Jerusalem was in keeping with his promise as the Apostle to the Gentiles (see Gal. 2:1–10). The Gentile Christians had a spiritual debt to their Jewish brothers in Jerusalem. In much the same way, we have a spiritual debt to our local church, so let us continue to give generously for the sake of the gospel and the ministries of mercy throughout our communities. How could we ever repay the One who for our sakes became poor (2 Cor. 8:9)?

6

The God of Peace

Now I beg you, brethren, **through the Lord Jesus Christ, and through the love of the Spirit, that you strive together with me in prayers to God for me, that I may be delivered from those in Judea who do not believe** (vv. 30–31a). Paul begs the Roman Christians to pray for him as he undertakes his journey to Jerusalem. He knows that there is a price on his head and a bull's-eye on his back. He knows that there are multitudes of unbelieving Jews eager to get their hands on him and, if possible, stone him to death. So he asks the saints in Rome to pray for him, **that my service for Jerusalem may be acceptable to the saints, that I may come to you with joy by the will of God, and may be refreshed together with you** (vv. 31b–32). He is going to Jerusalem to deliver the offering designed to bring relief to the saints there, but he is going to need safe conduct to get in and out of that city.

Paul closes this section with a brief benediction. It is not the ultimate benediction but the penultimate one: **Now the God of peace be with you all. Amen** (v. 33). The primary concern of the Apostle—and of every Jew—was the experience of the peace of God. Jews greet one another with *Shalom aleichem, aleichem shalom*, "Peace be unto you and unto you be peace."

> The LORD bless you and keep you;
> The LORD make His face shine upon you,
> And be gracious to you;
> The LORD lift up His countenance upon you,
> And give you peace. (Num. 6:24–26)

At the heart of virtually every Jewish benediction was the constant plea that God would give peace to His people.

Application

Paul begged the Romans for prayer. How often do we ask for prayer—let alone beg for it? We cannot live the Christian life alone, and though it may be difficult for us to be vulnerable, especially when it comes to our problems, needs, and sin, we ought to be often requesting prayer in these areas. There are no perfect Christians, so let us be people marked by humility and grace—humility to be open with others and grace that we might not judge others.

Romans 16

I COMMEND TO YOU PHOEBE OUR SISTER, *who is a servant of the church in Cenchrea, that you may receive her in the Lord in a manner worthy of the saints, and assist her in whatever business she has need of you; for indeed she has been a helper of many and of myself also.*

Greet Priscilla and Aquila, my fellow workers in Christ Jesus, who risked their own necks for my life, to whom not only I give thanks, but also all the churches of the Gentiles. Likewise greet the church that is in their house.

Greet my beloved Epaenetus, who is the firstfruits of Achaia to Christ. Greet Mary, who labored much for us. Greet Andronicus and Junia, my countrymen and my fellow prisoners, who are of note among the apostles, who also were in Christ before me.

Greet Amplias, my beloved in the Lord. Greet Urbanus, our fellow worker in Christ, and Stachys, my beloved. Greet Apelles, approved in Christ. Greet those who are of the household of Aristobulus. Greet Herodion, my countryman. Greet those who are of the household of Narcissus who are in the Lord.

Greet Tryphena and Tryphosa, who have labored in the Lord. Greet the beloved Persis, who labored much in the Lord. Greet Rufus, chosen in the Lord, and his mother and mine. Greet Asyncritus, Phlegon, Hermas, Patrobas, Hermes, and the brethren who are with them. Greet Philologus and Julia, Nereus and his sister, and Olympas, and all the saints who are with them.

Greet one another with a holy kiss. The churches of Christ greet you.

Now I urge you, brethren, note those who cause divisions and offenses, contrary to the doctrine which you learned, and avoid them. For those who are such do not serve our Lord Jesus Christ, but their own belly, and by smooth words and flattering speech deceive the hearts of the simple. For your obedience has become known to all. Therefore I am glad on your behalf; but I want you to be wise in what is good, and simple concerning evil. And the God of peace will crush Satan under your feet shortly.

The grace of our Lord Jesus Christ be with you. Amen.

Timothy, my fellow worker, and Lucius, Jason, and Sosipater, my countrymen, greet you.

I, Tertius, who wrote this epistle, greet you in the Lord.

Gaius, my host and the host of the whole church, greets you. Erastus, the treasurer of the city, greets you, and Quartus, a brother. The grace of our Lord Jesus Christ be with you all. Amen.

Now to Him who is able to establish you according to my gospel and the preaching of Jesus Christ, according to the revelation of the mystery kept secret since the world began but now made manifest, and by the prophetic Scriptures made known to all nations, according to the commandment of the everlasting God, for obedience to the faith—to God, alone wise, be glory through Jesus Christ forever. Amen.

WEEK 52

1

Phoebe's Faithfulness

AS PAUL CONCLUDES THE EPISTLE, he sends greetings to friends in the church at Rome. The Apostle has finished the instructional content of the epistle, and he is winding down now in his customary manner. Even in these greetings, we can learn something of value for our souls. We know the promise of God: "All Scripture is given by inspiration of God, and is profitable for doctrine, for reproof, for correction, for instruction in righteousness, that the man of God may be complete, thoroughly equipped for every good work" (2 Tim. 3:16–17).

This lengthy list of greetings and mentions of various people begins with a special commendation of a woman named Phoebe. She is described as a servant of the church in Cenchrea, which is on one of the coasts of Corinth. **I commend to you Phoebe our sister, who is a servant of the church in Cenchrea, that you may receive her in the Lord in a manner worthy of the saints, and assist her in whatever business she has need of you; for indeed she has been a helper of many and of myself also** (vv. 1–2). Paul's brief commendation has received no small amount of attention by those trying to glean from the New Testament an understanding of the role of women in the life of the church.

Phoebe is identified as our sister in the faith and a servant of the church in Corinth. This descriptive term "servant of the church" comes from the Greek word *diakonia* and is rendered in some translations as *deaconess*. Many churches in our day are organized by elders, ministers, deacons, and deaconesses, who are female deacons. Over the years there have been disputes, even within Reformed communities, about whether the office of deaconess should be an ordained office.

We see throughout Paul's greetings his profound appreciation for the assistance he received from women who were serving the cause of Christ and the church in very significant ways. What the church does today in terms of ordination is a different matter, which I will not address here. The point is that we must not underestimate the very important role that women have in the life of the church of Christ.

Paul directs the Christians in Rome to receive Phoebe in the Lord in a manner worthy of the saints. She is to be assisted in whatever she needs because of the high honor bestowed on her as a helper of many. The term *helper* is a very weak translation of the Greek, which indicates someone of important assistance to the Apostolic ministry. Phoebe is an assistant to Paul and part of his Apostolic ministry, so he directs the people in Rome to receive her with all honor and assistance.

Application

Paul's appreciation for the women who supported him and the church echoes back to Jesus and the role that women played in His earthly ministry: "Now it came to pass, afterward, that He went through every city and village, preaching and bringing the glad tidings of the kingdom of God. And the twelve were with Him, and certain women who had been healed of evil spirits and infirmities—Mary called Magdalene, . . . Joanna . . . , and Susanna, and many others who provided for Him from their substance" (Luke 8:1–3). Women are instrumental in the life of the church.

2

Priscilla and Aquila

PAUL SENDS MORE GREETINGS: **Greet Priscilla and Aquila, my fellow workers in Christ Jesus, who risked their own necks for my life, to whom not only I give thanks, but also all the churches of the Gentiles. Likewise greet the church that is in their house** (vv. 3–5a). We hear of Priscilla and Aquila in the book of Acts (see Acts 18). They ministered with the Apostle in Ephesus. Apparently, Priscilla and Aquila had been in Rome and had to flee when Christians were banished by the emperor Claudius. They went from Rome to Ephesus, where they met with the Apostle Paul and assisted him in his ministry. We do not have a specific record of the risks they took for the Apostle, but from the Acts record of Paul's sojourn in Ephesus, we know that the time was a tumultuous one and that his life was in danger more than once.

Paul also sends a greeting to the church that was in their house. In the first-century community, churches often met in homes. Those were not representative of today's so-called house church. Today's home-church movement generally, though not always, tends toward disenchantment with the organized visible church. There were home churches in the first century because there were no other places to meet. Those with larger homes would open them so that people could assemble together for worship and instruction. The family of Priscilla and Aquila did that.

Application

Paul always gives credit where credit is due. In speaking of his ministry to the Gentiles, he pointed to the work of Christ through him (see Rom. 15:18), and here he speaks of Priscilla and Aquila's work. They risked their lives for the one who labored diligently to bring the gospel to the Gentiles, and so all the churches of the Gentiles were called to be grateful for them. Who in your life needs to be encouraged by your gratitude?

3

Further Greetings

GREET MY BELOVED EPAENETUS, who is the firstfruits of Achaia to Christ (v. 5b). Some controversy surrounds this greeting. Elsewhere Paul writes about Stephanas, whom he also calls the "firstfruits of Achaia" (1 Cor. 16:15). A textual variant could explain the tension. The wording could be taken as referring to the firstfruits of Paul's ministry in Asia rather than in Achaia. Even if it was in Achaia, the firstfruits would presumably include more than one person, perhaps members of his family or a related group.

Greet Mary, who labored much for us. Greet Andronicus and Junia (vv. 6–7a). Junia could be a man or a woman, depending on how the Greek is rendered. Paul also sends greetings to my countrymen and my fellow prisoners, who are of note among the apostles, who also were in Christ before me (v. 7b). Apparently these believers had been part of Paul's entourage and had suffered imprisonment with the Apostle. He gives them tribute for their fidelity and also points out that they were Christians before he was; they were older in the Lord.

Greet Amplias, my beloved in the Lord. Greet Urbanus, our fellow worker in Christ, and Stachys, my beloved. Greet Apelles, approved in Christ. Greet those who are of the household of Aristobulus. Greet Herodion, my countryman. Greet those who are of the household of Narcissus who are in the Lord. Greet Tryphena and Tryphosa, who have labored in the Lord. Greet the beloved Persis,

who labored much in the Lord (vv. 8–12). Tryphena, Tryphosa, and Persis were women, so again we see Paul's concern to give his Apostolic good wishes to women who had labored with him.

Greet Rufus, chosen in the Lord, and his mother and mine (v. 13). Jesus' crossbeam had been carried by Simon of Cyrene, who is identified as the father of Alexander and Rufus (Mark 15:21). It was unusual for Mark to insert that kind of detail in his narrative, and we have to wonder why he did it. Mark's Gospel was sent to the church at Rome. Mark was likely aware that Rufus and perhaps his brother Alexander were members of the church at Rome when the Gospel was sent there. Mark, under the influence of the Holy Spirit, honored those local church members, the sons of the man who had carried the cross of Jesus. Rufus is described as "chosen in the Lord." In this context, it is unlikely that Paul means that Rufus is one of the elect, because all of them were elect. The context indicates that Rufus had a particular role and influence with the Apostle and with the Apostolic community in Rome.

Paul also sends greetings to Rufus' mother, presumably the wife of Simon of Cyrene, whom Paul calls his own mother. Paul was not speaking literally here; rather, he considered her his mother in the faith.

Greet Asyncritus, Phlegon, Hermas, Patrobas, Hermes, and the brethren who are with them. Greet Philologus and Julia, Nereus and his sister, and Olympas, and all the saints who are with them (vv. 14–15). After acknowledging others numbered among the saints, Paul adds, **Greet one another with a holy kiss. The churches of Christ greet you** (v. 16). That was the custom, particularly at the celebration of the Lord's Supper. Upon completion of the Lord's Supper meal, the people would customarily greet one another with a kiss on the cheek. We still see that form of greeting in the Middle East today. We do not know when or why that custom passed out of practice in the church, but it must be considered as a custom, not a principle.

Application

Let us be quick to give recognition to others who work hard for the church. Every Lord's Day, many work to make worship and the fellowship of the saints possible. Be sure to thank those who volunteer their time. The Lord sees, and He will ultimately commend all His servants, but we have an opportunity to encourage them in their labors now.

4

A Final Warning

PAUL TURNS HIS ATTENTION TO a serious Apostolic admonition. This is perhaps the last Apostolic entreaty we find in the book of Romans. **Now I urge you, brethren, note those who cause divisions and offenses, contrary to the doctrine which you learned, and avoid them** (v. 17). He admonishes the Christians at Rome to notice the troublemakers in the church. They are to watch out for those who sow seeds of dissension, particularly those who disrupt the body of Christ with false doctrine.

In the church today, doctrine is decried. Doctrine divides, some say, so we ought not to give much concern to it but focus instead on loving, peaceful relationships. They forget that we do not know what a loving relationship looks like apart from how it is described by the truth of biblical doctrine. Paul does not say to avoid doctrine here; he says to avoid heretics. We are to avoid those who would come into the church teaching false doctrine. **For those who are such do not serve our Lord Jesus Christ, but their own belly** (v. 18a). Such people are not in it for the building of the kingdom of God but for their own gratification, wealth, pleasure, and status in the community.

Paul is quite critical of them, who **by smooth words and flattering speech deceive the hearts of the simple** (v. 18b). James warns that not many should become teachers, for with teaching comes the greatest judgment (James 3:1). Watch out, says Paul. **I want you to be wise in what is good, and simple concerning evil** (v. 19c).

There are many Christians who do not want to be engaged in a laborious study of the Word of God. They say that they want to keep their faith simple and childlike, but there is a difference between a childlike faith and a childish faith. We are to be childlike in terms of our acquiescence to the authority of God, but we are to be adults in our understanding. The Christians of the New Testament were rebuked for being satisfied with spiritual infancy, with milk, when they should have been seeking after the deeper things of God, the meat of the Word (1 Cor. 3:2; Heb. 5:12). All we have been examining in Romans is not pabulum. We have been looking at the weightier things of God's Word so that we might not be simple in our understanding.

Application

In this study on Romans, we have been engaged in doctrinal study. We must be acquainted with true doctrine to spot false doctrine. Continue to be diligent in your study of the Word, so that if you ever need to speak up on behalf of the truth, you might do so boldly, knowing that Scripture is authoritative. Yet we must also proclaim the truth gently, for Scripture calls us to this as well.

5

A Final Greeting

AND THE GOD OF PEACE WILL CRUSH SATAN **under your feet shortly** (v. 20a). That prophetic statement may have specific reference to the destruction of Jerusalem, which would take place shortly after this letter was received. When it came, the great threat of the Judaizing heresy was removed from the church, the temple was destroyed, and those persecuting the early church were dispersed among the nations. Yet Paul might have been referring to something altogether different. He does not tell us.

Paul gives a preliminary brief benediction: **The grace of our Lord Jesus Christ be with you. Amen** (v. 20b). Paul's greatest hope was that the people would continue to have the grace of God in their presence. He told us earlier that we move from faith to faith, from life to life, from grace to grace. Our Christian pilgrimage begins in grace, is sustained by grace, and is finished by grace.

Timothy, my fellow worker, and Lucius, Jason, and Sosipater, my countrymen, greet you (v. 21). Next we find out who really wrote Romans: **I, Tertius, who wrote this epistle, greet you in the Lord** (v. 22). After all the greetings are communicated to Paul's friends in Rome and from his coworkers in Corinth, Tertius adds his personal greetings, identifying himself as the one who wrote the epistle. In the vast majority of cases, Paul did not write with his own hand. On one occasion he did write his letter: "See with what large letters I have written to you with my own hand!" (Gal. 6:11), but typically he, as well as many others, used a personal secretary called an *amanuensis*. The practice dates back to the Old Testament prophets. Jeremiah had an amanuensis who took down his words. Here Paul has been dictating the letter to the church at Rome, and Tertius, whose name means "the third," has been recording this magnificent epistle dutifully and carefully under the inspiration of the Holy Spirit.

Gaius, my host and the host of the whole church, greets you. Erastus, the treasurer of the city, greets you, and Quartus, a brother (v. 23). Not many in the early Christian community were in societal positions of honor or authority, but there were some, and here we learn of one such person, the treasurer of the city. He sent his greetings, along with Quartus, a brother. Then: **The grace of our Lord Jesus Christ be with you all. Amen** (v. 24).

Application

In speaking of Satan's being crushed underfoot, Paul evokes the *protoeuangelion* of Genesis 3:15, that the promised Seed would crush the head of the serpent. Paul's promise to the Romans is not merely a future promise. Jesus has already crushed the head of the serpent on the cross, and while He will cast him into the lake of fire at the end, even now He is putting an end to all His and our enemies. Praise Jesus for the ways that He is at work in your life, even the ways that you do not yet see.

6

Benediction

PAUL GIVES THE FINAL BENEDICTION: **Now to Him who is able to establish you according to my gospel** (v. 25a). He frequently uses the term *edification*. It is a term borrowed from the building industry. The teaching of our Lord at the end of the Sermon on the Mount warns against building a house upon the sand. Those who do so will find that when the floods come, the house will be swept away because its edifice had not been established. By the same token, Jesus said, the wise man is one who builds his house upon a rock so that when the storms come and beat against it, the house stands (Matt. 7:24–27). We are warned not to be tossed to and fro by every wind of doctrine. As we grow in grace, as our sanctification proceeds, we are to be edified and built up to the point at which our faith, our character, and our devotion are established (Eph. 4:11–13).

In this benediction, the Apostle reminds the people at Rome about who is able to make that happen: **the preaching of Jesus Christ** (v. 25b). We are to be established according to Paul's gospel. The biblical gospel is under attack today. The doctrine of justification by faith alone, which we have examined in much detail in Paul's letter, has been and continues to be attacked in the church today—not just from the so-called liberal wing of the church but from the evangelical and even the Reformed wings. At the heart of the dispute is whether our salvation rests upon the imputation of the righteousness of Jesus.

This is Paul's final benediction, that God is able to establish them in the gospel and in the preaching of Jesus Christ, **according to the revelation of the mystery kept secret since the world began but now made manifest, and by the prophetic Scriptures made known to all nations, according to the commandment of the everlasting God, for obedience to the faith** (vv. 25c–26). The final benediction of the final line of Paul's epistle repeats in succinct terms the quintessence of the message that he has labored to communicate throughout the epistle, the principle of *soli Deo gloria*: **to God, alone wise, be glory through Jesus Christ forever** (v. 27a).

The final word of the Apostle's letter comes from the Hebrew *aman*, which is translated *truth*. That word is **Amen** (v. 27b). So all God's people say, "Amen."

Application

Scripture is special in many ways. Paul wrote this letter to the Romans, but it was also by God's inspiration intended for the church in every place throughout history. Understood this way, Paul's benediction to the Romans is also the Apostle's benediction for you, and because Paul is an Apostle of Jesus Christ, it comes ultimately from Him. Revel in this blessing that is yours today.

About the Author

Dr. R.C. Sproul was founder of Ligonier Ministries, first minister of preaching and teaching at Saint Andrew's Chapel in Sanford, Fla., first president of Reformation Bible College, executive editor of *Tabletalk* magazine, and general editor of the *Reformation Study Bible*. His radio program, *Renewing Your Mind*, is still broadcast daily on hundreds of radio stations around the world and can also be heard online. He was author of more than one hundred books, including *The Holiness of God*, *Chosen by God*, and *Everyone's a Theologian*. He was recognized throughout the world for his articulate defense of the inerrancy of Scripture and the need for God's people to stand with conviction upon His Word.